Dorset Cousins
Sara Evans .

Return 1

C000271883

A READER IN
INTERNATIONAL RELATIONS
AND POLITICAL THEORY

A READER IN INTERNATIONAL RELATIONS AND POLITICAL THEORY

Edited by
Howard Williams, Moorhead Wright
and Tony Evans

Open University Press
Buckingham

Open University Press
Celtic Court
22 Ballmoor
Buckingham
MK18 1WX

First Published 1993

Copyright © Selection and editorial material, The Editors 1993

All rights reserved. No part of this publication may be
reproduced, stored in a retrieval system or transmitted in
any form or by any means, without written permission from the
publisher.

A catalogue record of this book is available from
the British library

ISBN   0 335 15668 1
ISBN   0 335 15667 3 (pbk)

Typeset by Colset Pte Ltd, Singapore
Printed in Great Britain by Biddles Ltd, Guildford and King's Lynn

To the memory of Jacquie Ryan

CONTENTS

ACKNOWLEDGEMENTS

The editors wish to thank the following for granting permission to reproduce material for the following sections: *Aquinas*, Blackwell Publishers, Oxford; *Machiavelli*, Random House, New York; *Grotius*, Wildy and Sons Ltd, London; *Kant*, Maria Zens, for the translation specially prepared for this reader; *Clausewitz*, Princeton University Press, New Jersey; *Marx & Engels*, L. D. Easton and Lawrence & Wishart, London; *Lenin*, Progress Publishers, Moscow; *Carr*, Curtis Brown Ltd, London; *Morgenthau*, McGraw-Hill Publishing Company, New York; *Herz*, Johns Hopkins University Press, Baltimore; *Waltz*, Columbia University Press, New York; *Wallerstein*, Cambridge University Press, Cambridge; *Bull*, Macmillan Publishers, Basingstoke; *Cox*, Millennium Publishing Group, LSE, London; and *Linklater*, Review of International Studies. The editors would also like to thank all those authors who have willingly allowed us to reproduce their work.

Every effort has been made to trace the copyright holders of all the extracts reproduced here. This has not proved possible in all cases. The editors would be pleased to receive any claim which will be considered under the same conditions offered to those who have already granted permission to reproduce material.

INTRODUCTION

The publication of a reader on international relations and political theory is particularly appropriate at the present time for two reasons. One concerns a continuing debate over the nature of 'theory' within the discipline of international relations, while the other is to do with recent changes in the structure of world politics.

The first concerns a continuing dissatisfaction among a growing number of international relations scholars with the still dominant theory of Realism. According to a well-known essay by Martin Wight,[1] what passes for international 'theory' cannot be thought of as theory at all, at least not in the same sense as we understand political theory. Wight argues that in the current epoch, which is dominated by the modern state, international relations is better understood as a debate between three traditions: the Realist or Machiavellian, the Rationalist or Grotian, and the Revolutionist or Kantian. Although Wight attempts to assert that no single strand of this debate can claim to have a monopoly of the truth about international relations, he none the less leans heavily on the side of the Realist explanation.[2] This, he argues, is because while the task of political

1. Martin Wight (1966) 'Why is there no International Theory?', in H. Butterfield and M. Wight (eds), *Diplomatic Investigations*. London, George Allen and Unwin, pp. 17–34.
2. It could be argued that Wight changed his position in his later years, moving more towards the Rationalist or Grotian approach. Compare *Power Politics* (The Royal Institute of International Affairs, London, 1946) with 'Western Values in International Relations', in H. Butterfield and M. Wight (eds), *Diplomatic Investigations*. London, George Allen and Unwin, pp. 89–131.

theory purports to describe some version of the 'good life' international theory offers only a 'theory of survival'.

The 'good life' is concerned with such normative issues as order, justice, fraternity and prosperity, while the 'theory of survival' focuses on instrumental means for protecting the state and its citizens from external threat. How such values as order and justice are to be achieved, how the state is to be developed or reformed, and how the institutions of the state are to be structured in an effort to achieve the 'good life', is the stuff of political theory. The state in its various forms is the goal or end to be achieved. Political theory assumes that the state should be understood as the best possible solution to achieving the 'good life'. If not a perfect form of association the state is at least perfectible and its perfection is one of the tasks of political theory.

From this three further points can be drawn. The first is that political theory often focuses on the individual citizen and his or her relationship to the state. The institutions of the state are to facilitate individual action in pursuit of the 'good life'. In this task these institutions may restrict the actions of particular individuals but these restrictions are the price that the citizen must pay for the provision of social goods intended to make the 'good life' possible. Second, the state alone is assumed capable of providing the means necessary for the individual to pursue the 'good life'. That is to say the state, understood as the most perfect form of political association, is capable of securing all the necessary means of achieving the 'good life' without resort to recruiting outside assistance. In short, the state is seen as politically self-sufficient and complete. Lastly, the values and social goods that the state underpins have no value in themselves but are understood as of value only so long as they serve the interests of citizens. This is the idea of change, progress and development within the political system and culture. It represents the interplay between political, social, economic, scientific and technological activity. Such developments help shape the aspirations of the population, leading it to seek new institutions more appropriate to its continually unfolding vision of the 'good life'.[3]

In contrast to this, for international theory, or at least in that version of Realism that has dominated the discipline of international relations since 1945, the state is a given. Since the state is assumed to represent the most perfect form of political association that humankind has thus far devised, the normative order that the state claims to represent, including its polity, economic system and value structure, must be secured from outside interference. Since no authority above the state exists, states must rely exclusively upon their own resources in ensuring their survival. The international political environment is therefore best characterized as anarchical. International relations becomes a political domain where each state is engaged in the endless activity of promoting and protecting

---

3. For an excellent overview of Martin Wight's approach to international relations see Robert H. Jackson (1990) 'Martin Wight, International Relations and the Good Life', *Millennium*, 19: 2, 261–72.

its own interests against the intrusions of others engaged in the same processes. Thus, Realism stresses conflict and the potential for conflict between independent states. Mindful of this condition, leaders of states are motivated to engage in the pursuit of military and coercive power as the means of defending against external threat. Perhaps the most familiar sentence to any student of international relations is that of Hans J. Morgenthau: 'We assume that statesmen [sic] think and act in terms of interest defined as power, and the evidence of history bears that assumption out'.[4] If political theory is concerned with normative issues – the aspirations of individuals and groups, social values and change – then international theory is to do with the 'hard shell' (Herz) of the state and the state's capabilities in protecting its citizens' distinctive way of life from the potentially destructive forces of foreign intervention.

Further features said to distinguish international from political theory can be found by looking at their separate approaches to such things as the 'state of nature', anarchy and security. One solution to the 'state of nature' at the domestic level has led to some notion of the social contract (exemplified in the works of Rousseau) through which insecurity, fear and conflict can be resolved and where citizens can hope to achieve mutual gains and benefits. At the international level however, problems of insecurity can be resolved only by constant vigilance and preparedness for war and conflict (Clausewitz). However, whereas anarchy is not to be tolerated within the state it is acceptable in the Realist view of international relations because the state's first and foremost responsibility is to preserve and protect the internal life of its citizens from any external interference that might threaten their economic, political and social values (Hobbes). If Realism has any claim to a normative content, it is to be found in the assumption that the norms and values contained within the state, which operates in an environment of anarchy, must be secured, even if this means resort to war.

But this rather stark Realist world does not lead to the open conflict that might be expected of an anarchic environment. In practice states, cognizant of the fact that in significant areas of political, economic and social life they share a common destiny or history, are bound by certain rules, norms and practices that allow at least some measure of peaceful coexistence (Grotius). These habits and practices take the form of social institutions that help both to shape the expectations of states and to offer a social framework for the realization of common goals. This is the Rationalist view of international theory. It stresses the importance of principles like reciprocity, sovereign equality and non-intervention upon which international institutions depend for the maintenance of order. Significant among these institutions are diplomacy and international law. It is the acceptance of these norms and institutions that, in part, legitimizes the state as a member of international society (Bull). As Bull expresses it, 'what these imperatives enjoin is not the overthrow of the system of states and its replacement by a universal

4. Hans J. Morgenthau (1966) *Politics Among Nations*. New York, Alfred A. Knopf, 4th edn, p. 5.

community of humankind, but rather acceptance of the requirements of co-existence and co-operation in a society of states.'[5]

Until the mid-1970s Realism and Rationalism, in their various forms, remained largely unchallenged. They gained their legitimacy in some measure from the Second World War and its cold war aftermath. While normative issues remained important to domestic politics, at the international level Realism offered a clear, plausible and, above all, simple explanation for what was seen as the immediate and abiding questions of international life: war, survival and power. However, while Realism was acknowledged as powerful in dealing with the great issues of war and peace, many scholars began to question its explanatory value in a world increasingly characterized by economic, political, scientific and social cooperation that transcended both the borders of states and the limits of accepted theory.

Furthermore, scholars began to question the usefulness of distinguishing between theories of the 'good life' and theories of survival. If, they asked, the state cannot always provide its people with the basic requirements for life like food and shelter, or if the political and civil rights of a people are violated by the despotic behaviour of some dictator such that they live in daily fear of their lives, should we really continue on the premise that political theory is concerned with the 'good life' while international theory is a theory of survival? With television pictures continually adding to our knowledge of famine over vast tracts of the world, and in the light of the violence done to whole populations by tyrants such as Pol Pot in Cambodia or Idi Amin in Uganda, was it really acceptable that the institutions of international relations – international law, diplomacy, non-intervention and sovereignty – should be sustained in the form that perpetuated the division of the international and the domestic? Such questions remain a challenge to accepted thinking in both international and political theory. If the state cannot be relied upon to provide the conditions for the 'good life', and international relations excludes external interference in helping others toward achieving their aspirations, then the role of theory in both spheres becomes unclear. In recent years these concerns have led to a growing interest in Revolutionist theories.

Those with an early interest in exploring alternatives to Realism noted the increasing sophistication and spread of technology, particularly in the form of transport and telecommunications, and the phenomenon of widespread transnational organizations covering almost every field of international relations. Some scholars began to argue that technological innovation brought with it new political structures outside of traditional thinking on international relations (Keohane and Nye). Others put forward theories that challenged accepted thinking on development, international economic cooperation and the role of aid (Wallerstein), all areas of international life for which Realism seemed to offer inadequate explanations. However, while much of this work contributed significantly to our understanding of international relations so that phrases such as

5. Hedley Bull (1988) *The Anarchical Society*. Basingstoke, Macmillan, p. 27.

dependency, interdependence, peripheral states and international regimes are now commonplace, the distinction between international and political theory remained largely untouched. Indeed, instead of challenging the conflictual, power-oriented, state-centric view of international relations many of these new developments came in time to be seen as additions to Realism rather than a serious attempt to replace it.

While none of these earlier attempts to replace Realism as the dominant theory of mainstream international thinking proved successful, they did stimulate a modest interest in reassessing our current assumptions. This can be seen in the so-called 'inter-paradigm debate'[6] which stimulated a literature that questioned the premises on which Realism is based. The most recent work in this project attempts to stand aside from currently held assumptions about the existing world order. It attempts to question the legitimacy of existing political and social institutions, to identify the forces for change, to understand more fully social and political changes within the global system as an integrated whole, and to understand the relationship between knowledge and the existing environment in which change must take place (Cox). Importantly, this recent work sees the distinction between normative theory and theories of survival as a false dichotomy. It questions the distinction between the individual and the citizen, where the rights and duties of individuals as members of the human race are understood as limited by their prior rights and duties as citizens of particular states (Linklater). In this way the claim of international relations to be a discrete area of action and discourse, separate from social and political theory, is seriously challenged.[7]

This reader supports the view that this challenge is long overdue. In our estimation the distinction between political theory and international theory, as posed by scholars like Wight, has always been false. To argue that theories of the 'good life' are exclusively concerned with the domestic politics of the state is to caricature political theory. It is true that the core of political theory has always focused on questions of citizenship and obligation. However, political theory and political theorists have also been concerned with sovereignty (Hobbes), war (Aquinas), diplomacy (Machiavelli) and a just international order (Rousseau and Kant), all issues with obvious international dimensions. As for the claim that Realism and the Realist approach distinguishes international theory from political theory one need look no further than the writings of Augustine, Hegel and Clausewitz. Indeed, it is in the writings of Machiavelli, Hegel and Clausewitz that Realist international thought was given first expression.

The second reason why a reader on political and international theory is so timely is that the decade of the 1980s witnessed revolutionary changes in the real world at both the national and international levels. At the national level popular movements such as Solidarity in Poland, the reunification movement in

6. Michael Banks (1985) 'The Inter-paradigm Debate', in M. Light and A.J.R. Groom (eds), *International Relations: A Handbook of Current Theory*. London, Frances Pinter, pp. 7–26.
7. Mark Hoffman (1986) 'Critical Theory and the Inter-paradigm Debate', *Millennium*, 16: 2, 231–49.

Germany, independence movements in the old satellite countries of the Soviet Union, the democracy movement in China and the anti-apartheid movement in South Africa, all articulated mass demands for greater political participation, the implementation of human rights and a more equitable share of economic rewards. Of course, not all of the demands made by these movements have been met. Indeed, in some cases, China for example, the old oppressive structures have proved sufficiently resilient in holding back the tide, at least for the present. However, it is difficult to believe that these structures, temporarily shored-up rather than permanently reinforced, will survive for long.

These revolutionary changes have seen constitutions rewritten, social and political institutions replaced, new economic systems developed and, for the first time in several generations, the necessity in many countries to develop foreign relations as independent states. These activities have stimulated immense interest in a wide range of political questions which, because of the oppressive nature of many of the regimes now replaced, have remained unasked for nearly five decades. What, for example, is the role of the individual in a modern state? What type of democracy is best suited to the traditions and cultures of the new states? How will the new constitution enable the fulfilment of international obligations? Is it possible to retain the best aspects of the old regime in the new politics? What are the responsibilities of government? What are the limits of government? What will constitute the requirements of citizenship? How should the newly emerging political order respond to other states, including the old democracies and those in a similar position of political reconstruction? Will the important responsibility of security be best served by traditional alliances or some other method? What form of economic system is likely to bring the benefits that many involved in the popular movements hoped to achieve? Will the new regime receive the support of existing international economic and political institutions? Which international organizations will be most beneficial in achieving the aspirations of the revolutions?

Perhaps most important of all are questions to do with sovereignty and self-determination. The nineteenth-century understanding of nationhood saw all political, economic and social expectations tied to some concept of the nation-state which alone was capable of providing complete fulfilment. This crude form of nationalism, still to be found in some west European countries as the European Community grinds towards political union, may not however be the rationale behind nationalist feelings in eastern Europe. In a world increasingly described in the language of interdependence, globalization and modernization, it seems doubtful whether nationalists and nationalism can be fully satisfied through the nation-state. The significant question is whether nationalism can be understood as complementary to the globalization of politics. If the nationalism of the newly emerging states of eastern Europe is qualitatively different from that of the nineteenth century, then it may not be tied to a rigid and uncompromising view of sovereignty. Instead, the new nationalism may express the needs of people to confront their own history in an attempt to define their own sense of identity and place in a world from which they have long been alienated. Such questions have always been at the heart of political theory. They are also of central interest to international relations.

Furthermore, parallel to the *disintegration* of the old Soviet bloc, and indeed the Soviet Union itself, is the idea of political *integration* now widely discussed in the European Community. This has further stimulated the debate over such issues as the future of sovereignty in an interdependent world, the nature and potential benefits of federalism, and the need to develop new forms of democratic institutions as the centres of government become increasingly more difficult to locate. In east and west Europe nationalism, autonomy and sovereignty have become key concerns for both practising politicians and academics. In the light both of growing nationalism and increasing globalization the old distinction between domestic and international politics, which has been the hallmark of university programmes since the introduction of international relations following the First World War, seems increasingly inappropriate. As international politics transcends its old forms of thought political theory comes into its own both as a general theory of politics and a theory of international relations.[8]

Although there remains a long way to go before we can hope to see the old thinking of Realism replaced, the revitalized debate over the nature of theory within the discipline of international relations has stimulated many international relations scholars to return to the texts of political theory in an effort to re-examine their approach. This reader is an attempt to encourage this endeavour.

Most previously published readers on international theory have been arranged thematically, including sections with headings such as 'Realism', 'war', 'peace studies', 'political economy' and 'functionalism'. This often demands that the editors label authors so that their essays can be neatly slotted into the chosen structure of the book. While this approach is useful, in our view it is not wholly justified. Labelling authors tends to predetermine the sections of the book that students will study, even though many authors defy easy categorization. This difficulty is particularly seen in attempting to assign classical political philosophers a modern label, and often results in the student ignoring potentially useful material.

The order of the essays and extracts chosen for inclusion in this reader is broadly historical and chronological. This, we believe, will have several advantages over the more usual thematic format adopted by many readers. First, it avoids the pitfall of classifying particular writers and encourages the student to assess independently the work of each contribution. Second, the chronological arrangement demonstrates continuity of theoretical development over time while acknowledging that this development is not linear. Third, it acknowledges that international theory and political theory are interconnected and not sharply distinct. Lastly, it encourages the student of international relations to draw from

---

8. David Held (ed.) (1991) *Political Theory Today*, Cambridge, Polity Press, especially chs 8, 9, 10 and 11.

a wider selection of texts than is usual and therefore to reflect more upon the nature of politics.

The problem of selecting texts for a reader is considerable and not easily resolved. Generally those writing in earlier periods confined themselves to domestic politics, while in the modern period international relations has developed as a distinctive discipline claiming its own epistemology, methods and theories. In part the object of this reader is to show that earlier political theory, while not always directly addressing the problems of international relations, none the less focuses on political problems that remain of central interest to the development of international relations theory. The principle for selection among the plethora of twentieth-century writing adopted here is that they debate with and extend the earlier traditions of thought. The main theme of the collection is therefore that of a number of interconnecting dialogues.

The first half of this reader is intended as a companion volume to Howard Williams, *International Relations in Political Theory* (also published by Open University Press, 1992), which provides a deeper justification for the relevance of classical political thought to contemporary international issues than space allows here. Classical political theory lies at the heart of contemporary issues in international relations in three senses. It does so in the first sense that the agents in contemporary international politics are for the most part steeped in a political tradition informed by classical thought; in the second sense that the contemporary debate in international political thought exemplified in these actions grows out of this classical tradition; and in the third sense that as the theory of political cooperation and conflict, political theory is also the theory of international relations.

The extracts in the first part of this reader are in some sense self-selecting because their authors are well established as important thinkers in the field of politics. This cannot be said for most of the extracts selected for the second part. These are the selections from the twentieth century, many of which were written after international relations was self-consciously established as an area of politics separate and apart form political theory. This has meant that the editors have had to exercise some judgement in selecting those extracts that extend the work of earlier writers. Moreover, while the outcome of this task can never be to the satisfaction of every student the editors have attempted to choose those extracts that are generally believed influential during this century and which are expected to remain so for the foreseeable future.

1

PLATO

Source: B. Jowett (trans.) (1892) *The Republic*, in *The Dialogues of Plato*. Oxford, Clarendon Press, pp. 12–20 and 47–67.

The theme of Plato's *Republic* is justice and the rule of philosophers. Plato argues against the conventional notion of justice which sees justice as embodied in particular forms of acting. Here he argues against the hard-headed view of Thrasymachus that justice is always the interest of the stronger party. For Plato justice cannot rest solely upon force. The view of justice he advocates can best come about in a community with a strict division of labour upon the basis of abilities. It is on these grounds that Plato concludes that the philosophically knowledgeable, as the most able, should rule. In Plato's vision of the just society order comes from above.

Several times in the course of the discussion Thrasymachus had made an attempt to get the argument into his own hands, and had been put down by the rest of the company, who wanted to hear the end. But when Polemarchus and I had done speaking and there was a pause, he could no longer hold his peace; and, gathering himself up, he came at us like a wild beast, seeking to devour us. We were quite panic-stricken at the sight of him.

He roared out to the whole company: What folly, Socrates, has taken possession of you all? And why, silly people, do you give in to one another? I say that if you want really to know what justice is, you should not only ask but answer, and you should not seek honour to yourself from the refutation of an opponent, but have your own answer; for there is many a one who can ask and cannot answer. And now I will not have you say that justice is duty or advantage or profit or gain or interest, for this sort of nonsense will not do for me; I must have clearness and accuracy.

I was panic-stricken at his words, and could not look at him without trembling. Indeed I believe that if I had not fixed my eye upon him, I should have been struck dumb: but when I saw his fury rising, I looked at him first, and was therefore able to reply to him.

Thrasymachus, I said, with a quiver, don't be hard upon us. Polemarchus and I may have been guilty of a little mistake in the argument, but I can assure you that the error was not intentional. If we were seeking for a piece of gold, you would not imagine that we were 'giving in to one another,' and so losing our chance of finding it. And why, when we are seeking for justice, a thing more precious than many pieces of gold, do you say that we are weakly yielding to one another and not doing our utmost to get at the truth? Nay, my good friend, we are most willing and anxious to do so, but the fact is that we cannot. And if so, you people who know all things should pity us and not be angry with us.

How characteristic of Socrates! he replied, with a bitter laugh; – that's your ironical style! Did I not foresee – have I not already told you, that whatever he was asked he would refuse to answer, and try irony or any other shuffle, in order that he might avoid answering?

You are a philosopher, Thrasymachus, I replied, and well know that if you ask a person what numbers make up twelve, taking care to prohibit him whom you ask from answering twice six, or three times four, or six times two, or four times three, 'for this sort of nonsense will not do for me,' – then obviously, if that is your way of putting the question, no one can answer you. But suppose that he were to retort, 'Thrasymachus, what do you mean? If one of these numbers which you interdict be the true answer to the question, am I falsely to say some other number which is not the right one? – is that your meaning?' – How would you answer him?

Just as if the two cases were at all alike! he said.

Why should they not be? I replied; and even if they are not, but only appear to be so to the person who is asked, ought he not to say what he thinks, whether you and I forbid him or not?

I presume then that you are going to make one of the interdicted answers?

I dare say that I may, notwithstanding the danger, if upon reflection I approve of any of them.

But what if I give you an answer about justice other and better, he said, than any of these? What do you deserve to have done to you?

Done to me! – as becomes the ignorant, I must learn from the wise – that is what I deserve to have done to me.

What, and no payment! a pleasant notion!

I will pay when I have the money, I replied.

But you have, Socrates, said Glaucon: and you, Thrasymachus, need be under no anxiety about money, for we will all make a contribution for Socrates.

Yes, he replied, and then Socrates will do as he always does – refuse to answer himself, but take and pull to pieces the answer of some one else.

Why, my good friend, I said, how can any one answer who knows, and says that he knows, just nothing; and who, even if he has some faint notions of his own, is told by a man of authority not to utter them? The natural thing is, that the speaker should be some one like yourself who professes to know and can tell what he knows. Will you then kindly answer, for the edification of the company and of myself?

Glaucon and the rest of the company joined in my request, and Thrasymachus, as any one might see, was in reality eager to speak; for he thought that he had an excellent answer, and would distinguish himself. But at first he affected to insist on my answering; at length he consented to begin. Behold, he said, the wisdom of Socrates; he refuses to teach himself, and goes about learning of others, to whom he never even says Thank you.

That I learn of others, I replied, is quite true; but that I am ungrateful I wholly deny. Money I have none, and therefore I pay in praise, which is all I have; and how ready I am to praise any one who appears to me to speak well you will very soon find out when you answer; for I expect that you will answer well.

Listen, then, he said; I proclaim that justice is nothing else than the interest of the stronger. And now why do you not praise me? But of course you won't.

Let me first understand you, I replied. Justice, as you say, is the interest of the stronger. What, Thrasymachus, is the meaning of this? You cannot mean to say that because Polydamas, the pancratiast, is stronger than we are, and finds the eating of beef conducive to his bodily strength, that to eat beef is therefore equally for our good who are weaker than he is, and right and just for us?

That's abominable of you, Socrates; you take the words in the sense which is most damaging to the argument.

Not at all, my good sir, I said; I am trying to understand them; and I wish that you would be a little clearer.

Well, he said, have you never heard that forms of government differ; there are tyrannies, and there are democracies, and there are aristocracies?

Yes, I know.

And the government is the ruling power in each state?

Certainly.

And the different forms of government make laws democratical, aristocratical, tyrannical, with a view to their several interests; and these laws, which are made by them for their own interests, are the justice which they deliver to their subjects, and him who transgresses them they punish as a breaker of the law, and unjust. And that is what I mean when I say that in all states there is the same principle of justice, which is the interest of the government; and as the government must be supposed to have power, the only reasonable conclusion is, that everywhere there is one principle of justice, which is the interest of the stronger.

Now I understand you, I said; and whether you are right or not I will try to discover. But let me remark, that in defining justice you have yourself used the word 'interest' which you forbade me to use. It is true, however, that in your definition the words 'of the stronger' are added.

A small addition, you must allow, he said.

Great or small, never mind about that: we must first enquire whether what you are saying is the truth. Now we are both agreed that justice is interest of some sort, but you go on to say 'of the stronger'; about this addition I am not so sure, and must therefore consider further.

Proceed.

I will; and first tell me, Do you admit that it is just for subjects to obey their rulers?

I do.

But are the rulers of states absolutely infallible, or are they sometimes liable to err?

To be sure, he replied, they are liable to err.

Then in making their laws they may sometimes make them rightly, and sometimes not?

True.

When they make them rightly, they make them agreeably to their interest; when they are mistaken, contrary to their interest; you admit that?

Yes.

And the laws which they make must be obeyed by their subjects – and that is what you call justice?

Doubtless.

Then justice, according to your argument, is not only obedience to the interest of the stronger but the reverse?

What is that you are saying? he asked.

I am only repeating what you are saying, I believe. But let us consider: Have we not admitted that the rulers may be mistaken about their own interest in what they command, and also that to obey them is justice? Has not that been admitted?

Yes.

Then you must also have acknowledged justice not to be for the interest of the stronger, when the rulers unintentionally command things to be done which are to their own injury. For if, as you say, justice is the obedience which the subject renders to their commands, in that case, O wisest of men, is there any escape from the conclusion that the weaker are commanded to do, not what is for the interest, but what is for the injury of the stronger?

Nothing can be clearer, Socrates, said Polemarchus.

Yes, said Cleitophon, interposing, if you are allowed to be his witness.

But there is no need of any witness, said Polemarchus, for Thrasymachus himself acknowledges that rulers may sometimes command what is not for their own interest, and that for subjects to obey them is justice.

Yes, Polemarchus, – Thrasymachus said that for subjects to do what was commanded by their rulers is just.

Yes, Cleitophon, but he also said that justice is the interest of the stronger, and, while admitting both these propositions, he further acknowledged that the stronger may command the weaker who are his subjects to do what is not for his own interest; whence follows that justice is the injury quite as much as the interest of the stronger.

But, said Cleitophon, he meant by the interest of the stronger what the stronger thought to be his interest, – this was what the weaker had to do; and this was affirmed by him to be justice.

Those were not his words, rejoined Polemarchus.

Never mind, I replied, if he now says that they are, let us accept his statement. Tell me, Thrasymachus, I said, did you mean by justice what the stronger thought to be his interest, whether really so or not?

Certainly not, he said. Do you suppose that I call him who is mistaken the stronger at the time when he is mistaken?

Yes, I said, my impression was that you did so, when you admitted that the ruler was not infallible but might be sometimes mistaken.

You argue like an informer, Socrates. Do you mean, for example, that he who is mistaken about the sick is a physician in that he is mistaken? or that he who errs in arithmetic or grammar is an arithmetician or grammarian at the time when he is making the mistake, in respect of the mistake? True, we say that the physician or arithmetician or grammarian has made a mistake, but this is only a way of speaking; for the fact is that neither the grammarian nor any other person of skill ever makes a mistake in so far as he is what his name implies; they none of them err unless their skill fails them, and then they cease to be skilled artists. No artist or sage or ruler errs at the time when he is what his name implies; though he is commonly said to err, and I adopted the common mode of speaking. But to be perfectly accurate, since you are such a lover of accuracy, we should say that the ruler, in so far as he is a ruler, is unerring, and, being unerring, always commands that which is for his own interest; and the subject is required to execute his commands; and therefore, as I said at first and now repeat, justice is the interest of the stronger.

Indeed, Thrasymachus, and do I really appear to you to argue like an informer?

Certainly, he replied.

And do you suppose that I ask these questions with any design of injuring you in the argument?

Nay, he replied, 'suppose' is not the word – I know it; but you will be found out, and by sheer force of argument you will never prevail.

I shall not make the attempt, my dear man; but to avoid any misunderstanding occurring between us in future, let me ask, in what sense do you speak of a ruler or stronger whose interest, as you were saying, he being the superior, it is just that the inferior should execute – is he a ruler in the popular or in the strict sense of the term?

In the strictest of all senses, he said. And now cheat and play the informer if you can; I ask no quarter at your hands. But you never will be able, never.

And do you imagine, I said, that I am such a madman as to try and cheat Thrasymachus? I might as well shave a lion.

Why, he said, you made the attempt a minute ago, and you failed.

Enough, I said, of these civilities. It will be better that I should ask you a question: Is the physician, taken in that strict sense of which you are speaking, a healer of the sick or a maker of money? And remember that I am now speaking of the true physician.

A healer of the sick, he replied.

And the pilot – that is to say, the true pilot – is he a captain of sailors or a mere sailor?

A captain of sailors.

The circumstance that he sails in the ship is not to be taken into account; neither is he to be called a sailor; the name pilot by which he is distinguished has nothing to do with sailing, but is significant of his skill and of his authority over the sailors.

Very true, he said.

Now, I said, every art has an interest?

Certainly.

For which the art has to consider and provide?

Yes, that is the aim of art.

And the interest of any art is the perfection of it – this and nothing else?

What do you mean?

I mean what I may illustrate negatively by the example of the body. Suppose you were to ask me whether the body is self-sufficing or has wants, I should reply: Certainly the body has wants; for the body may be ill and require to be cured, and has therefore interests to which the art of medicine ministers; and this is the origin and intention of medicine, as you will acknowledge. Am I not right?

Quite right, he replied.

But is the art of medicine or any other art faulty or deficient in any quality in the same way that the eye may be deficient in sight or the ear fail of hearing, and therefore requires another art to provide for the interests of seeing and hearing – has art in itself, I say, any similar liability to fault or defect, and does every art require another supplementary art to provide for its interests, and that another and another without end? Or have the arts to look only after their own interests? Or have they no need either of themselves or of another? – having no faults or defects, they have no need to correct them, either by the exercise of their own art or of any other; they have only to consider the interest of their subject-matter. For every art remains pure and faultless while remaining true – that is to say, while perfect and unimpaired. Take the words in your precise sense, and tell me whether I am not right.

Yes, clearly.

Then medicine does not consider the interest of medicine, but the interest of the body?

True, he said.

Nor does the art of horsemanship consider the interests of the art of horsemanship, but the interests of the horse; neither do any other arts care for themselves, for they have no needs; they care only for that which is the subject of their art?

True, he said.

But surely, Thrasymachus, the arts are the superiors and rulers of their own subjects?

To this he assented with a good deal of reluctance.

Then, I said, no science or art considers or enjoins the interest of the stronger or superior, but only the interest of the subject and weaker?

He made an attempt to contest this proposition also, but finally acquiesced.

Then, I continued, no physician, in so far as he is a physician, considers his own good in what he prescribes, but the good of his patient; for the true physician is also a ruler having the human body as a subject, and is not a mere money-maker; that has been admitted?

Yes.

And the pilot likewise, in the strict sense of the term, is a ruler of sailors and not a mere sailor?

That has been admitted.

And such a pilot and ruler will provide and prescribe for the interest of the sailor who is under him, and not for his own or the ruler's interest?

He gave a reluctant 'Yes.'

Then, I said, Thrasymachus, there is no one in any rule who, in so far as he is a ruler, considers or enjoins what is for his own interest, but always what is for the interest of his subject or suitable to his art; to that he looks, and that alone he considers in everything which he says and does.

[. . .]

I had always admired the genius of Glaucon and Adeimantus, but on hearing these words I was quite delighted, and said: Sons of an illustrious father, that was not a bad beginning of the Elegiac verses which the admirer of Glaucon made in honour of you after you had distinguished yourselves at the battle of Megara: – 'Sons of Ariston,' he sang, 'divine offspring of an illustrious hero.' The epithet is very appropriate, for there is something truly divine in being able to argue as you have done for the superiority of injustice, and remaining unconvinced by your own arguments. And I do believe that you are not convinced – this I infer from your general character, for had I judged only from your speeches I should have mistrusted you. But now, the greater my confidence in you, the greater is my difficulty in knowing what to say. For I am in a strait between two; on the one hand I feel that I am unequal to the task; and my inability is brought home to me by the fact that you were not satisfied with the answer which I made to Thrasymachus, proving, as I thought, the superiority which justice has over injustice. And yet I cannot refuse to help, while breath and speech remain to me; I am afraid that there would be an impiety in being present when justice is evil spoken of and not lifting up a hand in her defence. And therefore I had best give such help as I can.

Glaucon and the rest entreated me by all means not to let the question drop, but to proceed in the investigation. They wanted to arrive at the truth, first, about the nature of justice and injustice, and secondly, about their relative advantages. I told them, what I really thought, that the enquiry would be of a serious nature, and would require very good eyes. Seeing then, I said, that we are no great wits, I think that we had better adopt a method which I may illustrate thus; suppose that a short-sighted person had been asked by some one to read small letters from a distance; and it occurred to some one else that they might be found in another place which was larger and in which the letters were larger – if they were the same and he could read the larger letters first, and then proceed to the lesser – this would have been thought a rare piece of good fortune.

Very true, said Adeimantus; but how does the illustration apply to our enquiry?

I will tell you, I replied; justice, which is the subject of our enquiry, is, as you know, sometimes spoken of as the virtue of an individual, and sometimes as the virtue of a State.

True, he replied.

And is not a State larger than an individual?

It is.

Then in the larger the quantity of justice is likely to be larger and more easily discernible. I propose therefore that we enquire into the nature of justice and injustice, first as they appear in the State, and secondly in the individual, proceeding from the greater to the lesser and comparing them.

That, he said, is an excellent proposal.

And if we imagine the State in process of creation, we shall see the justice and injustice of the State in process of creation also.

I dare say.

When the State is completed there may be a hope that the object of our search will be more easily discovered.

Yes, far more easily.

But ought we to attempt to construct one? I said; for to do so, as I am inclined to think, will be a very serious task. Reflect therefore.

I have reflected, said Adeimantus, and am anxious that you should proceed.

A State, I said, arises, as I conceive, out of the needs of mankind; no one is self-sufficing, but all of us have many wants. Can any other origin of a State be imagined?

There can be no other.

Then as we have many wants, and many persons are needed to supply them, one takes a helper for one purpose and another for another; and when these partners and helpers are gathered together in one habitation the body of inhabitants is termed a State.

True, he said.

And they exchange with one another, and one gives, and another receives, under the idea that the exchange will be for their good.

Very true.

Then, I said, let us begin and create in idea a State; and yet the true creator is necessity, who is the mother of our invention.

Of course, he replied.

Now the first and greatest of necessities is food, which is the condition of life and existence.

Certainly.

The second is a dwelling, and the third clothing and the like.

True.

And now let us see how our city will be able to supply this great demand: We may suppose that one man is a husbandman, another a builder, some one else a weaver – shall we add to them a shoemaker, or perhaps some other purveyor to our bodily wants?

Quite right.

The barest notion of a State must include four or five men.

Clearly.

And how will they proceed? Will each bring the result of his labours into a common stock? – the individual husbandman, for example, producing for four, and labouring four times as long and as much as he need in the provision of food with which he supplies others as well as himself; or will he have nothing to do with others and not be at the trouble of producing for them, but provide for himself alone a fourth of the food in a fourth of the time, and in the remaining three fourths of his time be employed in making a house or a coat or a pair of shoes, having no partnership with others, but supplying himself all his own wants?

Adeimantus thought that he should aim at producing food only and not at producing everything.

Probably, I replied, that would be the better way; and when I hear you say this, I am myself reminded that we are not all alike; there are diversities of natures among us which are adapted to different occupations.

Very true.

And will you have a work better done when the workman has many occupations, or when he has only one?

When he has only one.

Further, there can be no doubt that a work is spoilt when not done at the right time?

No doubt.

For business is not disposed to wait until the doer of the business is at leisure; but the doer must follow up what he is doing, and make the business his first object.

He must.

And if so, we must infer that all things are produced more plentifully and easily and of a better quality when one man does one thing which is natural to him and does it at the right time, and leaves other things.

Undoubtedly.

Then more than four citizens will be required; for the husbandman will not make his own plough or mattock, or other implements of agriculture, if they are to be good for anything. Neither will the builder make his tools – and he too needs many; and in like manner the weaver and shoemaker.

True.

Then carpenters, and smiths, and many other artisans, will be sharers in our little State, which is already beginning to grow?

True.

Yet even if we add neatherds, shepherds, and other herdsmen, in order that our husbandmen may have oxen to plough with, and builders as well as husbandmen may have draught cattle, and curriers and weavers fleeces and hides, – still our State will not be very large.

That is true; yet neither will it be a very small State which contains all these.

Then, again, there is the situation of the city – to find a place where nothing need be imported is wellnigh impossible.

Impossible.

Then there must be another class of citizens who will bring the required supply from another city?

There must.

But if the trader goes empty-handed, having nothing which they require who would supply his need, he will come back empty-handed.

That is certain.

And therefore what they produce at home must be not only enough for themselves, but such both in quantity and quality as to accommodate those from whom their wants are supplied.

Very true.

Then more husbandmen and more artisans will be required?

They will.

Not to mention the importers and exporters, who are called merchants?

Yes.

Then we shall want merchants?

We shall.

And if any merchandise is to be carried over the sea, skilful sailors will also be needed, and in considerable numbers?

Yes, in considerable numbers.

Then, again, within the city, how will they exchange their productions? To secure such an exchange was, as you will remember, one of our principal objects when we formed them into a society and constituted a State.

Clearly they will buy and sell.

Then they will need a market-place, and a money-token for purposes of exchange.

Certainly.

Suppose now that a husbandman, or an artisan, brings some production to market, and he comes at a time when there is no one to exchange with him, – is he to leave his calling and sit idle in the market-place?

Not at all; he will find people there who, seeing the want, undertake the office of salesmen. In well-ordered states they are commonly those who are the weakest in bodily strength, and therefore of little use for any other purpose; their duty is to be in the market, and to give money in exchange for goods to those who desire to sell and to take money from those who desire to buy.

This want, then, creates a class of retail-traders in our State. Is not 'retailer' the term which is applied to those who sit in the market-place engaged in buying and selling, while those who wander from one city to another are called merchants?

Yes, he said.

And there is another class of servants, who are intellectually hardly on the level of companionship; still they have plenty of bodily strength for labour, which accordingly they sell, and are called, if I do not mistake, hirelings, hire being the name which is given to the price of their labour.

True.

Then hirelings will help to make up our population?

Yes.

And now, Adeimantus, is our State matured and perfected?

I think so.

Where, then, is justice, and where is injustice, and in what part of the State did they spring up?

Probably in the dealings of these citizens with one another. I cannot imagine that they are more likely to be found any where else.

I dare say that you are right in your suggestion, I said; we had better think the matter out, and not shrink from the enquiry.

Let us then consider, first of all, what will be their way of life, now that we have thus established them. Will they not produce corn, and wine, and clothes, and shoes, and build houses for themselves? And when they are housed, they will work, in summer, commonly, stripped and barefoot, but in winter substantially clothed and shod. They will feed on barley-meal and flour of wheat, baking and kneading them, making noble cakes and loaves; these they will serve up on a mat of reeds or on clean leaves, themselves reclining the while upon beds strewn with yew or myrtle. And they and their children will feast, drinking of the wine which they have made, wearing garlands on their heads, and hymning the praises of the gods, in happy converse with one another. And they will take care that their families do not exceed their means; having an eye to poverty or war.

But, said Glaucon, interposing, you have not given them a relish to their meal.

True, I replied, I had forgotten; of course they must have a relish – salt, and olives, and cheese, and they will boil roots and herbs such as country people prepare; for a dessert we shall give them figs, and peas, and beans; and they will roast myrtle-berries and acorns at the fire, drinking in moderation. And with such a diet they may be expected to live in peace and health to a good old age, and bequeath a similar life to their children after them.

Yes, Socrates, he said, and if you were providing for a city of pigs, how else would you feed the beasts?

But what would you have, Glaucon? I replied.

Why, he said, you should give them the ordinary conveniences of life. People who are to be comfortable are accustomed to lie on sofas, and dine off tables, and they should have sauces and sweets in the modern style.

Yes, I said, now I understand: the question which you would have me consider is, not only how a State, but how a luxurious State is created; and possibly there is no harm in this, for in such a State we shall be more likely to see how justice and injustice originate. In my opinion the true and healthy constitution of the State is the one which I have described. But if you wish also to see a State at fever-heat, I have no objection. For I suspect that many will not be satisfied with the simpler way of life. They will be for adding sofas, and tables, and other furniture; also dainties, and perfumes, and incense, and courtesans, and cakes, all these not of one sort only, but in every variety; we must go beyond the necessaries of which I was at first speaking, such as houses, and clothes, and shoes: the arts of the painter and the embroiderer will have to be set in motion, and gold and ivory and all sorts of materials must be procured.

True, he said.

Then we must enlarge our borders; for the original healthy State is no longer sufficient. Now will the city have to fill and swell with a multitude of callings which are not required by any natural want; such as the whole tribe of hunters and actors, of whom one large class have to do with forms and colours; another will be the votaries of music – poets and their attendant train of rhapsodists, players, dancers, contractors; also makers of divers kinds of articles, including women's dresses. And we shall want more servants. Will not tutors be also in request, and nurses wet and dry, tirewomen and barbers, as well as confectioners and cooks; and swineherds, too, who were not needed and therefore had no place in the former edition of our State, but are needed now? They must not be forgotten: and there will be animals of many other kinds, if people eat them.

Certainly.

And living in this way we shall have much greater need of physicians than before?

Much greater.

And the country which was enough to support the original inhabitants will be too small now, and not enough?

Quite true.

Then a slice of our neighbours' land will be wanted by us for pasture and tillage, and they will want a slice of ours, if, like ourselves, they exceed the limit of necessity, and give themselves up to the unlimited accumulation of wealth?

That, Socrates, will be inevitable.

And so we shall go to war, Glaucon. Shall we not?

Most certainly, he replied.

Then, without determining as yet whether war does good or harm, thus much we may affirm, that now we have discovered war to be derived from causes which are also the causes of almost all the evils in States, private as well as public.

Undoubtedly.

And our State must once more enlarge; and this time the enlargement will be nothing short of a whole army, which will have to go out and fight with the invaders for all that we have, as well as for the things and persons whom we were describing above.

Why? he said; are they not capable of defending themselves?

No, I said; not if we were right in the principle which was acknowledged by all of us when we were framing the State: the principle, as you will remember, was that one man cannot practise many arts with success.

Very true, he said.

But is not war an art?

Certainly.

And an art requiring as much attention as shoemaking?

Quite true.

And the shoemaker was not allowed by us to be a husbandman, or a weaver, or a builder – in order that we might have our shoes well made; but to him and to every other worker was assigned one work for which he was by nature fitted, and at that he was to continue working all his life long and at no other; he was not to let opportunities slip, and then he would become a good workman. Now nothing can be more important than that the work of a soldier should be well done. But is war an art so easily acquired that a man may be a warrior who is also a husbandman, or shoemaker, or other artisan; although no one in the world would be a good dice or draught player who merely took up the game as a recreation, and had not from his earliest years devoted himself to this and nothing else? No tools will make a man a skilled workman, or master of defence, nor be of any use to him who has not learned how to handle them, and has never bestowed any attention upon them. How then will he who takes up a shield or other implement of war become a good fighter all in a day, whether with heavy-armed or any other kind of troops?

Yes, he said, the tools which would teach men their own use would be beyond price.

And the higher the duties of the guardian, I said, the more time, and skill, and art, and application will be needed by him?

No doubt, he replied.

Will he not also require natural aptitude for his calling?

Certainly.

Then it will be our duty to select, if we can, natures which are fitted for the task of guarding the city?

It will.

And the selection will be no easy matter, I said; but we must be brave and do our best.

We must.

Is not the noble youth very like a well-bred dog in respect of guarding and watching?

What do you mean?

I mean that both of them ought to be quick to see, and swift to overtake the enemy when they see him; and strong too if, when they have caught him, they have to fight with him.

All these qualities, he replied, will certainly be required by them.

Well, and your guardian must be brave if he is to fight well?

Certainly.

And is he likely to be brave who has no spirit, whether horse or dog or any other animal? Have you never observed how invincible and unconquerable is spirit and how the presence of it makes the soul of any creature to be absolutely fearless and indomitable?

I have.

Then now we have a clear notion of the bodily qualities which are required in the guardian.

True.

And also of the mental ones; his soul is to be full of spirit?

Yes.

But are not these spirited natures apt to be savage with one another, and with everybody else?

A difficulty by no means easy to overcome, he replied.

Whereas, I said, they ought to be dangerous to their enemies, and gentle to their friends; if not, they will destroy themselves without waiting for their enemies to destroy them.

True, he said.

What is to be done then? I said; how shall we find a gentle nature which has also a great spirit, for the one is the contradiction of the other?

True.

He will not be a good guardian who is wanting in either of these two qualities; and yet the combination of them appears to be impossible; and hence we must infer that to be a good guardian is impossible.

I am afraid that what you say is true, he replied.

Here feeling perplexed I began to think over what had preceded. – My friend, I said, no wonder that we are in a perplexity; for we have lost sight of the image which we had before us.

What do you mean? he said.

I mean to say that there do exist natures gifted with those opposite qualities.

And where do you find them?

Many animals, I replied, furnish examples of them; our friend the dog is a very good one: you know that well-bred dogs are perfectly gentle to their familiars and acquaintances, and the reverse to strangers.

Yes, I know.

Then there is nothing impossible or out of the order of nature in our finding a guardian who has a similar combination of qualities?

Certainly not.

Would not he who is fitted to be a guardian, besides the spirited nature, need to have the qualities of a philosopher?

I do not apprehend your meaning.

The trait of which I am speaking, I replied, may be also seen in the dog, and is remarkable in the animal.

What trait?

Why, a dog, whenever he sees a stranger, is angry; when an acquaintance, he welcomes him, although the one has never done him any harm, nor the other any good. Did this never strike you as curious?

The matter never struck me before; but I quite recognise the truth of your remark.

And surely this instinct of the dog is very charming; – your dog is a true philosopher.

Why?

Why, because he distinguishes the face of a friend and of an enemy only by the criterion of knowing and not knowing. And must not an animal be a lover of learning who determines what he likes and dislikes by the test of knowledge and ignorance?

Most assuredly.

And is not the love of learning the love of wisdom, which is philosophy?

They are the same, he replied.

And may we not say confidently of man also, that he who is likely to be gentle to his friends and acquaintances, must by nature be a lover of wisdom and knowledge?

That we may safely affirm.

Then he who is to be a really good and noble guardian of the State will require to unite in himself philosophy and spirit and swiftness and strength?

Undoubtedly.

Then we have found the desired natures; and now that we have found them, how are they to be reared and educated? Is not this an enquiry which may be expected to throw light on the greater enquiry which is our final end – How do justice and injustice grow up in States? for we do not want either to omit what is to the point or to draw out the argument to an inconvenient length.

Adeimantus thought that the enquiry would be of great service to us.

Then, I said, my dear friend, the task must not be given up, even if somewhat long.

Certainly not.

Come then, and let us pass a leisure hour in story-telling, and our story shall be the education of our heroes.

By all means.

And what shall be their education? Can we find a better than the traditional sort? – and this has two divisions, gymnastic for the body, and music for the soul.

True.

Shall we begin education with music, and go on to gymnastic afterwards?

By all means.

And when you speak of music, do you include literature or not?

I do.

And literature may be either true or false?

Yes.

And the young should be trained in both kinds, and we begin with the false?

I do not understand your meaning, he said.

You know, I said, that we begin by telling children stories which, though not wholly destitute of truth, are in the main fictitious; and these stories are told them when they are not of an age to learn gymnastics.

Very true.

That was my meaning when I said that we must teach music before gymnastics.

Quite right, he said.

You know also that the beginning is the most important part of any work, especially in the case of a young and tender thing; for that is the time at which the character is being formed and the desired impression is more readily taken.

Quite true.

And shall we just carelessly allow children to hear any casual tales which may be devised by casual persons, and to receive into their minds ideas for the most part the very opposite of those which we should wish them to have when they are grown up?

We cannot.

Then the first thing will be to establish a censorship of the writers of fiction, and let the censors receive any tale of fiction which is good, and reject the bad; and we will desire mothers and nurses to tell their children the authorised ones only. Let them fashion the mind with such tales, even more fondly than they mould the body with their hands; but most of those which are now in use must be discarded.

Of what tales are you speaking? he said.

You may find a model of the lesser in the greater, I said; for they are necessarily of the same type, and there is the same spirit in both of them.

Very likely, he replied; but I do not as yet know what you would term the greater.

Those, I said, which are narrated by Homer and Hesiod, and the rest of the poets, who have ever been the great story-tellers of mankind.

But which stories do you mean, he said; and what fault do you find with them?

A fault which is most serious, I said; the fault of telling a lie, and, what is more, a bad lie.

But when is this fault committed?

Whenever an erroneous representation is made of the nature of gods and heroes, – as when a painter paints a portrait not having the shadow of a likeness to the original.

Yes, he said, that sort of thing is certainly very blameable; but what are the stories which you mean?

First of all, I said, there was that greatest of all lies in high places, which the poet told about Uranus, and which was a bad lie too, – I mean what Hesiod says that Uranus did, and how Cronus retaliated on him. The doings of Cronus, and the sufferings which in turn his son inflicted upon him, even if they were true, ought certainly not to be lightly told to young and thoughtless persons; if possible, they had better be buried in silence. But if there is an absolute necessity for their mention, a chosen few might hear them in a mystery, and they should sacrifice not a common [Eleusinian] pig, but some huge and unprocurable victim; and then the number of the hearers will be very few indeed.

Why, yes, said he, those stories are extremely objectionable.

Yes, Adeimantus, they are stories not to be repeated in our State; the young man should not be told that in committing the worst of crimes he is far from doing anything outrageous; and that even if he chastises his father when he does wrong, in whatever manner, he will only be following the example of the first and greatest among the gods.

I entirely agree with you, he said; in my opinion those stories are quite unfit to be repeated.

Neither, if we mean our future guardians to regard the habit of quarrelling among themselves as of all things the basest, should any word be said to them of the wars in heaven, and of the plots and fightings of the gods against one another, for they are not true. No, we shall never mention the battles of the giants, or let them be embroidered on garments; and we shall be silent about the innumerable other quarrels of gods and heroes with their friends and relatives. If they would only believe us we would tell them that quarrelling is unholy, and that never up to this time has there been any quarrel between citizens; this is what old men and old women should begin by telling children; and when they grow up, the poets also should be told to compose for them in a similar spirit. But the narrative of Hephaestus binding Here his mother, or how on another occasion Zeus sent him flying for taking her part when she was being beaten, and all the battles of the gods in Homer – these tales must not be admitted into our State, whether they are supposed to have an allegorical meaning or not. For a young person cannot judge what is allegorical and what is literal; anything that he receives into his mind at that age is likely to become indelible and unalterable; and therefore it is most important that the tales which the young first hear should be models of virtuous thoughts.

There you are right, he replied; but if any one asks where are such models to be found and of what tales are you speaking – how shall we answer him?

I said to him, You and I, Adeimantus, at this moment are not poets, but founders of a State: now the founders of a State ought to know the general forms in which poets should cast their tales, and the limits which must be observed by them, but to make the tales is not their business.

Very true, he said; but what are these forms of theology which you mean?

Something of this kind, I replied: – God is always to be represented as he truly is, whatever be the sort of poetry, epic, lyric or tragic, in which the representation is given.

Right.

And is he not truly good? and must he not be represented as such?

Certainly.

And no good thing is hurtful?

No, indeed.

And that which is not hurtful hurts not?

Certainly not.

And that which hurts not does no evil?

No.

And can that which does no evil be a cause of evil?

Impossible.

And the good is advantageous?

Yes.

And therefore the cause of well-being?

Yes.

It follows therefore that the good is not the cause of all things, but of the good only?

Assuredly.

Then God, if he be good, is not the author of all things, as the many assert, but he is the cause of a few things only, and not of most things that occur to men. For few are the goods of human life, and many are the evils, and the good is to be attributed to God alone; of the evils the causes are to be sought elsewhere, and not in him.

That appears to me to be most true, he said.

Then we must not listen to Homer or to any other poet who is guilty of the folly of saying that two casks: 'Lie at the threshold of Zeus, full of lots, one of good, the other of evil lots,' and that he to whom Zeus gives a mixture of the two: 'Sometimes meets with evil fortune, at other times with good;' but that he to whom is given the cup of unmingled ill, 'Him wild hunger drives o'er the beauteous earth.' And again – 'Zeus, who is the dispenser of good and evil to us.' And if any one asserts that the violation of oaths and treaties, which was really the work of Pandarus, was brought about by Athene and Zeus, or that the strife and contention of the gods was instigated by Themis and Zeus, he shall not have our approval; neither will we allow our young men to hear the words of Aeschylus, that 'God plants guilt among men when he desires utterly to destroy a house.' And if a poet writes of the sufferings of Niobe – the subject of the tragedy in which these iambic verses occur – or of the house of Pelops, or of the Trojan war or on any similar theme, either we must not permit him to say that these are the works of God, or if they are of God, he must devise some explanation of them such as we are seeking: he must say that God did what was just and right, and they were the better for being punished; but that those who are punished are miserable, and that God is the author of their misery – the poet is not to be permitted to say; though he may say that the wicked are miserable because they require to be punished, and are benefited by receiving punishment from God; but that God being good is the author of evil to any one is to be strenuously denied, and not to be said or sung or heard in verse or prose by any one whether old or young in any well-ordered commonwealth. Such a fiction is suicidal, ruinous, impious.

I agree with you, he replied, and am ready to give my assent to the law.

Let this then be one of our rules and principles concerning the gods, to which our poets and reciters will be expected to conform – that God is not the author of all things, but of good only.

That will do, he said.

And what do you think of a second principle? Shall I ask you whether God is a magician, and of a nature to appear insidiously now in one shape, and now in another – sometimes himself changing and passing into many forms, sometimes deceiving us with the semblance of such transformations; or is he one and the same immutably fixed in his own proper image?

I cannot answer you, he said, without more thought.

Well, I said; but if we suppose a change in anything, that change must be effected either by the thing itself, or by some other thing?

Most certainly.

And things which are at their best are also least liable to be altered or discomposed; for example, when healthiest and strongest, the human frame is least liable to be affected by meats and drinks, and the plant which is in the fullest vigour also suffers least from winds or the heat of the sun or any similar causes.

Of course.

And will not the bravest and wisest soul be least confused or deranged by any external influence?

True.

And the same principle, as I should suppose, applies to all composite things – furniture, houses, garments: when good and well made, they are least altered by time and circumstances.

Very true.

Then everything which is good, whether made by art or nature, or both, is least liable to suffer change from without?

True.

But surely God and the things of God are in every way perfect?

Of course they are.

Then he can hardly be compelled by external influence to take many shapes?

He cannot.

But may he not change and transform himself?

Clearly, he said, that must be the case if he is changed at all.

And will he then change himself for the better and fairer, or for the worse and more unsightly?

If he change at all he can only change for the worse, for we cannot suppose him to be deficient either in virtue or beauty.

Very true, Adeimantus; but then, would any one, whether God or man, desire to make himself worse?

Impossible.

Then it is impossible that God should ever be willing to change; being, as is supposed, the fairest and best that is conceivable, every God remains absolutely and for ever in his own form.

That necessarily follows, he said, in my judgment.

Then, I said, my dear friend, let none of the poets tell us that 'The gods, taking the disguise of strangers from other lands, walk up and down cities in all sorts of forms;' and let no one slander Proteus and Thetis, neither let any one, either in tragedy or in any other kind of poetry, introduce Here disguised in the likeness of a priestess asking an alms 'For the life-giving daughters of Inachus the river of Argos;' – let us have no more lies of that sort. Neither must we have mothers under the influence of the poets scaring their children with a bad version of these myths – telling how certain gods, as they say, 'Go about by night in the likeness of so many strangers and in divers forms;' but let them take heed lest they make cowards of their children, and at the same time speak blasphemy against the gods.

Heaven forbid, he said.

But although the gods are themselves unchangeable, still by witchcraft and deception they may make us think that they appear in various forms?

Perhaps, he replied.

Well, but can you imagine that God will be willing to lie, whether in word or deed, or to put forth a phantom of himself?

I cannot say, he replied.

Do you not know, I said, that the true lie, if such an expression may be allowed, is hated of gods and men?

What do you mean? he said.

I mean that no one is willingly deceived in that which is the truest and highest part of himself, or about the truest and highest matters; there, above all, he is most afraid of a lie having possession of him.

Still, he said, I do not comprehend you.

The reason is, I replied, that you attribute some profound meaning to my words; but I am only saying that deception, or being deceived or uninformed about the highest realities in the highest part of themselves, which is the soul, and in that part of them to have and to hold the lie, is what mankind least like; – that, I say, is what they utterly detest.

There is nothing more hateful to them.

And, as I was just now remarking, this ignorance in the soul of him who is deceived may be called the true lie; for the lie in words is only a kind of imitation and shadowy image of a previous affection of the soul, not pure unadulterated falsehood. Am I not right?

Perfectly right.

The true lie is hated not only by the gods, but also by men?

Yes.

Whereas the lie in words is in certain cases useful and not hateful; in dealing with enemies – that would be an instance; or again, when those whom we call our friends in a fit of madness or illusion are going to do some harm, then it is useful and is a sort of medicine or preventive; also in the tales of mythology, of which we were just now speaking – because we do not know the truth about ancient times, we make falsehood as much like truth as we can, and so turn it to account.

Very true, he said.

But can any of these reasons apply to God? Can we suppose that he is ignorant of antiquity, and therefore has recourse to invention?

That would be ridiculous, he said.

Then the lying poet has no place in our idea of God?

I should say not.

Or perhaps he may tell a lie because he is afraid of enemies?

That is inconceivable.

But he may have friends who are senseless or mad?

But no mad or senseless person can be a friend of God.

Then no motive can be imagined why God should lie?

None whatever.

Then the superhuman and divine is absolutely incapable of falsehood?

Yes.

Then is God perfectly simple and true both in word and deed; he changes not; he deceives not, either by sign or word, by dream or waking vision.

Your thoughts, he said, are the reflection of my own.

You agree with me then, I said, that this is the second type or form in which we should write and speak about divine things. The gods are not magicians who transform themselves, neither do they deceive mankind in any way.

I grant that.

Then, although we are admirers of Homer, we do not admire the lying dream which Zeus sends to Agamemnon; neither will we praise the verses of Aeschylus in which Thetis says that Apollo at her nuptials

> Was celebrating in song her fair progeny whose days were to be long, and to know no sickness. And when he had spoken of my lot as in all things blessed of heaven he raised a note of triumph and cheered my soul. And I thought that the word of Phoebus, being divine and full of prophecy, would not fail. And now he himself who uttered the strain, he who was present at the banquet, and who said this – he it is who has slain my son.

These are the kind of sentiments about the gods which will arouse our anger; and he who utters them shall be refused a chorus; neither shall we allow teachers to make use of them in the instruction of the young, meaning, as we do, that our guardians, as far as men can be, should be true worshippers of the gods and like them.

I entirely agree, he said, in these principles, and promise to make them my laws.

2

ARISTOTLE

Sources: Edward Wallford (trans.) (1885) *The Politics and Economics of Aristotle*. London, George Bell and Son, pp. 2–8, 144–55.

J.A.K. Thompson (trans.) (1970) *Aristotle: The Ethics*. London, Penguin Classics, pp. 178–85.

Aristotle presents an influential view of the state as a natural organization which exists for the good of its parts. Aristotle sees the state as prior to the individual, therefore, so that the state's well-being may legitimately take precedence over the individual. Aristotle goes on to examine various kinds of state from tyranny to democracy and concludes that the best form represents a mean between the extremes. He favours a mixed constitution with elements of both aristocracy and democracy. Similarly, Aristotle argues that the best kind of state is found where a large middle group, placed between the very very rich and the very poor, is dominant. In contrast to Plato's emphasis on the rule of philosophers, Aristotle presents a distinctive view of political wisdom which stresses the significance of practical experience in decision-making.

THE POLITICS

Book 1, Chapter I

As we see that every state is a society, and that every society is established for the sake of some good end; (for an apparent good is the spring of all human actions;) it is evident that all societies aim at some good or other:

and this is more especially true of that which aims at the highest possible end, and is itself the most excellent, and embraces all the rest.

Now this is that which is called a state, and forms a political society. For those are greatly at fault, who think that the principles of a political, a regal, a domestic, and a despotic government are the same; inasmuch as they suppose that each of these differ merely in point of number, and not in kind: so that with them a despotic government is one composed of a very few, a domestic of more, a civil and a regal of still more, as if there were no difference between a large family and a small city; and they hold that a regal and political government are the same things; only that in the one, a single person is continually at the head of affairs, while in the other, each individual in his turn becomes a magistrate and again a private person, according to the rules of political science. Now this is not true; and what we say will be evident to any one who will consider this question after the approved method. For as, in every other subject, it is necessary to separate its component nature, till we arrive at its first elements, which are the most minute parts thereof; so by viewing the first elements of which a state is composed, we shall see wherein states differ from each other, and whether it is possible to arrive at any systematic knowledge concerning each of the points above mentioned.

Chapter II

Now if any one would watch the parts of a state from the very first as they rise into existence, as in other matters, so here he would gain the truest view of the subject. In the first place, then, it is requisite that those should be joined together, which cannot exist without each other, as the male and the female, for the business of propagation; and this not through deliberate choice, but by that natural impulse which acts both in plants and in animals, namely, the desire of leaving behind them others like themselves. By nature too some beings command, and others obey, for the sake of mutual safety; for a being endowed with discernment and forethought is by nature the superior and governor; whereas he who is merely able to execute by bodily labour, is the inferior and a natural slave; and hence the interest of master and slave is identical. But there is a natural difference between the female and the slave; for nature does nothing meanly, like artists who make the Delphic swords; but she has one instrument for one end; for thus her instruments are most likely to be brought to perfection, being made to contribute to one end, and not to many. Yet, among Barbarians, the female and the slave are upon a level in the community; the reason for which is, that they are not fitted by nature to rule; and so their relationship becomes merely that between slaves of different sexes. For which reason the poets say, 'Tis meet that barbarous tribes to Greeks should bow.' as if a barbarian and a slave were by nature one and the same. Now of these two societies the domestic tie is the first, and Hesiod is right when he says, 'First house, then wife, then oxen for the plough;' for the ox is to the poor man in the place of a household slave. That society, then, which nature has established for daily support, is a family and those who compose it are called by 'Charondas 'Ομοσίπνοι, and by Epimenides the Cretan 'Ομόκαπνοι. But the society of many families, which was instituted for lasting and mutual advantage, is called a village and a village is most naturally composed of the emigrant members of one family, whom some persons call 'Ομογάλακτες, the children and the children's children. And hence, by the way, states were originally governed by kings, as the Barbarians now are; for they were composed of those who always were under kingly government. For every family is governed by the elder, as are its branches, on account of their relationship; and this is what Homer says, 'Then each his wife and child doth rule' for in this scattered manner they formerly lived. And the general opinion which makes the gods themselves subject to kingly government, arises from the fact that most men formerly were, and many are so now; and as they hold the gods to be like themselves in form, so they suppose their manner of life must needs be the same. But when many villages join themselves perfectly together into one society, that society is a state, and contains in itself, if I may so speak, the perfection of independence; and it is first founded that men may live, but continued that they may live happily. For which reason every state is the work of nature, since the first social ties are such; for to this they all tend as to an end, and the nature of a thing is judged by its tendency. For what every being is in its perfect state, that certainly is the nature of that being, whether it be a man, a horse, or a house; besides, its own final cause and its end must be the perfection of any thing; but a government complete in itself constitutes a final cause and what is best. Hence it is evident, that a state is one of the works of nature, and that man is naturally a political animal, and that whosoever is naturally, and not accidentally, unfit for society, must be either inferior or superior to man; just as the person reviled in Homer, 'No tribe, nor state, nor home hath he.' For he whose nature is such as this, must needs be a lover of strife, and as solitary as a bird of prey. It is clear, then, that man is truly a more social animal than bees, or any of the herding cattle; for nature, as we say, does nothing in vain, and man is the only animal who has reason. Speech indeed, as being the token of pleasure and pain, is imparted to other beings also, and thus far their nature extends; they can perceive pleasure and pain, and can impart these sensations to others; but speech is given to us to express what is useful or hurtful to us, and also what is just and unjust; for in this particular man differs from other animals, that he alone has a perception of good and evil, of justice and injustice, and it is the interchange of these common sentiments which forms a family and a city. And further, in the order of nature, the state is prior to the family or the individual; for the whole must necessarily be prior to the parts; for if you take away the whole body, you cannot say a foot or a hand remains, unless by equivocation, as if any one should call a hand made of stone, a hand; for such only can it have when mutilated. But every thing is defined according to its effects and inherent powers, so that when these no longer remain such as they were, it cannot be said to be the same, but something of the same name. It is plain, then, that the state is prior to the individual, for if an individual is not complete in himself, he bears the same relation to the state as other parts do to a whole; but he that is incapable of society, or so complete in himself as not to want it, makes no part of a state, but is either a beast or a god. There is then in all persons a natural impetus to associate with each other in this manner, and he who first established civil society was the cause of the greatest benefit; for as man, thus perfected, is the most excellent of all living beings, so without law and justice he would be the worst of all; for nothing is so savage as injustice in arms; but man is born with a faculty of gaining himself arms by prudence and virtue; arms which yet he may apply to the most opposite purposes. And hence he who is devoid of virtue will be the most wicked and cruel, the most lustful and gluttonous being imaginable. Now justice is a social virtue; for it is the rule of the social state, and the very criterion of what is right.

[. . .]

Chapter IX

Next in order to what has been said, let us state how that government which is peculiarly called a polity arises, beside a democracy and an oligarchy, and how it ought to be established; and this will at the same time show what are the proper limits by which these governments are bounded; for we must mark out wherein they differ from one another, and then from each of these we must take as it were a contribution, and so combine them. There are three ways in which states may be blended and joined together; for, in the first place, we may take from both sides whatever the laws of each have ordered; as for instance, in matters of judicial trials. For in an oligarchy the rich are fined if they do not serve as dicasts, but the poor are not paid for their attendance; but in democracies they are paid, while the rich are not fined for neglect. Now each of these points is a matter which belongs in common to both states; and hence they are adapted to a free state, which is composed of both. This, then, is one way in which they may be joined together. In the second place, a medium may be taken between the different methods which each state lays down; for instance, in a democracy the right to vote in the public assembly is either confined by no census at all, or by a low one; in an oligarchy it belongs only to those whose standard of wealth is high: therefore, as these two practices are incompatible, a census between each may be established in such a state. The third method is compounded of two ordinances, partly from the oligarchic principle and partly from the democratic. For instance, as it seems suitable to a democracy, that the magistrates should be chosen by lot, but to an aristocracy by vote; and it is oligarchical to choose them according to a census, while not to do so is democratical. To copy something from each other, then, is at once aristocratical and suitable to a free state; from an oligarchy, their choice of magistrates by vote, but from a democracy their refusal to impose a census. This is the way of blending them: but the best test of a happy mixture of a democracy and an oligarchy is, when a person may properly call the same state both a democracy and an oligarchy; for it is evident, that those who thus speak of it are led to do so, because both forms are there well blended together. And indeed this is common to all means, that the extremes of each side should be discerned in them; it is the case with the state of Lacedæmon; for many strive to maintain that it is a democracy, because it has many particulars which follow that form of government; as for instance, in the first place, in the bringing up of their children. For the children of both rich and poor are brought up in the same manner; and they are educated in such a manner that the children of the poor may partake of it: and the same rules are observed when they are successively youths and men, there is no distinction between a rich person and a poor one, and in their public tables the same provision is served to all. The rich also wear only such clothes as the poorest man might be able to purchase. Moreover, with respect to two magistracies of the highest rank, to one they have a right to elect, and to have a share of the other; for they elect the Senate and partake in the Ephoralty. Others consider it as an oligarchy, because it has many oligarchical points; as in choosing all their officers by vote, and not by lot; in there being but a few who have a right to judge on capital causes, and in matters of banishment, and the like. Indeed, a state which is well composed of two others ought to show that it resembles them both, and yet is neither one nor the other. Such a state ought to have its means of preservation in itself, and not from without; and when I say in itself, I do not mean that it should owe this to the forbearance of their neighbours, (for this may happen to a bad government,) but to the fact that every member of the community is unwilling that there should be the least alteration in its constitution. We have then spoken of the method in which a free state ought to be established, and likewise a so-called aristocracy.

Chapter X

It now remains for us to treat of a tyranny; not that there is much to be said on that subject, but still let it receive its proper place in our plan, since we have enumerated it also as one form of government. Now, in the beginning of this work we inquired into the nature of kingly government, where we entered into a particular examination of what was most properly called kingly sway, and whether it was advantageous to a state or not, and what it should be, and whence and how established. We also divided tyranny into two species, when we were upon the subject of monarchy, because their power somehow or other easily passes into a kingly government, owing to the fact that they are both of them established by law; for among some of the barbarians they elect monarchs with absolute power, and formerly among the Greeks there were some such, whom they called Æsymnetes. Now these have certain points of difference from each other; for they were kingly so far as they were regulated by law, ruled over voluntary subjects; but they were tyrannical, because they ruled despotically, according to their own will. There is a third species of tyranny, which seems to be most properly so called, the counterpart of kingly power; and this monarchy must needs be a tyranny, where one rules over his equals and superiors, without being accountable for his conduct, and whose object is his own advantage, and not the advantage of those whom he governs. And hence he rules by compulsion; for no freeman will ever willingly submit to such a government. These then, and so many, are the different species of tyrannies, owing to the above-mentioned causes.

Chapter XI

We now inquire what form of government and what manner of life is best for communities in general, and for the greater part of men; not with reference to that superior virtue which is above the reach of the vulgar, or to that education which needs every advantage of nature and fortune, nor with reference to the merely imaginary form of polity; but let it be with reference to that mode of life in which the greater part of mankind can share, and that government of which most cities can partake. For as to those, so called, aristocracies which we have now mentioned, they either fall beyond the attainment of states, or so nearly resemble that which is properly called a polity, that we shall treat of them both as one.

The opinions which we shall pass upon these subjects must depend upon the same principles: for if what we have said in our Ethics is true, that a happy life must arise from an uninterrupted course of virtue, and that virtue consists in a certain mean, of necessity the middle life must certainly be the happiest, the mean being supposed to be attainable by every one. The boundaries of virtue and vice must also necessarily be the same in a city and in a polity: for a polity is the very life of the city. In every state the people are divided into three sorts; the very rich, the very poor, and, thirdly, those who are between them. Since, then, it is universally admitted that the mean is best, it is evident, that even in point of fortune, a middle state is to be preferred; for that state is most apt to submit to reason. For those who are very handsome, or very strong, or very noble, or very rich, or, on the contrary, those who are very poor, or very weak, or very mean, with difficulty obey it. And this, because the one class is capricious and wicked on a large scale, the other rascally and mean; and the crimes of each arise respectively from insolence and villany: nor will they hold office as chiefs of a phyle or presidents of the council; and these things are both detrimental to the state. Besides, those who excel in strength, in riches, or friends, or the like, neither know how, nor are willing, to submit to command: – (and this begins at home when they are boys, for there they are brought up too delicately to be accustomed to obey their preceptors:) – as for the very poor, their excessive want reduces them to a state too mean; so that the one know not how to command, but only to be commanded as slaves, the others know not how to submit to any command, but only to command with despotic power. A city composed of such men must therefore consist of slaves and masters, not of freemen; where one party must hate, and the other despise; and this is very far removed from friendship and political community; for a community supposes affection, for men do not even on the road associate with their enemies. It is also the aim of a city to be composed as much as possible of equals; and this will be most so when the inhabitants are in the middle state; whence it follows, that that city must be best framed which is composed of those who we say are naturally its proper members. It is men of this station also who are best assured of safety; for they will neither covet what belongs to others, as the poor do; nor will others covet what is theirs, as the poor do what belongs to the rich; and thus, without plotting against any one, and having any one to plot against them, they will live free from danger. For which reason Phocylides wisely prayed,

> 'The middle state is best; that state be mine,
> Whate'er my city be.'

It is plain, then, that the most perfect political community must be amongst those who are in the middle rank, and that those states can best be carried on, wherein these are the majority and outweigh, if possible, both the other classes; or, if that cannot be, at least then either of them separate; for being thrown into the balance it will prevent either excess from preponderating. It is therefore the greatest happiness of citizens to possess a moderate and convenient fortune; for when some possess too much, and others nothing at all, the government must be either an extreme democracy, or else a pure oligarchy; or, from the excesses of both, a tyranny; for this arises from a headstrong democracy, or an oligarchy, but far more seldom when the members of the community are nearly on an equality with each other. We will assign a reason for this when we come to treat of the alterations which different states are likely to undergo. But it is clear that the middle state is the best, for it is alone free from seditions; for where the middle class is large, there is less of sedition and insurrection to disturb the community. And for the same reason extensive governments are least liable to these inconveniencies; for there the middle classes are very numerous; whereas in small ones it is easy to pass to the two extremes, so as hardly to have any in a middle state remaining, but the one half are rich, the other poor. And from the same principle it comes, that democracies are more firmly established, and of longer continuance than oligarchies; but even in those when there is a want of the proper number of men of middling fortune, the poor extend their power too far, abuses arise, and the government is soon at an end. We ought to consider as a proof of what we now advance, that the best lawgivers themselves were those in the middle rank of life; amongst whom was Solon, as is evident from his poems, and Lycurgus, (for he was not a king,) and Charondas, and indeed most others. And what has been said will show us why of so many free states, some have changed to democracies, others to oligarchies; for whenever the number of persons in the middle state has been too small, those who were the more numerous, whether the rich or the poor, always overpower them, and assume to themselves the adminstration of public affairs; and hence arises either a democracy or an oligarchy. Moreover, when in consequence of their disputes and quarrels with each other, either the rich get the better of the poor, or the poor of the rich, neither of them will establish a free state; but, as the record of their victory, they adopt one which inclines to their own principles, and form either a democracy or an oligarchy.

And further, those who gained the leadership of Greece, had each of them an eye to the respective forms of government in their own cities, and established either democracies or oligarchies, not considering what was serviceable to the state, but what was similar to their own. And for this reason a government has never, or very seldom, been established where the supreme power has been placed amongst those of the middle rank; and, amongst a few, one man only of those who have yet been conquerors has been persuaded to give the preference to this arrangement. It is indeed an established custom with the inhabitants of most cities, not to desire an equality, but either to aspire to govern, or when they are conquered to submit. Thus from what we have said, it is plain what is the best state, and why. But with regard to other polities, since we say that there are various forms both of democracy and oligarchy it will not be difficult to judge to which we should give the first place, to which the second, and which in a consequent order is better or worse, now that the best form has been defined: for that must be the best which is nearest to this, and that the worst which is most distant from the mean, unless any one forms a mere imaginary standard. I mean by this, that it may happen, that though one form of government may be better than another, yet oftentimes nothing prevents another from being preferable to it in particular circumstances, and for particular purposes.

Chapter XII

After what has been said, it follows that we should now show what and what kind of government is most suitable for particular cases. But first we must lay down the same maxim as applicable to all, that that party which desires to support the established policy of the state, ought to be superior to that which would alter it. Every city is made up of quality and quantity: by quality I mean liberty, riches, education, and nobility, and by quantity the excess of its population. Now it may so happen, that quality may exist in one of those parts of which the city is composed, and quantity in the other; thus, the number of the low-born may be greater than the number of those of family, and the number of the poor than that of the rich; but not so far that the quantity of the one shall outweigh the quality of the other. Hence these must be properly adjusted to each other; for where the number of the poor exceeds the proportion above-mentioned, there a democracy is wont to rise up, and the democracy will be of a particular species, according to that class of men which may happen to be most numerous: thus, should the number of husbandmen be excessive, it will be of the best kind; if of mechanics, and those who work for pay, of the worst; in the same manner it may be of any other set between these two. But where the rich and the noble prevail more in quality, than they fall short in quantity, there an oligarchy ensues; and this oligarchy in like manner may be of different species, according to the nature of the oligarchical party which prevails. Every legislator in framing his constitution ought to have a particular regard to those in the middle rank of life; for whether he intends an oligarchy, they should be the object of his aim; or whether a democracy, he ought to win these over to the laws. But whenever their number exceeds that of the two others, or at least over one of them, it is possible to find stability in the constitution; for there is no fear that the rich and the poor should agree to conspire together against them, for neither of these will choose to serve the other. But if any seek to fix the administration on a wider basis, they will find none preferable to this; for to rule by turns is what the rich and the poor will not submit to, on account of their distrust of each other. It is moreover allowed, that an arbitrator is the most proper person for both parties to trust to; and the middle class serve as an arbitrator.

Those too who would establish aristocratical governments are mistaken, not only in giving too much power to the rich, but also in misleading the common people; for in length of time, out of unreal goods real evils must needs arise; for the encroachments of the rich are more destructive to the state than those of the poor.

Chapter XIII

There are five particulars, in which, under fair pretences, they deal craftily with the rights of the people; and these are their public assemblies, their offices of state, their courts of justice, their military power, and their gymnastic exercises. With regard to their public assemblies; in having them open to all, but in fining the rich only; or a far larger sum, for not attending: with respect to offices, in permitting the poor to swear off, but not granting this indulgence to those who come up to the census; with respect to their courts of justice, in fining the rich for non-attendance, but the poor not at all; or those a great deal, and these very little, as was done in the laws of Charondas. In some places every citizen who is enrolled, has a right to attend the assemblies and to try causes; and if they do not do so, a very heavy fine is laid upon them; that through fear of the fine, they may avoid being enrolled, and that through not being on the roll, they need not serve in the assembly or the courts. The same spirit prevails with those who regulate their bearing arms, and their gymnastic exercises; for the poor are excused if they have no arms, but the rich are fined; and the same method takes place if they do not attend their gymnastic exercises, for there is no penalty laid on the one, but there is on the other: in order that the rich may be led to keep the one, and attend the other, while the poor, through fear of the penalty, do neither. These are the deceitful contrivances of oligarchical legislators. But contrary devices prevail in a democracy; for there they make the poor a proper allowance for attending the assemblies and the courts, but give the rich nothing for so doing; and hence it is evident, that if any one would properly blend these customs together, they must extend both the pay and the fine to every member of the community, and then every one would share it, whereas at present the polity is in the hands of one part only. The citizens of a free state ought to consist of those only who bear arms: with respect to their income, it is not easy to determine exactly, and to say that it ought to be so much: but keeping quality in view, it is fit to make the franchise as extensive as possible, so that those who share in it shall out-number those who do not; for those who are poor, although they partake not of the offices of the state, are willing to live quietly, provided that no one disturbs them in their property. But this is not an easy matter; for it may not always happen that those who are at the head of public affairs are of a humane behaviour. In time of war the poor are accustomed to show no alacrity except they have provisions found them; but when they are provided, then indeed they are willing to fight. In some governments the power is vested not only in those who bear arms, but also in those who have borne them.

Among the Malienses, the state was composed of these latter only, for to all the offices they elected soldiers who had served their time. And the first states in Greece which succeeded those where kingly power was established, were governed by the military. First of all they were governed by the horse, – (for at that time the strength and excellence of the army depended on the horse, as the heavy-armed foot were useless without proper discipline; but the art of tactics was not known to the ancients, for which reason their strength lay in their horse:) – but as the cities grew larger, and depended more on their foot-soldiers, greater numbers partook of the freedom of the state; and for this reason, what we call republics were formerly called democracies. The ancient governments were properly oligarchical and monarchical; for on account of the few persons in each state, they had but a small number of the middle rank; so that being but few, and used to subordination, they more easily submitted to be governed. We have now shown why there are many sorts of governments, and others different from those of which we have treated; (for there are more species of democracies than one, and the like is true of other forms;) as also what are their differences, and whence they arise; and besides this, we have shown which is the best form, at least in general; and which of the others is best suited for particular people.

THE ETHICS: BOOK 6

Chapter Six: What is meant by Intelligence or Scientific Insight?

Science is the coming to conclusions about universals and necessary truths. Now all science (for science involves a process of reasoning) and all facts scientifically proved depend ultimately upon certain first principles. When we see this we perceive that the first principles upon which all scientific results depend cannot be apprehended by science itself; nor, we may add, by art or common sense. The body of scientific knowledge is the product of logical deduction from premises which are eternally valid; but art and practical wisdom deal with matters susceptible of change. Nor can we say that speculative wisdom is merely a knowledge of first principles. For there are some truths which the philosopher can learn only from demonstration. Now if the qualities by means of which we reach the truth and are never led to what is false in matters variable and invariable are science, prudence, wisdom and the intelligence which apprehends the truth in reasoning; if, moreover, this mental endowment by means of which we are enabled to grasp first principles cannot be either prudence, science, or wisdom, we are left to conclude that what grasps them is 'intelligence'.

Chapter Seven: What is meant by Wisdom?

'Wisdom' is a word we use both in a particular and in a general sense. Thus, in the fine arts we attach the epithet of 'wise' to the masters – Phidias, for instance, as sculptor and Polyclitus as statuary. Here all that we mean by 'wisdom' is excellence in an art. But we also think of some people as wise not in any one of the human aptitudes but in all of them – not 'wise in some other things' or (as Homer puts it in his *Margites*):

> Neither a delver nor a ploughman he,
> Nor other wisdom had the gods bestowed.

This makes it evident that of all kinds of knowledge wisdom comes next to perfection. The wise man, you see, must not only know all that can be deduced from his first principles but he must understand their true meaning. So we conclude that wisdom must be a combination of science and reason or intelligence, being in fact the highest form of that knowledge whose objects are of transcendent value. I find it strange that anyone should regard political science or *practical* wisdom as the noblest of studies, for that is to assume that man is what is best in the world. But just as 'wholesome' and 'good' mean one thing to men and another to fish, whereas 'white' and 'straight' have always but one meaning, so 'wise', as men use the word, would always have the same signification, while 'prudent' would not. For every human creature says in effect, 'Whoever considers what is to my particular advantage is prudent and to him will I entrust myself.' And this leads people to maintain that some even of the lower animals have prudence, namely, those which evidently possess the ability to foresee what will be needed for their continued existence.

Another point that emerges clearly is that wisdom cannot be identified with political science. If men are to give the name of wisdom to the knowledge of what is to their own advantage, there will be more than one form of wisdom as there is more than one species of animal. You cannot have a single wisdom contriving the good of all living beings any more than an art of medicine consulting the health of everybody and everything. It is all very well to say that man is the noblest of the animals. There are creatures far more divine by nature than man, for instance – to take what stares us in the face – those luminaries of which the starry heavens are composed.

Enough has been said to show that wisdom is exact knowledge or science combined with the intelligence that grasps the truth of first principles when this combination is employed upon the grandest subjects of contemplation. The rareness of it leads many to say that men like Thales and Anaxagoras are no doubt wise but lack common sense. They say this when they observe such men at sea about their private interests. They allow that their knowledge is 'exceptional', 'wonderful', 'deep', 'superhuman', but they aver that it is useless because it is not the good of humanity that they explore. Common sense or prudence, however, does concern itself with human affairs and such matters as may form the subject of deliberation. To deliberate well – that, people say, is the special business of the practically wise man.[1]

Observe, too, that prudence is something more than a knowledge of general principles. It must acquire familiarity with particulars also, for conduct deals with particular circumstances, and prudence is a matter of conduct. This accounts for the fact that men who know nothing of the theory of their subject sometimes practise it with greater success than others who know it. Let me make my meaning clearer by an illustration. A man is aware that light meats are easily digested and beneficial to health but does not know what meats are light. Such a man is not so likely to make you well as one who only knows that chicken is good for you. It is in fact experience rather than theory that normally gets results. Practical wisdom being concerned with action, we need both kinds of knowledge; nay, we need the knowledge of particular facts more than general principles. But here, too, there must be a faculty – political science – in which the ultimate authority is vested.

Chapter Eight: The quality of *phronesis* reconsidered

Actually political science is an aspect of practical wisdom, though in essence they are different. Of political science one branch, regarded as sovran over the other, is legislative science; the other, dealing with the details of administration, is called political science, although that is also the name for both branches together. Political science in the narrower sense – politics in fact – is a matter of action and deliberation or policy.[2] This explains why it is only administrators who are described as practical politicians, because it is they alone who *do* things. They bear the same relation to the lawgiver as workmen to the master-craftsman. In the popular mind prudence is more particularly associated with the self and the individual – a usurpation of the title of prudence, which actually belongs to all the forms and kinds, including those designated as domestic economy, constitution-building, the art of the lawgiver, and political science, which again is subdivided into deliberative and juridical science. Now, knowing

---

1. We must not forget that no man deliberates about things that cannot be otherwise than as they are, or about things which, while admitting of variation, are not a means to some end, and that end a good that can be realized in action. Broadly speaking, a man good at deliberation is one who by careful calculation is able to make a good shot at some attainable advantage.
2. A decree of the executive in a democratic government, embodying the result of a deliberative process, is an instrument for action.

one's own interest would no doubt be one species of prudence, but there is a wide difference between it and the other species. Anyhow, the man who understands and minds his own business has the reputation of sagacity, while the practical politician is apt to be regarded as an interfering nuisance. Hence, Euripides was moved to represent a character as saying:

> I *prudent?* I, that might have lived unvexed
> By public cares, one man of many men,
> And with the wisest shared the common lot.
> Yet do we rather honour the proud fool
> Pestered for ever with a thousand cares.

Of course people do seek their own good and consider it their duty to do so, and it is the belief that this is so which has given rise to the notion that it is the self-regarding man who is prudent. Yet who can doubt that it is impossible for a man to secure his own interest without the aid of domestic economy, nay, without the aid of politics? Not to mention that even the best way of pursuing one's own interest is an obscure point and calls for investigation.

The truth of what I have said gets confirmation from another quarter. It is notorious that young persons are capable of becoming excellent geometricians and mathematicians and accomplished students in subjects of that nature. Yet the public is not easily persuaded that a young man can be prudent. The reason is that prudence involves a detailed knowledge which comes only from practical experience, and practical experience is what the young man lacks – it comes only after many years.[3] Moreover, a man who deliberates may go astray either in the principle he applies or in the particular *data* to which he applies it. Thus, in a study of water he may labour under the mistaken notion that (*a*) all heavy water is bad, or (*b*) that a particular specimen of water is heavy.

In one respect, then, prudence is the exact opposite of intuitive intelligence. Intelligence apprehends the truth of definitions which cannot be proved by argument, while prudence involves knowledge of the ultimate particular thing, which cannot be attained by science but only by 'perception'. By this I mean not perception by any one of the special senses but the power of perceiving such a truth as that the irreducible figure in mathematics is the triangle, beyond which we cannot carry our analysis. Yet this mathematical perception deserves the name better than does prudence, which perceives a certain kind of truth by a process of a different order.

---

3. The further question may be asked why a lad may become an expert mathematician, but not a metaphysician or a natural philosopher. The answer, it may be suggested, is this. The mathematician deals with abstractions, the metaphysician and the philosophic naturalist with first principles derived from observation and experience. A young man will have their principles on his lips, but he has no conviction of their truth. On the other hand the fundamental assumptions of mathematics are evidently true.

Chapter Nine: Our next task is to discover in what deliberative excellence consists

We ought also to ascertain the nature of that quality which enables a man to deliberate well, and we must try to discover whether it involves true knowledge, or opinion, or conjecture, or something else that differs from these in kind.

Well, it is not knowledge. Men do not investigate what they know already, whereas to deliberate well is a form of deliberation, and deliberation involves some investigation or calculation. Yet we must not identify deliberation with investigation in general but only when investigation is restricted to a particular field, namely, human behaviour. Nor must we say that it is clever guessing, for that gives the answer in a flash without the guesser's being able to render a reason for it. Deliberation, however, is a slow process; as the proverb says, *Act quickly, think slowly*. Nor is it mental alertness, for that is just an aspect of the ability to guess or conjecture with success. Finally, excellence in deliberation has nothing to do with opinion.

Seeing that a man who deliberates badly is in error, while he who deliberates well is right, it is clear that excellence in deliberation is a form of rightness or correctness, though not in knowledge or belief. One can no more speak of 'correctness' than of 'error' in knowledge, which is not knowledge, if it is not correct. On the other hand correctness of opinion is truth. Besides, one cannot have an opinion except about something which has already a definite meaning.[4] Opinion or belief has got beyond the stage of investigation and must be regarded as having become a form of affirmation. On the other hand a man who is engaged in deliberating – whether well or ill makes no difference here – is at the same time investigating and reasoning or calculating. But wise deliberation is a kind of correctness in deliberating or (as we called it) thinking. It is plain, however, that not every kind of correctness – for the word in this context admits of more than one meaning – is exhibited in wise deliberation. A weak or bad man may make a calculation which will enable him to do what he sets before himself as something which he ought to do. In that event he will have deliberated correctly, though the end he has achieved may be something very wicked or injurious. Yet to have deliberated well is, people feel sure, a good thing. We conclude that it is the sort of correctness in deliberation which ensures a good result that constitutes deliberative excellence. Such a result, however, may actually be achieved by fallacious reasoning. That is to say, one may reach the right conclusion by way of a wrong argument, the fallacy lying in the middle term. A procedure of this kind, then, by which one reaches the right conclusion but on the wrong grounds falls short like the other of the quality under discussion.

Another point arises. One man may deliberate too long, another not long enough. Here again we have not yet got the quality in its completeness. For that quality is correctness of deliberation, on the subject of what is advantageous,

4. It may be added that wise deliberation is impossible without reasoning. It remains therefore that it is a correctness in thinking or deliberating – thinking being only on the way to affirmation.

arriving at the right conclusion not only in the right manner but at the right time. Again, a man may have deliberated well towards achieving a particular end, or he may be good at deliberation as such. This general excellence in counsel is what secures the correct approach to the general end, while correctness of deliberation applied to a particular end is a particular exercise of good counsel. I conclude: If wise deliberation reveals a prudent man, it must be correct deliberation about what serves an end. Prudence consists in a true conception of what serves that end.

Chapter Ten: What is meant by Understanding or the faculty in respect of which a man is said to be 'intelligent'?

Understanding – that is sound understanding – the quality in virtue of which we say that certain persons are 'men of understanding' or 'of sound understanding' is not to be confused with knowledge in the sense of knowing what is always true, nor is it any one of the specialized sciences like medicine, which is concerned only with health, or geometry, which is concerned only with magnitudes.[5] Understanding is not employed upon the things that are eternal and unchangeable, nor upon anything that is brought into being. It is limited to things which admit of doubt and deliberation. That is to say, it is concerned with the same matters as prudence. Yet it is not the same as prudence. Prudence is imperative, understanding only judicial. (I mean that, whereas prudence gives orders, its end being a declaration of what we must or must not do, understanding is content to pass judgement.) Thus, understanding is neither the having nor the getting of prudence. What it is may be gathered from an analogy. When we learn a thing by using the faculty of knowing we are said to 'understand' it. Similarly, when we use our power of forming opinions to judge the truth of what somebody else says about matters on which prudence is qualified to speak we are said to 'understand'.[6] Our analogy in fact is something more, for the use of 'understanding' as a name for the quality in virtue of which men become 'of sound understanding' comes from the use of it as applied to the process of learning. For in our language 'learn' often means 'understand'.

5. It need hardly be said that it is not the same as opinion; if it were, we should all be men of sound understanding!
6. To 'judge' in this context means to judge rightly, a right judgement being equivalent to a sound understanding.

3

ST AUGUSTINE

Source: R.H. Barrow (trans.) (1950) Introduction to St Augustine: City of God. London, Faber & Faber, pp. 70–80, 84–92, 100–8 and 127–30.

Augustine's gloomy view of human existence has presented a starting point for much realist thought in politics and international relations. Augustine divides mankind into the select few who belong or will belong to the eternal kingdom and the condemned many who belong solely to the earthly city. The wise and good person will naturally wish to enter the *City of God* and Augustine provides advice as to how this might be achieved. This leads to a distinctive attitude to political authority which is accepted but not wholly respected. Augustine regards political conflict and war as part of the human condition. Normal international life is primarily a question of survival. Augustine had no doctrine of earthly progress.

Chapter 5: The life of fellowship

But, when the philosophers demand that the pagan saint should live a life of fellowship, we should be much more ready to applaud them. For how would that city of God – the description of which has now brought us into the nineteenth book of this work – how would that city originate and find a beginning or march forward in its course or attain its proper 'ends' if the life of its saints were not a life of fellowship? Nevertheless in this careworn mortal life the fellowship of men abounds in evils, and no one could reckon up their number or assess their magnitude. Let the pagan philosophers listen to the man in one of their comedies who uttered his own feelings and those of all his fellows, when he said: 'I married a wife: and what unhappiness I found there; sons were born to me, an added anxiety!' Remember too how the same comic play-wright, Terence, describes the ills which befall those who are in love; 'slights and suspicions, feuds, open war, and then peace again'. These have everywhere filled up human life to the brim, often appearing even in the purest friendships. Don't you agree that they fill up human life everywhere? We feel slights and suspicions, feuds and war to be certainly evils; on the other hand we feel the blessings of peace to be uncertain, for we are ignorant of the hearts of those with whom we wish to keep peace, and, even if we could know them to-day, we should be quite in the dark about their attitude to-morrow. Again, you would expect those who live within the walls of the same house usually to be friendly or to feel a duty to be friendly to one another; yet no one can derive any feeling of confidence from such conditions. For often secret intrigues give rise to serious evils, which are all the more bitter in contrast with the sweets of the peace which was thought to be real, though in fact it was due to most clever pretence. Everyone recognises the truth of this and is therefore moved to give mournful assent to the passage in Cicero: 'no intrigues are more difficult to detect than those which are covered up by the pretence of affection or hidden under the cloak of family relationship. For you could easily take precautions to avoid a declared enemy; but the hidden evil which lurks in the heart of your home not only is there – bad as that is – but it overwhelms you before you could look round and search it out.' The Scripture says that 'a man's foes shall be those of his own household'. The reason why this saying so pierces the heart is that, whereas a man can be brave enough to endure with composure the plots aimed against him under cover of friendship, or watchful enough to foresee them and guard against them, the good man is bound to suffer anguish from the treacherous hurt done to him by those whom he discovers to be wicked; and it makes no difference whether they always were evilly disposed to him and pretended to be the opposite or whether they have changed from a good to an evil disposition. If then the household, in which most men find shelter from these evils that beset the human race, offers no security, what are we to say about the city? For the larger the city the more crowded are its law-courts with civil and criminal cases; and, though open insurrection and civil war, which are always the cause of upheaval and more often than not of bloodshed, may not openly break out and cities may at times be spared their actual horrors, yet the threat of them is always overhanging.

Chapter 6

Consider now the nature of the judgements which men pass upon men in the law courts; for, however profound and enduring the peace which cities may enjoy, there are bound to be such judgements. How pitiable they are, how utterly regrettable? One set of men passes judgement upon others whose consciences they are unable to see. This explains why they are forced to examine innocent witnesses under torture, in order that they may seek the truth in a matter which concerns them not at all. Again, even in his own trial a suspect may be tortured and put on the rack during the inquiry into his guilt; and, though he is innocent, he pays for a hypothetical crime with the most definite penalties, not because his guilt is detected, but because his innocence is not established. And so the ignorance of the judge often spells catastrophe for the innocent. But the position may develop into something quite intolerable which demands our anguished grief and the outpouring, if it were possible, of rivers of tears. I mean that a judge, to avoid condemning to death in his ignorance an innocent man, tortures the prisoner before him, and then it results from the tragedy of his ignorance that he actually puts to death a tortured and innocent man whom he has tortured in order to avoid putting to death an innocent man. For, if the prisoner has elected to follow the wisdom of pagan philosophers and to escape from life rather than submit any longer to his torture, he actually pleads guilty to a crime which he has not committed. And so the prisoner is condemned and put to death; the judge is still in ignorance whether he has caused the death of an innocent or a guilty man, though he tortured him to avoid putting to death in his ignorance an innocent man. In short, he tortured him, though innocent, to discover the truth, and with the truth undiscovered he caused his death. If the life of fellowship is shrouded in such darkness as this, you may well ask whether the learned judge will sit or whether his courage will not fail him. Of course he will sit. For human fellowship, which he thinks it wrong to leave in the lurch, places its compulsion upon him and drags him off to fulfil his duty to the end. He does not feel it a wrong that innocent witnesses are tortured in causes which are not theirs, or that those who are themselves in the dock are often so overcome by the anguish of their pain that they make a false confession of guilt, and so are punished, though innocent, after being tortured as innocent – or that, even if they are not punished by death, they frequently die in the midst of their torture or as a result of it. There are men who prosecute through anxiety, perhaps, to benefit human fellowship by seeing that crimes do not go unpunished; they may fail to prove their charges, however true, because the witnesses lie or the prisoner bears up heroically under torture and does not confess. Yet the judge does not scruple to condemn these self-appointed pro-secutors, even though he does not know whether the charges are true or not. He does not regard all these glaring evils as sins. For, as a learned judge, he does not commit them from a wish to do hurt; he labours under the constraint which his ignorance imposes upon him. Yet in spite of his ignorance he is constrained to pass judgement because human fellowship compels him to pass it. Here you have without disguise that tragedy of the man of which we are speaking, even if we do not suggest evil in him as a learned judge. Constrained to be in ignorance and yet to pass judgement, he tortures the guiltless; and is he then not satisfied with escaping prosecution for this, but actually asks to be happy on top of it all? He shows greater power of reflection, as well as his worth as a man, when he recognises the tragedy of the constraint which is upon him and hates it in himself; and, if his learning springs from piety, he cries aloud to God, 'Deliver me from my constraints'.

Chapter 7

After the *civitas* or the city comes the world, in which the pagan philosophers find the third stage of human fellowship; they begin with the home, pass to the city and then they move on and come to the world, which, inasmuch as it is larger than the others, is all the more full of dangers, just as flood waters are all the more dangerous as they pile up. Here difference of language is the first cause of estrangement between man and man. If two men, neither of whom knows the other's language, meet each other and are compelled by some constraint not to pass by each other, but to be together, they do not find it as easy, though they are both men, to enter into fellowship with each other as would dumb animals, even of different species. They cannot share their feelings with one another, and so their inability to speak the same language prevents their natural kinship avail- ing to bring them into fellowship – so marked is this, that a man would rather be in the company of his dog than in the company of a foreigner.

To this you will reply that an imperial city, besides imposing its yoke upon the nations which it subdues, takes great pains to impose also its language; this it does through the peace which results from fellowship with it and which ensures that there shall be no dearth, but rather a plentiful supply of interpreters. This is all true; but at what a cost is this end achieved – repeated and gigantic wars, massacres and a vast outpouring of human blood. When these are over, the same ills and all their tragedy are not done with. For apart from the wars with hostile foreign nations, which, as history shows, inevitably occur, the mere vastness of an empire produce war of worse kind – I mean wars between part- ners in the empire and civil wars which convulse mankind with far greater suffer- ing than others; and this is true equally of actual war in order at last to suppress the rebels and of dread that there will be further outbreaks. As for the many and manifold catastrophes, the stern and stark constraints which follow in the wake of such evils, if I wished to describe them in fit terms – in reality I could certainly not do justice to them – I should write a long essay, indeed an essay without end.

But the wise ruler of pagan philosophy, I shall be told, is likely to wage only just wars. What nonsense! If he remembers that he is a man with human feelings, it will cause him all the more grief that the wars that he has become constrained to wage are just wars. For, if the wars were not just, he would not have to wage them; and so for the wise ruler there would be no wars at all. For it is the wickedness of the enemy that lays upon him the necessity of waging just wars, and this wickedness must assuredly cause grief to him as a man because it is the wickedness of man, even though it should not give rise to the constraint of going to war. Whosoever feels grief when he reflects upon these evils, must admit misery, for they are great and terrifying and cruel; but whosoever allows them to go on or contemplates them without any feeling of grief is all the more a miserable figure; for he thinks himself happy because he has lost all human feeling.

Chapter 8

Let us suppose, however, that we are not dealing with a case of ignorance bordering upon madness, which drives a man to mistake enemy for friend or friend for enemy; though as a matter of fact such cases are frequent in the miserable setting of this life. Surely amid the abundant errors and worries which beset this human fellowship of ours we derive comfort from the sincere trust of true and good friends and from our love for them and theirs for us. Yet the more such friends we have, and the more they are scattered, the more widely spread is our fear lest any evil should befall them from the vast piles of evil accumulated in this world. Not only does it worry us that they may be struck down by famine or war or disease or carried off as prisoners, or that in conditions of slavery they may suffer such horrors as it is beyond us to imagine; we are afraid also that they may change and become treacherous and evilly disposed and wicked, and this fear is much more bitter than the other. When our fears are realised – the more friends we have, the more often it happens – and when news is brought to us of our friends' behaviour, no one can describe, unless from similar experience, the burning emotions with which our hearts are on fire. We should prefer to hear that they were dead, though even this we could not hear without pain; for we cannot help feeling sorrow at the death of those whose lives gave us the joy and solace of friendship. If you forbid us such sorrow, you must forbid us also the friendly intercourse, you must put a ban on all friendly feeling or put an axe to its root, you must shatter all bonds of human relationship and make our minds a blank of cruel indifference; or else you must decree that we must adopt such an attitude to our friends as would rob friendship of its charm. If you cannot do all that, the death of those whose lives have given us pleasure is bound to be bitter. Hence grief is like a wound or an ulcer to the heart which is not devoid of feeling, and for the healing of it consolation is administered with loving care; for we must not argue that grief is not something which needs healing just because the healthier the mind, the more quickly and easily is grief healed in it. The deaths of close friends, particularly those whose services are of most value to human fellowship, affect the lives of mortal men with varying degrees of severity; none the less we should prefer to be told or to see that they were dead rather than that they had failed in loyalty or virtue, for then they would be dead in the soul itself. Of this huge mass of evils the earth is full; wherefore it is written: 'Is not human life on earth a time of testing?' and the Lord Himself says: 'Woe unto the world because of occasions of stumbling'; and again, 'Because wickedness has been multiplied, the love of many shall grow cold'. This is why we congratulate our friends, if they are good men, when they die: though their death saddens us their very death gives us all the surer comfort, for they have been freed of those evils by which even good men are worn down or are warped, or exposed to both of these dangers.

[. . .]

Chapter 12

You will agree with me in recognising the truth of this, if you consider human life and consider also nature, of which human life is a part; for there is no one so constituted as to be unwilling to possess peace any more than he is unwilling to feel joy. The very men who will wars will only victory; they are anxious therefore to reach a glorious peace by means of war; for victory is simply the subjugation of resistance, and, when that is achieved, peace will reign. Peace therefore is the objective even in the waging of war, and this is true also of those who aim at giving full play to martial qualities in the exercise of military control and in fighting. Hence it may be agreed that peace is the desired end of war; for everyone seeks peace even in the act of making war, but no one seeks war in the act of making peace. Those who are willing that the peace in which they live should be disturbed do not thereby show hatred of peace, but show their desire to alter it in accordance with their own wishes: they do not object to peace as such, but they want it to be such as they desire. They may have rebelled and separated themselves from the rest of the community, but, unless they maintain some semblance of peace with their fellow-conspirators or their supporters, they do not achieve their object; even brigands want peace among their confederates to enable them to threaten the peace of the rest with greater violence and in greater safety. Let us imagine an individual so overwhelmingly strong and so chary of confederates that he puts himself in the power of no ally, but all alone traps and overpowers his victim, falling upon all whom he can and murdering them and carrying off their goods. Even he maintains some shadow of peace with those whom he cannot kill or those from whom he wishes to conceal his deeds. In his house he is really anxious to be on peaceful terms with his wife and children and anyone else there; no doubt he gets pleasure from their obedience to his will. If he does not receive obedience, he fumes, he uses violence, he punishes, and, if necessary, even through his rage restores peace in the house since he realises that peace cannot exist unless some ruling principle – which in the home is himself – enforces the subjection of everything else in that same household-fellowship. Let us now imagine that he is offered the abject obedience of a larger number of men, a city or a nation, rendering him the same obedience that he exacted in his household; he would not now hide himself like a robber in his lair, but would exalt himself as a king for all to behold – though his greed and malignity would remain.

It can be seen therefore that everyone wishes to maintain peace with his own people, whom he wants to live according to his will. He wishes, if he can, to make his own all those against whom he wars, and to impose upon them when subjugated the laws of his own peace.

Let us now draw another picture, this time a picture of the kind of being sometimes met with in poetry or in fairy story, one whom the writers preferred to describe as a half-man, rather than as a man, just because of his untamed wildness which prevented him living in fellowship. This creature's kingdom was the loneliness of an eerie cave; so extraordinarily evil was his nature that his name – Cacus – was derived from it – in Greek κακός is the Latin *malus* [and in English 'evil']; he had no wife to offer him words of affection or to return his, no small children to play with and none growing up for him to control; no friends whose conversation he might enjoy. He did not even speak to his father Vulcan, over whom he did have one advantage, namely, that he was more fortunate in not having produced such a monster as a son of his own. He gave nothing away to anyone, but carried off when he could everything and everyone whom he wished. Now even in that lonely cave of his, where, so the story goes, the ground was always warm with blood from some fresh slaughter, this monster desired nothing but peace, peace in which none would disturb him, in which no violence and no terror from outside would interrupt his rest. In short, he was anxious to be at peace with his body, and all was well with him in proportion as he gained that. And so, since his limbs obeyed his orders implicitly, his aim was with all speed to impose peace upon his mortal frame whenever, through need of anything, it rebelled against itself or whenever it stirred up sedition within itself because threatened by the hunger, which, if unsatisfied, would part body from soul and keep them parted. Therefore he plundered and slew and devoured; yet, in spite of his cruelty and savagery, he was only striving in his own cruel and savage way after the peace and security of his own life. If he could have brought himself to possess in company with others the peace which he was concerned to establish in his own cave and in his own body, there would have been no need to call him evil or monster or half-man. Even if his physical appearance or the murky flames which he breathed out of his mouth terrified men from coming into fellowship with him, his savagery may not have been inspired by any desire to do harm but merely by the need to live. However, it is possible that such a creature never existed, or – which is easier to believe – at any rate was not quite as bad as the idle fancies of poets picture him: after all he had to be overdrawn or else the virtues of Hercules, his counterpart, would have lost in contrast. A creature of such a character – whether man or half-man – it is more reasonable to believe never existed, and the same is true of many poetical inventions. This view is supported by the evidence of the wildest of wild animals – and from them Cacus derived part of his wildness, for he is called half-beast as well as half-man. It is by a kind of peace that they preserve their species; they mate, produce young, tend and feed their young, though many of them are solitary and keep to themselves – not sheep, deer, doves, starlings or bees, but lions, wolves, foxes, eagles, owls. The tiger becomes gentle and purrs over its cubs and licks them, its wildness now at peace. The kite flies solitarily over its prey, but it mates, builds a nest, sits on its eggs, feeds its young, and with all the peace it can, it preserves with the hen – a real materfamilias – a fellowship of the home.

How much more powerfully is man drawn by the laws of his nature to enter into fellowship and, so far as in him lies, to maintain peace with all men. Even evil men make war in defence of the peace of their own world and try to reduce all men and all things to abject obedience to one man; and that can come about only if they agree to promote his peace whether through love or fear. This illustrates how pride distortedly imitates God. For it hates equality of fellow beings under Him, but tries to impose upon them its own domination instead of His; thus it hates the just peace of God and loves an inequitable peace of its own. It cannot do without loving peace of some kind. Indeed no corruption of good is so contrary to nature as to destroy even the last traces of nature.

Compared with the peace of the righteous the peace of the wicked is not worthy to be called peace, as you will see if you know how to prefer the straight to the crooked, and arrangement to wilful disarrangement. Even what is wilfully disarranged is bound to have some kind of peace imposed upon it: the elements of its nature or the elements of which it is composed have some kind of peace within or proceeding from or in association with some part of nature: otherwise it would simply be nothing at all. For example, suspend someone head downwards; the position of the body and the order of his limbs are disarranged, since what nature demands should be uppermost is now below, and vice versa: that disarrangement has disturbed the peace of the body and causes it discomfort. All the same the soul still remains at peace with its body [that is, it has not thereby become hostile to the body], and fusses over its welfare: that is why the man feels pain. If discomfort drives the soul to take its departure from the body, what is left behind still possesses a kind of peace in its parts as long as the limbs continue to be knit together; and that is why the man remains suspended. The body, composed of earth, tends towards the earth, straining on the rope which suspends it, and so it strives towards its own ordered peace: its weight cries out, as it were, for a resting place; and, though the body is lifeless and without feeling, it cannot withdraw from its own natural ordered peace, either when it possesses that peace or when it travels towards it. Suppose that chemicals are applied and the body is embalmed to prevent its wasting or dissolution; still a kind of peace joins part to part and adjusts the mass of the body to the place in which it rests, a place which is then adapted to it and so offers it peace. Suppose now that the body is not embalmed, but is left to its natural course; it then undergoes a process of violent change as it splits up into gases unpleasant to the senses (for that is what meets our senses when flesh rots), until finally it is ready to find its appropriate place among the elements and it departs gradually, particle by particle, into their peace. Nothing in fact can be exempted from the laws of the great Creator who orders all things and administers the peace of the universe: and even if from the corpse of some larger living creature minute animals are born, by the same law of the Creator each of these little bodies serves its small soul in the peace which is its health. Even if the flesh of dead men be devoured by animals, the same laws will be found to operate throughout creation and to make for the health of each species of mortal things, imposing peace through the adjustment of like to like, no matter in what direction movement may take place nor what combinations may occur, nor what changes and transformations.

[. . .]

Chapter 15

This is the conception of 'command' which the order inherent in nature prescribes, and these are the conditions under which God has created man. For He says, 'Let him have dominion over the fishes of the sea and the birds of the sky and all creeping things which creep upon the earth'. It was not His will that man, a creature possessed of reason and created in His image, should have dominion, unless over irrational creatures; it was His will that man should have dominion over beasts and not over men. Hence the first righteous men [the patriarchs] were appointed to be shepherds of flocks rather than kings of men; so that even in this way God gave an indication of what is demanded by the order which governs created beings and what is exacted by the deserts of sinners. For the condition of slavery is rightly understood to be a condition imposed upon the sinner. That explains why we never read of a slave in any passage of Scripture until Noah, a just man, used the term in condemning the sin of his son, who earned the title of slave by his own misdeed and not by nature. The derivation of the word for 'servile' in Latin is held to be as follows; prisoners who by the rights of war could have been put to death were reduced to a 'servile' state because they were 'preserved' alive by their conquerors, *servus* thus being derived from *servare*. This process of turning a 'preserved' captive into a slave takes place only as a penalty incurred by sin. For, even when a just war is being fought, the opposite side is battling in defence of sin, and even when victory goes in favour of the wicked it is a divine judgment humiliating the defeated by correcting or punishing their sins. To this, Daniel, a man of God, bears witness; when he was in captivity, he confessed to God his sins and those of his people, and his righteous grief testified that sin was the reason of the captivity which he endured.

So the primal cause of slavery is sin and its result is that one man is subordinated to another, fettered by his servile status; this always occurs through the judgment of God, with whom there is no injustice and who knows how to apportion differing punishments appropriate to the deserts of those who do wrong. But 'every man who commits sin is the slave of sin', says the most high Lord, and that is why many religious men, who are the slaves of wicked masters, are the slaves of masters who are not free; for 'a man is made over as a slave to that which has conquered him'. A man is much more fortunate in being a slave to another man than to a lustful passion, since – to quote only one example – a lust for power devastates the hearts of men by the savagery of the power which it exerts over them. In that ordered peace in which one set of men are made subordinate to another set, humility greatly profits those who are slaves, while arrogance greatly harms those who are masters. But no man is the slave either of another man or of sin because of the nature in which God originally created man. No! even slavery enforced as a punishment is ordered by that law which bids the order inherent in created things to be preserved and forbids its disarrangement; for, if there had been no misdeed transgressing that law, there would have been nothing which called for the constraint exerted by penal slavery. For these reasons the Apostle warns slaves to be subject to their masters and to be their slaves wholeheartedly and with good will; he means that, if they cannot win their freedom from their masters, they should of themselves bring a certain freedom into their slavery by being slaves not in craftiness and fear but in faithfulness and love, until inequality passes away and all overlordship and all power of man over man is made empty of meaning, and God is all in all.

Chapter 16

Even if our righteous forefathers did have slaves, at any rate they managed the peace of the household in such a way that, though as regards temporal goods they made a distinction between the lot of the sons of the household and the status of slaves, yet, when it was a question of the worship of God, which holds out hope of eternal goods, they took thought for every member of their household and showed each the same affection. This attitude is insisted upon by the order which is inherent in nature; from it the title of 'father of a family', that is, of a household, is sprung; and indeed it is so widely adopted now that even harsh masters like to be called by this name. But those who are truly fathers of their household take thought for each member of it just as if they were all sons, with a view to promoting the worship and service of God; for they ardently yearn to reach that heavenly home in which the obligation to rule mortal men will not be laid upon them, for the reason that there will no longer be obligation to take thought for those who have already attained felicity in the immortality of that heavenly home. Until they arrive there, fathers of households must be patient under their need to be masters, even more patient than slaves must be of their slavery. But, if anyone in a house is disobedient and so thwarts the peace of the household, he is corrected to the degree which human fellowship allows, either by the lash of the tongue or of the whip, or by any other form of punishment which is just and lawful; and correction is intended to be for the profit of him who is corrected, to make him fit himself again into the peace from which he has sprung apart. Just as no one can claim to be a benefactor who by his active aid causes someone to lose a greater good, so no one can with a clear conscience spare a wrongdoer and so allow him to fall into still greater evil. To have a clear conscience in such a matter you must not only do no evil to others, but you must hold them back from sin or punish their sin, in order that the experience of punishment may bring about the reformation of the sinner, or else that the example made of him may deter others from like sin.

A man's home ought to be the beginning of the state or a small fragment of it; every beginning looks towards some end proper to its own genus, and every part looks towards that whole, regarded as a whole, of which it is a part. From this it clearly follows that the peace of the household looks towards the peace of the city; that is to say, the ordered agreement of those who dwell together in a household, whether they command or whether they obey, looks towards the ordered agreement of citizens, whether they command or whether they obey. The result is that the head of a household ought to take his principles from the law of the city in order that by those principles he may so rule his own household as to bring it into harmony with the peace of the city.

Chapter 17

The household of men who do not live by faith pursues an earthly peace derived from the material things and the blessings of this temporal life. The household of men who live by faith awaits those eternal things which are promised for the future, and uses all earthly and temporal things as a stranger in a strange land; it is careful that these things shall not captivate and lead astray that faculty by which man travels towards God, but rather shall sustain it and so enable it to bear more easily the burdens of the body which is doomed to corruption and weighs down the spirit, and to do as little as possible to increase those burdens. Thus it comes about that both types of men and both types of household have something in common in the use which they make of the things necessary to this mortal life, but each type sets before itself its own specific end in the use which it makes of those things; and the end of one is very different from the end of the other.

Similarly, the earthly city, which does not live by faith, seeks an earthly peace and pins down to a particular purpose the agreement of its citizens, whether they command or obey, the purpose being that the wills of men may achieve a measure of concordance as regards the things which pertain to this mortal life. But the heavenly city, or rather that part of it which sojourns in mortality here on earth and lives by faith, must necessarily make use of the earthly peace of which we have just spoken, until mortality itself, to which such peace is a necessity, shall pass away. Hence, the heavenly city lives, as it were, the life of a prisoner in a strange land in the midst of the earthly city. But it has already been promised its redemption and has received the gift of the Spirit as a pledge of its future, and so it does not hesitate to obey the laws of the earthly city which control all that conduces to the maintenance of this mortal life; for thus it will preserve the harmony of the two cities in things relating to that mortality which both share alike.

The earthly city possessed saints or sages of its own, but of a kind of which divine philosophy strongly disapproves. Led astray by their own fancies or deluded by evil spirits they believed that a multiplicity of gods had to be appeased by man-made ritual and that various spheres were subordinated to these gods and belonged to them according to their variously assigned functions; to one god belonged the body, to another the mind; similarly with parts of the body – the head, the neck; so, too, with parts of the mind – intellect, learning, anger, desire; concrete things which go to make up life also had their gods – herds, corn, wine, oil, woods, money, sailing, wars and victories, marriage, birth, fecundity, and so on. But the heavenly city knew that only one God should be worshipped and in loyalty it held that service should be rendered to Him in that service which the Greeks called λατρεία and which is due to Him alone. Hence this city could not share the laws of religion with the earthly city, and in defence of its own laws it was bound to part company, and so to antagonise those who held different views. It had to endure anger and hatred and the full onset of their persecution – save when at moments it dismayed the hearts of its adversaries by the terror of its numbers, and always by divine help.

While, then, the heavenly city sojourns upon earth, it summons its citizens from all nations and in spite of differing languages it gathers together a fellowship of sojourners. It takes no account of differences of customs, laws and institutions which are necessary for securing or maintaining earthly peace. It repeals or cancels none of them; rather it preserves and adopts what is permissible to it amid the diversity of the various nations; but it keeps its eye fixed upon the one and the same end of earthly peace as does the earthly city, provided always that the religion which teaches the duty of worshipping the one all-highest and true God is not thereby hampered.

Hence, in its sojourn here, the heavenly city makes use of the peace provided by the earthly city; in all that relates to the mortal nature of man it preserves and indeed seeks the concordance of human wills, in so far as it can do this without prejudice to its piety and religion. It refers that earthly peace to the heavenly peace, which is truly such peace that it alone can be regarded and described as peace – at any rate the peace of a rational creature; for it is the highest degree of ordered and harmonious fellowship in the enjoyment of God and of one another in God. When this stage is reached, then there will be life, – not life subject to death, but life that is clearly and assuredly life-giving. There will be a body, – not a body which is animal, weighing down the soul as it decays, but a spiritual body experiencing no need and subordinated in every part to the will. This is the peace which the heavenly city has while it sojourns here in faith, and in this faith it lives a life of righteousness. To the establishing of that peace it refers all its good actions, whether they be towards God or towards one's neighbour; for the life of this city is utterly and entirely a life of fellowship.

[. . .]

Chapter 27

But the peace which is peculiar to us [Christians] is, in this world, a peace with God through faith, and, in eternity, a peace with God through sight. Nevertheless, whether we have in mind that temporal peace which is common to all or our own peace, in this world peace is of such quality as to offer rather comfort to our misery than the joy of happiness. So, too, with our righteousness; though it is true righteousness, because the final good, which it takes as its standard, is true, still in this life it is so limited that it comes into being rather through the remission of our sins than through any perfection of our virtues. Evidence of this is furnished by the prayer which is used by the whole of the heavenly city sojourning here in the lands of the earth; through every one of its members it cries to God, 'Forgive us our debts as we also forgive our debtors'. This prayer is of no avail to benefit those whose faith is dead because it is not accompanied by works: it is of benefit to those whose faith works through love. For, though the reason may be subjected to God, still, in our state as mortals occupying bodies which will perish and which weigh down the soul, the rule which reason exercises over evil desires is not complete, and therefore the righteous feel the need of such a prayer as this. It may be quite true that reason does rule over evil desires, but it is a rule that is certainly not exercised without a conflict: in fact, given the condition of human frailty, even if you contend well in that conflict or succeed in conquering, subjecting and maintaining dominion over such enemies, something always creeps in unnoticed which causes sin to be committed, not perhaps the sin of ready act, but certainly the sin of unguarded phrase or fleeting thought. For this reason, as long as rule over evil desire has to be exercised, peace cannot be complete: for against the evil elements which offer resistance a hazardous campaign has to be carried on to crush them, while the triumph over those which have been defeated brings a respite which is not yet assured; the rule which keeps them under is not yet free of anxiety. We are subject, then, to temptations, of which it is tersely said in the divine utterances, 'Is not the life of man upon earth a time of testing?' In the face of this, who would presume to say that his life is such that he can dispense with saying to God, 'Forgive us our debts'? Only the proud man; he cannot claim to be a great man, for he is puffed up and swollen with pride, and him God in His righteousness resists, God who bestows His grace upon the humble. Wherefore it is written, 'God resists the proud, but to the humble he gives grace'.

And so in this life each individual's righteousness consists in this, that God should rule man who should render Him obedience, that the mind should rule the body, and the reason the evil desires even when they fight against it, either by subduing them or resisting them, that God Himself should be asked to grant grace for merit and pardon for sin and that He should be thanked for all benefits received from Him.

But in that final peace things will be otherwise; to that peace righteousness looks for its standards and it is in order to obtain that peace that righteousness exists; man's nature, healed by its immortality and set free from corruption, will experience no evil desires, and each one of us will be rid of all that can thwart us whether it comes from outside or inside himself. Hence, there will be no need for reason to rule evil desires, for there will be none; God will rule man, the mind will rule the body, and obedience will be as acceptable and easy as life and kingship then will be happy. Such things shall be eternal there for all and for each, and it will be certain that they are eternal. Therefore the peace of this happiness or the happiness of this peace will be the supreme good.

4

AQUINAS

Source: A.P. d'Entreves (ed.) (1965) *Aquinas: Selected Political Writings*. Oxford, Blackwell, pp. 63–7, 73–83 and 159–67.

In Aquinas's Christian view of politics the ruler's role is defined not only by prudence but also by duty. The ruler is not only an agent of earthly order but, as a servant of God, of the divine order as well. Influenced by Aristotle, Aquinas has a vision of domestic and world society as governed by law. The ruler can gain access to these laws through the use of reason. These laws Aquinas describes as natural. This notion of a rationally accessible natural law conditions his approach to war. War is not to be welcomed but it may well be necessary. Aquinas gives three grounds for judging whether or not a war is just. First, the leader declaring war must have legitimate authority to do so; second, there has to be a just cause; third, the war must be declared with the right intent. Other interesting rules which derive from Aquinas's view of natural law are the right to resist tyranny and the right of the churchman to speak out on political matters.

DE REGIMINE PRINCIPUM

Chapter XI: The material benefits of good government, and the damaging effects of tyranny

From what we have said it is, then, evident, that stability in government, riches, and honour and glory, are all more surely attained by kings than by tyrants; and that a prince who would gain these ends by dishonest means risks becoming a tyrant. No one will leave the path of justice if he is kept to it by the hope of some gain. But furthermore, a tyrant is deprived of that supreme blessedness which is the reward of a good king; and, what is worse, brings down upon himself the most terrible penalties. If a man who robs or enslaves or kills another merits the maximum penalty, death from the tribunal of man and eternal damnation before the tribunal of God, how much more reason have we for saying that a tyrant deserves the most terrible penalties; when he has despoiled every one, and everywhere trampled on the liberties of all, and taken life at a mere whim? To this we must add that men of this sort rarely repent: puffed up with pride, abandoned by God for their sins, hardened by adulation, it is seldom indeed that they are capable of due reparation. When, indeed, could they restore all they have gained above what was due to them in justice? Yet it is not to be doubted that they are bound to make restitution. When could they do justice to those whom they have oppressed or otherwise ill-treated? We must further consider, besides their impenitence, the fact that they begin to think legitimate all that they have been able to do with impunity and without encountering resistance, so that, far from seeking to repair the evil they have done, they make evil a habit and an example which leads their successors to even more flagrant wrongdoing. So they become responsible before God not only for their own crimes but also for the crimes of those to whom they have given the occasion of sin. Their guilt is further aggravated by the dignity of the office they fill. Just as a king on this earth punishes his ministers more severely if he should find them rebelling against him, so also God has heavier punishments for those whom He has destined as His ministers and the dispensers of His authority, if they act evilly and pervert His judgments. So in the *Book of Wisdom* (VI, 5–7), it is said of evil kings: 'Because being ministers of his kingdom, you have not judged rightly, nor kept the law of justice, nor walked according to the will of the Lord: horribly and speedily will he appear to you: for a most severe judgement shall be for them that bear rule. For to him that is little, mercy is granted: but the mighty shall be mightily tormented.' And *Isaias* (XIV, 15–16), says to Nabuchodonosor: 'Thou shalt be brought down to hell, into the depth of the pit. They that shall see thee, shall turn toward thee, and behold thee,' as though to one who is engulfed in tribulation. If, then, kings receive temporal benefits in abundance, and God prepares for them a surpassing degree of blessedness; while tyrants are for the most part deprived of even those worldly satisfactions which they seek so eagerly, besides running many risks and, what is worse, being deprived of eternal benefits and condemned to most grievous pain; it is clear that those who assume the office of government must take every care to act as true kings to their subjects and not as tyrants.

We have now said sufficient about the powers of a king; about the advantages of a monarchy for the community, and about the importance of a ruler's bearing himself as a true king towards the community and not as a tyrant.

Chapter XII: The duties of a king: the similarity between royal power and the power of the soul over the body and of God over the universe

To complete what we have so far said it remains only to consider what is the duty of a king and how he should comport himself. And since art is but an imitation of nature, from which we come to learn how to act according to reason, it would seem best to deduce the duties of a king from the examples of government in nature. Now in nature there is to be found both a universal and a particular form of government. The universal is that by which all things find their place under the direction of God, who, by His providence, governs the universe. The particular is very similar to this divine control, and is found within man himself; who, for this reason, is called a microcosm, because he provides an example of universal government. Just as the divine control is exercised over all created bodies and over all spiritual powers, so does the control of reason extend over the members of the body and the other faculties of the soul: so, in a certain sense, reason is to man what God is to the universe. But because, as we have shown above, man is by nature a social animal living in community, this similarity with divine rule is found among men, not only in the sense that a man is directed by his reason, but also in the fact that a community is ruled by one man's intelligence; for this is essentially the king's duty. A similar example of such control is to be found among certain animals which live in community, such as bees, which are said to have a king. But in their case, of course, the control has no rational foundation, but springs from an instinct of their nature, given them by the supreme ruler who is the author of nature. A king, then, should realize that he has assumed the duty of being to his kingdom what the soul is to the body and what God is to the universe. If he thinks attentively upon this point he will, on the one hand, be fired with zeal for justice, seeing himself appointed to administer justice throughout his realm in the name of God, and, on the other hand, he will grow in mildness and clemency, looking upon the persons subject to his government, as the members of his own body.

[. . .]

Chapter XIV: Comparison between the priestly power and that of a king

Just as the creation of the world serves as a convenient model for the establishment of a city or a kingdom, so does its government allow us to deduce the principle of civil government. We must first have in mind that to govern is to guide what is governed to its appointed end. So we say that a ship is under control when it is sailed on its right course to port by the skill of a sailor. Now when something is ordered to an end which lies outside itself, as a ship is to harbour, it is the ruler's duty not only to preserve its integrity, but also to see that it reaches its appointed destination. If there were anything with no end beyond itself, then the ruler's sole task would be to preserve it unharmed in all its perfection. But though there is no such example to be found in creation, apart from God who is the end of all things, care for higher aims is beset with many and varied difficulties. For it is very clear that there may be one person employed about the preservation of a thing in its present state, and another concerned with bringing it to higher perfection; as we see in the case of a ship, which we have used as an example of government. Just as it is the carpenter's task to repair any damage which may occur and the sailor's task to steer the ship to port, so also in man himself the same processes are at work. The doctor sets himself to preserve man's life and bodily health; the economist's task is to see that there is no lack of material goods; the learned see to it that he knows the truth; and the moralist that he should live according to reason. Thus, if man were not destined to some higher end, these attentions would suffice.

But there is a further destiny for man after this mortal life; that final blessedness and enjoyment of God which he awaits after death. For, as the Apostle says (II *Corinthians* V, 6): 'While we are in the body we are absent from God.' So it is that the Christian, for whom that blessedness was obtained by the blood of Christ, and who is led to it through the gift of the Holy Ghost, has need of another, spiritual, guide to lead him to the harbour of eternal salvation: such guidance is provided for the faithful by the ministers of the Church of Christ.

Our conclusion must be the same, whether we consider the destiny of one person or of a whole community. Consequently, if the end of man were to be found in any perfection existing in man himself, the final object of government in a community would lie in the acquisition of such perfection and in its preservation once acquired. So that if such an end, whether of an individual or of a community, were life and bodily health, doctors would govern. If, on the other hand, it were abundance of riches, the government of the community could safely be left in the hands of the economist. If it were knowledge of truth, the king, whose task it is to guide the community, would have the duties of a professor. But the object for which a community is gathered together is to live a virtuous life. For men consort together that they may thus attain a fullness of life which would not be possible to each living singly: and the full life is one which is lived according to virtue. Thus the object of human society is a virtuous life.

A proof of this lies in the fact that only those members may be considered part of the community who contribute jointly to the fullness of social life. If men consorted together for bare existence, both animals and slaves would have a part in civil society. If for the multiplication of riches, all who had common commercial ties would belong to one city. But it is those who obey the same laws, and are guided by a single government to the fullness of life, who can be said to constitute a social unit. Now the man who lives virtuously is destined to a higher end, which consists, as we have already said, in the enjoyment of God: and the final object of human association can be no different from that of the individual man. Thus the final aim of social life will be, not merely to live in virtue, but rather through virtuous life to attain to the enjoyment of God. If, indeed, it were possible to attain this object by natural human virtue, it would, in consequence, be the duty of kings to guide men to this end. We believe, however, that it is the supreme power in temporal affairs which is the business of a king. Now government is of a higher order according to the importance of the ends it serves. For it is always the one who has the final ordering of affairs who directs those who carry out what pertains to the attainment of the final aim: just as the sailor who must navigate the ship advises the shipwright as to the type of ship which will suit his purpose; and the citizen who is to bear arms tells the smith what weapons to forge. But the enjoyment of God is an aim which cannot be attained by human virtue alone, but only through divine grace, as the Apostle tells us (*Romans*, VI, 23): 'The grace of God is eternal life.' Only a divine rule, then, and not human government, can lead us to this end. Such government belongs only to that King who is both man, and also God: that is to Jesus Christ, our Lord, Who, making men to be Sons of God has led them to the glory of heaven.

This, then, is the government entrusted to Him: a dominion which shall never pass away, and in virtue of which He is called in the Holy Scriptures, not only a priest but a king; as *Jeremias* says (XXIII, 5): 'A king shall reign and shall be wise.' It is from Him that the royal priesthood derives; and, what is more, all the Faithful of Christ, being members of Him, become thus, priests and kings. The ministry of this kingdom is entrusted not to the rulers of this earth but to priests, so that temporal affairs may remain distinct from those spiritual: and, in particular, it is delegated to the High Priest, the successor of Peter and Vicar of Christ, the Roman Pontiff; to whom all kings in Christendom should be subject, as to the Lord Jesus Christ Himself. For those who are concerned with the subordinate ends of life must be subject to him who is concerned with the supreme end and be directed by his command. And because the pagan priesthood and everything connected with the cult of pagan gods was directed to the attainment of temporal benefits, which form part of the common weal of the community, and which lie within the king's competence, it was right that pagan priests should be subject to their kings. Similarly in the Old Testament, temporal benefits were promised to the people in reward for their faith, though these promises were made by the true God and not by demons; so that under the Old Law we read that the priesthood was subject to kings. But under the New Law there is a higher priesthood through which men are led to a heavenly reward: and under Christ's Law, kings must be subject to priests.

For this reason it came about by the admirable dispensation of divine providence, that in the city of Rome which God chose to be the main centre of Christendom, it gradually became the custom for the rulers of the city to be subject to the pontiffs. So Valerius Maximus relates: 'It has been the custom in our city always to subordinate all things to religion, even in matters which concerned the dignity of the supreme power. So the authorities have never hesitated to place themselves at the service of the altar; thus showing their belief that only by good and faithful service of divine authority can temporal government be rightly exercised.' And because it was to come about that in Gaul Christian priesthood would be more highly respected, providence permitted that the pagan priests of the Gauls, who were called Druids, should establish their authority, throughout the country; as Caesar tells us in his book, *De Bello Gallico*.

Chapter XV: How to attain the aim of a good life in the political community

Just as the good life of men on this earth is directed, as to its end, to the blessed life which is promised us in heaven, so also all those particular benefits which men can procure for themselves, such as riches, or gain, or health, or skill, or learning, must be directed to the good of the community. But, as we have said, he who has charge of supreme ends must take precedence over those who are concerned with aims subordinate to these ends, and must guide them by his authority; it follows, therefore, that a king, though subject to that power and authority must, nevertheless, preside over all human activities, and direct them in virtue of his own power and authority. Now, whoever has a duty of completing some task, which is itself connected with some higher aim, must satisfy himself that his action is rightly directed towards that aim. Thus the smith forges a sword which is fit to fight with; and the builder must construct a house so that it is habitable. And because the aim of a good life on this earth is blessedness in heaven, it is the king's duty to promote the welfare of the community in such a way that it leads fittingly to the happiness of heaven; insisting upon the performance of all that leads thereto, and forbidding, as far as is possible, whatever is inconsistent with this end. The road to true blessedness and the obstacles which may be found along it, are learnt through the medium of the divine law; to teach which is the duty of priests, as we read in *Malachy* (Chapter II, 7): 'The lips of the priest shall keep knowledge, and they shall seek the law at his mouth.' So the Lord commands (*Deuteronomy* XVII, 18): 'But after he is raised to the throne of his kingdom, he shall copy out to himself the Deuteronomy of this law in a volume, taking the copy of the priests of the Levitical tribe, and he shall have it with him and shall read it all the days of his life, that he may learn to fear the Lord his God, and keep his words and ceremonies, that are commanded in the law'. A king then, being instructed in the divine law, must occupy himself particularly with directing the community subject to him to the good life. In this connection he has three tasks. He must first establish the welfare of the community he rules; secondly, he must ensure that nothing undermines the well-being thus established; and thirdly he must be at pains continually to extend this welfare.

For the well-being of the individual two things are necessary: the first and most essential is to act virtuously (it is through virtue, in fact, that we live a good life); the other, and secondary requirement, is rather a means, and lies in a sufficiency of material goods, such as are necessary to virtuous action. Now man is a natural unit, but the unity of a community, which is peace, must be brought into being by the skill of the ruler. To ensure the well-being of a community, therefore, three things are necessary. In the first place the community must be united in peaceful unity. In the second place the community, thus united, must be directed towards well-doing. For just as a man could do no good if he were not an integral whole, so also a community of men which is disunited and at strife within itself, is hampered in well-doing. Thirdly and finally, it is necessary that there be, through the ruler's sagacity, a sufficiency of those material goods which are indispensable to well-being. Once the welfare of the community is thus ensured, it remains for the king to consider its preservation.

Now there are three things which are detrimental to the permanence of public welfare and one of these springs from the nature of things. For the common prosperity should not be for any limited period, but should endure, if possible, in perpetuity. But men, being mortal, cannot live for ever. Nor, even while they are still alive, they have always the same vigour; for human life is subject to many changes, and a man is not always capable of fulfilling the same tasks throughout the span of his lifetime. Another obstacle to the preservation of public welfare is one which arises from within, and lies in the perversity of the will; for many are inattentive in carrying out duties necessary to the community, or even harm the peace of the community by failing to observe justice and disturbing the peace of others. Then there is a third obstacle to the preservation of the community which comes from without: when peace is shattered by hostile invasion, and sometimes the kingdom or city itself is entirely destroyed. Corresponding to these three points, the task of a king has a threefold aspect. The first regards the succession and substitution of those who hold various offices: just as divine providence sees to it that corruptible things, which cannot remain unchanged for ever, are renewed through successive generations, and so conserves the integrity of the universe, it is the king's duty also to preserve the well-being of the community subject to him, by providing successors for those who are failing. Secondly, he must, in governing, be concerned, by laws and by advice, by penalties and by rewards, to dissuade men from evil-doing and to induce them to do good; following thus the example of God, who gave to men a law, and rewards those who observe it but punishes those who transgress. Thirdly it is a king's duty to make sure that the community subject to him is made safe against its enemies. There is no point in guarding against internal dangers, when defence from enemies without is impossible.

So, for the right ordering of society there remains a third task for the king: he must be occupied with its development. This task is best fulfilled by keeping in mind the various points enumerated above; by attention to what may be a cause of disorder, by making good whatever is lacking and by perfecting whatever can be better done. Therefore the Apostle (I *Corinthians*, XII), warns the faithful always to prize the better gifts.

These, then, are the things which go to make up the duty of a king: but each should be treated in much greater detail.

[. . .]

SUMMA THEOLOGIA

15: War

The conditions of a just war *follows logically –*

For a war to be just three conditions are necessary. First, the authority of the *ruler or* ruler within whose competence it lies to declare war. A private individual may *comm* not declare war; for he can have recourse to the judgement of a superior to safeguard his rights. Nor has he the right to mobilize the people, which is *good,* necessary in war. But since responsibility for public affairs is entrusted to the *dwed* rulers, it is they who are charged with the defence of the city, realm, or province, subject to them. And just as in the punishment of criminals they rightly defend the state against all internal disturbance with the civil arm; as the Apostle says (*Romans*, XIII, 4): 'He beareth not the sword in vain. For he is God's minister: an avenger to execute wrath upon him that doth evil.' So also they have the duty of defending the state, with the weapons of war, against external enemies. For this reason rulers are told in *Psalm* LXXXI to 'Rescue the poor; and deliver the needy out of the hand of the sinner.' And St. Augustine says in his book, *Contra Faustum* (XXIII, 73): 'The natural order of men, to be peacefully disposed, requires that the power and decision to declare war should lie with the rulers.'

Secondly, there is required a just cause: that is that those who are attacked for some offence merit such treatment. St. Augustine says (Book LXXXIII q.; *Super Josue*, qu. X): 'Those wars are generally defined as just which avenge some wrong, when a nation or a state is to be punished for having failed to make amends for the wrong done, or to restore what has been taken unjustly.'

Thirdly, there is required a right intention on the part of the belligerents: either of achieving some good object or of avoiding some evil. So St. Augustine says in the book *De Verbis Domini*: 'For the true followers of God even wars are peaceful, not being made for greed or out of cruelty, but from desire of peace, to restrain the evil and assist the good.' So it can happen that even when war is declared by legitimate authority and there is just cause, it is, nevertheless, made unjust through evil intention. St. Augustine says in *Contra Faustum* (LXXIV): 'The desire to hurt, the cruelty of vendetta, the stern and implacable spirit, arrogance in victory, the thirst for power, and all that is similar, all these are justly condemned in war.'

16: The right to resist tyrannical government

Tyrannical government is unjust government because it is directed not to the common welfare but to the private benefit of the ruler. This is clear from what the Philosopher says in the *Politics*, Book III, and in the *Ethics*, Book VIII. Consequently the overthrowing of such government is not strictly sedition; except perhaps in the case that it is accompanied by such disorder that the community suffers greater harm from the consequent disturbances than it would from a continuance of the former rule. A tyrant himself is, in fact, far more guilty of sedition when he spreads discord and strife among the people subject to him, so hoping to control them more easily. For it is a characteristic of tyranny to order everything to the personal satisfaction of the ruler at the expense of the community.

17: Political prudence

Its nature

Whoever promotes the common welfare of the community promotes his own welfare at the same time: and this for two reasons. First, because individual well-being cannot exist without the welfare of the family, or city, or realm. Valerius Maximus says of the Romans of old that, 'They preferred rather to be poor men in a rich empire, than rich men in a poor empire.' Secondly, because man, being part of the family, or of the city, it is right that he should consider his personal well-being in the light of what prudence advises with regard to the common welfare. For the good disposition of any part must be determined by its relationship to the whole. For, as St. Augustine says in the *Confessions*: 'All parts are base which do not fit or harmonise with their whole.'

Its object

The object of prudence is government and command. So wherever there is to be found a special form of government and command in human actions, there is to be found also a special form of prudence. But it is clear that in a man whose duty it is to govern, not only himself, but also a perfect community such as a city or realm, there is to be found a special and perfect form of governing. For government is the more perfect the more universal it is, and the further it extends and the higher its aims. Therefore a king, whose duty it is to rule a city or kingdom, must possess prudence of a special and most perfect quality. For this reason we distinguish a species of 'political' prudence.

18: Natural and positive justice

The origin of positive justice

Right, or what is just, lies in the due proportion between some exterior action and another according to a certain relationship of equality. Now there are two ways in which such a proportion may be established for man. First, from the nature of the thing itself: as for example when some one gives so much that he may receive equal in return. And this is called natural justice (*ius naturale*). – Secondly, something may be comparable or commensurate with another by agreement or common consent: as when, for example, some one declares himself content to receive such an amount. This again can happen in two ways. Either by private agreement, as when a pact is reached among a number of private individuals: or by public agreement, when such a proportion or standard of measurement is agreed by the consent of the whole community, or by decree of the ruler who administers and represents the community. And this is called positive justice (*ius positivum*).

The subordination of positive to natural justice

The human will can, by common consent, attribute juridical value to anything which is not in itself contrary to natural justice. And this is precisely the field of positive law. So the Philosopher (V, *Ethics*) defines the legally just as 'that which does not in itself present any difference of values, but which acquires them on being laid down.' But if a thing is in itself contrary to natural justice, it cannot be made just by human volition: if, for example, it were laid down that it is permissible to steal or commit adultery, so it is said in *Isaias* (X, 1): 'Woe to those who make evil laws.'

19: Justice and the state

The various ways in which justice is achieved in the state (Art. 1, ad 5um.)

The judge renders to each his due in that he commands and directs: because, as is said in the *Ethics* (V, 4), 'the judge is the embodiment of justice' and 'the ruler is the custodian of justice.' Subjects, on the other hand, render to each his due in the capacity of executors. (Cp. Art. 6, concl.: Justice . . . is in the ruler as in principle and constructively; in subjects, however, it is derivative and executive).

Justice and the common welfare

The scope of justice, as we have said, is to regulate men in their relations with others. Here there are two cases to be considered. Either when the reference is to others considered individually. Or when the reference is to others considered as a community: to the extent, that is, to which one who is a subject of a certain community is subject also to all the persons who go to form it. Justice, as such, enters into both cases. For it is evident that all those who make up the community, have to it the same relationship as that of parts to a whole. Now the part, as such, belongs to the whole: consequently any partial interest is subordinate to the good of the whole. From this point of view, whatever is good and virtuous, whether in respect of a man to himself or with respect to the relationships between men, can have reference to the common well-being which is the object of justice. In this sense all virtues may come within the province of justice, in so far as it orders men to the common welfare.

The common welfare and individual interest

The common welfare of the city and the individual welfare of one person are distinguished not only by a quantative but also by a formal difference: for the common welfare is different in nature from that of the individual, just as the nature of the part is different from that of the whole. So the Philosopher (I, *Politics*, 1), says: 'they are in error who say that the city, and the family and other similar groups, differ only in size and not specifically.'

20: The relationship between the temporal and the spiritual power

The right of the spiritual power to interpose in temporal affairs

The temporal power is subject to the spiritual as the body to the soul, as St. Gregory Nazianzenus says (*Orat.* XVII). Therefore there is no usurpation of power if a spiritual Prelate should interest himself in temporal affairs with respect to those things in which the temporal power is subject to him or in matters which have been left to him by the secular power.

Possibility of the submission of the spiritual to the temporal authority

In human affairs it can happen that persons submit themselves spontaneously to the judgement of others, even though these may not be their superiors; as for instance when people have recourse to arbitration. But arbiters, not being superiors, have not in themselves the full power of enforcing their decision and therefore it is necessary for such decision to be accompanied by some sanction. In this sense, Christ freely subjected Himself to human judgement, and Pope Leo also submitted himself to the judgement of the Emperor.

Distinction between the temporal and the spiritual sphere

Just as it falls to temporal princes to enact legal statutes which are particular determinations of the natural law, in all those matters which concern the common welfare in mundane affairs; so also it is the province of ecclesiastical prelates to regulate by precept those matters which affect the common interest of the faithful to their spiritual well-being.

5

MACHIAVELLI

Source: Max Lerner (1950) *The Prince and the Discourses*. New York, Random House, chs XII, XIII, XV, XVII and XXV.

Machiavelli's thinking on politics represents a break with the Christian tradition in advocating a form of statesmanship divorced from conventional morality. Machiavelli concerns himself with the prudent use of power in achieving the goals of a state. Drawing on Italian and Roman history he advances the idea of a shrewdly calculating Prince who acts to attain his most advantageous outcome and is judged by the political consequences of his actions. Machiavelli's political doctrines have inspired realist thinking about international relations. His sceptical view of human nature leads to harsh and surprising recommendations that have greatly influenced political thought and behaviour. But Machiavelli's elevation of politics above ordinary morality is directed towards what he conceives as a progressive purpose. He wished to see a prudent Italian prince capitalize on fortune and unify the Italian nation. The view of Hegel, Clausewitz and the Realist schools in international relations owe a great deal to Machiavelli.

Chapter XII: The different kinds of militia and mercenary soldiers

Having now discussed fully the qualities of these principalities of which I proposed to treat, and partially considered the causes of their prosperity or failure, and having also showed the methods by which many have sought to obtain such states, it now remains for me to treat generally of the methods, both offensive and defensive, that can be used in each of them. We have said already how necessary it is for a prince to have his foundations good, otherwise he is certain to be ruined. The chief foundations of all states, whether new, old, or mixed, are good laws and good arms. And as there cannot be good laws where there are not good arms, and where there are good arms there must be good laws, I will not now discuss the laws, but will speak of the arms.

I say, therefore, that the arms by which a prince defends his possessions are either his own, or else mercenaries, or auxiliaries, or mixed. The mercenaries and auxiliaries are useless and dangerous, and if any one supports his state by the arms of mercenaries, he will never stand firm or sure, as they are disunited, ambitious, without discipline, faithless, bold amongst friends, cowardly amongst enemies, they have no fear of God, and keep no faith with men. Ruin is only deferred as long as the assault is postponed; in peace you are despoiled by them, and in war by the enemy. The cause of this is that they have no love or other motive to keep them in the field beyond a trifling wage, which is not enough to make them ready to die for you. They are quite willing to be your soldiers so long as you do not make war, but when war comes, it is either fly or decamp altogether. I ought to have little trouble in proving this, since the ruin of Italy is now caused by nothing else but through her having relied for many years on mercenary arms. These did indeed help certain individuals to power, and appeared courageous when matched against each other, but when the foreigner came they showed their worthlessness. Thus it came about that King Charles of France was allowed to take Italy without the slightest trouble, and those who said that it was owing to our sins, spoke the truth, but it was not the sins they meant but those that I have related. And as it was the sins of princes, they too have suffered the punishment.

I will explain more fully the defects of these arms. Mercenary captains are either very capable men or not; if they are, you cannot rely upon them, for they will always aspire to their own greatness, either by oppressing you, their master, or by oppressing others against your intentions; but if the captain is not an able man, he will generally ruin you. And if it is replied to this, that whoever has armed forces will do the same, whether these are mercenary or not, I would reply that as armies are to be used either by a prince or by a republic, the prince must go in person to take the position of captain, and the republic must send its own citizens. If the man sent turns out incompetent, it must change him; and if capable, keep him by law from going beyond the proper limits. And it is seen by experience that only princes and armed republics make very great progress, whereas mercenary forces do nothing but harm, and also an armed republic submits less easily to the rule of one of its citizens than a republic armed by foreign forces.

Rome and Sparta were for many centuries well armed and free. The Swiss are well armed and enjoy great freedom. As an example of mercenary armies in antiquity there are the Carthaginians, who were oppressed by their mercenary soldiers, after the termination of the first war with the Romans, even while they still had their own citizens as captains. Philip of Macedon was made captain of their forces by the Thebans after the death of Epaminondas, and after gaining the victory he deprived them of liberty. The Milanese, on the death of Duke Philip, hired Francesco Sforza against the Venetians, who having overcome the enemy at Caravaggio, allied himself with them to oppress the Milanese his own employers. The father of this Sforza, being a soldier in the service of Queen Giovanna of Naples, left her suddenly unarmed, by which she was compelled, in order not to lose the kingdom, to throw herself into the arms of the King of Aragon. And if the Venetians and Florentines have in times past increased their dominions by means of such forces, and their captains have not made themselves princes but have defended them, I reply that the Florentines in this case have been favoured by chance, for of the capable leaders whom they might have feared, some did not conquer, some met with opposition, and others directed their ambition elsewhere. The one who did not conquer was Sir John Hawkwood, whose fidelity could not be known as he was not victorious, but every one will admit that, had he conquered, the Florentines would have been at his mercy. Sforza had always the Bracceschi against him which served as a mutual check. Francesco directed his ambition towards Lombardy; Braccio against the Church and the kingdom of Naples.

But let us look at what occurred a short time ago. The Florentines appointed Paolo Vitelli their captain, a man of great prudence, who had risen from a private station to the highest reputation. If he had taken Pisa no one can deny that it was highly important for the Florentines to retain his friendship, because had he become the soldier of their enemies they would have had no means of opposing him; and if they had retained him they would have been obliged to obey him. As to the Venetians, if one considers the progress they made, it will be seen that they acted surely and gloriously so long as they made war with their own forces; that it was before they commenced their enterprises on land that they fought courageously with their own gentlemen and armed populace, but when they began to fight on land they abandoned this virtue, and began to follow the Italian custom. And at the commencement of their land conquests they had not much to fear from their captains, their territories not being very large, and their reputation being great, but as their possessions increased, as they did under Carmagnola, they had an example of their mistake. For seeing that he was very powerful, after he had defeated the Duke of Milan, and knowing, on the other hand, that he was but lukewarm in this war, they considered that they would not make any more conquests with him, and they neither would nor could dismiss him, for fear of losing what they had already gained. In order to make sure of him they were therefore obliged to execute him. They then had for captains Bartolommeo da Bergamo, Roberto da San Severino, Count di Pitigliano, and such like, from whom they had to fear loss instead of gain, as happened subsequently at Vailà, where in one day they lost what they had laboriously gained in eight hundred years; for with these forces, only slow and trifling acquisitions are made, but sudden and miraculous losses. And as I have cited these examples from Italy, which has now for many years been governed by mercenary forces, I will now deal more largely with them, so that having seen their origin and progress, they can be better remedied.

You must understand that in these latter times, as soon as the empire began to be repudiated in Italy and the Pope to gain greater reputation in temporal matters, Italy was divided into many states; many of the principal cities took up arms against their nobles, who, favoured by the emperor, had held them in subjection, and the Church encouraged this in order to increase its temporal power. In many other cities one of the inhabitants became prince. Thus Italy having fallen almost entirely into the hands of the Church and a few republics, and the priests and other citizens not being accustomed to bear arms, they began to hire foreigners as soldiers. The first to bring into reputation this kind of militia was Alberigo da Como, a native of Romagna. Braccio and Sforza, who were in their day the arbiters of Italy were, amongst others, trained by him. After these came all those others who up to the present day have commanded the armies of Italy, and the result of their prowess has been that Italy has been overrun by Charles, preyed on by Louis, tyrannised over by Ferrando, and insulted by the Swiss. The system adopted by them was, in the first place, to increase their own reputation by discrediting the infantry. They did this because, as they had no country and lived on their earnings, a few foot soldiers did not augment their reputation, and they could not maintain a large number and therefore they restricted themselves almost entirely to cavalry, by which with a smaller number they were well paid and honoured. They reduced things to such a state that in an army of 20,000 soldiers there were not 2,000 foot. They had also used every means to spare themselves and the soldiers any hardship or fear by not killing each other in their encounters, but taking prisoners without expectation of ransom. They made no attacks on fortifications by night; and those in the fortifications did not attack the tents at night, they made no stockades or ditches round their camps, and did not take the field in winter. All these things were permitted by their military code, and adopted, as we have said, to avoid trouble and danger, so that they have reduced Italy to slavery and degradation.

Chapter XIII: Of auxiliary, mixed, and native troops

When one asks a powerful neighbour to come to aid and defend one with his forces, they are termed auxiliaries and are as useless as mercenaries. This was done in recent times by Julius, who seeing the wretched failure of his mercenary forces, in his Ferrara enterprise, had recourse to auxiliaries, had arranged with Ferrando, King of Spain, that he should help him with his armies. These forces may be good in themselves, but they are always dangerous for those who borrow them, for if they lose you are defeated, and if they conquer you remain their prisoner. And although ancient history is full of examples of this, I will not depart from the example of Pope Julius II, which is still fresh. Nothing could be less prudent than the course he adopted; for, wishing to take Ferrara, he put himself entirely into the power of a foreigner. But by good fortune there arose a third cause which prevented him reaping the effects of his bad policy; for when his auxiliaries were beaten at Ravenna, the Swiss rose up and drove back the victors, against all expectation of himself or others, so that he was not taken prisoner by the enemy which had fled, nor by his own auxiliaries, having conquered by other arms than theirs. The Florentines, being totally disarmed, hired 10,000 Frenchmen to attack Pisa, by which measure they ran greater risk than at any period of their struggles. The emperor of Constantinople, to oppose his neighbours, put 10,000 Turks into Greece, who after the war would not go away again, which was the beginning of the servitude of Greece to the infidels.

And one, therefore, who wishes not to conquer, would do well to use these forces, which are much more dangerous than mercenaries, as with them ruin is complete, for they are all united, and owe obedience to others, whereas with mercenaries, when they have conquered, it requires more time and a good opportunity for them to injure you, as they do not form a single body and have been engaged and paid by you, therefore a third party that you have made leader cannot at once acquire enough authority to be able to injure you. In a word, the greatest danger with mercenaries lies in their cowardice and reluctance to fight, but with auxiliaries the danger lies in their courage.

A wise prince, therefore, always avoids these forces and has recourse to his own, and would prefer rather to lose with his own men than conquer with the forces of others, not deeming it a true victory which is gained by foreign arms. I never hesitate to cite the example of Cesare Borgia and his actions. This duke entered Romagna with auxiliary troops, leading forces composed entirely of French soldiers, and with these he took Imola and Forlì; but as they seemed unsafe, he had recourse to mercenaries as a less risky policy, and hired the Orsini and Vitelli. Afterwards finding these uncertain to handle, unfaithful, and dangerous, he suppressed them, and relied upon his own men. And the difference between these forces can be easily seen if one considers the difference between the reputation of the duke when he had only the French, when he had the Orsini and Vitelli, and when he had to rely on himself and his own soldiers. His reputation will be found to have constantly increased, and he was never so highly esteemed as when every one saw that he was the sole master of his forces.

I do not wish to depart from recent Italian instances, but I cannot omit Hiero of Syracuse, whom I have already mentioned. This man being, as I said, made head of the army by the Syracusans, immediately recognised the uselessness of that militia which was organized like our Italian mercenary troops, and as he thought it unsafe either to retain them or dismiss them, he had them cut in pieces and thenceforward made war with his own arms and not those of others. I would also call to mind a symbolic tale from the Old Testament which well illustrates this point. When David offered to Saul to go and fight against the Philistine champion Goliath, Saul, to encourage him, armed him with his own arms, which when David had tried on, he refused saying, that with them he could not fight so well; he preferred, therefore, to face the enemy with his own sling and knife. In short, the arms of others either fail, overburden, or else impede you. Charles VII, father of King Louis XI, having through good fortune and bravery liberated France from the English, recognised this necessity of being armed with his own forces, and established in his kingdom a system of men-at-arms and infantry. Afterwards King Louis his son abolished the infantry and began to hire Swiss, which mistake being followed by others is, as may now be seen, a cause of danger to that kingdom. For by giving such reputation to the Swiss, France has disheartened all her own troops, the infantry having been abolished and the men-at-arms being obliged to foreigners for assistance; for being accustomed to fight with Swiss troops, they think they cannot conquer without them. Whence it comes that the French are insufficiently strong to oppose the Swiss, and without the aid of the Swiss they will not venture against others. The armies of the French are thus of a mixed kind, partly mercenary and partly her own; taken together they are much better than troops entirely composed of mercenaries or auxiliaries, but much inferior to national forces.

And let this example be sufficient, for the kingdom of France would be invincible if Charles's military organization had been developed or maintained. But men with their lack of prudence initiate novelties and, finding the first taste good, do not notice the poison within, as I pointed out previously in regard to wasting fevers.

The prince, therefore, who fails to recognise troubles in his state as they arise, is not truly wise, and it is given to few to be thus. If we consider the first cause of the collapse of the Roman Empire we shall find it merely due to the hiring of Goth mercenaries, for from that time we find the Roman strength begin to weaken. All the advantages derived from the Empire fell to the Goths.

I conclude then by saying that no prince is secure without his own troops, on the contrary he is entirely dependent on fortune, having no trustworthy means of defence in time of trouble. It has always been held and proclaimed by wise men 'quod nihil sit tam infirmum aut instabile quam fama potentiae non sua vi nixae.' One's own troops are those composed either of subjects or of citizens or of one's own dependants; all others are mercenaries or auxiliaries. The way to organise one's own troops is easily learnt if the methods of the four princes mentioned above be studied, and if one considers how Philip, father of Alexander the Great, and many republics and sovereigns have organised theirs. With such examples as these there is no need to labour the point.

[. . .]

Chapter XV: Of the things for which men, and especially princes, are praised or blamed

It now remains to be seen what are the methods and rules for a prince as regards his subjects and friends. And as I know that many have written of this, I fear that my writing about it may be deemed presumptuous, differing as I do, especially in this matter, from the opinions of others. But my intention being to write something of use to those who understand, it appears to me more proper to go to the real truth of the matter than to its imagination; and many have imagined republics and principalities which have never been seen or known to exist in reality; for how we live is so far removed from how we ought to live, that he who abandons what is done for what ought to be done, will rather learn to bring about his own ruin than his preservation. A man who wishes to make a profession of goodness in everything must necessarily come to grief among so many who are not good. Therefore it is necessary for a prince, who wishes to maintain himself, to learn how not to be good, and to use this knowledge and not use it, according to the necessity of the case.

Leaving on one side, then, those things which concern only an imaginary prince, and speaking of those that are real, I state that all men, and especially princes, who are placed at a greater height, are reputed for certain qualities which bring them either praise or blame. Thus one is considered liberal, another *misero* or miserly (using a Tuscan term, seeing that *avaro* with us still means one who is rapaciously acquisitive and *misero* one who makes grudging use of his own); one a free giver, another rapacious; one cruel, another merciful; one a breaker of his word, another trustworthy; one effeminate and pusillanimous, another fierce and high-spirited; one humane, another haughty; one lascivious, another chaste; one frank; another astute; one hard, another easy; one serious, another frivolous; one religious, another an unbeliever, and so on. I know that every one will admit that it would be highly praiseworthy in a prince to possess all the above-named qualities that are reputed good, but as they cannot all be possessed or observed, human conditions not permitting of it, it is necessary that he should be prudent enough to avoid the scandal of those vices which would lose him the state, and guard himself if possible against those which will not lose it him, but if not able to, he can indulge them with less scruple. And yet he must not mind incurring the scandal of those vices, without which it would be difficult to save the state, for if one considers well, it will be found that some things which seem virtues would, if followed, lead to one's ruin, and some others which appear vices result in one's greater security and wellbeing.

[. . .]

Chapter XVII: Of cruelty and clemency, and whether it is better to be loved or feared

Proceeding to the other qualities before named, I say that every prince must desire to be considered merciful and not cruel. He must, however, take care not to misuse this mercifulness. Cesare Borgia was considered cruel, but his cruelty had brought order to the Romagna, united it, and reduced it to peace and fealty. If this is considered well, it will be seen that he was really much more merciful than the Florentine people, who, to avoid the name of cruelty, allowed Pistoia to be destroyed. A prince, therefore, must not mind incurring the charge of cruelty for the purpose of keeping his subjects united and faithful; for, with a very few examples, he will be more merciful than those who, from excess of tenderness, allow disorders to arise, from whence spring bloodshed and rapine; for these as a rule injure the whole community, while the executions carried out by the prince injure only individuals. And of all princes, it is impossible for a new prince to escape the reputation of cruelty, new states being always full of dangers. Wherefore Virgil through the mouth of Dido says:

Res dura, et regni novitas me talia cogunt
Moliri, et late fines custode tueri.

Nevertheless, he must be cautious in believing and acting, and must not be afraid of his own shadow, and must proceed in a temperate manner with prudence and humanity, so that too much confidence does not render him incautious, and too much diffidence does not render him intolerant.

From this arises the question whether it is better to be loved more than feared, or feared more than loved. The reply is, that one ought to be both feared and loved, but as it is difficult for the two to go together, it is much safer to be feared than loved, if one of the two has to be wanting. For it may be said of men in general that they are ungrateful, voluble, dissemblers, anxious to avoid danger, and covetous of gain; as long as you benefit them, they are entirely yours; they offer you their blood, their goods, their life, and their children, as I have before said, when the necessity is remote; but when it approaches, they revolt. And the prince who has relied solely on their words, without making other preparations, is ruined; for the friendship which is gained by purchase and not through grandeur and nobility of spirit is bought but not secured, and at a pinch is not to be expended in your service. And men have less scruple in offending one who makes himself loved than one who makes himself feared; for love is held by a chain of obligation which, men being selfish, is broken whenever it serves their purpose; but fear is maintained by a dread of punishment which never fails.

Still, a prince should make himself feared in such a way that if he does not gain love, he at any rate avoids hatred; for fear and the absence of hatred may well go together, and will be always attained by one who abstains from interfering with the property of his citizens and subjects or with their women. And when he is obliged to take the life of any one, let him do so when there is a proper justification and manifest reason for it; but above all he must abstain from taking the property of others, for men forget more easily the death of their father than the loss of their patrimony. Then also pretexts for seizing property are never wanting, and one who begins to live by rapine will always find some reason for taking the goods of others, whereas causes for taking life are rarer and more fleeting.

But when the prince is with his army and has a large number of soldiers under his control, then it is extremely necessary that he should not mind being thought cruel; for without this reputation he could not keep an army united or disposed to any duty. Among the noteworthy actions of Hannibal is numbered this, that although he had an enormous army, composed of men of all nations and fighting in foreign countries, there never arose any dissension either among them or against the prince, either in good fortune or in bad. This could not be due to anything but his inhuman cruelty, which together with his infinite other virtues, made him always venerated and terrible in the sight of his soldiers, and without it his other virtues would not have sufficed to produce that effect. Thoughtless writers admire on the one hand his actions, and on the other blame the principal cause of them.

And that it is true that his other virtues would not have sufficed may be seen from the case of Scipio (famous not only in regard to his own times, but all times of which memory remains), whose armies rebelled against him in Spain, which arose from nothing but his excessive kindness, which allowed more licence to the soldiers than was consonant with military discipline. He was reproached with this in the senate by Fabius Maximus, who called him a corrupter of the Roman militia. Locri having been destroyed by one of Scipio's officers was not revenged by him, nor was the insolence of that officer punished, simply by reason of his easy nature; so much so, that some one wishing to excuse him in the senate, said that there were many men who knew rather how not to err, than how to correct the errors of others. This disposition would in time have tarnished the fame and glory of Scipio had he persevered in it under the empire, but living under the rule of the senate this harmful quality was not only concealed but became a glory to him.

I conclude, therefore, with regard to being feared and loved, that men love at their own free will, but fear at the will of the prince, and that a wise prince must rely on what is in his power and not on what is in the power of others, and he must only contrive to avoid incurring hatred, as has been explained.

[. . .]

Chapter XXV: How much fortune can do in human affairs and how it may be opposed

It is not unknown to me how many have been and are of opinion that worldly events are so governed by fortune and by God, that men cannot by their prudence change them, and that on the contrary there is no remedy whatever, and for this they may judge it to be useless to toil much about them, but let things be ruled by chance. This opinion has been more held in our day, from the great changes that have been seen, and are daily seen, beyond every human conjecture. When I think about them, at times I am partly inclined to share this opinion. Nevertheless, that our free-will may not be altogether extinguished, I think it may be true that fortune is the ruler of half our actions, but that she allows the other half or thereabouts to be governed by us, I would compare her to an impetuous river that, when turbulent, inundates the plains, casts down trees and buildings, removes earth from this side and places it on the other; every one flees before it, and everything yields to its fury without being able to oppose it; and yet though it is of such a kind, still then it is quiet, men can make provision against it by dykes and banks, so that when it rises it will either go into a canal or its rush will not be so wild and dangerous. So it is with fortune, which shows her power where no measures have been taken to resist her, and directs her fury where she knows that no dykes or barriers have been made to hold her. And if you regard Italy, which has been the seat of these changes, and who has given the impulse to them, you will see her to be a country without dykes or banks of any kind. If she had been protected by proper measures, like Germany, Spain, and France, this inundation would not have caused the great changes that it has, or would not have happened at all.

This must suffice as regards opposition to fortune in general. But limiting myself more to particular cases, I would point out how one sees a certain prince to-day fortunate and to-morrow ruined, without seeing that he has changed in character or otherwise. I believe this arises in the first place from the causes that we have already discussed at length; that is to say, because the prince who bases himself entirely on fortune is ruined when fortune changes. I also believe that he is happy whose mode of procedure accords with the needs of the times, and similarly he is unfortunate whose mode of procedure is opposed to the times. For one sees that men in those things which lead them to the aim that each one has in view, namely, glory and riches, proceed in various ways; one with circumspection, another with impetuosity, one by violence, another by cunning, one with patience, another with the reverse; and each by these diverse ways may arrive at his aim. One sees also two cautious men, one of whom succeeds in his designs, and the other not, and in the same way two men succeed equally by different methods, one being cautious, the other impetuous, which arises only from the nature of the times, which does or does not conform to their method of procedure. From this it results, as I have said, that two men, acting differently, attain the same effect, and of two others acting in the same way, one attains his goal and not the other. On this depend also the changes in prosperity, for if it happens that time and circumstances are favourable to one who acts with caution and prudence he will be successful, but if time and circumstances change he will be ruined, because he does not change his mode of procedure. No man is found so prudent as to be able to adapt himself to this, either because he cannot deviate from that to which his nature disposes him, or else because having always prospered by walking in one path, he cannot persuade himself that it is well to leave it; and therefore the cautious man, when it is time to act suddenly, does not know how to do so and is consequently ruined; for if one could change one's nature with time and circumstances, fortune would never change.

Pope Julius II acted impetuously in everything he did and found the times and conditions so in conformity with that mode of procedure, that he always obtained a good result. Consider the first war that he made against Bologna while Messer Giovanni Bentivogli was still living. The Venetians were not pleased with it, neither was the King of Spain, France was conferring with him over the enterprise, notwithstanding which, owing to his fierce and impetuous disposition, he engaged personally in the expedition. This move caused both Spain and the Venetians to halt and hesitate, the latter through fear, the former through the desire to recover the entire kingdom of Naples. On the other hand, he engaged with him the King of France, because seeing him make this move and desiring his friendship in order to put down the Venetians, that king judged that he could not refuse him his troops without manifest injury. Thus Julius by his impetuous move achieved what no other pontiff with the utmost human prudence would have succeeded in doing, because, if he had waited till all arrangements had been made and everything settled before leaving Rome, as any other pontiff would have done, it would never have succeeded. For the king of France would have found a thousand excuses, and the others would have inspired him with a thousand fears. I will omit his other actions, which were all of this kind and which all succeeded well, and the shortness of his life did not suffer him to experience the contrary, for had times followed in which it was necessary to act with caution, his ruin would have resulted, for he would never have deviated from these methods to which his nature disposed him.

I conclude then that fortune varying and men remaining fixed in their ways, they are successful so long as these ways conform to circumstances, but when they are opposed then they are unsuccessful. I certainly think that it is better to be impetuous than cautious, for fortune is a woman, and it is necessary, if you wish to master her, to conquer her by force; and it can be seen that she lets herself be overcome by the bold rather than by those who proceed coldly. And therefore, like a woman, she is always a friend to the young, because they are less cautious, fiercer, and master her with greater audacity.

6

GROTIUS

Source: F.W. Kelsey (trans.) (1964) *Hugo Grotius: De Jure Belli ac Pacis Libri Tres*. London, Wildy & Sons, pp. 16–20, 33–4 and 51–7.

In his treatise the *Law of War and Peace* Grotius presents war as part of the natural condition of international society. In his view there is no controversy among states that might not give rise to war. Side by side with the condition of war there is also the peaceful condition. Since war is a natural part of international relations the condition of war does not mean that there are no rules ordering the relations between states. For Grotius the condition of war is as subject to rules as the condition of peace. Grotius sees war a compatible with the law of nations and he argues against those Christian and moral thinkers who favour pacificism.

Prolegomenci

For since, by his own admission, the national who in his own country obeys its laws is not foolish, even though, out of regard for that law, he may be obliged to forgo certain things advantageous for himself, so that nation is not foolish which does not press its own advantage to the point of disregarding the laws common to nations. The reason in either case is the same. For just as the national, who violates the law of his country in order to obtain an immediate advantage, breaks down that by which the advantages of himself and his posterity are for all future time assured, so the state which transgresses the laws of nature and of nations cuts away also the bulwarks which safeguard its own future peace. Even if no advantage were to be contemplated from the keeping of the law, it would be a mark of wisdom, not of folly, to allow ourselves to be drawn towards that to which we feel that our nature leads.

19. Wherefore, in general, it is by no means true that

> You must confess that laws were framed
> From fear of the unjust,

a thought which in Plato some one explains thus, that laws were invented from fear of receiving injury, and that men are constrained by a kind of force to cultivate justice. For that relates only to the institutions and laws which have been devised to facilitate the enforcement of right; as when many persons in themselves weak, in order that they might not be overwhelmed by the more powerful, leagued themselves together to establish tribunals and by combined force to maintain these, that as a united whole they might prevail against those with whom as individuals they could not cope.

And in this sense we may readily admit also the truth of the saying that right is that which is acceptable to the stronger; so that we may understand that law fails of its outward effect unless it has a sanction behind it. In this way Solon accomplished very great results, as he himself used to declare,

> By joining force and law together,
> Under a like bond.

20. Nevertheless law, even though without a sanction, is not entirely void of effect. For justice brings peace of conscience, while injustice causes torments and anguish, such as Plato describes, in the breast of tyrants. Justice is approved, and injustice condemned, by the common agreement of good men. But, most important of all, in God injustice finds an enemy, justice a protector. He reserves His judgements for the life after this, yet in such a way that He often causes their effects to become manifest even in this life, as history teaches by numerous examples.

21. Many hold, in fact, that the standard of justice which they insist upon in the case of individuals within the state is inapplicable to a nation or the ruler of a nation. The reason for the error lies in this, first of all, that in respect to law they have in view nothing except the advantage which accrues from it, such advantage being apparent in the case of citizens who, taken singly, are powerless to protect themselves. But great states, since they seem to contain in themselves all things required for the adequate protection of life, seem not to have need of that virtue which looks toward the outside, and is called justice.

22. But, not to repeat what I have said, that law is not founded on expediency alone, there is no state so powerful that it may not some time need the help of others outside itself, either for purposes of trade, or even to ward off the forces of many foreign nations united against it. In consequence we see that even the most powerful peoples and sovereigns seek alliances, which are quite devoid of significance according to the point of view of those who confine law within the

boundaries of states. Most true is the saying, that all things are uncertain the moment men depart from law.

23. If no association of men can be maintained without law, as Aristotle showed by his remarkable illustration drawn from brigands, surely also that association which binds together the human race, or binds many nations together, has need of law; this was perceived by him who said that shameful deeds ought not to be committed even for the sake of one's country. Aristotle takes sharply to task those who, while unwilling to allow any one to exercise authority over themselves except in accordance with law, yet are quite indifferent as to whether foreigners are treated according to law or not.

24. That same Pompey, whom I just now quoted for the opposite view, corrected the statement which a king of Sparta had made, that that state is the most fortunate whose boundaries are fixed by spear and sword; he declared that that state is truly fortunate which has justice for its boundary line. On this point he might have invoked the authority of another king of Sparta, who gave the preference to justice over bravery in war, using this argument, that bravery ought to be directed by a kind of justice, but if all men were just they would have no need for bravery in war.

Bravery itself the Stoics defined as virtue fighting on behalf of equity. Themistius in his address to Valens argues with eloquence that kings who measure up to the rule of wisdom make account not only of the nation which has been committed to them, but of the whole human race, and that they are, as he himself says, not 'friends of the Macedonians' alone, or 'friends of the Romans', but 'friends of mankind'. The name of Minos became odious to future ages for no other reason than this, that he limited his fair-dealing to the boundaries of his realm.

25. Least of all should that be admitted which some people imagine, that in war all laws are in abeyance. On the contrary war ought not to be undertaken except for the enforcement of rights; when once undertaken, it should be carried on only within the bounds of law and good faith. Demosthenes well said that war is directed against that who cannot be held in check by judicial processes. For judgements are efficacious against those who feel that they are too weak to resist; against those who are equally strong, or think that they are, wars are undertaken. But in order that wars may be justified, they must be carried on with not less scrupulousness than judicial processes are wont to be.

26. Let the laws be silent, then, in the midst of arms, but only the laws of the State, those that the courts are concerned with, that are adapted only to a state of peace; not those other laws, which are of perpetual validity and suited to all times. It was exceedingly well said by Dio of Prusa, that between enemies written laws, that is, laws of particular states, are not in force, but that unwritten laws are in force, that is, those which nature prescribes, or the agreement of nations has established. This is set forth by that ancient formula of the Romans, 'I think that those things ought to be sought by means of a war that is blameless and righteous.'

The ancient Romans, as Varro noted, were slow in undertaking war, and permitted themselves no licence in that matter, because they held the view that a war ought not to be waged except when free from reproach. Camillus said that wars should be carried on justly no less than bravely; Scipio Africanus, that the Roman people commenced and ended wars justly. In another passage you may read: 'War has its laws no less than peace.' Still another writer admires Fabricius as a great man who maintained his probity in war – a thing most difficult – and believed that even in relation to an enemy there is such a thing as wrongdoing.

27. The historians in many a passage reveal how great in war is the influence of the consciousness that one has justice on his side; they often attribute victory chiefly to this cause. Hence the proverbs, that a soldier's strength is broken or increased by his cause; that he who has taken up arms unjustly rarely comes back in safety; that hope is the comrade of a good cause; and others of the same purport.

No one ought to be disturbed, furthermore, by the successful outcome of unjust enterprises. For it is enough that the fairness of the cause exerts a certain influence, even a strong influence upon actions, although the effect of that influence, as happens in human affairs, is often nullified by the interference of other causes. Even for winning friendships, of which for many reasons nations as well as individuals have need, a reputation for having undertaken war not rashly nor unjustly, and of having waged it in a manner above reproach, is exceedingly efficacious. No one readily allies himself with those in whom he believes that there is only a slight regard for law, for the right, and for good faith.

28. Fully convinced, by the considerations which I have advanced, that there is a common law among nations, which is valid alike for war and in war, I have had many and weighty reasons for undertaking to write upon this subject. Throughout the Christian world I observed a lack or restraint in relation to war, such as even barbarous races should be ashamed of; I observed that men rush to arms for slight causes, or no cause at all, and that when arms have once been taken up there is no longer any respect for law, divine or human; it is as if, in accordance with a general decree, frenzy had openly been let loose for the committing of all crimes.

[. . .]

Chapter I: What is war? What is law?

I: *Scope of the treatise*

Controversies among those who are not held together by a common bond of municipal law are related either to times of war or to times of peace. Such controversies may arise among those who have not yet united to form a nation, and those who belong to different nations, both private persons and kings; also those who have the same body of rights that kings have, whether members of a ruling aristocracy, or free peoples.

War, however, is undertaken in order to secure peace, and there is no controversy which may not give rise to war. In undertaking to treat the law of war, therefore, it will be in order to treat such controversies, of any and every kind, as are likely to arise. War itself will finally conduct us to peace as its ultimate goal.

II: *Definition of war, and origin of the word*

1. As we set out to treat the law of war, then, we ought to see what is war, which we are treating, and what is the law which forms the subject of our investigation.

Cicero defined war as a contending by force. A usage has gained currency, however, which designates by the word not a contest but a condition; thus war is the condition of those contending by force, viewed simply as such. This general definition includes all the classes of wars which it will hereafter be necessary to discuss. For I do not exclude private war, since in fact it is more ancient than public war and has, incontestably, the same nature as public war; wherefore both should be designated by one and the same term.

2. The origin of the word, moreover, is not inconsistent with this use. For *bellum*, 'war', comes from the old word *duellum*, as *bonus*, 'good', from an earlier *duonus*, and *bis*, 'twice', from *duis*. The word *duellum*, again, bears to *duo*, 'two', a relation in sense similar to that which we have in mind when we call peace 'union'. In like manner the Greeks derived their word for 'war' from a word meaning 'multitude'; the ancients also took a word for 'faction' from the idea of dissolution in it, just as the dissolution of the body suggested δύη, 'anguish'.

3. And usage does not reject this broader meaning of the word. If, to be sure, the term 'war' is at times limited to public war, that implies no objection to our view, since it is perfectly certain that the name of a genus is often applied in a particular way to a species, especially a species that is more prominent.

I do not include justice in my definition because this very question forms a part of our investigation, whether there can be a just war, and what kind of a war is just; and a subject which is under investigation ought to be distinguished from the object towards which the investigation is directed.

[. . .]

Chapter II: Whether it is ever lawful to wage war

I: *That war is not in conflict with the law of nature is proved by several considerations*

1. Having seen what the sources of law are, let us come to the first and most general question, which is this: whether any war is lawful, or whether it is ever permissible to war. This question, as also the others which will follow, must first be taken up from the point of view of the law of nature.

Marcus Tullius Cicero, both in the third book of his treatise *On Ends* and in other places, following Stoic writings learnedly argues that there are certain first principles of nature – 'first according to nature', as the Greeks phrased it – and certain other principles which are later manifest but which are to have the preference over those first principles. He calls first principles of nature those in accordance with which every animal from the moment of its birth has regard for itself and is impelled to preserve itself, to have zealous consideration for its own condition and for those things which tend to preserve it, and also shrinks from destruction and things which appear likely to cause destruction. Hence also it happens, he says, that there is no one who, if the choice were presented to him, would not prefer to have all the parts of his body in proper order and whole rather than dwarfed or deformed; and that it is one's first duty to keep oneself in the condition which nature gave to him, then to hold to those things which are in conformity with nature and reject those things that are contrary thereto.

2. But after these things have received due consideration [Cicero continues], there follows a notion of the conformity of things with reason, which is superior to the body. Now this conformity, in which moral goodness becomes the paramount object, ought to be accounted of higher import than the things to which alone instinct first directed itself, because the first principles of nature commend us to right reason, and right reason ought to be more dear to us than those things through whose instrumentality we have been brought to it.

Since this is true and without other demonstration would easily receive the assent of all who are endowed with sound judgement, it follows that in investigating the law of nature it is necessary first to see what is consistent with those fundamental principles of nature, and then to come to that which, though of later origin, is nevertheless more worthy – that which ought not only to be grasped, if it appear, but to be sought out by every effort.

3. According to the diversity of the matter, that which we call moral goodness at times consists of a point, so to speak, so that if you depart from it even the least possible distance you turn aside in the direction of wrong-doing; at times it has a wider range, so that an act may be praiseworthy if performed, yet if it be omitted altogether or performed in some other way no blame would attach, the distinction being generally without an intermediate stage, like the transition from being to not-being. Between things opposed in a different way, however, as white and black, a mean may be founded either by effecting a combination of the two or by finding an intermediate between them.

It is with this latter class of actions that both divine and human laws are wont to concern themselves, in order that those acts which were in themselves merely praiseworthy might become also obligatory. But we said above, in discussing the law of nature, that the question is this, whether an act can be performed without injustice; and injustice is understood to be that which is utterly repugnant to a rational and social nature.

4. In the first principles of nature there is nothing which is opposed to war; rather, all points are in its favour. The end and aim of war being the preservation of life and limb, and the keeping or acquiring of things useful to life, war is in

perfect accord with those first principles of nature. If in order to achieve these ends it is necessary to use force, no inconsistency with the first principles of nature is involved, since nature has given to each animal strength sufficient for self-defence and self-assistance. 'All kinds of animals', says Xenophon, 'understand some mode of fighting, and they have learned this from no other source than nature.' In the fragment of the *Piscation* we read:

> To all has it been given
> To recognize a foe, likewise to know
> Their safeguards each its own, and power and use
> Each of its weapon.

Horace had said:

> With tooth the wolf, with horn the bull attacks;
> And why, unless by inner feeling guided?

Lucretius presents the thought more fully:

> Each creature feels the strength which it can use.
> Felt by the calf his horns are, ere they stand
> Upon his forehead; and with them he butts
> Angrily, and, threatening, forward thrusts.

The same idea is thus expressed by Galen: 'We see that each animal uses for its protection that in which it is strongest. For the calf whose horns have not yet sprouted threatens with that part, and the colt kicks before its hoofs are hard, and the puppy tries to bite when its teeth are not yet strong.' Galen also remarks (*On the Use of Parts*, 1) that man is an animal born for peace and war. Weapons, to be sure, are not born with him, but he has hands suited for fashioning and handling weapons; and we see that babies of their own accord, and without being taught by any one, use their hands in place of weapons. So Aristotle, too (*On the Parts of Animals*, IV.10), says that in the case of man the hand has the place of spear, sword, and all other weapons, because he is able to take and hold everything with the hand.

5. Right reason, moreover, and the nature of society, which must be studied in the second place and are of even greater importance, do not prohibit all use of force, but only that use of force which is in conflict with society, that is which attempts to take away the rights of another. For society has in view this object, that through community of resource and effort each individual be safeguarded in the possession of what belongs to him.

It is easy to understand that this consideration would hold even if private ownership (as we now call it) had not been introduced; for life, limbs, and liberty would in that case be the possessions belonging to each, and no attack could be made upon these by another without injustice. Under such conditions the first one taking possession would have the right to use things not claimed and to consume them up to the limit of his needs, and any one depriving him of that right would commit an unjust act. But now that private ownership has by law or usage assumed a definite form, the matter is much easier to understand. I shall express the thought in the words of Cicero:

> Just as, in case each member of the body should have a feeling of its own, so that it might think that it could gain in vigour by drawing to itself the vigour of the nearest member, the whole body would of necessity be weakened and utterly perish, so, if every one of us should seize upon the possessions of others for himself and carry off from each whatever he could, for his own gain, human society and the community of life would of necessity be absolutely destroyed. For, since nature does not oppose, it has been granted that each prefer that whatever contributes to the advantage of life be acquired for himself rather than for another; but nature does not allow us to increase our means of susbsistence, our resources, and our riches, from the spoil of others.

6. It is not, then, contrary to the nature of society to look out for oneself and advance one's own interests, provided the rights of others are not infringed; and consequently the use of force which does not violate the rights of others is not unjust. This thought also Cicero has presented: 'Since there are two ways of settling a difference, the one by argument, the other by force, and since the former is characteristic of man, the latter of brutes, we should have recourse to the second only when it is not permitted to use the first.' 'What can be done', says the same writer in another passage, 'against force without force?'

In Ulpian we read: 'Cassius writes that it is permissible to repel force by force, and this right is bestowed by nature. From this moreover it appears, he says, that it is permissible to repel arms by means of arms.' Ovid had said: 'The laws permit arms 'gainst armed men to bear.'

II: *That war is not in conflict with the law of nature is proved from history*

1. Our statement that not all war is in conflict with the law of nature is more fully proved from sacred history. For Abraham with his servants and allies had taken up arms and had won the victory over the four kings who had sacked Sodom; and God approved the deed through his priest Melchizedek. Thus in fact Melchizedek addressed him (*Genesis*, xiv. 20): 'Praise be to God Most High, who has delivered thine enemies into thine hand.' But Abraham had taken up arms, as is evident from the narrative, without a special command of God; in accordance with the law of nature, therefore, did he act, a man not only most holy but also most wise – so recognized even by the testimony of foreigners, Berosus and Orpheus.

I shall not appeal to the history of the seven peoples whom God delivered to the Israelites to be destroyed; for in that case there was a special command to execute a judgement of God upon peoples guilty of the greatest crimes. These wars therefore in holy writ are properly called the wars of God, since they were undertaken by the command of God, not at the discretion of men. Having a more direct bearing on our subject is the war in which the Jews, under the leadership of Moses and Joshua, by arms repelled the Amalekites who were attacking them (*Exodus*, xvii). This act, which God had not commanded in advance, He approved afterward.

2. But further, God laid down for His own people general and perpetual laws in regard to the mode of carrying on war (*Deuteronomy*, xx. 10, 15), showing by this very act that a war can be just even without having been specifically commanded by Him. For in these passages He plainly distinguishes the case of the seven peoples from that of other peoples; and since in the same passages He presents no ordinance dealing with the just causes for undertaking war, by this very fact He shows that these are clearly enough known from nature. A just cause of war, for example, is the defence of territory, in the war of Jephthah against the Ammonites (*Judges*, xi); another is the maltreatment of envoys, in the war of David against the same people (2 *Samuel*, x).

In the same connexion we should note what the inspired writer to the Hebrews says, that Gideon, Barak, Samson, Jephthah, David, Samuel, and others 'through faith subdued kingdoms, waxed valiant in fight, turned to flight the armies of the aliens' (*Hebrews*, xi. 33, 34). In this passage, as the context makes plain, he includes in the term 'faith' the conviction that what is done is pleasing to God. So also a wise woman says that David 'fights the battles of God' (1 *Samuel*, xxv. 28), that is, battles that are righteous and just.

III: *That war is not in conflict with the law of nature is proved from general agreement*

1. Our thesis is proved also by the general agreement of all nations, and especially among the wise. Well known is the passage of Cicero in regard to force used in the defence of life, in which he bears witness to nature herself:

> There is this law which is not written, but born with us; which we have not learned, have not received, have not read, but which we have caught up, have sucked in, yes have wrung out from nature herself; a law regarding which we have not been instructed, but in accord with which we have been made; to which we have not been trained, but with which we are imbued – the law that if our life has been placed in jeopardy by any snare, or violence, or weapons either of brigands or of enemies, every possible means of securing safety is morally right.

The same writer in another passage adds:

> This law reason has enjoined upon the learned, necessity upon barbarians, custom upon nations, and nature herself upon wild beasts, that always, with whatever means of defence they possess, they ward off all violence from body, from head, from life itself.

The jurist Gaius says: 'Natural reason permits defence of oneself against danger'; the jurist Florentinus, 'In accordance with this law it comes about that whatever each may have done in defence of his person he is thought to have done lawfully.' 'For there is', says Josephus, 'that law of nature which applies in the case of all creatures, that they wish to live; and therein lies the reason why we consider those as enemies who clearly wish to rob us of life.'

2. So obvious is the fairness of this principle that even among brutes which, as we have said, have not the substance of legal rights but only a shadowy appearance of them, we may distinguish between the use of force which attempts an injury and that which wards it off. For Ulpian, having said that an animal devoid of sense, that is, of the use of reason, is incapable of doing what is legally wrong, nevertheless immediately adds that when rams or bulls have fought, and one has killed the other, on the authority of Quintus Mucius a distinction ought to be made. If the animal which started the fight should be killed, an action would not lie; but if the animal which had not started the fight should be killed, an action would lie. A passage of Pliny will serve to throw light on what has been said:

> The fierceness of lions does not manifest itself in attacks upon lions, the bites of serpents are not directed to serpents; but if violence is attempted there is no creature which does not manifest anger, which does not possess a spirit impatient of injury and will not show a ready liveliness in defending itself if you do it harm.

IV: *Proof is adduced that war is not in conflict with the law of nations*

1. It is sufficiently well established, therefore, that not all wars are at variance with the law of nature; and this may also be said to be true of the law of nations.

2. That wars, moreover, are not condemned by the volitional law of nations, histories, and the laws and customs of all peoples fully teach us. Rather, Hermogenianus said that wars were introduced by the law of nations; but I think that this statement ought to be understood as having a meaning slightly different from that ordinarily given to it, namely, that a definite formality in the conduct of war was introduced by the law of nations, and that particular effects follow wars waged in accordance with such formality under the law of nations. Hence arises the distinction, which we shall have to make use of later, between a war which, according to the law of nations, is formally declared and is called legal, that is a complete war; and a war not formally declared, which nevertheless does not on that account cease to be a legal war, that is according to law. For as regards other wars, provided the cause be just, the law of nations does not indeed lend them support, but it does not oppose them, as will be explained more fully later. 'It has been established by the law of nations,' says Livy, 'that arms are to be warded off by arms.' And Florentinus declares that the law of nations authorizes us to ward off violence and injury in order to protect our body.

7

HOBBES

Source: J. Plamentaz (ed.) (1969) *Leviathan*. London, Fontana, William Collins, pp. 141–5, 309–10, 141–7 and 156–66

Hobbes is a thoroughgoing materialist. He sees human beings as machines moved by the desire for self-preservation. In Hobbes' view the natural condition of the human race is one of war of each against all. In the absence of power to enforce rules human life is dangerous and highly unpredictable. Hobbes argues that the only rational answer to this condition is to create a mighty power that holds everyone in awe: the Leviathan. But, surprisingly, Hobbes does not hold that world government is the best answer to the state of anarchy among nations. He suggests that there are natural laws which should be observed by individuals in a state of nature which also hold for states in international society.

Chapter XIII: Of the natural condition of mankind as concerning their felicity, and misery

Nature hath made men so equal, in the faculties of the body, and mind; as that though there be found one man sometimes manifestly stronger in body, or of quicker mind than another; yet when all is reckoned together, the difference between man, and man, is not so considerable, as that one man can thereupon claim to himself any benefit, to which another may not pretend, as well as he. For as to the strength of body, the weakest has strength enough to kill the strongest, either by secret machination, or by confederacy with others, that are in the same danger with himself.

And as to the faculties of the mind, setting aside the arts grounded upon words, and especially that skill of proceeding upon general, and infallible rules, called science; which very few have, and but in few things; as being not a native faculty, born with us; nor attained, as prudence, while we look after somewhat else, I find yet a greater equality amongst men, than that of strength. For prudence, is but experience; which equal time, equally bestows on all men, in those things they equally apply themselves unto. That which may perhaps make such equality incredible, is but a vain conceit of one's own wisdom, which almost all men think they have in a greater degree, than the vulgar; that is, than all men but themselves, and a few others, whom by fame, or for concurring with themselves, they approve. For such is the nature of men, that howsoever they may acknowledge many others to be more witty, or more eloquent, or more learned; yet they will hardly believe there be many so wise as themselves; for they see their own wit at hand, and other men's at a distance. But this proveth rather that men are in that point equal, than unequal. For there is not ordinarily a greater sign of the equal distribution of any thing, than that every man is contented with his share.

From this equality of ability, ariseth equality of hope in the attaining of our ends. And therefore if any two men desire the same thing, which nevertheless they cannot both enjoy, they become enemies; and in the way to their end, which is principally their own conservation, and sometimes their delectation only, endeavour to destroy, or subdue one another. And from hence it comes to pass, that where an invader hath no more to fear, than another man's single power; if one plant, sow, build, or possess a convenient seat, others may probably be expected to come prepared with forces united, to dispossess, and deprive him, not only of the fruit of his labour, but also of his life, or liberty. And the invader again is in the like danger of another.

And from this diffidence of one another, there is no way for any man to secure himself, so reasonable, as anticipation; that is, by force, or wiles, to master the persons of all men he can, so long, till he see no other power great enough to endanger him: and this is no more than his own conservation requireth, and is generally allowed. Also because there be some, that taking pleasure in contemplating their own power in the acts of conquest, which they pursue farther than their security requires; if others, that otherwise would be glad to be at ease within modest bounds, should not by invasion increase their power, they would not be able, long time, by standing only on their defence, to subsist. And by consequence, such augmentation of dominion over men being necessary to a man's conservation, it ought to be allowed him.

Again, men have no pleasure, but on the contrary a great deal of grief, in keeping company, where there is no power able to over-awe them all. For every man looketh that his companion should value him, at the same rate he sets upon himself: and upon all signs of contempt, or undervaluing, naturally endeavours, as far as he dares, (which amongst them that have no common power to keep them in quiet, is far enough to make them destroy each other), to extort a greater value from his contemners, by damage; and from others, by the example.

So that in the nature of man, we find three principal causes of quarrel. First, competition; secondly, diffidence; thirdly, glory.

The first, maketh men invade for gain; the second, for safety; and the third, for reputation. The first use violence, to make themselves masters of other men's persons, wives, children, and cattle; the second, to defend them; the third, for trifles, as a word, a smile, a different opinion, and any other sign of undervalue, either direct in their persons, or by reflection in their kindred, their friends, their nation, their profession, or their name.

Hereby it is manifest, that during the time men live without a common power to keep them all in awe, they are in that condition which is called war; and such a war, as is of every man, against every man. For WAR, consisteth not in battle only, or the act of fighting; but in a tract of time, wherein the will to contend by battle is sufficiently known: and therefore the notion of *time*, is to be considered in the nature of war; as it is in the nature of weather. For as the nature of foul weather, lieth not in a shower or two of rain; but in an inclination thereto of many days together: so the nature of war, consisteth not in actual fighting; but in the known disposition thereto, during all the time there is no assurance to the contrary. All other time is PEACE.

Whatsoever therefore is consequent to a time of war, where every man is enemy to every man; the same is consequent to the time, wherein men live without other security, than what their own strength, and their own invention shall furnish them withal. In such condition, there is no place for industry; because the fruit thereof is uncertain: and consequently no culture of the earth; no navigation, nor use of the commodities that may be imported by sea; no commodious building; no instruments of moving, and removing, such things as require much force; no knowledge of the face of the earth; no account of time; no arts; no letters; no society; and which is worst of all, continual fear, and danger of violent death; and the life of man, solitary, poor, nasty, brutish, and short.

It may seem strange to some man, that has not well weighed these things; that nature should thus dissociate, and render men apt to invade, and destroy one another: and he may therefore, not trusting to this inference, made from the passions, desire perhaps to have the same confirmed by experience. Let him therefore consider with himself, when taking a journey, he arms himself, and seeks to go well accompanied; when going to sleep, he locks his doors; when even in his house he locks his chests; and this when he knows there be laws, and public officers, armed, to revenge all injuries shall be done him; what opinion he has of his fellow-subjects, when he rides armed; of his fellow citizens, when he locks his doors; and of his children, and servants, when he locks his chests. Does he not there as much accuse mankind by his actions, as I do by my words? But neither of us accuse man's nature in it. The desires, and other passions of man, are in themselves no sin. No more are the actions, that proceed from those passions, till they know a law that forbids them: which till laws be made they cannot know: nor can any law be made, till they have agreed upon the person that shall make it.

It may peradventure be thought, there was never such a time, nor condition of war as this; and I believe it was never generally so, over all the world: but there are many places, where they live so now. For the savage people in many places of America, except the government of small families, the concord whereof dependeth on natural lust, have no government at all; and live at this day in that brutish manner, as I said before. Howsoever, it may be perceived what manner of life there would be, where there were no common power to fear, by the manner of life, which men that have formerly lived under a peaceful government, use to degenerate into, in a civil war.

But though there had never been any time, wherein particular men were in a condition of war one against another; yet in all times, kings, and persons of sovereign authority, because of their independency, are in continual jealousies, and in the state and posture of gladiators; having their weapons pointing, and their eyes fixed on one another; that is, their forts, garrisons, and guns upon the frontiers of their kingdoms; and continual spies upon their neighbours; which is a posture of war. But because they uphold thereby, the industry of their subjects; there does not follow from it, that misery, which accompanies the liberty of particular men.

To this war of every man, against every man, this also is consequent; that nothing can be unjust. The notions of right and wrong, justice and injustice have there no place. Where there is no common power, there is no law: where no law, no injustice. Force, and fraud, are in war the two cardinal virtues. Justice, and injustice are none of the faculties neither of the body, nor mind. If they were, they might be in a man that were alone in the world, as well as his senses, and passions. They are qualities, that relate to men in society, not in solitude. It is consequent also to the same condition, that there be no propriety, no dominion, no *mine* and *thine* distinct; but only that to be every man's, that he can get; and for so long, as he can keep it. And thus much for the ill condition, which man by mere nature is actually placed in; though with a possibility to come out of it, consisting partly in the passions, partly in his reason.

The passions that incline men to peace, are fear of death; desire of such things as are necessary to commodious living; and a hope by their industry to obtain them. And reason suggesteth convenient articles of peace, upon which men may be drawn to agreement. These articles, are they, which otherwise are called the Laws of Nature: whereof I shall speak more particularly, in the two following chapters.

[. . .]

Concerning the offices of one sovereign to another, which are comprehended in that law, which is commonly called the *law of nations*, I need not say anything in this place; because the law of nations, and the law of nature, is the same thing. And every sovereign hath the same right, in procuring the safety of his people, that any particular man can have, in procuring the safety of his own body. And the same law, that dictateth to men that have no civil government, what they ought to do, and what to avoid in regard of one another, dictateth the same to commonwealths, that is, to the consciences of sovereign princes and sovereign assemblies; there being no court of natural justice, but in the conscience only; where not man, but God reigneth; whose laws, such of them as oblige all mankind, in respect of God, as he is the author of nature, are *natural*, and in respect of the same God, as he is King of kings, are *laws*. But of the kingdom of God, as King of kings, and as King also of a peculiar people, I shall speak in the rest of this discourse.

[. . .]

Chapter XIV: Of the first and second natural laws, and of contracts

The right of nature, which writers commonly call *jus naturale*, is the liberty each man hath, to use his own power, as he will himself, for the preservation of his own nature; that is to say, of his own life; and consequently, of doing any thing, which in his own judgment, and reason, he shall conceive to be the aptest means thereunto.

By LIBERTY, is understood, according to the proper signification of the word, the absence of external impediments: which impediments, may oft take away part of a man's power to do what he would; but cannot hinder him from using the power left him, according as his judgment, and reason shall dictate to him.

A LAW OF NATURE, *lex naturalis*, is a precept or general rule, found out by reason, by which a man is forbidden to do that, which is destructive of his life, or taketh away the means of preserving the same; and to omit that, by which he thinketh it may be best preserved. For though they that speak of this subject, use to confound *jus*, and *lex*, *right* and *law*: yet they ought to be distinguished; because RIGHT, consisteth in liberty to do, or to forbear; whereas LAW, determineth, and bindeth to one of them: so that law, and right, differ as much, as obligation, and liberty; which in one and the same matter are inconsistent.

And because the condition of man, as hath been declared in the precedent chapter, is a condition of war of every one against every one: in which case every one is governed by his own reason; and there is nothing he can make use of, that may not be a help unto him, in preserving his life against his enemies; it followeth, that in such a condition, every man has a right to every thing; even to one another's body. And therefore, as long as this natural right of every man to every thing endureth, there can be no security to any man, how strong or wise soever he be, of living out the time, which nature ordinarily alloweth men to live, and consequently it is a precept, or general rule of reason, *that every man, ought to endeavour peace, as far as he has hope of obtaining it; and when he cannot obtain it, that he may seek, and use, all helps, and advantages of war*. The first branch of which rule, containeth the first, and fundamental law of nature; which is, *to seek peace, and follow it*. The second, the sum of the right of nature; which is, *by all means we can, to defend ourselves*.

From this fundamental law of nature, by which men are commanded to endeavour peace, is derived this second law; *that a man be willing, when others are so too, as far-forth, as for peace, and defence of himself he shall think it necessary, to lay down this right to all things; and be contented with so much liberty against other men, as he would allow other men against himself.* For as long as every man holdeth this right, of doing any thing he liketh; so long are all men in the condition of war. But if other men will not lay down their right, as well as he; then there is no reason for any one, to divest himself of his: for that were to expose himself to prey, which no man is bound to, rather than to dispose himself to peace. This is that law of the Gospel; *whatsoever you require that others should do to you, that do ye to them.* And that law of all men, *quod tibi fieri non vis, alteri ne feceris.*

[. . .]

Chapter XV: Of other laws of nature

From that law of nature, by which we are obliged to transfer to another, such rights, as being retained, hinder the peace of mankind, there followeth a third; which is this, *that men perform their covenants made*: without which, covenants are in vain, and but empty words; and the right of all men to all things remaining, we are still in the condition of war.

And in this law of nature, consisteth the fountain and original of JUSTICE. For where no covenant hath preceded, there hath no right been transferred, and every man has right to every thing; and consequently, no action can be unjust. But when a covenant is made, then to break it is *unjust*: and the definition of INJUSTICE, is no other than *the not performance of covenant*. And whatsoever is not unjust, is *just*.

[. . .]

As justice dependeth on antecedent covenant; so does GRATITUDE depend on antecedent grace; that is to say, antecedent free gift: and is the fourth law of nature; which may be conceived in this form, *that a man which receiveth benefit from another of mere grace, endeavour that he which giveth it, have no reasonable cause to repent him of his good will.* For no man giveth, but with intention of good to himself; because gift is voluntary; and of all voluntary acts, the object is to every man his own good; of which if men see they shall be frustrated, there will be no beginning of benevolence, or trust; nor consequently of mutual help; nor of reconciliation of one man to another; and therefore they are to remain still in the condition of *war*; which is contrary to the first and fundamental law of nature, which commandeth men to *seek peace*. The breach of this law, is called *ingratitude*; and hath the same relation to grace, that injustice hath to obligation by covenant.

A fifth law of nature, is COMPLAISANCE; that is to say, *that every man strive to accommodate himself to the rest.* For the understanding whereof, we may consider, that there is in men's aptness to society, a diversity of nature, rising from their diversity of affections; not unlike to that we see in stones brought together for building of an edifice. For as that stone which by the asperity, and irregularity of figure, takes more room from others, than itself fills; and for the hardness, cannot be easily made plain, and thereby hindereth the building, is by the builders cast away as unprofitable, and troublesome: so also, a man that by asperity of nature, will strive to retain those things which to himself are superfluous, and to others necessary; and for the stubbornness of his passions, cannot be corrected, is to be left, or cast out of society, as cumbersome thereunto. For seeing every man, not only by right, but also by necessity of nature, is supposed to endeavour all he can, to obtain that which is necessary for his conservation; he that shall oppose himself against it, for things superfluous, is guilty of the war that thereupon is to follow; and therefore doth that, which is contrary to the fundamental law of nature, which commandeth *to seek peace.* The observers of this law, may be called SOCIABLE, the Latins call them *commodi*; the contrary, *stubborn, insociable, forward, intractable.*

A sixth law of nature, is this, *that upon caution of the future time, a man ought to pardon the offences past of them that repenting, desire it.* For PARDON, is nothing but granting of peace; which though granted to them that persevere in their hostility, be not peace, but fear; yet not granted to them that give caution of the future time, is sign of an aversion to peace; and therefore contrary to the law of nature.

A seventh is, *that in revenges*, that is, retribution of evil for evil, *men look not at the greatness of the evil past, but the greatness of the good to follow.* Whereby we are forbidden to inflict punishment with any other design, than for correction of the offender, or direction of others. For this law is consequent to the next before it, that commandeth pardon, upon security of the future time. Besides, revenge without respect to the example, and profit to come, is a triumph, or glorying in the hurt of another, tending to no end; for the end is always somewhat to come; and glorying to no end, is vain-glory, and contrary to reason, and to hurt without reason, tendeth to the introduction of war; which is against the law of nature; and is commonly styled by the name of *cruelty*.

And because all signs of hatred, or contempt, provoke to fight; insomuch as most men choose rather to hazard their life, than not to be revenged; we may in the eighth place, for a law of nature, set down this precept, *that no man by deed, word, countenance, or gesture, declare hatred, or contempt of another.* The breach of which law, is commonly called *contumely*.

The question who is the better man, has no place in the condition of mere nature; where, as has been shewn before, all men are equal. The inequality that now is, has been introduced by the laws civil. I know that Aristotle in the first book of his *Politics*, for a foundation of his doctrine, maketh men by nature, some more worthy to command, meaning the wiser sort, such as he thought himself to be for his philosophy; others to serve, meaning those that had strong bodies, but were not philosophers as he; as if master and servant were not introduced by consent of men, but by difference of wit: which is not only against reason; but also against experience. For there are very few so foolish, that had not rather govern themselves, than be governed by others: nor when the wise in their own conceit, contend by force, with them who distrust their own wisdom, do they always, or often, or almost at any time, get the victory. If nature therefore have made men equal, that equality is to be acknowledged: or if nature have made men unequal; yet because men that think themselves equal, will not enter into conditions of peace, but upon equal terms, such equality must be admitted. And therefore for the ninth law of nature, I put this, *that every man acknowledge another for his equal by nature.* The breach of this precept is *pride.*

On this law, dependeth another, *that at the entrance into conditions of peace, no man require to reserve to himself any right, which he is not content should be reserved to every one of the rest.* As it is necessary for all men that seek peace, to lay down certain rights of nature; that is to say, not to have liberty to do all they list: so is it necessary for man's life, to retain some; as right to govern their own bodies; enjoy air, water, motion, ways to go from place to place; and all things else, without which a man cannot live, or not live well. If in this case, at the making of peace, men require for themselves, that which they would not have to be granted to others, they do contrary to the precedent law, that commandeth the acknowledgment of natural equality, and therefore also against the law of nature. The observers of this law, are those we call *modest*, and the breakers *arrogant* men. The Greeks call the violation of this law πλεονεξια; that is, a desire of more than their share.

Also if *a man be trusted to judge between man and man*, it is a precept of the law of nature, *that he deal equally between them.* For without that, the controversies of men cannot be determined but by war. He therefore that is partial in judgment, doth what in him lies, to deter men from the use of judges, and arbitrators; and consequently, against the fundamental law of nature, is the cause of war.

The observance of this law, from the equal distribution to each man, of that which in reason belongeth to him, is called EQUITY, and, as I have said before, distributive justice: the violation, *acception of persons*, προσωποληψία.

And from this followeth another law, *that such things as cannot be divided, be enjoyed in common, if it can be; and if the quantity of the thing permit, without stint; otherwise proportionably to the number of them that have right.* For otherwise the distribution is unequal, and contrary to equity.

But some things there be, that can neither be divided, nor enjoyed in common. Then, the law of nature, which prescribeth equity, requireth, *that the entire right; or else, making the use alternate, the first possession, be determined by lot.* For equal distribution, is of the law of nature; and other means of equal distribution cannot be imagined.

Of *lots* there be two sorts, *arbitrary*, and *natural*. Arbitrary, is that which is agreed on by the competitors: natural, is either *primogeniture*, which the Greek calls κληρονομία, which signifies, *given by lot*; or *first seizure*.

And therefore those things which cannot be enjoyed in common, nor divided, ought to be adjudged to the first possessor; and in some cases to the first born, as acquired by lot.

It is also a law of nature, *that all men that mediate peace, be allowed safe conduct.* For the law that commandeth peace, as the *end*, commandeth intercession, as the *means*; and to intercession the means is safe conduct.

And because, though men be never so willing to observe these laws, there may nevertheless arise questions concerning a man's action; first, whether it were done, or not done; secondly, if done, whether against the law, or not against the law, the former whereof, is called a question *of fact*; the latter a question *of right*, therefore unless the parties to the question, covenant mutually to stand to the sentence of another, they are as far from peace as ever. This other to whose sentence they submit is called an ARBITRATOR. And therefore it is of the law of nature, *that they that are at controversy, submit their right to the judgment of an arbitrator.*

And seeing every man is presumed to do all things in order to his own benefit, no man is a fit arbitrator in his own cause; and if he were never so fit; yet equity allowing to each party equal benefit, if one be admitted to be judge, the other is to be admitted also; and so the controversy, that is, the cause of war, remains, against the law of nature.

For the same reason no man in any cause ought to be received for arbitrator, to whom greater profit, or honour, or pleasure apparently ariseth out of the victory of one party, than of the other: for he hath taken, though an unavoidable bribe, yet a bribe; and no man can be obliged to trust him. And thus also the controversy, and the condition of war remaineth, contrary to the law of nature.

And in a controversy of *fact*, the judge being to give no more credit to one, than to the other, if there be no other arguments, must give credit to a third; or to a third and fourth; or more: for else the question is undecided, and left to force, contrary to the law of nature.

These are the laws of nature, dictating peace, for a means of the conservation of men in multitudes; and which only concern the doctrine of civil society. There be other things tending to the destruction of particular men; as drunkenness, and all other parts of intemperance; which may therefore also be reckoned amongst those things which the law of nature hath forbidden; but are not necessary to be mentioned, nor are pertinent enough to this place.

And though this may seem too subtle a deduction of the laws of nature, to be taken notice of by all men; whereof the most part are too busy in getting food, and the rest too negligent to understand; yet to leave all men inexcusable, they have been contracted into one easy sum, intelligible even to the meanest capacity; and that is, *Do not that to another, which thou wouldest not have done to thyself*; which sheweth him, that he has no more to do in learning the laws of nature, but, when weighing the actions of other men with his own, they seem too heavy, to put them into the other part of the balance, and his own into their place, that his own passions, and self-love, may add nothing to the weight; and then there is none of these laws of nature that will not appear unto him very reasonable.

8

ROUSSEAU

Source: 'Extract of the Abbé de Saint-Pierre's Project for Perpetual Peace', in C.E. Vaughan (trans. and ed.) (1917) *A Lasting Peace Through a Federation of Europe*. London, Constable, pp. 141–56.

Rousseau's essays on international peace reflect the conclusions of his general political philosophy. Rousseau is a proponent of the social contract. The social contract is a notional agreement among individuals within a society which brings that society into existence as a functioning unit. Sovereignty with Rousseau lies always with the contracting parties to this unit so that political authority is always held in trust. Rousseau thinks that at the domestic level the problems of ceding one's natural freedom have to be resolved for civic life to exist. But at the level of international society states might always withhold their consent without this leading to a complete breakdown in the system. For Rousseau the tragedy of international society is that it is in everyone's social interest to have a commonly agreed sovereign power, but it is in the interests of each individual state to flout that authority when it is to its advantage.

If I have dwelt upon the equal distribution of forces which springs from the present constitution of Europe, it was in order to draw from it a conclusion of the highest importance to the project for establishing a general league among her peoples. For, if we are to form a solid and lasting Confederation, we must have put all the members of it in a state of such mutual dependence that no one of them is singly in a position to overbear all the others, and that separate leagues, capable of thwarting the general League, shall meet with obstacles formidable enough to hinder their formation. Failing this, the Confederation will be nothing but an empty name; and under an appearance of subjection, every member of it will in reality be independent. But, if those obstacles are such as I have described at the present moment – a moment when all the Powers are entirely free to form separate leagues and offensive alliances – judge what they would become if they were a general League, fully armed and ready at any moment to forestall those who should conceive the design of destroying or resisting it. That in itself is enough to show that such a Federation, so far from ending in mere vain discussions to be set at defiance with impunity, would on the contrary give birth to an effective Power, capable of forcing any ambitious ruler to observe the terms of the general treaty which he has joined with others to set up.

From the above survey three certain conclusions may be drawn: the first that, Turkey excepted, there already exists among the nations of Europe a bond, imperfect indeed but still closer than the loose and general ties which exist between man and man in the state of nature; the second, that the imperfections of this association make the state of those who belong to it worse than it would be if they formed no community at all; the third, that these rudimentary ties, which make such an association injurious, make it at the same time readily capable of improvement, that all its members might easily find their happiness in what actually makes their misery, that from the state of war which now reigns among them they might perfectly well draw an abiding peace.

Let us now consider the means by which this great work, begun by chance, may be completed by wisdom. Let us ask how the free and voluntary association which now unites the States of Europe may be converted, by taking to itself the strength and firmness of a genuine Body politic, into an authentic Confederation. There is no doubt that such a creation, by giving to the existing bond the completeness which it now lacks, will increase all its advantages and compel all the parts to unite for the benefit of the whole body. But in order that this can be brought about this Confederation must be sufficiently general that it includes all important powers; it must have a judicial body equipped to establish laws and ordinances binding upon all its members; sufficient power to oblige any state either to perform or abstain from actions commonly agreed upon. Finally it must be solid and durable enough to prevent members from withdrawing the moment they perceive their own interests opposed to the general interest. These factors will ensure that the institution is wise, useful and indestructible. It is now a question of developing these ideas to see what consequences follow, what measures are called for in order to establish it and what reasonable expectations one may have that it can be put into practice.

From time to time there takes place among us kinds of general Diets under the name of Congresses to which men come from all the states of Europe only to return to them; where men assemble in order to say nothing of importance; where public issues are treated as private matters; where there is general deliberation over whether the table is to be round or square, the room is to have this or that number of doors, a certain negotiator his face or his back towards the window, or whether another is to advance a couple of inches this way or that during his reception. These and a thousand similar topics of like importance have been uselessly argued about over the last three hundred years and are worthy, to be sure, of detaining politicians of our own century.

It could come about that at one of these assemblies the members may be endowed with some common sense; it is not entirely impossible that they sincerely want the public good; and that, for reasons which will be worked-out hereafter, one can further conceive, that having overcome many difficulties, they will be instructed by their respective sovereigns to sign the general Confederation that I take in its essentials to be contained in the following five Articles.

By the first, the sovereigns will establish between themselves a perpetual and irrevocable alliance, and designate negotiators to convene in a specific place, a Diet or a permanent Congress in which all the outstanding issues arising between the contracting parties are to be regulated and brought to an end by means of arbitration or decision.

By the second shall be specified the number of the Sovereigns whose plenipotentiaries shall have a vote in the Diet; those who shall be invited to accede to the Treaty; the order, date and method by which the presidency shall pass, at equal intervals, from one to another; finally the quota of their respective contributions and the method of raising them for the defrayal of the common expenses.

By the third, the Confederation shall guarantee to each of its members the possession and government of all the dominions which he holds at the moment of the Treaty, as well as the manner of succession to them, elective or hereditary, as established by the fundamental laws of each Province. Further, with a view to suppressing at a single stroke and at the source those incessant disputes which arise between them, it shall be agreed to take as the basis of the respective rights of the contracting Parties the possession of the moment, as settled in each case by the last treaty concluded, with a general renunciation on all sides of every anterior claim: exception being made for all disputed successions and other claims to fall due in the future, all which shall be determined by arbitration of the Diet, to the absolute exclusion of all attempts to settle the matter by force or to take arms against each other under any pretext whatsoever.

By the fourth shall be specified the conditions under which any Confederate who may break this Treaty shall be put to the ban of Europe and proscribed as a public enemy: namely, if he shall have refused to execute the decisions of the Grand Alliance, if he shall have made preparations for war, if he shall have made a treaty hostile to the ends of the Confederation; if he shall have taken up arms to resist it or to attack any one of the Confederates.

By the same article, it shall be argued that all the Confederates shall arm and take the offensive, conjointly and at the common expense, against any State put to the ban of Europe, and that they shall not desist until the moment when he shall have laid down his arms, carried out the decisions and orders of the Diet, made amends for his offence, paid all the costs and atoned even for such warlike preparations as he may have made in defiance of the Treaty.

Finally, by the fifth Article, the plenipotentiaries of the Confederation of

Europe shall receive standing powers to frame – provisionally by a bare majority, definitively (after an interval of five years) by a majority of three-quarters – those measures which, on the instruction of their Courts, they shall consider expedient with a view to the greatest possible advantage of the Commonwealth of Europe and of its members, all and single. In none of the above five Articles, however, shall any change ever be made except with the unanimous consent of the Confederates.

These five Articles, summarized and reduced to the most general form, are, I am aware, exposed to countless petty objections, several of which would call for lengthy explanations. But petty objections are easily removed in case of need; and, in an enterprise of this importance, they are beside the point. When the policy of the Congress comes to be considered, a thousand obstacles will present themselves and ten thousand ways of removing them. It is *our* business to ask whether in the nature of the case, the enterprise is possible or no. We should lose ourselves in volumes of trifles, if we had to foresee all and find an answer to all. Confining ourselves, as we do, to incontestable principles, we have no call to satisfy every reader, not to solve every objection, nor to say how every detail will be settled. It is enough to show that a settlement is possible.

In judging of this scheme, then, what are the questions that have to be considered? Two only; for I will not insult the reader by proving to him the general proposition that the state of peace is a better thing than the state of war.

The first question is whether the Confederation suggested would be certain to answer its purpose and give a solid and abiding peace to Europe. The second, whether it is in the interest of the various sovereigns to establish such a Confederation and to pay the price I have mentioned to obtain a lasting peace.

When we have thus proved our scheme to be for the advantage both of Europe as a whole and of all the States composing her, what obstacle is left, we ask, that can possibly prevent the execution of a design which, after all, depends solely upon the will of those concerned?

In discussing the first Article, for instance, let us apply what has been said above of the general order now established in Europe and of the common resolve which confines each Power practically within its traditional limits and does not allow it wholly to crush any of the others. In order to make my argument clear, I give here a list of the nineteen Powers here assumed to constitute the Commonwealth of Europe, to each of which I give an equal voice, making altogether nineteen votes, in the deliberations of the Diet: the Emperor of the Romans, the Emperor of Russia, the King of France, the King of Spain, the King of England, the States General, the King of Denmark, Sweden, Poland, the King of Portugal, the Sovereign of Rome, the King of Prussia, the Elector of Bavaria and his associates, the Elector Palatine and his associates, the Swiss and their associates, the ecclesiastical Electors and their associates, the Republic of Venice and her associates, the King of Naples, the King of Sardinia.

Several minor sovereigns – for instance, the Republic of Genoa, the dukes of Parma and Modena, and others – are omitted from the list. They will be associated with one or other of the less powerful States, with whom they will share a vote, after the fashion of the joint vote (*votum curiatum*) of the Counts of the Empire. It is useless to make the list more precise because, at any moment before the scheme is put in force, things may happen which, without affecting the principle of the measure, may call for alterations of detail.

A glance at the list will be enough to prove conclusively that it is impossible either for any single Power to resist the united action of all the others, or for any partial league to be formed capable of defying the Confederation as a whole.

How, indeed, could such a league be formed? Between the more powerful of the Confederates? We have already proved that such a league could never last; and with the list before us, it is easy enough to see that it could never be reconciled with the traditional policy of any of the great Powers, or with the interests inherent in their respective positions. Between a large State and a number of small ones? Then the other large States, with the Federation behind them, will crush such a league in no time; and it is clear that the Grand Alliance, being perpetually armed and concerted for action, will find no difficulty in forestalling and crushing in advance any partial and seditious alliance, likely to trouble the peace and the public order of Europe. Look at the cohesion of the Germanic Body: and that, in spite of its defective discipline and the glaring inequality of its members. Is there a single Prince, not even excepting the most powerful, who would dare to expose himself to the ban of the Empire by openly defying its laws, unless indeed he had good reason to suppose that the Empire would never have the courage to take action against the culprit in good earnest?

That is why I regard it as proved that the Diet of Europe, once established, will have no rebellion to fear and that no abuses which may creep in are ever likely to defeat the aims with which it was founded. It remains to ask whether those aims are really secured by the proposed institution.

With a view to answering this question, let us consider the motives by which Princes are commonly led to take up arms. These motives are: either to make conquests, or to protect themselves from aggression, or to weaken a too powerful neighbour, or to maintain their rights against attack, or to settle a difference which has defied friendly negotiation, or lastly, to fulfil some treaty obligation. There is no cause or pretext of war which cannot be brought under one or other of these six heads; and it is manifest that not one of the six is left standing under the new order which I propose.

As for the first, the thought of conquest will have to be given up from the absolute impossibility of making them. The aggressor is sure to find his way barred by forces stronger than his own; he is powerless to gain anything, and he risks the loss of all he has. At present, an ambitious Prince, who wishes to extend his dominions in Europe, relies upon two weapons; he begins by securing strong allies, and then seeks to catch his enemy unawares. But, under the new conditions, no special alliance could stand for a moment before the General Alliance which is stronger and subsists permanently; and as there is no longer any pretext for arming, no Prince can do so without being at once detected, stopped and punished by the Federation always under arms.

Again, the very thing which destroys all hope of conquest relieves him at the same time from all fear of being attacked. And, under the guarantee of all Europe, not only are his territories as strongly assured to him as the possessions of any citizen in a well-ordered community, but they are even more so than they were when he was their sole and only defender; in exactly the same proportion as the whole of Europe is stronger than any one of her Princes taken singly.

Thirdly, having no more reason to fear his neighbour, neither has he any more reason for desiring to weaken him; and having no hope of success in such an enterprise, he is under no temptation to attempt it.

As for the maintenance of his rights, I begin by remarking that a whole host of pettifogging claims and obscure pretensions will be swept away at one stroke by the third Article of Federation, which settles for ever all the conflicting rights of the allied Princes, on the basis of what they actually hold. By the same Article, we have a clear principle for settling all claims and pretensions which may be raised in the future: each will be decided in the Diet, as it arises. It may be added that, if my rights are attacked, I am bound to defend them by the weapon used against me. They cannot be attacked by force of arms without bringing the ban of the Diet upon the assailant. It is not by arms then that I shall have to defend them. The same may be said of injuries, wrongs and claims for damage – in short, of all the unforeseen differences which may arise between two Sovereigns. The same Power which is bound to maintain their rights is bound also to redress their grievances.

As for the last head, the question settles itself. It is clear at a glance that, having no longer any assailant to fear, I have no longer any use for treaties of defence; and that, as no treaty can be so strong or so trustworthy as that guaranteed by the Grand Confederation, any other treaty would be useless, illegitimate and consequently null and void.

For all these reasons it is impossible that the Confederation, once established, can leave any seed of war between its members; impossible that our object, an abiding peace, should not be absolutely attained by the proposed system, if it were once set on foot.

It now remains to settle the other question: that relating to the interests of the several parties concerned. For everyone knows that the general interest is powerless to silence that of the individual. To prove that peace, as a general principle, is a better thing than war is to say nothing to the man who has private reasons for preferring war to peace; to show him the means for securing a lasting peace is only to encourage him to work against them.

In truth, we shall be told: 'You are taking from Sovereigns the right of doing themselves justice; that is to say, the precious right of being unjust when they please. You are taking from them the power of making themselves great at the expense of their neighbours. You are forcing them to renounce those antiquated claims whose value depends on their obscurity and which grow with every fresh growth in power; that parade of might and terror with which they love to awe the world; that pride of conquest which is the chief source of their glory. In one word, you are forcing them to be equitable and peaceful. What amends do you propose to make them for all these cruel privations?'

I do not venture to answer, with the Abbé de Saint-Pierre, that the true glory of Princes lies in serving the good of the community and the happiness of their subjects, that their highest interest is to win a good name, and that such a name is awarded by the wise in exact proportion to the good which the ruler had done in the world; that the scheme of founding a lasting peace is the most lofty ever conceived and the most certain, if executed, to cover its author with undying glory; that such a scheme would not only do a greater service than any other to the people but also confer higher honour upon the Sovereign; that this is the only ideal not stained with blood, rapine, curses and tears; in a word, that the surest way for a sovereign to raise himself above the common herd of kings is to labour for the good of the community. Let such language, which has covered the author and his projects with ridicule in all the council-chambers of Europe, be left to irresponsible declaimers. But let us never join in the cry against the arguments it embodies; and, whatever may be the truth as to the virtues of princes, let us confine ourselves to their interests.

All the Powers of Europe have rights, or claims, as against each other. These rights are, from the nature of the case, incapable of ever being finally adjusted, because there is no common and unvarying standard for judging of their merits and because they are often based upon facts which are either disputed or of doubtful interpretation. Nor are the quarrels which spring from them any more capable of being settled beyond appeal, whether in default of any recognized umpire, or because, when the chance offers, every Prince goes back shamelessly upon the cessions which have been forcibly torn from him by a stronger Power through treaties, or after an unsuccessful war. It is therefore a mistake to think only of the claims we have on others, and to forget those they have on us, when in reality there is no more justice on one side than on the other and both are equally capable of acquiring the means for enforcing their demands. Directly fortune is taken for arbiter, actual possession acquires a value which no wise man will stake against a possible gain in the future, even where chances are equal on both sides; and the rich man who, in the hope of doubling his fortune, ventures to risk it all upon one throw is blamed by the whole world. We have shown, however, that in schemes of self-aggrandizement the chances are never equal and that, even in the present order of things, the aggressor is always bound to find his enemy stronger than himself. The inevitable conclusion is that, the more powerful having no motive for staking his possessions and the weaker no hope of gaining on the throw, both will find their advantage in renouncing what they would like to win, in order to secure what they possess.

Think of the waste of men, of money, of strength in every form; think of the exhaustion in which any State is plunged by the most successful war; compare these ravages with the profit which results; and we shall find that we commonly lose where we suppose ourselves to gain; that the conqueror, always enfeebled by the war, can only console himself with the thought that the conquered is still more enfeebled than himself. And even this advantage is more in appearance than reality; for the strength which has been gained upon our opponent has been lost against the neutrals, who without changing themselves, are nevertheless stronger relatively to us by all the strength that we have lost.

If all Kings have not yet thrown off the folly of conquests, it would seem that the wiser of them at any rate are beginning to realize that they sometimes cost more than they are worth. Without going into a thousand distinctions which would only distract us from our purpose, we may say broadly that a Prince who, in extending his frontiers, loses as many of his old subjects as he gains new ones in the process only weakens himself by his aggrandizement; because, with a larger territory to defend, he has no more soldiers to defend it. Everyone knows, however, that, as war is waged nowadays, the smallest part of the resultant loss of life is due to losses in the field. Certainly, that is the loss which everyone sees and feels. But all the time there is taking place through the whole kingdom a loss far more serious and more irreparable than that of those who die: a loss due to those who are not born, to the increase of taxes, to the interruption of trade, to the desertion of the fields, to the neglect of their cultivation. This evil, which no one sees at first, makes itself felt cruelly in the end. And then the King is astonished to find himself so weak, as the result of making himself so strong.

There is another thing which makes conquests even less profitable than they used to be. It is that Kings have at last learned the secret of doubling or trebling their power not only without enlarging their territory but even, it may be, by contracting it, after the wise example of Hadrian. The secret is that the strength of Kings lies only in that of their subjects; and it follows from what I have just said that, given two States supporting an equal number of inhabitants, that which covers the smaller extent of territory is in reality the more powerful. It is then by good laws, by a wise discipline, by large views on economic policy that a sagacious Sovereign is sure of increasing his power without incurring any hazard. It is in carrying out works more useful than his neighbours' that he makes conquests – the early true conquests – at their expense; and every subject born to him in excess of theirs is another enemy killed.

It may be objected that I prove too much and that, if the matter were as I put it, everyone being manifestly interested in avoiding war and the public interest combining with that of individuals for the preservation of peace, that peace ought to come of itself and of itself last for ever without any need of Federation. Given the present state of things, however, that would be to reason very ill. It is quite true that it would be much better for all men to remain always at peace. But so long as there is no security for this, everyone, having no guarantee that he can avoid war, is anxious to begin it at the moment which suits his own interest and so forestall a neighbour, who would not fail to forestall the attack in his turn at any moment favourable to himself, so that many wars, even offensive wars, are rather in the nature of unjust precautions for the protection of the assailant's own possessions than a device for seizing those of others. However salutary it may be in theory to obey the dictates of public spirit, it is certain that, politically and even morally, those dictates are liable to prove fatal to the man who persists in observing them with all the world when no one thinks of observing them towards him.

I have nothing to say on the question of military parade because, when supported by no solid foundation either of hope or fear, such parade is mere child's play, and Kings have no business to keep dolls. I am equally silent as to the glory of conquest because, if there really were men who would break their hearts at the thought of having no one to massacre, our duty would be not to reason with such monsters but to deprive them of all means for putting their murderous frenzy into act. All solid grounds of war being swept away by the third Article, no King can have any motive for kindling its horrors against a rival which would not furnish that rival with equally strong grounds for kindling them against him. And it is a great gain to be delivered from a danger in which each finds himself alone against the world.

As for the dependence of all upon the Tribunal of Europe, it is abundantly clear by the same Article that the rights of sovereignty, so far from being weakened, will, on the contrary, be strengthened and confirmed. For that Article guarantees to each Sovereign not only that his dominions shall be protected against foreign invasion, but also that his authority shall be upheld against the rebellion of his subjects. The Prince accordingly will be none the less absolute, and his crown will be more fully assured. By submitting to the decision of the Diet in all disputes with his equals, and by surrendering the perilous right of seizing other men's possessions, he is, in fact, doing nothing more than securing his real rights and renouncing those which are purely fictitious. Besides, there is all the difference in the world between dependence upon a rival and dependence upon a Body of which he is himself a member and of which each member in turn becomes the head. In the latter case, the pledges that are given him are really the security for his freedom: it would be forfeited, if lodged with a superior; it is confirmed, when lodged with equals. In support of this, I appeal to the example of the Germanic Body. It is quite true that the constitution of this is such as to trench in many ways upon the sovereignty of its members. It is quite true that their position is consequently less favourable than it would be in the Confederation of Europe. But, in spite of those drawbacks, there is not one of them, however jealous he may be of his dignity, who would choose, even if he had the power, to win absolute independence at the cost of severance from the Empire.

Observe further that the head of the Germanic Body, being permanent, is bound to usurp ceaselessly upon the rights of the other members. In the Diet of Europe, where the presidency passes from one to another without any regard to disparities of power, no such danger is to be feared.

There is yet another consideration which is likely to weigh even more with men so greedy of money as Princes always are. Not only will an unbroken peace give them, as well as their subjects, every means of amassing abundant riches; they will also be spared vast expenses by the reduction of their military budget, of those innumerable fortresses, of those enormous armies, which swallow up their revenue and become daily more and more of a burden to their subjects and themselves. I know that it will not suit all Sovereigns to suppress their army bodily and leave themselves with no force in hand to crush an unexpected revolt or repel a sudden invasion. I know also that they will have their contingent to furnish to the Confederation with a view both to guarding the frontiers of

Europe and to maintaining the federal arm whose duty it will be, in case of need, to carry out the decrees of the Diet. But, when all these charges are met and, at the same time, the extraordinary expenses of war suppressed for ever, there will still be a saving of more than half the ordinary military budget; and that saving can be divided between the relief of the subject and the coffers of the Prince. The result will be that the people will have to pay much less; that the Prince, being much better off, will be in a position to encourage commerce, agriculture and the arts and to create useful foundations which will still further increase his subjects' riches, and his own; and, over and above all this, that the State will enjoy a security far greater than it now draws from all its armies and from all that warlike parade which drains its strength in the very bosom of peace.

It will be said perhaps that the frontier countries of Europe will then be relatively worse off, they will still have to face the chance of war either with the Turk, or the African Corsairs, or the Tartars.

The answer to this is (1) that those countries are under the same necessity at present, from which it follows that they will not be put to any positive disadvantage, but will only have an advantage the less; and this, in fact, is an inevitable consequence of their geographical position; (2) that, being freed from all anxiety on the side of Europe, they will be much more capable of resisting attacks from other quarters; (3) that the suppression of all fortresses in the inner parts of Europe and of all expenses needed for their maintenance would enable the Federation to build a large number on the eastern frontiers without bringing any fresh charge upon its members; (4) that these fortresses, built, maintained and garrisoned at the common charge, will mean so many fresh guarantees, and so much expense saved to the frontier Powers for whose benefit they are built; (5) that the troops of the Federation, posted on the frontiers of Europe, will stand permanently ready to drive back the invader; (6) and finally, that a Body so formidable as the Commonwealth of Europe will make the foreigner think twice before attacking any of its members: just as the Germanic Body, though infinitely less powerful, is still strong enough to command the respect of its neighbours and offer valuable protection to all the Princes who compose it.

It may be further objected that, when the nations of Europe have ceased to war among themselves, the art of war will be gradually forgotten, that her armies will lose their courage and discipline, that there will be no more soldiers or generals, and that Europe will lie at the mercy of the first comer.

My answer is that one of two things will happen. Either the neighbours of Europe will attack her and wage war against her; or they will be afraid of the Confederation and leave her in peace.

In the former case, there will be plenty of opportunities for training military genius and talent, for practising and hardening our troops. The armies of the Confederation will, in this way, be the school of Europe. Men will go to the frontiers to learn war, while in the heart of Europe there will reign the blessings of peace. The advantages of war and peace will be combined. Does anyone believe that no nation can become warlike without perpetual civil war? And are the

French the less brave because Anjou and Touraine are not constantly fighting with each other?

In the latter case, it is true that there can be no more hardening for war. But neither will there be any more need for it. Of what use would it be to train for war, when you have no intention of ever making it? And which is the better course – to cultivate a pernicious art, or to destroy the need of it for ever? If the secret of perpetual health were discovered, would there be any sense in rejecting it, on the ground that doctors must not be deprived of the chance of gaining experience? And in making this parallel we have still to ask which of the two arts is the more beneficent in itself and the more deserving of encouragement.

Let no one threaten us with a sudden invasion. It is perfectly obvious that Europe has no invader to fear, and that the 'first comer' will never come. The day of those barbarian eruptions, which seemed to fall from the clouds, is gone for ever. Now that the whole surface of the earth lies bare to our scrutiny, no danger can reach us which we have not foreseen for years. There is no Power in the World now capable of threatening all Europe; and if one ever appears, Europe will either have time to make ready or, at the worst, will be much more capable of resisting him when she is united in one corporate body than she is now, when she would have to put a sudden end to all her quarrels and league herself in haste against the common invader.

We have thus seen that all the alleged evils of Confederation, when duly weighed, come to nothing. I now ask whether anyone in the world would dare to say as much of those which flow from the recognized method of settling disputes between one prince and another – the appeal to the sword; a method inseparable from the state of anarchy and war, which necessarily springs from the absolute independence conceded to all Sovereigns under the imperfect conditions now prevailing in Europe. In order to put the reader in a better position to estimate these evils, I will give a short summary of them and leave him to judge of their significance.

(1) The existence of no solid right, except that of the stronger. (2) The perpetual and inevitable shifting of the balance from nation to nation, which makes it impossible for any one of them to keep in its grasp the power it holds at any moment. (3) The absence of complete security for any nation, so long as its neighbours are not subdued or annihilated. (4) The impossibility of annihilating them, in view of the fact that, directly one is conquered, another springs up in its place. (5) The necessity of endless precautions and expenses to keep guard against possible enemies. (6) Weakness, and consequent exposure to attack, during minorities or revolts; for, when the State is divided, who can support one faction against the other? (7) The absence of any guarantee for international agreements. (8) The impossibility of obtaining justice from others without enormous cost and loss, which even so do not always obtain it, while the object in dispute is seldom worth the price. (9) The invariable risk of the Prince's possessions, and sometimes of his life, in the quest of his rights. (10) The necessity of taking part against his will in the quarrels of his neighbours and of engaging in war at the moment when he would least have chosen it. (11) The

stoppage of trade and revenue at the moment when they are most indispensable. (12) The perpetual danger threatened by a powerful neighbour, if the Prince is weak, and by an armed alliance, if he is strong. (13) Finally, the uselessness of prudence, when everything is left to chance; the perpetual impoverishment of nations; the enfeeblement of the State alike in victory and defeat; and the total inability of the Prince ever to establish good government, ever to count upon his own possessions, ever to secure happiness either for himself or for his subjects.

9

KANT

Source: 'Perpetual peace', specially translated for this volume by Maria Zens, edited by Howard Williams.

Kant is the leading classical theorist of international society. In his view the problems of domestic political society will not be properly resolved until harmony is achieved at the international level. To bring about international harmony he sets forward a proposal for international peace whose success would rest upon permissive laws. These are laws which states are not legally obliged to follow but if they are serious about peace they are morally obligated to observe. Kant sees the prospects of peace being enhanced by the creation of republics based upon the separation of powers. These states then engage in peaceful federations. These federations would afford hospitality to visitors from other states and thereby develop rights of world citizenship. Kant does not see his plan as entirely a dream. He thinks that the forces of world history, trade and war itself may make states follow a peaceful path.

'PERPETUAL PEACE': A PHILOSOPHICAL SKETCH

It might be debated whether this satirical inscription 'Perpetual Peace', which a Dutch innkeeper once put on his sign depicting a graveyard, refers to mankind in general, or to sovereigns in particular who cannot have enough of warfare, or only to the philosophers who dream this sweet dream of eternal peace. The author of this essay wishes, however, to make this reservation: The practical politician does not get along with the theorist; with great complacency he looks down on him as the academic. With his abstract ideas the latter is considered no danger to the state which must be founded upon the rules of experience. The theorist, therefore, may be allowed to fire off his whole broadside and the *worldly-wise* statesman need not bother at all. Consequently, even if there is a dispute between the two the statesman must not suspect subversion behind those randomly and publicly uttered opinions. Through this *clausuia salvatoria* the author considers himself properly insured against all ill-minded interpretation.

First Section: which contains the preliminary articles for a perpetual peace among states

1. 'No conclusion of peace shall be regarded as such if it were made with the secret reservation for a future war'

Since if this were the case it would be a mere ceasefire, a suspension of hostilities, not a *peace*, which means the ending of all hostilities. Attaching the qualifier *'perpetual'* to it is already a suspicious pleonasm. The conclusion of peace eradicates all causes of a future war, even if they are not yet known to the concluding parties themselves, no matter with what discerning aptitude they might later be constructed out of archived documents. The reservation (*reservatio mentalis*) of old, if still to be elaborated pretensions, which neither party will now make explicit since both parties are too exhausted to continue the war but will bear it in mind with the malicious will to seize the first favourable opportunity to pursue their end, is the casuistry of Jesuits and beneath the dignity of a ruler. Just as it is beneath the dignity of a minister to collude with such conclusions if we look at the matter itself.

If, however, in accordance with enlightened concepts of political prudence the true honour of a state is seen to consist in a permanent increase of power with no regard to the means, the above judgement most certainly will appear abstract and pedantic.

2. 'No state existing independently for itself (whether large or small) shall be acquired by another state by inheritance, exchange, purchase or gift'

For a state (unlike the ground on which it is founded) is not a possession (*patrimonium*). A state is a society of men who no-one else than this state can command or dispose of. Having its own roots grafted on to another state as a shoot is to end its existence as a moral person and render it a commodity. This, in fact, would contradict the idea of the original contract without which there can be no social right at all. It is known to everyone what danger this assumed right of acquiring other states has brought for Europe (for in other continents it is not known) even in our own and, indeed, the most recent times. Everyone knows that states can marry one another, on the one hand as a kind of industry in order to acquire hegemonic power without effort, and on the other to extend their landed property. The hiring of the troops of one state to another can be subsumed here as well; for the subjects are used and exploited as commodities at will.

3. 'Standing armies (miles perpetuus) shall be gradually abolished'

For they constantly threaten other states with war by being prepared for it. They incite other states to arm an infinite number of soldiers in order to outdo them. Since the costs of this armament eventually render peace more oppressive than a short war, they themselves are the cause of offensive wars fought to abandon that burden. Moreover, being paid to kill or to be killed implies the use of men as machines and tools in someone else's (the state's) hand, which cannot be easily reconciled with the personal rights of mankind. Voluntary military exercises citizens might undertake with a certain regularity in order to protect themselves and their country from external aggression are a completely different matter. The accumulation of wealth would have much the same effects; being perceived as a threat by other states, it would result in preventive attacks (for among the three powers – *military power*, *alliance power* and *financial power* – the latter seems to be the most reliable instrument of war) if it were not for the difficulty of actually discovering the wealth of a state.

4. 'No national debt shall be incurred in relation to the foreign affairs of the state'

In order to seek sustenance for the national economy (for the improvements of roads, new settlements, the storage of food for years of poor yield) inside or outside the state, this source of funds is inconspicuous. But as a machinery implemented against each other by the powers a credit system of indefinitely increasing and yet seemingly secured (because not all creditors will raise them at the same time) debts represents the dangerous power of money. For it is a fund for fighting a war, a fund which exceeds the funds of all states put together and which can only be exhausted by the foreseeable tax deficit (which, however, is postponed by the commercial stimulus that industry and consumption receive). This ease in fighting wars, in combination with the martial attitude of those in power, which appears to be a feature of human nature, is therefore a major obstacle on the path to perpetual peace. Its prohibition ought to be a preliminary article of such a peace the more since the eventually inevitable bankruptcy of the state will involve other states in the loss and thus, since they do not deserve it, inflict on them a public injury. Therefore other states are justified in allying against such a state and its presumptions.

5. 'No state shall by force interfere in the constitution and government of another state'

For what can entitle a state to such interference? The sense of outrage it gives to the subjects of another state? Rather it might serve as a warning example of the great evil which a people has incurred by its lawlessness. And the bad example a free person gives to another (as a *scandalum acceptum*) is not an injury to the latter. It would not be an interference if a state through internal disunity were to split into two parts, both of which representing a separate state and claiming authority over the whole, and an external state set up to support one since they are in a condition of anarchy. But as long as the internal conflict is not resolved, the interference of external powers would mean the violation of an independent people only struggling to overcome its internal malaise, and, thus, itself be an offence and a threat to the autonomy of all states.

6. 'No state at war with another shall permit such hostilities which would make mutual confidence impossible in the future time of peace: such hostilities include the hiring of assassins (percussores) or poisoners (venefici), the breaching of capitulation agreements, the instigation of treason (perduellio) etc. within the enemy state'

These are dishonourable stratagems. For even in wartime there must remain a certain amount of confidence in the enemy's patterns of thought, otherwise peace could not be concluded and hostilities would turn into a war of extermination (*bellum internecium*). War is only a poor expedient to pursue forcibly one's right in a state of nature (where no court of justice has legal authority). In such a state neither party can be declared an unjust enemy for this would already presuppose a legal verdict; it is the *outcome* of the war (just as a judgement of God) which decides on whose side the right is. There cannot be a war of punishment among states since there is no hierarchical relationship of superior to inferior between them. Thus follows that a war of extermination, in which both parties might altogether be extinguished and, moreover, right would allow perpetual peace only on the great graveyard of the human species. A war like that and the implementation of the means leading towards it must be utterly prohibited. For it is clear that the hostile means listed above inevitably lead there: these evil arts are despicable in themselves, and once employed they would not be confined to warfare for long. The employment of spies (*uti exploratoribus*), for instance, only exploits the dishonesty *of others* (which can never entirely be eradicated). The use of such evil methods will spread into peacetime and thus entirely undermine their own intentions.

Although all of the laws listed above are objective – i.e. in accordance with the intention of those in power, *prohibitive laws* (*leges prohibitivae*) – some of them are more *strict* (*leges strictae*) and should be implemented *immediately* without regard to the circumstances (nos. 1, 5, 6). Yet others (nos. 2, 3, 4), although not exceptions to the rule of law, allow for some *subjective* latitude in respect of their *implementation (leges latae)* and without losing sight of the ultimate end which justifies the permission for this *delay*. One example is, under article no. 2, the *re-establishment* of freedom of which states have been deprived – But this does not justify a delay until doomsday (as Augustus used to put it, *ad calendas graecas*). Thus a complete failure to restore freedom is not permitted, only a delay in order to prevent hasty action which might run contrary to the initial purpose. For the prohibition concerns only the *mode of acquisition* not the actual *possession*, which although not bearing the requisite legal title, was considered lawful in the light of public opinion in all states at the time (of the putative acquisition).

Second section: which contains the definitive articles for perpetual peace among states

The condition of peace among people living together is not a state of nature (*status naturalis*), which is rather a state of war. In such a state of nature even if there are no actual hostilities taking place, there is the constant threat of their breaking out. Peace must therefore be *established*: for a suspension of hostilities is no guarantee of peace, and unless one neighbour gives a guarantee to the other on request (which can happen only under conditions of *legality*) the latter may treat the former as an enemy.

First definitive article for perpetual peace: 'The civil constitution of every state shall be republican'

The constitution which is founded upon, firstly, the principle of *freedom* of all members of a society (as men), secondly, the principle of *dependence* of all on a single common legislature (as subjects) and, thirdly, on the principle of *equality* of all (as *citizens*). This is the only one which emerges from the idea of the original contract – the *republican* constitution. Therefore, a republican constitution, as far as right is concerned, is one which forms the basis for any kind of civil constitution. The question now is whether it is also the only one which can lead to perpetual peace. In addition to the purity of its origin – for it has sprung from the pure source of the very concept of right – the republican constitution provides the prospect of attaining the desired goal, perpetual peace. The reason for this is: If – and under this constitution this must be the case – the citizens' consent is required to decide whether to embark on a war or not it is only natural that they will be very cautious about starting an enterprise as dangerous as this, since they will decide to call down the miseries of war on themselves (such as: to be personally involved in the fighting, to pay for the war from their own possessions, to repair painfully the devastation war leaves behind, and, in order to complete the evil, finally to take on a burden of debts which will embitter peace itself and cannot be paid off because more and more new wars become imminent). Under a constitution, on the other hand, where the subject is not a citizen, which in other words is not republican, declaring a war is the easiest thing in the world to do. Since the head of state is not a citizen and member of the state, but owns the state, he will not lose out in the slightest way on his banquets, hunts, pleasure palaces and courtly feasts and can therefore decide on war as a kind of amusement, on insignificant grounds, and can with indifference leave its justification (for the sake of propriety) to the diplomatic corps, who are always prepared to provide one.

In order to prevent the republican constitution from being confused with the democratic (as commonly happens) we need to note the following. The different types of state (*civitas*) can be classified with regard to the person who holds the highest authority in the state or with regard to the *mode of government*, which is exercised over a people by its ruler whoever that might be. The first considers the form of *sovereignty* (*forma imperii*). And there are only three such forms, the ruling power either lies in the hands of an *individual*, or an association of *several persons* or in the hands of *all* who constitute civil society (*autocracy, aristocracy* and *democracy* – the power of a prince, the power of a nobility and the power of the people). The second categorization considers the mode of government (*forma regiminis*) and concerns the way in which a state as set out in its constitution (i.e. the act of general will which renders the mass a people) makes use of its comprehensive power: in this respect it will either be *republican* or *despotic*. *Republicanism* is the political principle of separating the executive power (the government) from the legislative power. *Despotism* is the principle of the execution of laws by the state – laws which the state itself has legislated. The ruler then treats the general will as his own private will. Of the three forms of sovereignty *democracy* in the true meaning of the word is necessarily a *despotism* because it creates an executive power through which each may decide about all and, this may also be the case, against the one (who, then, does not consent). So *all who yet are not all* make decisions. The general will is in contradiction with itself and, thus, with freedom. For any mode of government, which is not *representative* is in fact a perversion of government, since the legislator cannot at the same time be the executor of his will (just as the universal of the major premise in a syllogism cannot, at the same time, be the subsumption of the particular under the universal in the minor premise). Although the two other types of constitution (the autocratic and the aristocratic) are deficient in that they allow for such a mode of government to exist it is at least possible that they take on a mode of government which is consistent with the *spirit* of a representative system. For instance, Frederick II at least *said* that he was merely the highest servant of the state, whereas the democratic form makes this impossible since everyone wants to be a ruler. Thus, one might say: the smaller the number of the government staff (the number of rulers) and the greater their representative status the more this constitution approached the possibility of republicanism which one might hope to realize through gradual reforms. For this reason it is more difficult in an aristocracy than in a monarchy, and it is impossible in a democracy to arrive at this only perfectly lawful constitution by other than means of violent revolution. But the people put more weight on the mode of government than on the form of sovereignty (although much depends on the greater or lesser suitability of the latter to the end of government). Yet, if the mode of government is to be consistent with the concept of right it must be founded on a representative system. Only in this system is a republican state possible; without it, the constitution of whatever kind will be despotic and violent. None of the old so-called republics knew such a system as their own, and they therefore had to end in a despotism, which under the rule of a single individual might be the most bearable of all forms of despotism.

Second definitive article for perpetual peace: 'International law shall be based upon a federation of free states'

As states peoples can be seen as single individuals who in a state of nature (i.e. independent of external influences) afflict each other simply by living alongside one another. For the sake of their security each people can and ought to demand of others that they enter a constitution similar to the civil one in which the rights of each people can be secured. This would be a *federation of nations* which should not be an international state. For this would be a contradiction: since every state implies a relationship between a *superior* (the legislator) and an *inferior* (the people obeying the laws), in an international state many peoples would form one people. And this contradicts our initial premise, for we are weighing the rights of *nations* in relation to one another as they constitute different states and should not be merged into a single one.

Just as we look down with deep contempt on the savages' clinging to their lawless freedom, who would romp around constantly rather than submit to a lawful constraint constituted by themselves, and, thus, prefer senseless freedom to rational freedom. Since we regard this as barbarism, rudeness and a brutish degradation of humanity, one might expect civilized peoples (each united in itself as a state) to hasten and escape such a depraved condition – the sooner the better. Instead, each *state* perceives its own majesty (for it is absurd to speak of the majesty of the people) precisely in not being restrained by any external law. And the glory of its ruler consists in his power to command many thousands to be sacrificed for a cause that is not theirs without placing himself in any danger. The main difference between European and American savages is that while many tribes of the latter have been entirely eaten up by their enemies the former have found a better use for their defeated opponents than simply eating them: They rather add them to the number of their subjects and, thus, the mass of instruments for even more extensive wars.

Given the viciousness of human nature, which can be observed without disguise in the free interaction of peoples (although in lawful civil societies it is largely concealed by governmental restraints), it is amazing that the very word *right* has not yet been completely banned from the politics of war for being pedantic and that no state yet has been pretentious enough to publicly advocate this opinion. For Hugo Grotius, Pufendorf, Vattel and others (weary comforters all of them) are candidly cited in *justification* of military aggression although their philosophical or diplomatic codes have not and cannot have any *legal* force whatsoever, since states as such are not subjected to any common external constraint. And yet there is no instance of a state ever having been moved to step back from its plan by arguments armed by the views of these important men. This homage, which every state pays (at least in words) to the concept of right, proves that man has a greater, if dormant, moral disposition to master the evil principle in him (which he cannot deny) and to hope others will do likewise. Otherwise the word *right* would never be uttered from states which intend to make war upon one another, unless to mock at it, in the way a certain Gallic prince explained it: 'It [right] is the prerogative which nature has given the stronger: that the weaker should obey them.'

The way in which states pursue their right can never be a trial under an external court of justice, it can only be war. But war and its favourable outcome, *victory*, cannot determine right. A *peace treaty* may put an end to the current war, but not to the general state of war (which always allows one to find a new pretext for war and which cannot be declared utterly unjust since in this condition everyone is the judge in his own cause). Natural law suggests that men in a lawless condition ought to give it up, yet the law of nations cannot suggest the same for states (for as states they already have a lawful internal constitution and therefore have outgrown the coercion by others to subject them to an extended lawful constitution according to their own conception of right). Still, reason as the seat of the highest legislating power of morality condemns war as a legal recourse and makes a state of peace an immediate duty which can neither be established nor secured without a treaty of nations: – thus, a particular kind of league one might call it the *peace federation (foedus pacificum)* is demanded, which differs from a *peace treaty (pactum pacis)* in that the latter ends only *one* war, while the former would seek to end *all* wars forever. This federation is not aimed at the acquisition of state power but only at the maintenance and security of the freedom of a state for itself and, at the same time, the freedom of confederate states, without the need to submit to public laws and the coercion which enforces such laws, like men do in a state of nature. The practicability (objective reality) of this idea of *federalism* spreading gradually over all states and thus leading to perpetual peace can be demonstrated. If by good fortune a powerful and enlightened people can form a republic (which by its nature is inclined to seek perpetual peace) this republic will be the centre of federative alliance for other states in order to associate and in doing so secure the condition of freedom of states in accordance with the idea of international right and to expand through more and more alignments of this kind.

It is easy to understand when a people says: 'There shall be no war among us; for we want to form into a state, i.e. we want to create a supreme legislative, executive and juridicial power which is to resolve our conflicts peacefully'. But if this state declares: 'There shall be no war between myself and other states, although I do not acknowledge any supreme legislative power which secures my rights and whose rights I secure in turn', then it is not at all comprehensible, where to ground the confidence in my rights, unless it is the substitute for the association of civil society, i.e. a free federation. Reason must associate the concept of international right with federalism if there shall be any meaning left to it at all.

The concept of international right becomes meaningless if right is conceived as the right to war (for it is then a law of deciding what is right by unilateral maxims through force and not by universal public laws which restrict the freedom of each individual). Its meaning would be that men who think that way only deserve to destroy one another and thus find perpetual peace in the vast grave which covers all the horrors of violence with those who brought them about. For states in their relation to other states there is no other rational way to escape the unlawful and warlike condition than to abandon their savage (lawless) freedom just like individual men to submit to public and coercive laws and in doing so create a (constantly expanding) *international state (civitas gentium)* which eventually will encompass all peoples of the world. But according to their conception of international right this is not what they actually want. What is right *in hypothesi* they reject *in thesi*. The place of the positive idea of *one world republic* – if all is not to be lost – can only be taken by the *negative* substitute of a war-preventing, enduring and expanding federation. It may stop the stream of unlawful and hostile inclinations, but there will remain the constant danger of their breaking loose again (*Furor impius intus – fremit horridus ore cruento*, Virgil).

Third definitive article for perpetual peace: 'The right of world-citizenship (cosmopolitan right) shall be limited to conditions of universal hospitality'

As in the preceding articles we are not concerned with philanthropy but with *right*. In this context *hospitality* means the right of a stranger not to be treated in a hostile way because of his arriving on someone else's territory. We can send the stranger back if this can be done without causing his death, but we cannot treat him with hostility if he remains peaceful. This is not the *right of a guest* the stranger can claim (for this would require a particular charitable agreement which makes him a member of the household for a certain time) but a *visitor's right*; for it is due to all men to present themselves in society on the grounds of the collective ownership of the surface of the earth on which they cannot disperse indefinitely but have to tolerate one another. Originally, no one has a greater right to inhabit one place of the earth's surface than any other person. The uninhabitable parts of this surface, the oceans and the deserts, divide this community, but the *ship* or the camel (the *ship* of the desert) make it possible to approach one another across these uninhabited parts and to utilize the right to the *surface* which the human race collectively holds for commerce. The inhospitable manner in coastal areas (e.g. the Barbary coast) of plundering ships or enslaving stranded seamen, or of the people of the desert (e.g. the Arabic Bedouins) who regard the proximity to the nomadic tribes as a justification for plundering them is in contradiction with natural law. The right of hospitality – i.e. the stranger's right – does not go beyond the possibility of *attempting* to communicate with the native inhabitants. – In this way distant parts of the world can develop peaceful relationships which will eventually become publicly established by laws and thus take the human race closer to a worldwide civil constitution.

If one compares [with this ultimate end] the *inhospitable* behaviour of the civilized, trading states of our continent, the injustice they inflict upon foreign countries and peoples by *visiting* them (which on their part is the same as *conquering* them) is appalling. America, the territories inhabited by negroes, the Spice Islands, the Cape etc. were regarded as unowned countries when they were discovered; they counted the native inhabitants as nothing. Under the pretext of merely settling commerce posts they brought foreign troops into East India (Hindustan), and with those troops they brought the oppression of the natives, the incitement of the different Indian states to excessive wars, famine, mass arousal, treason and what more is part of the whole litany of evils which are the burden of the human race.

China and Japan (*Nippon*), which have both encountered such visitors, wisely, in China's case, allow access to, but not penetration, of their country and in Japan's case, allowed entry of a single European people, the Dutch. And yet they, like prisoners, are still prevented from entering into community with the native population. The worst thing about this (or, from the point of view of a moral judgement, the best thing) is that they do not even profit from their violence. All these trade companies are on the verge of collapse. The sugar islands, site of the cruellest and most refined slavery, do not yield any real profit but only an indirect and not entirely laudable one. They serve for the training of sailors for warships and thus, again, the conduct of wars in Europe. These powers make much ado about piety and would like to be seen as the chosen people in terms of devotion to justice, yet they are drinking injustice like water.

Since the peoples of the earth have reached a stage of (narrower or broader) community where a violation of rights in *one* place is felt in *all* places, the idea of a right of world-citizenship (cosmopolitan right) is not a fantastic or overstrained vision of right but a necessary amendment to the unwritten code of civil and international right, to the rights of man in general and thus to perpetual peace. Only under this condition can we flatter ourselves that we are continually approaching perpetual peace.

10

HEGEL

Source: S.W. Dyde (trans.) (1896) *Hegel's Philosophy of Right*. London, George Bell & Sons, sections 257–61, 268–9 and 321–60.

Hegel takes a markedly statist view of domestic and international politics. Hegel regards individual freedom as only fully realizable through the state. Each individual may legitimately pursue his or her own ends within the context of civil society in the economic class to which he or she belongs, but this pursuit of particular ends has to be subordinate to the higher purposes of the state. Hegel would not have the individual regard the state as external to his or her will. In ethical terms the state takes precedence over the individual. This statism is carried over into international relations where Hegel does not recognize international law as a fully binding force. The individuality of the state requires that it act ultimately as the arbiter of its own fate. War is always a possibility in such an international order and it should not be regarded as entirely an evil. A war may well have beneficial internal effects. The development of international relations is not entirely in the hands of states and their leaders. Hegel sees those relations as subject to world spirit. This world spirit may require great sacrifices from individuals and states in achieving its ultimate goal of freedom. This freedom is epitomized for Hegel in the Protestant ethic.

The state

257. The state is the realized ethical idea or ethical spirit. It is the will which manifests itself, makes itself clear and visible, substantiates itself. It is the will which thinks and knows itself, and carries out what it knows, and in so far as it knows. The state finds in ethical custom its direct and unreflected existence, and its indirect and reflected existence in the self-consciousness of the individual and in his knowledge and activity. Self-consciousness in the form of social disposition has its substantive freedom in the state, as the essence, purpose, and product of its activity.

[. . .]

259. (a) The idea of the state has direct actuality in the individual state. It, as a self-referring organism, is the constitution or internal state-organization or polity.

(b) It passes over into a relation of the individual state to other states. This is its external organization or polity.

(c) As universal idea, or kind, or species, it has absolute authority over individual states. This is the spirit which gives itself reality in the process of world-history.

The state as an actual thing is pre-eminently individual, and, what is more, particular. Individuality as distinguished from particularity is an element of the idea of the state itself, while particularity belongs to history. Any two states, as such, are independent of each other. Any relation between the two must be external. A third must therefore stand above and unite them. Now this third is the spirit, which gives itself reality in world-history, and constitutes itself absolute judge over states. Several states indeed might form an alliance and pass judgment upon others, or interstate relations may arise of the nature of the Holy Alliance. But these things are always relative and limited, as was the everlasting peace. The sole, absolute judge, which always avails against the particular, is the self-caused self-existing spirit, which presents itself as the universal and efficient leaven of world-history.

Internal polity

260. The state is the embodiment of concrete freedom. In this concrete freedom, personal individuality and its particular interests, as found in the family and civic community, have their complete development. In this concrete freedom, too, the rights of personal individuality receive adequate recognition. These interests and rights pass partly of their own accord into the interest of the universal. Partly, also, do the individuals recognize by their own knowledge and will the universal as their own substantive spirit, and work for it as their own end. Hence, neither is the universal completed without the assistance of the particular interest, knowledge, and will, nor, on the other hand, do individuals, as private persons, live merely for their own special concern. They regard the general end, and are

in all their activities conscious of this end. The modern state has enormous strength and depth, in that it allows the principle of subjectivity to complete itself to an independent extreme of personal particularity, and yet at the same time brings it back into the substantive unity, and thus preserves particularity in the principle of the state.

The peculiarity of the idea of the modern state is that it is the embodiment of freedom, not according to subjective liking, but to the conception of the will, the will, that is, in its universal and divine character. Incomplete states are they, in which this idea is still only a germ, whose particular phases are not permitted to mature into self-dependence. In the republics of classical antiquity universality, it is true, is to be found. But in those ages particularity had not as yet been released from its fetters, and led back to unversality or the universal purpose of the whole. The essence of the modern state binds together the universal and the full freedom of particularity, including the welfare of individuals. It insists that the interests of the family and civic community shall link themselves to the state, and yet is aware that the universal purpose can make no advance without the private knowledge and will of a particularity, which must adhere to its right. The universal must be actively furthered, but, on the other side, subjectivity must be wholly and vitally developed. Only when both elements are present in force is the state to be regarded as articulate and truly organized.

261. In contrast with the spheres of private right and private good, of the family and of the civic community, the state is on one of its sides an external necessity. It is thus a higher authority, in regard to which the laws and interests of the family and community are subject and dependent. On the other side, however, the state is the indwelling end of these things, and is strong in its union of the universal end with the particular interests of individuals. Thus, just so far as people have duties to fulfil towards it, they have also rights.

[. . .]

268. Political disposition, or, in general terms, patriotism, may be defined as the assurance which stands on truth, and the will which has become a custom. Mere subjective assurance does not proceed out of truth, and is only opinion. Genuine patriotism is simply a result of the institutions which subsist in the state as in the actuality of reason. Hence, patriotic feeling is operative in the act, which is in accord with these institutions. Political sentiment is, in general a confidence, which may pass over into a more or less intelligent insight; it is a consciousness that my substantive and particular interest is contained and preserved in the interest and end of another, here the state, in its relation to me, the individual. Wherefore the state is for me forthwith not another, and I in this consciousness am free.

By patriotic feeling is frequently understood merely a readiness to submit to exceptional sacrifices or do exceptional acts. But in reality it is the sentiment which arises in ordinary circumstances and ways of life, and is wont to regard the commonweal as its substantive basis and end. This consciousness is kept intact in the routine of life, and upon it the readiness to submit to exceptional effort is based. But as men would rather be magnanimous than merely right, they easily persuade themselves that they possess this extraordinary patriotism, in order to spare themselves the burden of the true sentiment, and to excuse the lack of it. If this feeling be regarded as something, which provides its own beginning, and can proceed out of subjective imaginations and thoughts, it is confounded with mere opinion, and in that case is devoid of its true basis in objective reality.

Uneducated men delight in surface-reasonings and fault-findings. Faultfinding is an easy matter, but hard is it to know the good and its inner necessity. Education always begins with fault-finding, but when full and complete sees in everything the positive. In the case of religion one may say off-hand that this or that is superstition, but it is infinitely harder to conceive of the truth involved in it. Political sentiment, as a mere appearance, is also to be distinguished from what men truly will. They will in fact the real matter, but they hold fast to bits, and delight in the vanity of making improvements. Men trust in the stability of the state, and suppose that in it only the particular interest can come into being. But custom makes invisible that upon which our whole existence turns. If any one goes safe through the streets at night, it does not occur to him that it could be otherwise. The habit of feeling secure has become a second nature, and we do not reflect that it is first brought about by the agency of special institutions. Often it is imagined that force holds the state together, but the binding cord is nothing else than the deep-seated feeling of order, which is possessed by all.

269. Political disposition is given definite content by the different phases of the organism of the state. This organism is the development of the idea into its differences, which are objectively actualized. These differences are the different functions, affairs, and activities of state. By means of them the universal uninterruptedly produces itself, by a process which is a necessary one, since these various offices proceed from the nature of the conception. The universal is, however, none the less self-contained, since it is already presupposed in its own productive process. This organism is the political constitution.

The state is an organism or the development of the idea into its differences. These different sides are the different functions, affairs and activities of state by means of which the universal unceasingly produces itself by a necessary process. At the same time it is self-contained, since it is presupposed in its own productive activity. This organism is the political constitution. It proceeds eternally out of the state, just as the state in turn is self-contained by means of the constitution. If these two things fall apart, and make the different aspects independent, the unity produced by the constitution is no longer established. The true relation is illustrated by the fable of the belly and the limbs. Although the parts of an organism do not constitute an identity, yet it is of such a nature that, if one of its parts makes itself independent, all must be harmed. We cannot by means of predicates, propositions, etc., reach any right estimate of the state, which should be apprehended as an organism. It is much the same with the state as with the nature of God, who cannot be through predicates conceived, whose life rather is within itself and must be perceived.

[. . .]

External sovereignty

321. Internal sovereignty is this ideality in so far as the elements of spirit, and of the state as the embodiment of spirit, are unfolded in their necessity, and subsist as organs of the state. But spirit, involving a reference to itself, which is negative and infinitely free, becomes an independent existence, which has incorporated the subsistent differences, and hence is exclusive. So constituted, the state has an individuality, which exists essentially as an individual, and in the sovereign is a real, direct individual.

322. Individuality, as exclusive and independent existence, appears as a relation to other self-dependent states. The independent existence of the actual spirit finds an embodiment in this general self-dependence, which is, therefore, the first freedom and highest dignity of a people.

Those who, out of a desire for a collective whole, which will constitute a more or less self-dependent state, and have its own centre, are willing to abandon their own centre and self-dependence, and form with others a new whole, are ignorant of the nature of a collective whole, and underrate the pride of a people in its independence. – The force, which states have on their first appearance in history, is this self-dependence, even though it is quite abstract and has no further internal development. Hence, in its most primitive manifestation, the state has at its head an individual, whether he be patriarch, chief, or what not.

323. In actual reality, this negative reference of the state to itself appears as reference to each other of two independent things, as though the negative were some external thing. This negative reference has, therefore, in its existence the form of an event, involving accidental occurrences coming from without. But it is in fact its own highest element, its real infinitude, the idealization of all its finite materials. The substance, as the absolute power, is here brought into contrast with all that is individual and particular, such as life, property, the rights of property, or even wider circles, and makes their relative worthlessness a fact for consciousness.

324. The phase, according to which the interest and right of individuals is made a vanishing factor, is at the same time a positive element, forming the basis of their, not accidental and fleeting, but absolute individuality. This relation and the recognition of it constitute their substantial duty. Property and life, not to speak of opinions and the ordinary routine of existence, they must sacrifice, if necessary, in order to preserve the substantive individuality, independence, and sovereignty of the state.

It is a very distorted account of the matter when the state, in demanding sacrifices from the citizens, is taken to be simply the civic community, whose object is merely the security of life and property. Security cannot possibly be obtained by the sacrifice of what is to be secured.

Herein is to be found the ethical element in war. War is not to be regarded as an absolute evil. It is not a merely external accident, having its accidental ground in the passions of powerful individuals or nations, in acts of injustice, or in anything which ought not to be. Accident befalls that which is by nature accidental, and this fate is a necessity. So from the standpoint of the conception and in philosophy the merely accidental vanishes, because in it, as it is a mere appearance, is recognized its essence, namely, necessity. It is necessary that what is finite, such as life and property, should have its contingent nature exposed, since contingency is inherent in the conception of the finite. This necessity has in one phase of it the form of a force of nature, since all that is finite is mortal and transient. But in the ethical life, that is to say, the state, this force and nature are separated. Necessity becomes in this way exalted to the work of freedom, and becomes a force which is ethical. What from the standpoint of nature is transient, is now transient because it is willed to be so; and that, which is fundamentally negative, becomes substantive and distinctive individuality in the ethical order.

It is often said, for the sake of edification, that war makes short work of the vanity of temporal things. It is the element by which the idealization of what is particular receives its right and becomes an actuality. Moreover, by it, as I have elsewhere expressed it, 'finite pursuits are rendered unstable, and the ethical health of peoples is preserved. Just as the movement of the ocean prevents the corruption which would be the result of perpetual calm, so by war people escape the corruption which would be occasioned by a continuous or eternal peace.' – The view that this quotation contains merely a philosophical idea, or, as it is sometimes called, a justification of providence, and that actual war needs another kind of justification, will be taken up later. The idealization, which comes to the surface in war, viewed as an accidental foreign relation, is the same as the ideality by virtue of which the internal state functions are organic elements of the whole. This principle is found in history in such a fact as that successful wars have prevented civil broils and strengthened the internal power of the state. So, too, peoples, who have been unwilling or afraid to endure internal sovereignty, have been subjugated by others, and in their struggles for independence have had honour and success small in proportion to their failure to establish within themselves a central political power; their freedom died through their fear of its dying. Moreover, states, which have no guarantee of independence in the strength of their army, states, e.g., that are very small in comparison with their neighbours, have continued to subsist because of their internal constitution, which merely of itself would seem to promise them neither internal repose nor external security. These phenomena are illustrations of our principle drawn from history.

In peace the civic life becomes more and more extended. Each separate sphere walls itself in and becomes exclusive, and at last there is a stagnation of mankind. Their particularity becomes more and more fixed and ossified. Unity of the body is essential to health, and where the organs become hard death ensues. Everlasting peace is frequently demanded as the ideal towards which mankind must move. Hence, Kant proposed an alliance of princes, which should settle the controversies of states and the Holy Alliance was probably intended to be an institution of this kind. But the state is individual, and in individuality negation is essentially implied. Although a number of states may make themselves into a family, the union, because it is an individuality, must create an opposition, and so beget an enemy. As a result of war peoples are strengthened, nations, which are involved in civil quarrels, winning repose at home by means of war abroad. It is true that war occasions insecurity of possessions, but this real insecurity is simply a necessary commotion. From the pulpit we hear much regarding the uncertainty, vanity, and instability of temporal things. At the very same time every one, no matter how much he is impressed by these utterances, thinks that he will manage to retain his own stock and store. But if the uncertainty comes in the form of hussars with glistening sabres, and begins to work in downright earnest, this touching edification turns right about face, and hurls curses at the invader. In spite of this, wars arise, when they lie in the nature of the matter. The seeds spring up afresh, and words are silenced before the earnest repetitions of history.

325. Sacrifice for the sake of the individuality of the state is the substantive relation of all the citizens, and is, thus, a universal duty. It is ideality on one of its sides, and stands in contrast to the reality of particular subsistence. Hence it itself becomes a specific relation, and to it is dedicated a class of its own, the class whose virtue is bravery.

326. Dissensions between states may arise out of any one specific side of their relations to each other. Through these dissensions the specific part of the state devoted to defence receives its distinguishing character. But if the whole state, as such, is in danger of losing its independence, duty summons all the citizens to its defence. If the whole becomes a single force, and is torn from its internal position and goes abroad, defence becomes converted into a war of conquest.

The weaponed force of the state constitutes its standing army. The specific function of defending the state must be intrusted to a separate class. This proceeding is due to the same necessity by which each of the other particular elements, interests, or affairs, has a separate place, as in marriage, the industrial class, the business class, and the political class. Theorizing, which wanders up and down with its reasons, goes about to contemplate the greater advantages or the greater disadvantages of a standing army. Mere opinion decides against an army, because the conception of the matter is harder to understand than are separate and external sides. Another reason is that the interests and aims of particularity, expenses, consequent higher taxation, etc., are counted of greater concern by the civic community than is the absolutely necessary. On this view the necessary is valuable only as a means to the preservation of the various special civic interests.

327. Bravery taken by itself is a formal virtue, since in it freedom is farthest

removed from all special aims, possessions, and enjoyments, and even from life. But it involves a negation or renunciation of only external realities, and does not carry with it a completion of the spiritual nature. Thus, the sentiment of courage may be based upon any one of a variety of grounds, and its actual result may be not for the brave themselves, but only for others.

The military class is the class of universality. To it are assigned the defence of the state and the duty of bringing into existence the ideality implicit in itself. In other words it must sacrifice itself. Bravery is, it is true, of different sorts. The courage of the animal, or the robber, the bravery due to a sense of honour, the bravery of chivalry, are not yet the true forms of it. True bravery in civilized peoples consists in a readiness to offer up oneself in the service of the state, so that the individual counts only as one amongst many. Not personal fearlessness, but the taking of one's place in a universal cause, is the valuable feature of it. In India five hundred men conquered twenty thousand, who were by no means cowardly but lacked the sense of co-operation.

328. The content of bravery as a sentiment is found in the true absolute final end, the sovereignty of the state. Bravery realizes this end, and in so doing gives up personal reality. Hence, in this feeling are found the most rigorous and direct antagonisms. There is present in it a self-sacrifice, which is yet the existence of freedom. In it is found the highest self-control or independence, which yet in its existence submits to the mechanism of an external order and a life of service. An utter obedience or complete abnegation of one's own opinion and reasonings, even an absence of one's own spirit, is coupled with the most intense and comprehensive direct presence of the spirit and of resolution. The most hostile and hence most personal attitude towards individuals is allied with perfect indifference, or even, it may be, a kindly feeling towards them as individuals.

To risk one's life is indeed something more than fear of death, but it is yet a mere negative, having no independent character and value. Only the positive element, the aim and content of the act, gives significance to the feeling of fearlessness. Robbers or murderers, having in view a crime, adventurers bent upon gratifying merely their own fancy, risk their lives without fear. – The principle of the modern world, that is, the thought and the universal, have given bravery a higher form. It now seems to be mechanical in its expression, being the act not of a particular person, but of a member of the whole. As antagonism is now directed, not against separate persons, but against a hostile whole, personal courage appears as impersonal. To this change is due the invention of the gun; and this by no means chance invention has transmuted the merely personal form of bravery into the more abstract.

329. The state has a foreign aspect, because it is an individual subject. Hence, its relation to other states falls within the princely function. Upon this function it devolves solely and directly to command the armed force, to entertain relations with other states through ambassadors, to decide upon peace and war, and to conduct other negotiations.

In almost all European countries the individual summit is the princely function, which has charge of foreign affairs. Wherever the constitution requires the existence of classes or estates, it may be asked whether the classes, which in any case control the supplies, should not also resolve upon war and peace. In England, for example, no unpopular war can be waged. But if it is meant that princes and cabinets are more subject to passion than the houses, and hence that the houses should decide whether there should be war or peace, it must be replied, that often whole nations have been roused to a pitch of enthusiasm surpassing that of their princes. Frequently in England the whole people have insisted upon war, and in a certain measure compelled the ministers to wage it. The popularity of Pitt was due to his knowing how to meet what the nation willed. Not till afterwards did calm give rise to the consciousness that the war was utterly useless, and undertaken without adequate means. Moreover, a state is connected not only with another but with several others, and the complications are so delicate that they can be managed only by the highest power.

International law

330. International law arises out of the relation to one another of independent states. Whatever is absolute in this relation receives the form of a command, because its reality depends upon a distinct sovereign will.

A state is not a private person, but in itself a completely independent totality. Hence, the relation of states to one another is not merely that of morality and private right. It is often desired that states should be regarded from the standpoint of private right and morality. But the position of private persons is such that they have over them a law court, which realizes what is intrinsically right. A relation between states ought also to be intrinsically right, and in mundane affairs that which is intrinsically right ought to have power. But as against the state there is no power to decide what is intrinsically right and to realize this decision. Hence, we must here remain by the absolute command. States in their relation to one another are independent and look upon the stipulations which they make one with another as provisional.

331. The nation as a state is the spirit substantively realized and directly real. Hence, it is the absolute power on earth. As regards other states it exists in sovereign independence. Hence, to exist for and be recognized by another as such a state is its primary absolute right. But this right is yet only formal, and the state's demand to be recognized, when based on these external relations, is abstract. Whether the state exists absolutely and in concrete fact, depends upon its content, constitution, and condition. Even then the recognition, containing the identity of both inner and outer relations, depends upon the view and will of another.

Just as the individual person is not real unless related to others so the state is not really individual unless related to other states. The legitimate province of a state in its foreign relations, and more especially of the princely function, is on one side wholly internal; a state shall not meddle with the internal affairs of another state. Yet, on the other side, it is essential for its completeness that it be recognized by others. But this recognition demands as a guarantee that it shall recognize those who recognize it, and will have respect for their independence. Therefore they cannot be indifferent to its internal affairs. – In the case of a nomadic people, or any people occupying a lower grade of civilization, the question arises how far it can be considered as a state. The religious opinions formerly held by Jews and Mahomedans may contain a still higher opposition, which does not permit of the universal identity implied in recognition.

When Napoleon, before the peace of Campoformio, said, 'The French Republic needs recognition as little as the sun requires to be recognized,' he really indicated the strength of the existence, which already carried with it a guarantee of recognition, without its having been expressed.

332. The direct reality, in which states stand to one another, sunders itself into various relations, whose nature proceeds from independent caprice on both sides, and hence has as a general thing the formal character of a contract. The subject matter of these contracts is, however, of infinitely narrower range than of those in the civic community. There individuals are dependent upon one another in a great variety of ways, while independent states are wholes, which find satisfaction in the main within themselves.

333. International law, or the law which is universal, and is meant to hold absolutely good between states, is to be distinguished from the special content of positive treaties, and has at its basis the proposition that treaties, as they involve the mutual obligations of states, must be kept inviolate. But because the relation of states to one another has sovereignty as its principle, they are so far in a condition of nature one to the other. Their rights have reality not in a general will, which is constituted as a superior power, but in their particular wills. Accordingly the fundamental proposition of international law remains a good intention, while in the actual situation the relation established by the treaty is being continually shifted or abrogated.

There is no judge over states, at most only a referee or mediator, and even the mediatorial function is only an accidental thing, being due to particular wills. Kant's idea was that eternal peace should be secured by an alliance of states. This alliance should settle every dispute, make impossible the resort to arms for a decision, and be recognized by every state. This idea assumes that states are in accord, an agreement which, strengthened though it might be by moral, religious, and other considerations, nevertheless always rested on the private sovereign will, and was therefore liable to be disturbed by the element of contingency.

334. Therefore, when the particular wills of states can come to no agreement, the controversy can be settled only by war. Owing to the wide field and the varied relations of the citizens of different states to one another, injuries occur easily and frequently. What of these injuries is to be viewed as a specific breach of a treaty or as a violation of formal recognition and honour remains from the nature of the case indefinite. A state may introduce its infinitude and honour into every one of its separate compartments. It is all the more tempted to make or seek some occasion for a display of irritability, if the individuality within it has

been strengthened by long internal rest, and desires an outlet for its pent-up activity.

335. Moreover, the state as a spiritual whole cannot be satisfied merely with taking notice of the fact of an injury, because injury involves a threatened danger arising from the possible action of the other state. Then, too, there is the weighing of probabilities, guesses at intentions, and so forth, all of which have a part in the creation of strife.

336. Each self-dependent state has the standing of a particular will; and it is on this alone that the validity of treaties depends. This particular will of the whole is in its content its well-being, and well-being constitutes the highest law in its relation to another. All the more is this so since the idea of the state involves that the opposition between right or abstract freedom on one side and the complete specific content or well-being on the other is superseded. It is to states as concrete wholes that recognition is first granted.

337. The substantive weal of the state is its weal as a particular state in its definite interests and condition, its peculiar external circumstances, and its particular treaty obligations. Thus the government is a particular wisdom and not universal providence. So, too, its end in relation to other states, the principle justifying its wars and treaties, is not a general thought, such as philanthropy, but the actually wronged or threatened weal in its definite particularity.

At one time a lengthy discussion was held with regard to the opposition between morals and politics, and the demand was made that politics should be in accordance with morality. Here it may be remarked merely that the commonweal has quite another authority than the weal of the individual, and that the ethical substance or the state has directly its reality or right not in an abstract but in a concrete existence. This existence, and not one of the many general thoughts held to be moral commands, must be the principle of its conduct. The view that politics in this assumed opposition is presumptively in the wrong depends on a shallow notion both of morality and of the nature of the state in relation to morality.

338. Although in war there prevails force, contingency, and absence of right, states continue to recognize one another as states. In this fact is implied a covenant, by virtue of which each state retains absolute value. Hence, war, even when actively prosecuted, is understood to be temporary, and in international law is recognized as containing the possibility of peace. Ambassadors, also, are to be respected. War is not to be waged against internal institutions, or the peaceable family and private life, or private persons.

Modern wars are carried on humanely. One person is not set in hate over against another. Personal hostilities occur at most in the case of the pickets. But in the army as an army, enmity is something undetermined, and gives place to the duty which each person owes to another.

339. For the rest, the capture of prisoners in time of war, and in time of peace the concession of rights of private intercourse to the subjects of another state, depend principally upon the ethical observances of nations. In them is embodied that inner universality of behaviour, which is preserved under all relations.

The nations of Europe form a family by virtue of the universal principle of their legislation, their ethical observances, and their civilization. Amongst them international behaviour is ameliorated, while there prevails elsewhere a mutual infliction of evils. The relation of one state to another fluctuates; no judge is present to compose differences; the higher judge is simply the universal and absolute spirit, the spirit of the world.

340. As states are particular, there is manifested in their relation to one another a shifting play or internal particularity of passions, interests, aims, talents, virtues, force, wrong, vice, and external contingency on the very largest scale. In this play even the ethical whole, national independence, is exposed to chance. The spirit of a nation is an existing individual having in particularity its objective actuality and self-consciousness. Because of this particularity it is limited. The destinies and deeds of states in their connection with one another are the visible dialectic of the finite nature of these spirits. Out of this dialectic the universal spirit, the spirit of the world, the unlimited spirit, produces itself. It has the highest right of all, and exercises its right upon the lower spirits in world-history. The history of the world is the world's court of judgment.

World-history

341. The universal spirit exists concretely in art in the form of perception and image, in religion in the form of feeling and pictorial imaginative thinking, and in philosophy in the form of pure free thought. In world-history this concrete existence of spirit is the spiritual actuality in the total range of its internality and externality. It is a court of judgment because in its absolute universality the particular, namely, the Penates, the civic community, and the national spirit in their many-coloured reality are all merely ideal. The movement of spirit in this case consists in visibly presenting these spheres as merely ideal.

342. Moreover, world-history is not a court of judgment, whose principle is force, nor is it the abstract and irrational necessity of a blind fate. It is self-caused and self-realized reason, and its actualized existence in spirit is knowledge. Hence, its development issuing solely out of the conception of its freedom is a necessary development of the elements of reason. It is, therefore, an unfolding of the spirit's self-consciousness and freedom. It is the exhibition and actualization of the universal spirit.

343. The history of spirit is its overt deeds, for only what it does it is, and its deed is to make itself as a spirit the object of its consciousness, to explain and lay hold upon itself by reference to itself. To lay hold upon itself is its being and principle, and the completion of this act is at the same time self-renunciation and transition. To express the matter formally, the spirit which again apprehends what has already been grasped and actualized, or, what is the same thing, passes through self-renunciatiion into itself, is the spirit of a higher stage.

Here occurs the question of the perfection and education of humanity. They who have argued in favour of this idea, have surmised something of the nature of spirit. They have understood that spirit has Γνῶθι σεαυτὸν as a law of its being, and that when it lays hold upon what it itself is, it assumes a higher form. To those who have rejected this idea, spirit has remained an empty word and history a superficial play of accidental and so-called mere human strife and passion. Though in their use of the words 'providence' and 'design of providence,' they express their belief in a higher control, they do not fill up the notion, but announce that the design of providence is for them unknowable and inconceivable.

344. States, peoples, and individuals are established upon their own particular definite principle, which has systematized reality in their constitutions and in the entire compass of their surroundings. Of this systematized reality they are aware, and in its interests are absorbed. Yet are they the unconscious tools and organs of the world-spirit, through whose inner activity the lower forms pass away. Thus the spirit by its own motion and for its own end makes ready and works out the transition into its next higher stage.

345. Justice and virtue, wrong, force, and crime, talents and their results, small and great passions, innocence and guilt, the splendour of individuals, national life, independence, the fortune and misfortune of states and individuals, have in the sphere of conscious reality their definite meaning and value, and find in that sphere judgment and their due. This due is, however, as yet incomplete. In world-history, which lies beyond this range of vision, the idea of the world-spirit, in that necessary phase of it which constitutes at any time its actual stage, is given its absolute right. The nation, then really flourishing, attains to happiness and renown, and its deeds receive completion.

346. Since history is the embodiment of spirit in the form of events, that is, of direct natural reality, the stages of development are present as direct natural principles. Because they are natural, they conform to the nature of a multiplicity, and exist one outside the other. Hence, to each nation is to be ascribed a single principle, comprised under its geographical and anthropological existence.

347. To the nation, whose natural principle is one of these stages, is assigned the accomplishment of it through the process characteristic of the self-developing self-consciousness of the world-spirit. In the history of the world this nation is for a given epoch dominant, although it can make an epoch but once. In contrast with the absolute right of this nation to be the bearer of the current phase in the development of the world-spirit, the spirits of other existing nations are void of right, and they, like those whose epochs are gone, count no longer in the history of the world.

The special history of a world-historic nation contains the unfolding of its principle from its undeveloped infancy up to the time when, in the full manhood of free ethical self-consciousness, it presses in upon universal history. It contains, moreover, the period of decline and destruction, the rise of a higher principle being marked in it simply as the negative of its own. Hence, the spirit passes over into that higher principle, and thus indicates to world-history another nation. From that time onward the first nation has lost absolute interest, absorbs the higher principle positively, it may be, and fashions itself in accordance with it, but is, after all, only a recipient, and has no indwelling vitality and freshness. Perhaps it loses its independence, perhaps continues to drag itself on as a particular state or circle of states, and spends itself in various random civil enterprises and foreign broils.

348. At the summit of all actions, including world-historical actions, stand individuals. Each of these individuals is a subjectivity who realizes what is substantive. He is a living embodiment of the substantive deed of the world-spirit, and is, therefore, directly identical with this deed. It is concealed even from himself, and is not his object and end. Thus they do not receive honour and thanks for their acts either from their contemporaries or from the public opinion of posterity. By this opinion they are viewed merely as formal subjectivities, and, as such, are simply given their part in immortal fame.

349. A people is not as yet a state. The transition from the family, horde, clan, or multitude into a state constitutes the formal realization in it of the idea. If the ethical substance, which every people has implicitly, lacks this form, it is without that objectivity which comes from laws and thought-out regulations. It has neither for itself nor for others any universal or generally admitted reality. It will not be recognized. Its independence, being devoid of objective law or secure realized rationality, is formal only and not a sovereignty.

From the ordinary point of view we do not call the patriarchal condition a constitution, or a people in this condition a state, or its independence sovereignty. Before the beginning of actual history there are found uninteresting stupid innocence and the bravery arising out of the formal struggle for recognition and out of revenge.

350. It is the absolute right of the idea to come visibly forth, and proceeding from marriage and agriculture realize itself in laws and objective institutions. This is true whether its realization appears in the form of divine law and beneficence or in the form of force and wrong. This right is the right of heroes to found states.

351. In the same way civilized nations may treat as barbarians the peoples who are behind them in the essential elements of the state. Thus, the rights of mere herdsmen, hunters, and tillers of the soil are inferior, and their independence is merely formal.

Wars and contests arising under such circumstances are struggles for recognition in behalf of a certain definite content. It is this feature of them which is significant in world-history.

352. The concrete ideas, which embody the national minds or spirits, has its truth in the concrete idea in its absolute universality. This is the spirit of the world, around whose throne stand the other spirits as perfecters of its actuality, and witnesses and ornaments of its splendour. Since it is, as spirit, only the movement of its activity in order to know itself absolutely, to free its consciousness from mere direct naturalness, and to come to itself, the principles of the different forms of its self-consciousness, as they appear in the process of liberation, are four. They are the principles of the four world-historic kingdoms.

353. In its first and direct revelation the world-spirit has as its principle the

form of the substantive spirit, in whose identity individuality is in its essence submerged and without explicit justification.

In the second principle the substantive spirit is aware of itself. Here spirit is the positive content and filling, and is also at the same time the living form, which is in its nature self-referred.

The third principle is the retreat into itself of this conscious self-referred existence. There thus arises an abstract universality, and with it an infinite opposition to objectivity, which is regarded as bereft of spirit.

In the fourth principle this opposition of the spirit is overturned in order that spirit may receive into its inner self its truth and concrete essence. It thus becomes at home with objectivity, and the two are reconciled. Because the spirit has come back to its formal substantive reality by returning out of this infinite opposition, it seeks to produce and know its truth as thought, and as a world of established reality.

354. In accordance with these four principles the four world-historic empires are (1) the Oriental, (2) the Greek, (3) the Roman, and (4) the Germanic.

355. (1) The Oriental Empire: The first empire is the substantive world-intuition, which proceeds from the natural whole of patriarchal times. It has no internal divisions. Its worldly government is theocracy, its ruler a high priest or God, its constitution and legislation are at the same time its religion, and its civic and legal regulations are religious and moral commands or usages. In the splendour of this totality the individual personality sinks without rights; external nature is directly divine or an ornament of God, and the history of reality is poetry. The distinctions, which develop themselves in customs, government, and the state, serve instead of laws, being converted by mere social usage into clumsy, diffuse, and superstitious ceremonies, the accidents of personal power and arbitrary rule. The division into classes becomes a caste fixed as the laws of nature. Since in the Oriental empire there is nothing stable, or rather what is firm is petrified, it has life only in a movement, which goes on from the outside, and becomes an elemental violence and desolation. Internal repose is merely a private life, which is sunk in feebleness and lassitude.

The element of substantive natural spirituality is present in the first forming of every state, and constitutes the absolute starting-point of its history. This assertion is presented and historically established by Dr Stuhr in his well-reasoned and scholarly treatise 'Vom Untergange der Naturstaaten' (Berlin, 1812), who, moreover, suggests in this work a rational method of viewing constitutional history and history in general. The principle of subjectivity and self-conscious freedom he ascribes to the German nation. But since the treatise is wholly taken up with the decline of the nature-states, it simply leads to the point at which this modern principle makes its appearance. At that time it assumed in part the guise of restless movement, human caprice, and corruption, in part the particular guise of feeling, not having as yet developed itself into the objectivity of self-conscious substantivity or the condition of organized law.

356. (2) The Greek Empire: This empire still contains the earlier substantive unity of the finite and infinite, but only as a mysterious background, suppressed

and kept down in gloomy reminiscence, in caves and in traditional imagery. This background under the influence of the self-distinguishing spirit is recreated into individual spirituality, and exalted into the daylight of consciousness, where it is tempered and clarified into beauty and a free and cheerful ethical life. Here arises the principle of personal individuality, although it is not as yet self-centred, but held in its ideal unity. One result of this incompleteness is that the whole is broken up into a number of particular national minds or spirits. Further, the final decision of will is not as yet intrusted to the subjectivity of the independent self-consciousness, but resides in a power, which is higher than, and lies beyond it. Moreover, the particularity, which is found in wants, is not yet taken up into freedom, but segregated in a class of slaves.

357. (3) The Roman Empire: In this empire the distinctions of spirit are carried to the length of an infinite rupture of the ethical life into two extremes, personal private self-consciousness, and abstract universality. The antagonism, arising between the substantive intuition of an aristocracy and the principle of free personality in democratic form, developed on the side of the aristocracy into superstition and the retention of cold self-seeking power, and on the side of the democracy into the corrupt mass. The dissolution of the whole culminates in universal misfortune, ethical life dies, national individualities, having merely the bond of union of a Pantheon, perish, and individuals are degraded to the level of that equality, in which they are merely private persons and have only formal rights.

358. (4) The German Empire: Owing to the loss of itself and its world, and to the infinite pain caused by it, a loss of which the Jewish people were already held to be the type, spirit is pressed back into itself, and finds itself in the extreme of absolute negativity. But this extreme is the absolute turning-point, and in it finds the infinite and yet positive nature of its own inner being. This new discovery is the unity of the divine and the human. By means of it objective truth is reconciled with freedom, and that, too, inside of self-consciousness and subjectivity. This new basis, infinite and yet positive, it has been charged upon the northern principle of the Germanic nations to bring to completion.

359. The internal aspect of this northern principle exists in feeling as faith, love, and hope. Although it is in this form still abstract, it is the reconciliation and solution of all contradiction. It proceeds to unfold its content in order to raise it to reality and self-conscious rationality. It thus constructs a kingdom of this world, based upon the feeling, trust, and fellowship of free men. This kingdom in this its subjectivity is an actual kingdom of rude caprice and barbarism in contrast with the world beyond. It is an intellectual empire, whose content is indeed the truth of its spirit. But as it is yet not thought out, and still is veiled in the barbarism of picture-thinking, it exists as a spiritual force, which exercises over the actual mind a despotic and tyrannical influence.

360. These kingdoms are based upon the distinction, which has now won the form of absolute antagonism, and yet at the same time are rooted in a single unity and idea. In the obdurate struggle, which thus ensues, the spiritual has to lower its heaven to the level of an earthly and temporal condition, to common

worldliness, and to ordinary life and thought. On the other hand the abstract actuality of the worldly is exalted to thought, to the principle of rational being and knowing, and to the rationality of right and law. As a result of these two tendencies, the contradiction has become a marrowless phantasm. The present has stripped off its barbarism and its lawless caprice, and truth has stripped off its beyond and its casualness. The true atonement and reconciliation has become objective, and unfolds the state as the image and reality of reason. In the state, self-consciousness finds the organic development of its real substantive knowing and will, in religion it finds in the form of ideal essence the feeling and the vision of this its truth, and in science it finds the free conceived knowledge of this truth, seeing it to be one and the same in all its mutually completing manifestations, namely, the state, nature, and the ideal world.

11

CLAUSEWITZ

Source: Michael Howard and Peter Paret (eds and trans.) (1984) *Carl von Clausewitz: On War*. New Jersey, Princeton University Press, pp. 75–89 and 119–23. Reprinted by permission of Princeton University Press, copyright © 1976.

Clausewitz regards war as a duel in which the object is to disarm the enemy. In war Clausewitz sees no logical limit to the use of force. The party that is least prepared to use force plays into the hands of the enemy. But the use of force must be governed by intelligence. Brutal though war may be, it is none the less a human activity and victory goes to the protagonist who best uses all the capacities at their disposal. War for Clausewitz is an imprecise art where passion and subjective abilities play their part. A great military commander is one who can rise above the pressures of circumstance and direct passions towards the achievement of victory. Wars are subject to friction in which the execution of even apparently ordinary tasks may become difficult.

But war should not be seen as an end in itself. The prosecution of war has to be subordinate to the achievement of political ends. Warfare has a part to play in preserving the health of national and international society but those who prosecute war ought not to see war as the predominant force. Much of the strategic aspect of contemporary thinking on international relations derives from the work of Clausewitz.

Chapter One: What is war?

1. Introduction

I propose to consider first the various *elements* of the subject, next its *various parts* or *sections*, and finally *the whole* in its internal structure. In other words, I shall proceed from the simple to the complex. But in war more than in any other subject we must begin by looking at the nature of the whole; for here more than elsewhere the part and the whole must always be thought of together.

2. Definition

I shall not begin by expounding a pedantic, literary definition of war, but go straight to the heart of the matter, to the duel. War is nothing but a duel on a larger scale. Countless duels go to make up war, but a picture of it as a whole can be formed by imagining a pair of wrestlers. Each tries through physical force to compel the other to do his will; his *immediate* aim is to *throw* his opponent in order to make him incapable of further resistance.

War is thus an act of force to compel our enemy to do our will.

Force, to counter opposing force, equips itself with the inventions of art and science. Attached to force are certain self-imposed, imperceptible limitations hardly worth mentioning, known as international law and custom, but they scarcely weaken it. Force – that is, physical force, for moral force has no existence save as expressed in the state and the law – is thus the *means* of war; to impose our will on the enemy is its *object*. To secure that object we must render the enemy powerless; and that, in theory, is the true aim of warfare. That aim takes the place of the object, discarding it as something not actually part of war itself.

3. The maximum use of force

Kind-hearted people might of course think there was some ingenious way to disarm or defeat an enemy without too much bloodshed, and might imagine this is the true goal of the art of war. Pleasant as it sounds, it is a fallacy that must be exposed: war is such a dangerous business that the mistakes which come from kindness are the very worst. The maximum use of force is in no way incompatible with the simultaneous use of the intellect. If one side uses force without compunction, undeterred by the bloodshed it involves, while the other side refrains, the first will gain the upper hand. That side will force the other to follow suit; each will drive its opponent toward extremes, and the only limiting factors are the counterpoises inherent in war.

This is how the matter must be seen. It would be futile – even wrong – to try and shut one's eyes to what war really is from sheer distress at its brutality.

If wars between civilized nations are far less cruel and destructive than wars between savages, the reason lies in the social conditions of the states themselves and in their relationships to one another. These are the forces that give rise to war; the same forces circumscribe and moderate it. They themselves however are not part of war; they already exist before fighting starts. To introduce the principle of moderation into the theory of war itself would always lead to logical absurdity.

Two different motives make men fight one another: *hostile feelings* and *hostile intentions*. Our definition is based on the latter, since it is the universal element. Even the most savage, almost instinctive, passion of hatred cannot be conceived as existing without hostile intent; but hostile intentions are often unaccompanied by any sort of hostile feelings – at least by none that predominate. Savage peoples are ruled by passion, civilized peoples by the mind. The difference, however, lies not in the respective natures of savagery and civilization, but in their attendant circumstances, institutions, and so forth. The difference, therefore, does not operate in every case, but it does in most of them. Even the most civilized of peoples, in short, can be fired with passionate hatred for each other.

Consequently, it would be an obvious fallacy to imagine war between civilized peoples as resulting merely from a rational act on the part of their governments and to conceive of war as gradually ridding itself of passion, so that in the end one would never really need to use the physical impact of the fighting forces – comparative figures of their strength would be enough. That would be a kind of war by algebra.

Theorists were already beginning to think along such lines when the recent wars taught them a lesson. If war is an act of force, the emotions cannot fail to be involved. War may not spring from them, but they will still affect it to some degree, and the extent to which they do so will depend not on the level of civilization but on how important the conflicting interests are and on how long their conflict lasts.

If, then, civilized nations do not put their prisoners to death or devastate cities and countries, it is because intelligence plays a larger part in their methods of warfare and has taught them more effective ways of using force than the crude expression of instinct.

The invention of gunpowder and the constant improvement of firearms are enough in themselves to show that the advance of civilization has done nothing practical to alter or deflect the impulse to destroy the enemy, which is central to the very idea of war.

The thesis, then, must be repeated: war is an act of force, and there is no logical limit to the application of that force. Each side, therefore, compels its opponent to follow suit; a reciprocal action is started which must lead, in theory, to extremes. This is the *first case of interaction and the first 'extreme'* we meet with.

4. The aim is to disarm the enemy

I have already said that the aim of warfare is to disarm the enemy and it is time to show that, at least in theory, this is bound to be so. If the enemy is to be coerced you must put him in a situation that is even more unpleasant than the sacrifice you call on him to make. The hardships of that situation must not of course be merely transient – at least not in appearance. Otherwise the enemy would not give in but would wait for things to improve. Any change that might be brought about by continuing hostilities must then, at least in theory, be of a kind to bring the enemy still greater disadvantages. The worst of all conditions in which a belligerent can find himself is to be utterly defenseless. Consequently, if you are to force the enemy, by making war on him, to do your bidding, you must either make him literally defenseless or at least put him in a position that makes this danger probable. It follows, then, that to overcome the enemy, or disarm him – call it what you will – must always be the aim of warfare.

War, however, is not the action of a living force upon a lifeless mass (total nonresistance would be no war at all) but always the collision of two living forces. The ultimate aim of waging war, as formulated here, must be taken as applying to both sides. Once again, there is interaction. So long as I have not overthrown my opponent I am bound to fear he may overthrow me. Thus I am not in control: he dictates to me as much as I dictate to him. This is the *second case of interaction and it leads to the second 'extreme.'*

5. The maximum exertion of strength

If you want to overcome your enemy you must match your effort against his power of resistance, which can be expressed as the product of two inseparable factors, viz. *the total means at his disposal* and *the strength of his will.* The extent of the means at his disposal is a matter – though not exclusively – of figures, and should be measurable. But the strength of his will is much less easy to determine and can only be gauged approximately by the strength of the motive animating it. Assuming you arrive in this way at a reasonably accurate estimate of the enemy's power of resistance, you can adjust your own efforts accordingly; that is, you can either increase them until they surpass the enemy's or, if this is beyond your means, you can make your efforts as great as possible. But the enemy will do the same; competition will again result and, in pure theory, it must again force you both to extremes. This is *the third case of interaction and the third 'extreme.'*

6. Modifications in practice

Thus in the field of abstract thought the inquiring mind can never rest until it reaches the extreme, for here it is dealing with an extreme: a clash of forces freely operating and obedient to no law but their own. From a pure concept of war you might try to deduce absolute terms for the objective you should aim at and for the means of achieving it; but if you did so the continuous interaction would land you in extremes that represented nothing but a play of the imagination issuing from an almost invisible sequence of logical subtleties. If we were to think purely in absolute terms, we could avoid every difficulty by a stroke of the pen and proclaim with inflexible logic that, since the extreme must always be the goal, the greatest effort must always be exerted. Any such pronouncement would be an abstraction and would leave the real world quite unaffected.

Even assuming this extreme effort to be an absolute quantity that could easily be calculated, one must admit that the human mind is unlikely to consent to being ruled by such a logical fantasy. It would often result in strength being wasted, which is contrary to other principles of statecraft. An effort of will out of all proportion to the object in view would be needed but would not in fact be realized, since subtleties of logic do not motivate the human will.

But move from the abstract to the real world, and the whole thing looks quite different. In the abstract world, optimism was all-powerful and forced us to assume that both parties to the conflict not only sought perfection but attained it. Would this ever be the case in practice? Yes, it would if: (a) war were a wholly isolated act, occurring suddenly and not produced by previous events in the political world; (b) it consisted of a single decisive act or a set of simultaneous ones; (c) the decision achieved was complete and perfect in itself, uninfluenced by any previous estimate of the political situation it would bring about.

7. War is never an isolated act

As to the first of these conditions, it must be remembered that neither opponent is an abstract person to the other, not even to the extent of that factor in the power of resistance, namely the will, which is dependent on externals. The will is not a wholly unknown factor; we can base a forecast of its state tomorrow on what it is today. War never breaks out wholly unexpectedly, nor can it be spread instantaneously. Each side can therefore gauge the other to a large extent by what he is and does, instead of judging him by what he, strictly speaking, ought to be or do. Man and his affairs, however, are always something short of perfect and will never quite achieve the absolute best. Such shortcomings affect both sides alike and therefore constitute a moderating force.

8. War does not consist of a single short blow

The second condition calls for the following remarks:

If war consisted of one decisive act, or of a set of simultaneous decisions, preparations would tend toward totality, for no omission could ever be rectified. The sole criterion for preparations which the world of reality could provide would be the measures taken by the adversary – so far as they are known; the rest would once more be reduced to abstract calculations. But if the decision in war consists of several successive acts, then each of them, seen in context, will provide a gauge for those that follow. Here again, the abstract world is ousted by the real one and the trend to the extreme is thereby moderated.

But, of course, if all the means available were, or could be, simultaneously employed, all wars would automatically be confined to a single decisive act or a set of simultaneous ones – the reason being that any *adverse* decision must reduce the sum of the means available, and if *all* had been committed in the first act there could really be no question of a second. Any subsequent military operation would virtually be part of the first – in other words, merely an extension of it.

Yet, as I showed above, as soon as preparations for a war begin, the world of reality takes over from the world of abstract thought; material calculations take the place of hypothetical extremes and, if for no other reason, the interaction of the two sides tends to fall short of maximum effort. Their full resources will therefore not be mobilized immediately.

Besides, the very nature of those resources and of their employment means they cannot all be deployed at the same moment. The resources in question are *the fighting forces proper, the country*, with its physical features and population, and its *allies*.

The country – its physical features and population – is more than just the source of all armed forces proper; it is in itself an integral element among the factors at work in war – though only that part which is the actual theater of operations or has a notable influence on it.

It is possible, no doubt, to use all mobile fighting forces simultaneously; but with fortresses, rivers, mountains, inhabitants, and so forth, that cannot be done; not, in short, with the country as a whole, unless it is so small that the opening action of the war completely engulfs it. Furthermore, allies do not cooperate at the mere desire of those who are actively engaged in fighting; international relations being what they are, such cooperation is often furnished only at some later stage or increased only when a balance has been disturbed and needs correction.

In many cases, the proportion of the means of resistance that cannot immediately be brought to bear is much higher than might at first be thought. Even when great strength has been expended on the first decision and the balance has been badly upset, equilibrium can be restored. The point will be more fully treated in due course. At this stage it is enough to show that the very nature of war impedes the *simultaneous concentration of all forces*. To be sure, that fact in itself cannot be grounds for making any but a maximum effort to obtain the first decision, for a defeat is always a disadvantage no one would deliberately risk. And even if the first clash is not the only one, the influence it has on subsequent actions will be on a scale proportionate to its own. But it is contrary to human nature to make an extreme effort, and the tendency therefore is always to plead that a decision may be possible later on. As a result, for the first decision, effort and concentration of forces are not all they might be. Anything omitted out of weakness by one side becomes a real, *objective* reason for the other to reduce its efforts, and the tendency toward extremes is once again reduced by this interaction.

9. *In war the result is never final*

Lastly, even the ultimate outcome of a war is not always to be regarded as final. The defeated state often considers the outcome merely as a transitory evil, for which a remedy may still be found in political conditions at some later date. It is obvious how this, too, can slacken tension and reduce the vigor of the effort.

10. *The probabilities of real life replace the extreme and the absolute required by theory*

Warfare thus eludes the strict theoretical requirement that extremes of force be applied. Once the extreme is no longer feared or aimed at, it becomes a matter of judgment what degree of effort should be made; and this can only be based on the phenomena of the real world and the *laws of probability*. Once the antagonists have ceased to be mere figments of a theory and become actual states and governments, when war is no longer a theoretical affair but a series of actions obeying its own peculiar laws, reality supplies the data from which we can deduce the unknown that lies ahead.

From the enemy's character, from his institutions, the state of his affairs and his general situation, each side, using the *laws of probability*, forms an estimate of its opponent's likely course and acts accordingly.

11. *The political object now comes to the fore again*

A subject which we last considered in Section 2 now forces itself on us again, namely the *political object of the war*. Hitherto it had been rather overshadowed by the law of extremes, the will to overcome the enemy and make him powerless. But as this law begins to lose its force and as this determination wanes, the political aim will reassert itself. If it is all a calculation of probabilities based on given individuals and conditions, the *political object*, which was the *original motive*, must become an essential factor in the equation. The smaller the penalty you demand from your opponent, the less you can expect him to try and deny it to you; the smaller the effort he makes, the less you need make yourself. Moreover, the more modest your own political aim, the less importance you attach to it and the less reluctantly you will abandon it if you must. *This is another reason why your effort will be modified.*

The political object – the original motive for the war – will thus determine both the military objective to be reached and the amount of effort it requires. The political object cannot, however, *in itself* provide the standard of measurement. Since we are dealing with realities, not with abstractions, it can do so only in the context of the two states at war. The same political object can elicit *differing* reactions from different peoples, and even from the same people at different times. We can therefore take the political object as a standard only if we think of *the influence it can exert upon the forces it is meant to move*. The nature of those forces therefore calls for study. Depending on whether their characteristics increase or diminish the drive toward a particular action, the outcome will vary. Between two peoples and two states there can be such tensions, such a mass of inflammable material, that the slightest quarrel can produce a wholly disproportionate effect – a real explosion.

This is equally true of the efforts a political object is expected to arouse in either state, and of the military objectives which their policies require. Sometimes the *political and military objective is the same* – for example, the conquest of a province. In other cases the political object will not provide a suitable military objective. In that event, another military objective must be adopted that will serve the political purpose and symbolize it in the peace negotiations. But here, too, attention must be paid to the character of each state involved. There are times when, if the political object is to be achieved, the substitute must be a good deal more important. The less involved the population and the less serious the strains within states and between them, the more political requirements in themselves will dominate and tend to be decisive. Situations can thus exist in which the political object will almost be the sole determinant.

Generally speaking, a military objective that matches the political object in scale will, if the latter is reduced, be reduced in proportion; this will be all the more so as the political object increases its predominance. Thus it follows that without any inconsistency wars can have all degrees of importance and intensity, ranging from a war of extermination down to simple armed observation. This brings us to a different question, which now needs to be analyzed and answered.

12.   *An interruption of military activity is not explained by anything yet said*

However modest the political demands may be on either side, however small the means employed, however limited the military objective, can the process of war ever be interrupted, even for a moment? The question reaches deep into the heart of the matter.

Every action needs a certain time to be completed. That period is called its duration, and its length will depend on the speed with which the person acting works. We need not concern ourselves with the difference here. Everyone performs a task in his own way; a slow man, however, does not do it more slowly because he wants to spend more time over it, but because his nature causes him to need more time. If he made more haste he would do the job less well. His speed, then, is determined by subjective causes and is a factor in the actual duration of the task.

Now if every action in war is allowed its appropriate duration, we would agree that, at least at first sight, any additional expenditure of time – any suspension of military action – seems absurd. In this connection it must be remembered that what we are talking about is not the progress made by one side or the other but the progress of military interaction as a whole.

13. Only one consideration can suspend military action, and it seems that it can never be present on more than one side

If two parties have prepared for war, some motive of hostility must have brought them to that point. Moreover so long as they remain under arms (do not negotiate a settlement) that motive of hostility must still be active. Only one consideration can restrain it: *a desire to wait for a better moment before acting*. At first sight one would think this desire could never operate on more than one side since its opposite must automatically be working on the other. If action would bring an advantage to one side, the other's interest must be to wait.

But an absolute balance of forces cannot bring about a standstill, for if such a balance should exist the initiative would necessarily belong to the side with the positive purpose – the attacker.

One could, however, conceive of a state of balance in which the side with the positive aim (the side with the stronger grounds for action) was the one that had the weaker forces. The balance would then result from the combined effects of aim and strength. Were that the case, one would have to say that unless some shift in the balance were in prospect the two sides should make peace. If, however, some alteration were to be foreseen, only one side could expect to gain by it – a fact which ought to stimulate the other into action. Inaction clearly cannot be explained by the concept of balance. The only explanation is that both are waiting for a better time to act. Let us suppose, therefore, that one of the two states has a positive aim – say, the conquest of a part of the other's territory, to use for bargaining at the peace table. Once the prize is in its hands, the political object has been achieved; there is no need to do more, and it can let matters rest. If the other state is ready to accept the situation, it should sue for peace. If not, it must do something; and if it thinks it will be better organized for action in four weeks' time it clearly has an adequate reason for not taking action at once.

But from that moment on, logic would seem to call for action by the other side – the object being to deny the enemy the time he needs for getting ready. Throughout all this I have assumed, of course, that both sides understand the situation perfectly.

14. Continuity would thus be brought about in military action and would again intensify everything

If this continuity were really to exist in the campaign its effect would again be to drive everything to extremes. Not only would such ceaseless activity arouse men's feelings and inject them with more passion and elemental strength, but events would follow more closely on each other and be governed by a stricter causal chain. Each individual action would be more important, and consequently more dangerous.

But war, of course, seldom if ever shows such continuity. In numerous conflicts only a very small part of the time is occupied by action, while the rest is spent in inactivity. This cannot always be an anomaly. Suspension of action in war must be possible; in other words, it is not a contradiction in terms. Let me demonstrate this point, and explain the reasons for it.

15. Here a principle of polarity is proposed

By thinking that the interests of the two commanders are opposed in equal measure to each other, we have assumed a genuine *polarity*. A whole chapter will be devoted to the subject further on, but the following must be said about it here.

The principle of polarity is valid only in relation to one and the same object, in which positive and negative interests exactly cancel one another out. In a battle each side aims at victory; that is a case of true polarity, since the victory of one side excludes the victory of the other. When, however, we are dealing with two different things that have a common relation external to themselves, the polarity lies not in the *things* but in their relationship.

16. Attack and defense being things different in kind and unequal in strength, polarity cannot be applied to them

If war assumed only a single form, namely, attacking the enemy, and defense were nonexistent; or, to put it in another way, if the only differences between attack and defense lay in the fact that attack has a positive aim whereas defense has not, and the forms of fighting were identical; then every advantage gained by one side would be a precisely equal disadvantage to the other – true polarity would exist.

But there are two distinct forms of action in war: attack and defense. As will be shown in detail later, the two are very different and unequal in strength. Polarity, then, does not lie in attack or defense, but in the object both seek to achieve: the decision. If one commander wants to postpone the decision, the other must want to hasten it, always assuming that both are engaged in the same kind of fighting. If it is in A's interest not to attack B now but to attack him in four weeks, then it is in B's interest not to be attacked in four weeks' time, but now. This is an immediate and direct conflict of interest; but it does not follow from this that it would also be to B's advantage to make an immediate attack on A. That would obviously be quite another matter.

17. The superiority of defense over attack often destroys the effect of polarity, and this explains the suspension of military action

As we shall show, defense is a stronger form of fighting than attack. Consequently we must ask whether the advantage of *postponing a decision* is as great for one side as the advantage of *defense* is for the other. Whenever it is not, it cannot balance the advantage of defense and in this way influence the progress of the war. It is clear, then, that the impulse created by the polarity of interests may be exhausted in the difference between the strength of attack and defense, and may thus become inoperative.

Consequently, if the side favored by present conditions is not sufficiently strong to do without the added advantages of the defense, it will have to accept the prospect of acting under unfavorable conditions in the future. To fight a defensive battle under these less favorable conditions may still be better than to attack immediately or to make peace. I am convinced that the superiority of the defense (if rightly understood) is very great, far greater than appears at first sight. It is this which explains without any inconsistency most periods of inaction that occur in war. The weaker the motives for action, the more will they be overlaid and neutralized by this disparity between attack and defense, and the more frequently will action be suspended – as indeed experience shows.

18. A second cause is imperfect knowledge of the situation

There is still another factor that can bring military action to a standstill: imperfect knowledge of the situation. The only situation a commander can know fully is his own; his opponent's he can know only from unreliable intelligence. His evaluation, therefore, may be mistaken and can lead him to suppose that the initiative lies with the enemy when in fact it remains with him. Of course such faulty appreciation is as likely to lead to ill-timed action as to ill-timed inaction, and is no more conducive to slowing down operations than it is to speeding them up. Nevertheless, it must rank among the natural causes which, *without entailing inconsistency, can bring military activity to a halt.* Men are always more inclined to pitch their estimate of the enemy's strength too high than too low, such is human nature. Bearing this in mind, one must admit that partial ignorance of the situation is, generally speaking, a major factor in delaying the progress of military action and in moderating the principle that underlies it.

The possibility of inaction has a further moderating effect on the progress of the war by diluting it, so to speak, in time by delaying danger, and by increasing the means of restoring a balance between the two sides. The greater the tensions that have led to war, and the greater the consequent war effort, the shorter these periods of inaction. Inversely, the weaker the motive for conflict, the longer the intervals between actions. For the stronger motive increases willpower, and willpower, as we know, is always both an element in and the product of strength.

19. Frequent periods of inaction remove war still further from the realm of the absolute and make it even more a matter of assessing probabilities

The slower the progress and the more frequent the interruptions of military action the easier it is to retrieve a mistake, the bolder will be the general's assessments, and the more likely he will be to avoid theoretical extremes and to base his plans on probability and inference. Any given situation requires that probabilities be calculated in the light of circumstances, and the amount of time available for such calculation will depend on the pace with which operations are taking place.

20. Therefore only the element of chance is needed to make war a gamble, and that element is never absent

It is now quite clear how greatly the objective nature of war makes it a matter of assessing probabilities. Only one more element is needed to make war a gamble – chance: the very last thing that war lacks. No other human activity is so continuously or universally bound up with chance. And through the element of chance, guesswork and luck come to play a great part in war.

21. Not only its objective but also its subjective nature makes war a gamble

If we now consider briefly the *subjective nature* of war – the means by which war has to be fought – it will look more than ever like a gamble. The element in which war exists is danger. The highest of all moral qualities in time of danger is certainly *courage*. Now courage is perfectly compatible with prudent calculation but the two differ nonetheless, and pertain to different psychological forces. Daring, on the other hand, boldness, rashness, trusting in luck are only variants of courage, and all these traits of character seek their proper element – chance.

In short, absolute, so-called mathematical, factors never find a firm basis in military calculations. From the very start there is an interplay of possibilities, probabilities, good luck and bad that weaves its way throughout the length and breadth of the tapestry. In the whole range of human activities, war most closely resembles a game of cards.

22. How in general this best suits human nature

Although our intellect always longs for clarity and certainty, our nature often finds uncertainty fascinating. It prefers to day-dream in the realms of chance and luck rather than accompany the intellect on its narrow and tortuous path of philosophical enquiry and logical deduction only to arrive – hardly knowing how – in unfamiliar surroundings where all the usual landmarks seem to have disappeared. Unconfined by narrow necessity, it can revel in a wealth of possibilities; which inspire courage to take wing and dive into the element of daring and danger like a fearless swimmer into the current.

Should theory leave us here, and cheerfully go on elaborating absolute conclusions and prescriptions? Then it would be no use at all in real life. No, it must also take the human factor into account, and find room for courage, boldness, even foolhardiness. The art of war deals with living and with moral forces. Consequently, it cannot attain the absolute, or certainty; it must always leave a margin for uncertainty, in the greatest things as much as in the smallest. With uncertainty in one scale, courage and self-confidence must be thrown into the other to correct the balance. The greater they are, the greater the margin that can be left for accidents. Thus courage and self-confidence are essential in war, and theory should propose only rules that give ample scope to these finest and least dispensable of military virtues, in all their degrees and variations. Even in daring there can be method and caution; but here they are measured by a different standard.

23. But war is nonetheless a serious means to a serious end: a more precise definition of war

Such is war, such is the commander who directs it, and such the theory that governs it. War is no pastime; it is no mere joy in daring and winning, no place for irresponsible enthusiasts. It is a serious means to a serious end, and all its colorful resemblance to a game of chance, all the vicissitudes of passion, courage, imagination, and enthusiasm it includes are merely its special characteristics.

When whole communities go to war – whole peoples, and especially *civilized* peoples – the reason always lies in some political situation, and the occasion is always due to some political object. War, therefore, is an act of policy. Were it a complete, untrammeled, absolute manifestation of violence (as the pure concept would require), war would of its own independent will usurp the place of policy the moment policy had brought it into being; it would then drive policy out of office and rule by the laws of its own nature, very much like a mine that can explode only in the manner or direction predetermined by the setting. This, in fact, is the view that has been taken of the matter whenever some discord between policy and the conduct of war has stimulated theoretical distinctions of this kind. But in reality things are different, and this view is thoroughly mistaken. In reality war, as has been shown, is not like that. Its violence is not of the kind that explodes in a single discharge, but is the effect of forces that do not always develop in exactly the same manner or to the same degree. At times they will expand sufficiently to overcome the resistance of inertia or friction; at others they are too weak to have any effect. War is a pulsation of violence, variable in strength and therefore variable in the speed with which it explodes and discharges its energy. War moves on its goal with varying speeds; but it always lasts long enough for influence to be exerted on the goal and for its own course to be changed in one way or another – long enough, in other words, to remain subject to the action of a superior intelligence. If we keep in mind that war springs from some political purpose, it is natural that the prime cause of its existence will remain the supreme consideration in conducting it. That, however, does not imply that the political aim is a tyrant. It must adapt itself to its chosen means, a process which can radically change it; yet the political aim remains the first consideration. Policy, then, will permeate all military operations, and, in so far as their violent nature will admit, it will have a continuous influence on them.

24. *War is merely the continuation of policy by other means*

We see, therefore, that war is not merely an act of policy but a true political instrument, a continuation of political intercourse, carried on with other means. What remains peculiar to war is simply the peculiar nature of its means. War in general, and the commander in any specific instance, is entitled to require that the trend and designs of policy shall not be inconsistent with these means. That, of course, is no small demand; but however much it may affect political aims in a given case, it will never do more than modify them. The political object is the goal, war is the means of reaching it, and means can never be considered in isolation from their purpose.

25. *The diverse nature of war*

The more powerful and inspiring the motives for war, the more they affect the belligerent nations and the fiercer the tensions that precede the outbreak, the closer will war approach its abstract concept, the more important will be the destruction of the enemy, the more closely will the military aims and the political objects of war coincide, and the more military and less political will war appear to be. On the other hand, the less intense the motives, the less will the military element's natural tendency to violence coincide with political directives. As a result, war will be driven further from its natural course, the political object will be more and more at variance with the aim of ideal war, and the conflict will seem increasingly *political* in character.

At this point, to prevent the reader from going astray, it must be observed that the phrase, the *natural tendency* of war, is used in its philosophical, strictly *logical* sense alone and does not refer to the tendencies of the forces that are actually engaged in fighting – including, for instance, the morale and emotions of the combatants. At times, it is true, these might be so aroused that the political factor would be hard put to control them. Yet such a conflict will not occur very often, for if the motivations are so powerful there must be a policy of proportionate magnitude. On the other hand, if policy is directed only toward minor objectives, the emotions of the masses will be little stirred and they will have to be stimulated rather than held back.

26. *All wars can be considered acts of policy*

It is time to return to the main theme and observe that while policy is apparently effaced in the one kind of war and yet is strongly evident in the other, both kinds are equally political. If the state is thought of as a person, and policy as the product of its brain, then among the contingencies for which the state must be prepared is a war in which every element calls for policy to be eclipsed by violence. Only if politics is regarded not as resulting from a just appreciation of affairs, but – as it conventionally is – as cautious, devious, even dishonest, shying away from force, could the second type of war appear to be more 'political' than the first.

27. The effects of this point of view on the understanding of military history and the foundations of theory

First, therefore, it is clear that war should never be thought of as *something autonomous* but always as an *instrument of policy*; otherwise the entire history of war would contradict us. Only this approach will enable us to penetrate the problem intelligently. *Second*, this way of looking at it will show us how wars must vary with the nature of their motives and of the situations which give rise to them.

The first, the supreme, the most far-reaching act of judgment that the statesman and commander have to make is to establish by that test the kind of war on which they are embarking; neither mistaking it for, nor trying to turn it into, something that is alien to its nature. This is the first of all strategic questions and the most comprehensive. It will be given detailed study later, in the chapter on war plans.

It is enough, for the moment, to have reached this stage and to have established the cardinal point of view from which war and the theory of war have to be examined.

28. The consequences for theory

War is more than a true chameleon that slightly adapts its characteristics to the given case. As a total phenomenon its dominant tendencies always make war a paradoxical trinity – composed of primordial violence, hatred, and enmity, which are to be regarded as a blind natural force; of the play of chance and probability within which the creative spirit is free to roam, and of its element of subordination, as an instrument of policy, which makes it subject to reason alone.

The first of these three aspects mainly concerns the people; the second the commander and his army; the third the government. The passions that are to be kindled in war must already be inherent in the people; the scope which the play of courage and talent will enjoy in the realm of probability and chance depends on the particular character of the commander and the army; but the political aims are the business of government alone.

These three tendencies are like three different codes of law, deep-rooted in their subject and yet variable in their relationship to one another. A theory that ignores any one of them or seeks to fix an arbitrary relationship between them would conflict with reality to such an extent that for this reason alone it would be totally useless

Our task therefore is to develop a theory that maintains a balance between these three tendencies, like an object suspended between three magnets.

What lines might best be followed to achieve this difficult task will be explored in the book on the theory of war [Book Two]. At any rate, the preliminary concept of war which we have formulated casts a first ray of light on the basic

structure of theory, and enables us to make an initial differentiation and identification of its major components.

[. . .]

Chapter Seven: Friction in war

If one has never personally experienced war, one cannot understand in what the
difficulties constantly mentioned really consist, nor why a commander should
need any brilliance and exceptional ability. Everything looks simple; the
knowledge required does not look remarkable, the strategic options are so
obvious that by comparison the simplest problem of higher mathematics has an
impressive scientific dignity. Once war has actually been seen the difficulties
become clear; but it is still extremely hard to describe the unseen, all-pervading
element that brings about this change of perspective.

Everything in war is very simple, but the simplest thing is difficult. The difficulties accumulate and end by producing a kind of friction that is inconceivable
unless one has experienced war. Imagine a traveler who late in the day decides
to cover two more stages before nightfall. Only four or five hours more, on a
paved highway with relays of horses: it should be an easy trip. But at the next
station he finds no fresh horses, or only poor ones; the country grows hilly, the
road bad, night falls, and finally after many difficulties he is only too glad to
reach a resting place with any kind of primitive accommodation. It is much
the same in war. Countless minor incidents – the kind you can never really
foresee – combine to lower the general level of performance, so that one always
falls far short of the intended goal. Iron will-power can overcome this friction;
it pulverizes every obstacle, but of course it wears down the machine as well. We
shall often return to this point. The proud spirit's firm will dominates the art of
war as an obelisk dominates the town square on which all roads converge.

Friction is the only concept that more or less corresponds to the factors that
distinguish real war from war on paper. The military machine – the army and
everthing related to it – is basically very simple and therefore seems easy to
manage. But we should bear in mind that none of its components is of one piece:
each part is composed of individuals, every one of whom retains his potential
of friction. In theory it sounds reasonable enough: a battalion commander's duty
is to carry out his orders; discipline welds the battalion together, its commander
must be a man of tested capacity, and so the great beam turns on its iron pivot
with a minimum of friction. In fact, it is different, and every fault and exaggera-
tion of the theory is instantly exposed in war. A battalion is made up of
individuals, the least important of whom may chance to delay things or
somehow make them go wrong. The dangers inseparable from war and the
physical exertions war demands can aggravate the problem to such an extent
that they must be ranked among its principal causes.

This tremendous friction, which cannot, as in mechanics, be reduced to a few
points, is everywhere in contact with chance, and brings about effects that
cannot be measured, just because they are largely due to chance. One, for

example, is the weather. Fog can prevent the enemy from being seen in time, a gun from firing when it should, a report from reaching the commanding officer. Rain can prevent a battalion from arriving, make another late by keeping it not three but eight hours on the march, ruin a cavalry charge by bogging the horses down in mud, etc.

We give these examples simply for illustration, to help the reader follow the argument. It would take volumes to cover all difficulties. We could exhaust the reader with illustrations alone if we really tried to deal with the whole range of minor troubles that must be faced in war. The few we have given will be excused by those readers who have long since understood what we are after.

Action in war is like movement in a resistant element. Just as the simplest and most natural of movements, walking, cannot easily be performed in water, so in war it is difficult for normal efforts to achieve even moderate results. A genuine theorist is like a swimming teacher, who makes his pupils practice motions on land that are meant to be performed in water. To those who are not thinking of swimming the motions will appear grotesque and exaggerated. By the same token, theorists who have never swum, or who have not learned to generalize from experience, are impractical and even ridiculous: they teach only what is already common knowledge: how to walk.

Moreover, every war is rich in unique episodes. Each is an uncharted sea, full of reefs. The commander may suspect the reefs' existence without ever having seen them; now he has to steer past them in the dark. If a contrary wind springs up, if some major mischance appears, he will need the greatest skill and personal exertion, and the utmost presence of mind, though from a distance everything may seem to be proceeding automatically. An understanding of friction is a large part of that much-admired sense of warfare which a good general is supposed to possess. To be sure, the best general is not the one who is most familiar with the idea of friction, and who takes it most to heart (he belongs to the anxious type so common among experienced commanders). The good general must know friction in order to overcome it whenever possible, and in order not to expect a standard of achievement in his operations which this very friction makes impossible. Incidentally, it is a force that theory can never quite define. Even if it could, the development of instinct and tact would still be needed, a form of judgment much more necessary in an area littered by endless minor obstacles than in great, momentous questions, which are settled in solitary deliberation or in discussion with others. As with a man of the world instinct becomes almost habit so that he always acts, speaks, and moves appropriately, so only the experienced officer will make the right decision in major and minor matters – at every pulsebeat of war. Practice and experience dictate the answer: 'this is possible, that is not.' So he rarely makes a serious mistake, such as can, in war, shatter confidence and become extremely dangerous if it occurs often.

Friction, as we choose to call it, is the force that makes the apparently easy so difficult. We shall frequently revert to this subject, and it will become evident that an eminent commander needs more than experience and a strong will. He must have other exceptional abilities as well.

Chapter Eight: Concluding observations on Book One

We have identified danger, physical exertion, intelligence, and friction as the elements that coalesce to form the atmosphere of war, and turn it into a medium that impedes activity. In their restrictive effects they can be grouped into a single concept of general friction. Is there any lubricant that will reduce this abrasion? Only one, and a commander and his army will not always have it readily available: combat experience.

Habit hardens the body for great exertions, strengthens the heart in great peril, and fortifies judgment against first impressions. Habit breeds that priceless quality, calm, which, passing from hussar and rifleman up to the general himself, will lighten the commander's task.

In war the experienced soldier reacts rather in the same way as the human eye does in the dark: the pupil expands to admit what little light there is, discerning objects by degrees, and finally seeing them distinctly. By contrast, the novice is plunged into the deepest night.

No general can accustom an army to war. Peacetime maneuvers are a feeble substitute for the real thing; but even they can give an army an advantage over others whose training is confined to routine, mechanical drill. To plan maneuvers so that some of the elements of friction are involved, which will train officers' judgment, common sense, and resolution is far more worthwhile than inexperienced people might think. It is immensely important that no soldier, whatever his rank, should wait for war to expose him to those aspects of active service that amaze and confuse him when he first comes across them. If he has met them even once before, they will begin to be familiar to him. This is true even of physical effort. Exertions must be practiced, and the mind must be made even more familiar with them than the body. When exceptional efforts are required of him in war, the recruit is apt to think that they result from mistakes, miscalculations, and confusion at the top. In consequence, his morale is doubly depressed. If maneuvers prepare him for exertions, this will not occur.

Another very useful, though more limited, way of gaining familiarity with war in peacetime is to attract foreign officers who have seen active service. Peace does not often reign everywhere in Europe, and never throughout the whole world. A state that has been at peace for many years should try to attract some experienced officers – only those, of course, who have distinguished themselves. Alternatively, some of its own officers should be sent to observe operations, and learn what war is like.

However few such officers may be in proportion to an army, their influence can be very real. Their experience, their insights, and the maturity of their character will affect their subordinates and brother officers. Even when they cannot be given high command they should be considered as guides who know the country and can be consulted in specific eventualities.

12

MARX AND ENGELS

Sources: *Selected Works in One Volume*. London, Lawrence &
Wishart, 1988, *Communist Manifesto*, pp. 35–40; 62–3; Preface to
A Contribution to the Critique of Political Economy, pp. 182–3.
L.D. Easton and K.H. Guddat (eds) (1967) *Writings of the Young
Marx*. Garden City, NY, Anchor Books, Doubleday, pp. 408–16.

Marx and Engels regard economic relations as the basis of social and historical
development. Political relations – both international and national – are conditioned by changes in the material productive relations of society. This is their
doctrine of historical materialism which is taken up by later Marxists such as
Lenin, Hilferding and Gramsci. Marx argues that the capitalist economic system
is just one historical form of production which will ultimately be succeeded by
a higher socialist form. Marx and Engels concede the superiority of capitalism
to previous modes of production. They marvel at the immense wealth it creates.
In particular, they point to the way in which capitalism brings together world
society through trade and makes possible one world culture. But Marx and
Engels saw capitalism, in an analogous way to feudalism, as subject to internal
pressures which would lead to its collapse. They pointed to the tendency of
capitalism to overproduce. They also noted the high levels of unemployment to
which capitalist states were periodically subject. Above all they pointed to the
alienated condition of the working class which was to them a class which did not
recognize national boundaries and loyalties. Marx and Engels pinned their
hopes for international peace upon the workers of the world.

COMMUNIST MANIFESTO

Bourgeois and proletarians

The history of all hitherto existing society is the history of class struggles.

Freeman and slave, patrician and plebeian, lord and serf, guild-master and journeyman, in a word, oppressor and oppressed, stood in constant opposition to one another, carried on an uninterrupted, now hidden, now open fight, a fight that each time ended, either in a revolutionary re-constitution of society at large, or in the common ruin of the contending classes.

In the earlier epochs of history, we find almost everywhere a complicated arrangement of society into various orders, a manifold gradation of social rank. In ancient Rome we have patricians, knights, plebeians, slaves; in the Middle Ages, feudal lords, vassals, guild-masters, journeymen, apprentices, serfs; in almost all of these classes, again, subordinate gradations.

The modern bourgeois society that has sprouted from the ruins of feudal society has not done away with class antagonisms. It has but established new classes, new conditions of oppression, new forms of struggle in place of the old ones.

Our epoch, the epoch of the bourgeoisie, possesses, however, this distinctive feature: it has simplified the class antagonisms. Society as a whole is more and more splitting up into two great hostile camps, into two great classes directly facing each other: Bourgeoisie and Proletariat.

From the serfs of the Middle Ages sprang the chartered burghers of the earliest towns. From these burgesses the first elements of the bourgeoisie were developed.

The discovery of America, the rounding of the Cape, opened up fresh ground for the rising bourgeoisie. The East-Indian and Chinese markets, the colonisation of America, trade with the colonies, the increase in the means of exchange and in commodities generally, gave to commerce, to navigation, to industry, an impulse never before known, and thereby, to the revolutionary element in the tottering feudal society, a rapid development.

The feudal system of industry, under which industrial production was monopolised by closed guilds, now no longer sufficed for the growing wants of the new markets. The manufacturing system took its place. The guild-masters were pushed on one side by the manufacturing middle class; division of labour between the different corporate guilds vanished in the face of division of labour in each single workshop.

Meantime the markets kept ever growing, the demand ever rising. Even manufacture no longer sufficed. Thereupon, steam and machinery revolutionised industrial production. The place of manufacture was taken by the giant, Modern Industry, the place of the industrial middle class, by industrial millionaires, the leaders of whole industrial armies, the modern bourgeois.

Modern industry has established the world-market for which the discovery of America paved the way. This market has given an immense development to commerce, to navigation, to communication by land. This development has, in its turn, reacted on the extension of industry; and in proportion as industry, commerce, navigation, railways extended, in the same proportion the bourgeoisie developed, increased its capital, and pushed into the background every class handed down from the Middle Ages.

We see, therefore, how the modern bourgeoisie is itself the product of a long course of development, of a series of revolutions in the modes of production and of exchange.

Each step in the development of the bourgeoisie was accompanied by a corresponding political advance of that class. An oppressed class under the sway of the feudal nobility, an armed and self-governing association in the mediaeval commune; here independent urban republic (as in Italy and Germany), there taxable 'third estate' of the monarchy (as in France), afterwards, in the period of manufacture proper, serving either the semi-feudal or the absolute monarchy as a counterpoise against the nobility, and, in fact, corner-stone of the great monarchies in general, the bourgeoisie has at last, since the establishment of Modern Industry and of the world-market, conquered for itself, in the modern representative State, exclusive political sway. The executive of the modern State is but a committee for managing the common affairs of the whole bourgeoisie.

The bourgeoisie, historically, has played a most revolutionary part.

The bourgeoisie, wherever it has got the upper hand, has put an end to all feudal, patriarchal, idyllic relations. It has pitilessly torn asunder the motley feudal ties that bound man to his 'natural superiors,' and has left remaining no other nexus between man and man than naked self-interest, than callous 'cash payment.' It has drowned the most heavenly ecstasies of religious fervour, of chivalrous enthusiasm, of philistine sentimentalism, in the icy water of egotistical calculation. It has resolved personal worth into exchange value, and in place of the numberless indefeasible chartered freedoms, has set up that single, unconscionable freedom – Free Trade. In one word, for exploitation, veiled by religious and political illusions, it has substituted naked, shameless, direct, brutal exploitation.

The bourgeoisie has stripped of its halo every occupation hitherto honoured and looked up to with reverent awe. It has converted the physician, the lawyer, the priest, the poet, the man of science, into its paid wage-labourers.

The bourgeoisie has torn away from the family its sentimental veil, and has reduced the family relation to a mere money relation.

The bourgeoisie has disclosed how it came to pass that the brutal display of vigour in the Middle Ages, which Reactionists so much admire, found its fitting complement in the most slothful indolence. It has been the first to show what man's activity can bring about. It has accomplished wonders far surpassing Egyptian pyramids, Roman aqueducts, and Gothic cathedrals; it has conducted expeditions that put in the shade all former Exoduses of nations and crusades.

The bourgeoisie cannot exist without constantly revolutionising the instruments of production, and thereby the relations of production, and with them the whole relations of society. Conservation of the old modes of production in unaltered form, was, on the contrary, the first condition of existence for all earlier industrial classes. Constant revolutionising of production, uninterrupted disturbance of all social conditions, everlasting uncertainty and agitation distinguish the bourgeois epoch from all earlier ones. All fixed, fast-frozen relations, with their train of ancient and venerable prejudices and opinions, are swept away, all newformed ones become antiquated before they can ossify. All that is solid melts into air, all that is holy is profaned, and man is at last compelled to face with sober senses, his real conditions of life, and his relations with his kind.

The need of a constantly expanding market for its products chases the bourgeoisie over the whole surface of the globe. It must nestle everywhere, settle everywhere, establish connexions everywhere.

The bourgeoisie has through its exploitation of the world-market given a cosmopolitan character to production and consumption in every country. To the great chagrin of Reactionists, it has drawn from under the feet of industry the national ground on which it stood. All old-established national industries have been destroyed or are daily being destroyed. They are dislodged by new industries, whose introduction becomes a life and death question for all civilised nations, by industries that no longer work up indigenous raw material, but raw material drawn from the remotest zones; industries whose products are consumed, not only at home, but in every quarter of the globe. In place of the old wants, satisfied by the productions of the country, we find new wants, requiring for their satisfaction the products of distant lands and climes. In place of the old local and national seclusion and self-sufficiency, we have intercourse in every direction, universal inter-dependence of nations. And as in material, so also in intellectual production. The intellectual creations of individual nations become common property. National one-sidedness and narrow-mindedness become more and more impossible, and from the numerous national and local literatures, there arises a world literature.

The bourgeoisie, by the rapid improvement of all instruments of production, by the immensely facilitated means of communication, draws all, even the most barbarian, nations into civilisation. The cheap prices of its commodities are the heavy artillery with which it batters down all Chinese walls, with which it forces the barbarians' intensely obstinate hatred of foreigners to capitulate. It compels all nations, on pain of extinction, to adopt the bourgeois mode of production; it compels them to introduce what it calls civilisation into their midst, i.e., to become bourgeois themselves. In one word, it creates a world after its own image.

The bourgeoisie has subjected the country to the rule of the towns. It has created enormous cities, has greatly increased the urban population as compared with the rural, and has thus rescued a considerable part of the population from the idiocy of rural life. Just as it has made the country dependent on the towns, so it has made barbarian and semi-barbarian countries dependent on the civilised ones, nations of peasants on nations of bourgeois, the East on the West.

The bourgeoisie keeps more and more doing away with the scattered state of

the population, of the means of production, and of property. It has agglome-
rated population, centralised means of production, and has concentrated
property in a few hands. The necessary consequence of this was political cen-
tralisation. Independent, or but loosely connected provinces, with separate
interests, laws, governments and systems of taxation, became lumped together
into one nation, with one government, one code of laws, one national class-
interest, one frontier and one customs-tariff.

The bourgeoisie, during its rule of scarce one hundred years, has created more
massive and more colossal productive forces than have all preceding generations
together. Subjection of Nature's forces to man, machinery, application of
chemistry to industry and agriculture, steam-navigation, railways, electric tele-
graphs, clearing of whole continents for cultivation, canalisation of rivers,
whole populations conjured out of the ground – what earlier century had even
a presentiment that such productive forces slumbered in the lap of social labour?

We see then: the means of production and of exchange, on whose foundation
the bourgeoisie built itself up, were generated in feudal society. At a certain stage
in the development of these means of production and of exchange, the conditions
under which feudal society produced and exchanged, the feudal organisation of
agriculture and manufacturing industry, in one word, the feudal relations of property became no longer compatible with the already developed productive
forces; they became so many fetters. They had to be burst asunder; they were
burst asunder.

Into their place stepped free competition, accompanied by a social and
political constitution adapted to it, and by the economical and political sway of
the bourgeois class.

[. . .]

Position of the Communists in relation to the various existing
opposition parties

Section II has made clear the relations of the Communists to the existing
working-class parties, such as the Chartists in England and the Agrarian
Reformers in America.

The Communists fight for the attainment of the immediate aims, for the
enforcement of the momentary interests of the working class; but in the movement of the present, they also represent and take care of the future of that movement. In France the Communists ally themselves with the Social-Democrats,
against the conservative and radical bourgeoisie, reserving, however, the right
to take up a critical position in regard to phrases and illusions traditionally
handed down from the great Revolution.

In Switzerland they support the Radicals, without losing sight of the fact that
this party consists of antagonistic elements, partly of Democratic Socialists, in
the French sense, partly of radical bourgeois.

In Poland they support the party that insists on an agrarian revolution as the prime condition for national emancipation, that party which fomented the insurrection of Cracow in 1846.

In Germany they fight with the bourgeoisie whenever it acts in a revolutionary way, against the absolute monarchy, the feudal squirearchy, and the petty bourgeoisie.

But they never cease, for a single instant, to instil into the working class the clearest possible recognition of the hostile antagonism between bourgeoisie and proletariat, in order that the German workers may straightway use, as so many weapons against the bourgeoisie, the social and political conditions that the bourgeoisie must necessarily introduce along with its supremacy, and in order that, after the fall of the reactionary classes in Germany, the fight against the bourgeoisie itself may immediately begin.

The Communists turn their attention chiefly to Germany, because that country is on the eve of a bourgeois revolution that it bound to be carried out under more advanced conditions of European civilisation, and with a much more developed proletariat, than that of England was in the seventeenth, and of France in the eighteenth century, and because the bourgeois revolution in Germany will be but the prelude to an immediately following proletariat revolution.

In short, the Communists everywhere support every revolutionary movement against the existing social and political order of things.

In all these movements they bring to the front, as the leading question in each, the property question, no matter what its degree of development at the time.

Finally, they labour everywhere for the union and agreement of the democratic parties of all countries.

The Communists disdain to conceal their views and aims. They openly declare that their ends can be attained only by the forcible overthrow of all existing social conditions. Let the ruling classes tremble at a Communistic revolution. The proletarians have nothing to lose but their chains. They have a world to win.

WORKING MEN OF ALL COUNTRIES, UNITE!

[. . .]

CRITIQUE OF POLITICAL ECONOMY

The general result at which I arrived and which, once won, served as a guiding thread for my studies, can be briefly formulated as follows: In the social production of their life, men enter into definite relations that are indispensable and independent of their will, relations of production which correspond to a definite stage of development of their material productive forces. The sum total of these relations of production constitutes the economic structure of society, the real foundation, on which rises a legal and political superstructure and to which correspond definite forms of social consciousness. The mode of production of material life conditions the social, political and intellectual life process in general. It is not the consciousness of men that determines their being, but, on the contrary, their social being that determines their consciousness. At a certain stage of their development, the material productive forces of society come in conflict with the existing relations of production, or – what is but a legal expression for the same thing – with the property relations within which they have been at work hitherto. From forms of development of the productive forces these relations turn into their fetters. Then begins an epoch of social revolution. With the change of the economic foundation the entire immense superstructure is more or less rapidly transformed. In considering such transformations a distinction should always be made between the material transformation of the economic conditions of production, which can be determined with the precision of natural science, and the legal, political, religious, aesthetic or philosophic – in short, ideological forms in which men become conscious of this conflict and fight it out. Just as our opinion of an individual is not based on what he thinks of himself, so can we not judge of such a period of transformation by its own consciousness; on the contrary, this consciousness must be explained rather from the contradictions of material life, from the existing conflict between the social productive forces and the relations of production. No social order ever perishes before all the productive forces for which there is room in it have developed; and new, higher relations of production never appear before the material conditions of their existence have matured in the womb of the old society itself. Therefore mankind always sets itself only such tasks as it can solve; since, looking at the matter more closely, it will always be found that the task itself arises only when the material conditions for its solution already exist or are at least in the process of formation. In broad outlines Asiatic, ancient, feudal, and modern bourgeois modes of production can be designated as progressive epochs in the economic formation of society. The bourgeois relations of production are the last antagonistic form of the social process of production – antagonistic not in the sense of individual antagonism, but of one arising from the social conditions of life of the individuals; at the same time the productive forces developing in the womb of bourgeois society create the material conditions for the solution of that antagonism. This social formation brings, therefore, the prehistory of human society to a close.

[. . .]

WRITINGS OF THE YOUNG MARX

1. Ideology in general, especially German philosophy

We know only one science, the science of history. History can be viewed from two sides: it can be divided into the history of nature and that of man. The two sides, however, are not to be seen as independent entities. As long as man has existed, nature and man have affected each other. The history of nature, so-called natural history, does not concern us here at all. But we will have to discuss the history of man, since almost all ideology amounts to either a distorted interpretation of this history or a complete abstraction from it. Ideology itself is only one of the sides of this history.

The premises from which we start are not arbitrary; they are not dogmas but rather actual premises from which abstraction can be made only in imagination. They are the real individuals, their actions, and their material conditions of life, those which they find existing as well as those which they produce through their actions. These premises can be substantiated in a purely empirical way.

The first premise of all human history, of course, is the existence of living human individuals. The first *historical* act of these individuals, the act by which they distinguish themselves from animals is not the fact that they think but the fact that they begin to *produce their means of subsistence*. The first fact to be established, then, is the physical organisation of these individuals and their consequent relationship to the rest of nature. Of course, we cannot discuss here the physical nature of man or the natural conditions in which man finds himself – geological, orohydrographical, climatic, and others. These relationships affect not only the original and natural organisation of men, especially as to race, but also his entire further development or non-development up to the present. All historiography must proceed from these natural bases and their modification in the course of history through the actions of men.

Man can be distinguished from the animal by consciousness, religion, or anything else you please. He begins to distinguish himself from the animal the moment he begins to *produce* his means of subsistence, a step required by his physical organisation. By producing food, man indirectly produces his material life itself.

The way in which man produces his food depends first of all on the nature of the means of subsistence that he finds and has to reproduce. This mode of production must not be viewed simply as reproduction of the physical existence of individuals. Rather it is a definite form of their activity, a definite way of expressing their life, a definite *mode of life*. As individuals express their life, so they are. What they are, therefore, coincides with what they produce, with *what* they produce and *how* they produce. The nature of individuals thus depends on the material conditions which determine their production.

This production begins with *population growth* which in turn presupposes *interaction* [*Verkehr*] among individuals. The form of such interaction is again determined by production.

The relations of various nations with one another depend upon the extent to which each of them has developed its productive forces, the division of labour, and domestic commerce. This proposition is generally accepted. But not only the relation of one nation to others, but also the entire internal structure of the nation itself depends on the stage of development achieved by its production and its domestic and international commerce. How far the productive forces of a nation are developed is shown most evidently by the degree to which the division of labour has been developed. Each new productive force, in so far as it is not only a quantitative extension of productive forces already known (e.g. cultivation of land) will bring about a further development of the division of labour.

The division of labour in a nation leads first of all to the separation of industrial–commercial labour from agricultural labour and consequently to the separation of *town* and *country* and to a clash of their interests. Its further development leads to the separation of commercial from industrial labour. At the same time, within these various branches, there develop through the division of labour further various divisions among the individuals co-operating in specific kinds of labour. The relative position of these individual groups is determined by the methods employed in agricultural, industrial, and commercial labour (patriarchalism, slavery, estates, classes). The same conditions can be observed in the relations of various nations if commerce has been further developed.

The different stages of development in the division of labour are just so many different forms of ownership; that is, the stage in the division of labour also determines the relations of individuals to one another so far as the material, instrument, and product of labour are concerned.

The first form of ownership is tribal ownership. It corresponds to the undeveloped stage of production where people live by hunting and fishing, by breeding animals or, in the highest stage, by agriculture. Great areas of uncultivated land are required in the latter case. The division of labour at this stage is still very undeveloped and confined to extending the natural division of labour in the family. The social structure thus is limited to an extension of the family: patriarchal family chieftains, below them the members of the tribe, finally the slaves. The slavery latent in the family develops only gradually with the increase in population, the increase of wants, and the extension of external relations in war as well as in barter.

The second form is the ancient communal and state ownership which proceeds especially from the union of several tribes into a *city* by agreement or by conquest; this form is still accompanied by slavery. Alongside communal ownership there already develops movable, and later even immovable, private property, but as an abnormal form subordinate to communal ownership. The citizens hold power over their labouring slaves only in community and are therefore bound to the form of communal ownership. The communal private property of the active citizens compels them to remain in this natural form of association over against their slaves. Hence the whole social structure based on communal ownership and with it the power of the people decline as immovable private property develops. The division of labour is developed to a larger extent. We already find antagonism between town and country and later antagonism between states representing urban interests and those representing rural interests. Within the cities themselves we find the antagonism between industry and maritime commerce. The class relation between citizens and slaves is then fully developed.

With the development of private property we encounter for the first time those conditions which we shall find again with modern private property, only on a larger scale. On the one hand, there is the concentration of private property which began very early in Rome (as proved by the Licinian agrarian law) and proceeded very rapidly from the time of the civil wars and particularly under the emperors. On the other hand, there is linked to this the transformation of the plebeian small peasantry into a proletariat that never achieved an independent development because of its intermediate position between propertied citizens and slaves.

The third form is feudal or estate ownership. Antiquity started out from the *town* and the small territory around it; the Middle Ages started out from the *country*. This different starting-point was caused by the sparse population at that time, scattered over a large area and receiving no large population increase from the conquerors. In contrast to Greece and Rome, the feudal development began in a much larger area, prepared by the Roman conquests and the spreading of agriculture initially connected with these conquests. The last centuries of the declining Roman Empire and its conquest by the barbarians destroyed many productive forces. Agriculture had declined, trade had come to a standstill or had been interrupted by force, and the rural and urban population had decreased. These conditions and the mode of organisation of the conquest determined by them developed feudal property under the influence of the Germanic military constitution. Like tribal and communal ownership, it is based again on a community. While the slaves stood in opposition to the ancient community, here the serfs as the direct producing class stand in opposition. As soon as feudalism is fully developed, there also emerges antagonism to the towns. The hierarchical system of land ownership and the armed bodies of retainers gave the nobility power over the serfs. Like the ancient communal ownership this feudal organisation was an association directed against a subjected producing class. But the form of association and the relation to the direct producers were different because of the different conditions of production.

This feudal organisation of land ownership had its counterpart in the *towns* in the form of corporate property, the feudal organisation of the trades. Property consisted mainly in the labour of each individual. The necessity for association against the organised robber nobility, the need for communal markets in an age when the industrialist was at the same time a merchant, the growing competition of escaped serfs pouring into the rising cities, and the feudal structure of the whole country gave rise to *guilds*. The gradually accumulated capital of individual craftsmen and their stable number in comparison to the growing population produced the relationship of journeyman and apprentice. In the towns, this led to a hierarchy similar to that in the country.

The main form of property during the feudal times consisted on the one hand of landed property with serf labour and on the other hand, individual labour with small capital controlling the labour of journeymen. The organisation of both was determined by the limited conditions of production: small-scale, primitive cultivation of land and industry based on crafts. There was little division of labour when feudalism was at its peak. Every district carried in itself the antagonism of town and country. Though division into estates was strongly marked, there was no division of importance apart from the differentiation of princes, nobility, clergy, and peasants in the country, and masters, journeymen, apprentices, and soon the mob of day labourers in the cities. The strip-system hindered such a division in agriculture; cottage industry of the peasants themselves emerged; and in industry there was no division of labour at all within particular trades, and very little among them. The separation of industry and commerce occurred in older towns, and in newer towns it developed later when they entered into mutual relations.

The merger of larger territories into feudal kingdoms was a necessity for the landed nobility as well as for the cities. The organisation of the ruling class, the nobility, had a monarch at its head in all instances.

The fact is, then, that definite individuals who are productively active in a specific way enter into these definite social and political relations. In each particular instance, empirical observation must show empirically, without any mystification or speculation, the connection of the social and political structure with production. The social structure and the state continually evolve out of the life-process of definite individuals, but individuals not as they may appear in their own or other people's imagination but rather as they *really* are, that is, as they work, produce materially, and act under definite material limitations, presuppositions, and conditions independent of their will.

The ideas which these individuals form are ideas either about their relation to nature, their mutual relations, or their own nature. It is evident that in all these cases these ideas are the conscious expression – real or illusory – of their actual relationships and activities, of their production and commerce, and of their social and political behaviour. The opposite assumption is possible only if, in addition to the spirit of the actual and materially evolved individuals, a separate spirit is presupposed. If the conscious expression of the actual relations of these individuals is illusory, if in their imagination they turn reality upside down, this in turn is a result of their limited mode of activity and their limited social relations arising from it.

The production of ideas, of conceptions, of consciousness is directly interwoven with the material activity and the material relationships of men; it is the language of actual life. Conceiving, thinking, and the intellectual relationships of men appear here as the direct result of their material behaviour. The same applies to intellectual production as manifested in a people's language of politics, law, morality, religion, metaphysics, etc. Men are the producers of their conceptions, ideas, etc., but these are real, active men, as they are conditioned by a definite development of their productive forces and of the relationships corresponding to these up to their highest forms. Consciousness can never be anything else except conscious existence, and the existence of men is their actual life-process. If men and their circumstances appear upside down in all ideology as in a camera obscura, this phenomenon is caused by their historical life-process, just as the inversion of objects on the retina is caused by their immediate physical life.

In direct contrast to German philosophy, which descends from heaven to earth, here one ascends from earth to heaven. In other words, to arrive at man in the flesh, one does not set out from what men say, imagine, or conceive, nor from man as he is described, thought about, imagined, or conceived. Rather one sets out from real, active men and their actual life-process and demonstrates the development of ideological reflexes and echoes of that process. The phantoms formed in the human brain, too, are necessary sublimations of man's material life-process which is empirically verifiable and connected with material premises. Morality, religion, metaphysics, and all the rest of ideology and their corresponding forms of consciousness no longer seem to be independent. They have no history or development. Rather, men who develop their material production and their material relationships alter their thinking and the products of their thinking alone with their real existence. Consciousness does not determine life, but life determines consciousness. In the first view the starting point is consciousness taken as a living individual; in the second it is the real living individuals themselves as they exist in real life, and consciousness is considered only as *their* consciousness.

This view is not devoid of premises. It proceeds from real premises and does not abandon them for a moment. These premises are men, not in any fantastic isolation and fixation, but in their real, empirically perceptible process of development under certain conditions. When this active life-process is presented, history ceases to be a collection of dead facts as it is with the empiricists who are themselves still abstract, or an imagined activity of imagined subjects, as with the idealists.

Where speculation ends, namely in actual life, there real, positive science begins as the representation of the practical activity and practical process of the development of men. Phrases about consciousness cease and real knowledge takes their place. With the description of reality, independent philosophy loses its medium of existence. At best, a summary of the most general results, abstractions derived from observation of the historical development of men, can take its place. Apart from actual history, these abstractions have in themselves no value whatsoever. They can only serve to facilitate the arrangement of historical material and to indicate the sequence of its particular strata. By no means do they give us a recipe or schema, as philosophy does, for trimming the epochs of history. On the contrary, the difficulties begin only when we start the observation and arrangement of the material, the real description, whether of a past epoch or of the present. The removal of these difficulties is governed by premises we cannot state here. Only the study of the real life-process and the activity of the individuals of any given epoch will yield them.

13

LENIN

Source: V.I. Lenin (13th edn, 1966) *Imperialism, the Highest Form of Capitalism*. Moscow, Progress Publishers, pp. 81–92.

Lenin's ideas on economic imperialism owe much to John A. Hobson's book *Imperialism* published in 1902. Lenin argues that inequalities in the distribution of wealth and income in Britain dampened consumption and reduced the potential of domestic investment. Unable to make profitable investments at home, capitalists sought to export capital to under-exploited regions of the world, particularly to Asia and Africa. The struggle to acquire colonies was therefore linked to contradictions in the capital economic system that demanded new outlets for surplus investment. Imperialism, far from being a policy option as suggested by Kautsky, was to be understood as a monopoly stage of capitalism. Lenin suggests five features of imperialism:

1. The concentration of production and capital, developed so highly that it creates monopolies which play a decisive role in economic life.
2. The fusion of banking capital with industrial capital and the creation, on the basis of this financial capital, of a financial oligarchy.
3. The export of capital, which has become extremely important, as distinguished from export of commodities.
4. The formation of international capitalist monopolies which share out the world among themselves.
5. The territorial division of the whole earth completed by the great capitalist powers.

VII. Imperialism, as a special stage of capitalism

We must now try to sum up, to draw together the threads of what has been said above on the subject of imperialism. Imperialism emerged as the development and direct continuation of the fundamental characteristics of capitalism in general. But capitalism only became capitalist imperialism at a definite and very high stage of its development, when certain of its fundamental characteristics began to change into their opposites, when the features of the epoch of transition from capitalism to a higher social and economic system had taken shape and revealed themselves in all spheres. Economically, the main thing in this process is the displacement of capitalist free competition by capitalist monopoly. Free competition is the basic feature of capitalism, and of commodity production generally; monopoly is the exact opposite of free competition, but we have seen the latter being transformed into monopoly before our eyes, creating large-scale industry and forcing out small industry, replacing large-scale by still larger-scale industry, and carrying concentration of production and capital to the point where out of it has grown and is growing monopoly: cartels, syndicates and trusts, and merging with them, the capital of a dozen or so banks, which manipulate thousands of millions. At the same time the monopolies, which have grown out of free competition, do not eliminate the latter, but exist above it and alongside it, and thereby give rise to a number of very acute, intense antagonisms, frictions and conflicts. Monopoly is the transition from capitalism to a higher system.

If it were necessary to give the briefest possible definition of imperialism we should have to say that imperialism is the monopoly stage of capitalism. Such a definition would include what is most important, for, on the one hand, finance capital is the bank capital of a few very big monopolist banks, merged with the capital of the monopolist associations of industrialists; and, on the other hand, the division of the world is the transition from a colonial policy which has extended without hindrance to territories unseized by any capitalist power, to a colonial policy of monopolist possession of the territory of the world, which has been completely divided up.

But very brief definitions, although convenient, for they sum up the main points, are nevertheless inadequate, since we have to deduce from them some especially important features of the phenomenon that has to be defined. And so, without forgetting the conditional and relative value of all definitions in general, which can never embrace all the concatenations of a phenomenon in its full development, we must give a definition of imperialism that will include the following five of its basic features:

(1) the concentration of production and capital has developed to such a high stage that it has created monopolies which play a decisive role in economic life; (2) the merging of bank capital with industrial capital, and the creation, on the basis of this 'finance capital', of a financial oligarchy; (3) the export of capital as distinguished from the export of commodities acquires exceptional

importance; (4) the formation of international monopolist capitalist associations which share the world among themselves, and (5) the territorial division of the whole world among the biggest capitalist powers is completed. Imperialism is capitalism at that stage of development at which the dominance of monopolies and finance capital is established; in which the export of capital has acquired pronounced importance; in which the division of the world among the international trusts has begun, in which the division of all territories of the globe among the biggest capitalist powers has been completed.

We shall see later that imperialism can and must be defined differently if we bear in mind not only the basic, purely economic concepts – to which the above definition is limited – but also the historical place of this stage of capitalism in relation to capitalism in general, or the relation between imperialism and the two main trends in the working-class movement. The thing to be noted at this point is that imperialism, as interpreted above, undoubtedly represents a special stage in the development of capitalism. To enable the reader to obtain the most well-grounded idea of imperialism, I deliberately tried to quote as extensively as possible *bourgeois* economists who have to admit the particularly incontrovertible facts concerning the latest stage of capitalist economy. With the same object in view, I have quoted detailed statistics which enable one to see to what degree bank capital, etc., has grown, in what precisely the transformation of quality into quantity, of developed capitalism into imperialism, was expressed. Needless to say, of course, all boundaries in nature and in society are conventional and changeable, and it would be absurd to argue, for example, about the particular year or decade in which imperialism 'definitely' became established.

In the matter of defining imperialism, however, we have to enter into controversy, primarily, with Karl Kautsky, the principal Marxist theoretician of the epoch of the so-called Second International – that is, of the twenty-five years between 1889 and 1914. The fundamental ideas expressed in our definition of imperialism were very resolutely attacked by Kautsky in 1915, and even in November 1914, when he said that imperialism must not be regarded as a 'phase' or stage of economy, but as a policy, a definite policy 'preferred' by finance capital; that imperialism must not be 'identified' with 'present-day capitalism'; that if imperialism is to be understood to mean 'all the phenomena of present-day capitalism' – cartels, protection, the domination of the financiers, and colonial policy – then the question as to whether imperialism is necessary to capitalism becomes reduced to the 'flattest tautology', because, in that case, 'imperialism is naturally a vital necessity for capitalism', and so on. The best way to present Kautsky's idea is to quote his own definition of imperialism, which is diametrically opposed to the substance of the ideas which I have set forth (for the objections coming from the camp of the German Marxists, who have been advocating similar ideas for many years already, have been long known to Kautsky as the objections of a definite trend in Marxism).

Kautsky's definition is as follows:

> Imperialism is a product of highly developed industrial capitalism. It consists in the striving of every industrial capitalist nation to bring under its control or to annex all large areas of *agrarian* [Kautsky's italics] territory, irrespective of what nations inhabit it.

This definition is of no use at all because it one-sidedly, i.e., arbitrarily, singles out only the national question (although the latter is extremely important in itself as well as in its relation to imperialism), it arbitrarily and *inaccurately* connects this question *only* with industrial capital in the countries which annex other nations, and in an equally arbitrary and inaccurate manner pushes into the forefront the annexation of agrarian regions.

Imperialism is a striving for annexations – this is what the *political* part of Kautsky's definition amounts to. It is correct, but very incomplete, for politically, imperialism is, in general, a striving towards violence and reaction. For the moment, however, we are interested in the *economic* aspect of the question, which Kautsky *himself* introduced into *his* definition. The inaccuracies in Kautsky's definition are glaring. The characteristic feature of imperialism is *not* industrial *but* finance capital. It is not an accident that in France it was precisely the extraordinarily rapid development of *finance* capital, and the weakening of industrial capital, that from the eighties onwards gave rise to the extreme intensification of annexationist (colonial) policy. The characteristic feature of imperialism is precisely that it strives to annex *not only* agrarian territories, but even most highly industrialised regions (German appetite for Belgium; French appetite for Lorraine), because (1) the fact that the world is already partitioned obliges those contemplating a *redivision* to reach out for *every* kind of territory, and (2) an essential feature of imperialism is the rivalry between several great powers in the striving for hegemony, i.e., for the conquest of territory, not so much directly for themselves as to weaken the adversary and undermine *his* hegemony. (Belgium is particularly important for Germany as a base for operations against Britain; Britain needs Baghdad as a base for operations against Germany, etc.)

Kautsky refers especially – and repeatedly – to English writers who, he alleges, have given a purely political meaning to the word 'imperialism' in the sense that he, Kautsky, understands it. We take up the work by the English writer Hobson, *Imperialism*, which appeared in 1902, and there we read:

> The new imperialism differs from the older, first, in substituting for the ambition of a single growing empire the theory and the practice of competing empires, each motivated by similar lusts of political aggrandisement and commercial gain; secondly, in the dominance of financial or investing over mercantile interests.

We see that Kautsky is absolutely wrong in referring to English writers generally (unless he meant the vulgar English imperialists, or the avowed apologists for imperialism). We see that Kautsky, while claiming that he continues to advocate Marxism, as a matter of fact takes a step backward compared with the *social-liberal* Hobson, who *more correctly* takes into account two 'historically concrete' (Kautsky's definition is a mockery of historical concreteness!) features of modern imperialism: (1) the competition between *several* imperialisms, and (2) the predominance of the financier over the merchant. If it is chiefly a question of the annexation of agrarian countries by industrial countries, then the role of the merchant is put in the forefront.

Kautsky's definition is not only wrong and un-Marxist. It serves as a basis for a whole system of views which signify a rupture with Marxist theory and Marxist practice all along the line. I shall refer to this later. The argument about words which Kautsky raises as to whether the latest stage of capitalism should be called imperialism or the stage of finance capital is not worth serious attention. Call it what you will, it makes no difference. The essence of the matter is that Kautsky detaches the politics of imperialism from its economics, speaks of annexations as being a policy 'preferred' by finance capital, and opposes to it another bourgeois policy which, he alleges, is possible on this very same basis of finance capital. It follows, then, that monopolies in the economy are compatible with non-monopolistic, non-violent, non-annexationist methods in politics. It follows, then, that the territorial division of the world, which was completed during this very epoch of finance capital, and which constitutes the basis of the present peculiar forms of rivalry between the biggest capitalist states, is compatible with a non-imperialist policy. The result is a slurring-over and a blunting of the most profound contradictions of the latest stage of capitalism, instead of an exposure of their depth; the result is bourgeois reformism instead of Marxism.

Kautsky enters into controversy with the German apologist of imperialism and annexations, Cunow, who clumsily and cynically argues that imperialism is present-day capitalism; the development of capitalism is inevitable and progressive; therefore imperialism is progressive; therefore, we should grovel before it and glorify it! This is something like the caricature of the Russian Marxists which the Narodniks drew in 1894–95. They argued: if the Marxists believe that capitalism is inevitable in Russia, that it is progressive, then they ought to open a tavern and begin to implant capitalism! Kautsky's reply to Cunow is as follows: imperialism is not present-day capitalism; it is only one of the forms of the policy of present-day capitalism. This policy we can and should fight, fight imperialism, annexations, etc.

The reply seems quite plausible, but in effect it is a more subtle and more disguised (and therefore more dangerous) advocacy of conciliation with imperialism, because a 'fight' against the policy of the trusts and banks that does not affect the economic basis of the trusts and banks is mere bourgeois reformism and pacifism, the benevolent and innocent expression of pious wishes. Evasion of existing contradictions, forgetting the most important of them, instead of revealing their full depth – such is Kautsky's theory, which has nothing in common with Marxism. Naturally, such a 'theory' can only serve the purpose of advocating unity with the Cunows!

'From the purely economic point of view,' writes Kautsky, 'it is not impossible that capitalism will yet go through a new phase, that of the extension of the policy of the cartels to foreign policy, the phase of ultra-imperialism,' i.e., of a superimperialism, of a union of the imperialisms of the whole world and not struggles among them, a phase when wars shall cease under capitalism, a phase of 'the joint exploitation of the world by internationally united finance capital'.

We shall have to deal with this 'theory of ultra-imperialism' later on in order to show in detail how decisively and completely it breaks with Marxism. At present, in keeping with the general plan of the present work, we must examine the exact economic data on this question. 'From the purely economic point of view', is 'ultra-imperialism' possible, or is it ultra-nonsense?

If the purely economic point of view is meant to be a 'pure' abstraction, then all that can be said reduces itself to the following proposition: development is proceeding towards monopolies, hence, towards a single world monopoly, towards a single world trust. This is indisputable, but it is also as completely meaningless as is the statement that 'development is proceeding' towards the manufacture of foodstuffs in laboratories. In this sense the 'theory' of ultra-imperialism is no less absurd than a 'theory of ultra-agriculture' would be.

If, however, we are discussing the 'purely economic' conditions of the epoch of finance capital as a historically concrete epoch which began at the turn of the twentieth century, then the best reply that one can make to the lifeless abstractions of 'ultra-imperialism' (which serve exclusively a most reactionary aim: that of diverting attention from the depth of *existing* antagonisms) is to contrast them with the concrete economic realities of the present-day world economy. Kautsky's utterly meaningless talk about ultra-imperialism encourages, among other things, that profoundly mistaken idea which only brings grist to the mill of the apologists of imperialism, i.e., that the rule of finance capital *lessens* the unevenness and contradictions inherent in the world economy, whereas in reality it *increases* them.

R. Calwer, in his little book, *An Introduction to the World Economy*, made an attempt to summarise the main, purely economic, data that enable one to obtain a concrete picture of the internal relations of the world economy at the turn of the twentieth century. He divides the world into five 'main economic areas', as follows: (1) Central Europe (the whole of Europe with the exception of Russia and Great Britain); (2) Great Britain; (3) Russia; (4) Eastern Asia; (5) America; he includes the colonies in the 'areas' of the states to which they belong and 'leaves aside' a few countries not distributed according to areas, such as Persia, Afghanistan, and Arabia in Asia, Morocco and Abyssinia in Africa, etc.

Here is a brief summary of the economic data he quotes on these regions (see table opposite):

We see three areas of highly developed capitalism (high development of means of transport, of trade and of industry): the Central European, the British and the American areas. Among these are three states which dominate the world: Germany, Great Britain, and the United States. Imperialist rivalry and the struggle between these countries have become extremely keen because Germany has only an insignificant area and few colonies; the creation of 'Central Europe' is still a matter for the future, it is being born in the midst of a desperate struggle. For

Principal economic areas	Area (000,000 sq. km)	Population (000,000)	Transport		Trade	Industry output (000,000 tons)		Number of cotton spindles (000,000)
			Railways (000 km)	Mercantile fleet (000,000 tons)	Imports and exports (000,000,000 marks)	Coal	Iron	
1) Central Europe	27.6 (23.6)**	388 (146)	204	8	41	251	15	26
2) Britain	28.9 (28.6)**	398 (355)	140	11	25	249	9	51
3) Russia	22	131	63	1	3	16	3	7
4) Eastern Asia	12	389	8	1	2	8	0.02	2
5) America	30	148	379	6	14	245	14	19

** The figures in parentheses show the area of population of the colonies.

the moment the distinctive feature of the whole of Europe is political disunity. In the British and American areas, on the other hand, political concentration is very highly developed, but there is a vast disparity between the immense colonies of the one and the insignificant colonies of the other. In the colonies, however, capitalism is only beginning to develop. The struggle for South America is becoming more and more acute.

There are two areas where capitalism is little developed: Russia and Eastern Asia. In the former, the population is extremely sparse, in the latter it is extremely dense; in the former political concentration is high, in the latter it does not exist. The partitioning of China is only just beginning, and the struggle for it between Japan, the U.S., etc., is continually gaining in intensity.

Compare this reality – the vast diversity of economic and political conditions, the extreme disparity in the rate of development of the various countries, etc., and the violent struggles among the imperialist states – with Kautsky's silly little fable about 'peaceful' ultra-imperialism. Is this not the reactionary attempt of a frightened philistine to hide from stern reality? Are not the international cartels which Kautsky imagines are the embryos of 'ultra-imperialism' (in the same way as one 'can' describe the manufacture of tablets in a laboratory as ultra-agriculture in embryo) an example of the division *and the redivision* of the world, the transition from peaceful division to non-peaceful division and vice versa? Is not American and other finance capital, which divided the whole world peacefully with Germany's participation in, for example, the international rail syndicate, or in the international mercantile shipping trust, now engaged in *redividing* the world on the basis of a new relation of forces that is being changed by methods *anything but* peaceful?

Finance capital and the trusts do not diminish but increase the differences in the rate of growth of the various parts of the world economy. Once the relation of forces is changed, what other solution of the contradictions can be found *under capitalism* than that of *force*? Railway statistics provide remarkably exact data on the different rates of growth of capitalism and finance capital in world economy. In the last decades of imperialist development, the total length of railways has changed as follows:

	Railways (000 kilometres)		
	1890	*1913*	*+*
Europe	224	346	+122
U.S.	268	411	+143
All colonies	82	210	+128
Independent and semi-independent states of Asia and America	125	347	+222
	43	137	+94
Total	617	1,104	

Thus, the development of railways has been most rapid in the colonies and in the independent (and semi-independent) states of Asia and America. Here, as we know, the finance capital of the four or five biggest capitalist states holds undisputed sway. Two hundred thousand kilometres of new railways in the colonies and in the other countries of Asia and America represent a capital of more than 40,000 million marks newly invested on particularly advantageous terms, with special guarantees of a good return and with profitable orders for steel works, etc., etc.

Capitalism is growing with the greatest rapidity in the colonies and in overseas countries. Among the latter, *new* imperialist powers are emerging (e.g., Japan). The struggle among the world imperialisms is becoming more acute. The tribute levied by finance capital on the most profitable colonial and overseas enterprises is increasing. In the division of this 'booty', an exceptionally large part goes to countries which do not always stand at the top of the list in the rapidity of the development of their productive forces. In the case of the biggest countries, together with their colonies, the total length of railways was as follows:

	(000 kilometres)		
	1890	1913	
U.S.	268	413	+145
British Empire	107	208	+101
Russia	32	78	+ 46
Germany	43	68	+ 25
France	41	63	+ 22
Total for 5 powers	491	830	+339

Thus, about 80 per cent of the total existing railways are concentrated in the hands of the five biggest powers. But the concentration of the *ownership* of these railways, the concentration of finance capital, is immeasurably greater since the French and British millionaires, for example, own an enormous amount of shares and bonds in American, Russian and other railways.

Thanks to her colonies, Great Britain has increased the length of 'her' railways by 100,000 kilometres, four times as much as Germany. And yet, it is well known that the development of productive forces in Germany, and especially the development of the coal and iron industries, has been incomparably more rapid during this period than in Britain – not to speak of France and Russia. In 1892, Germany produced 4,900,000 tons of pig-iron and Great Britain produced 6,800,000 tons; in 1912, Germany produced 17,600,000 tons and Great Britain, 9,000,000 tons. Germany, therefore, had an overwhelming superiority over Britain in this respect. The question is: what means other than war could there be *under capitalism* to overcome the disparity between the development of productive forces and the accumulation of capital on the one side, and the division of colonies and spheres of influence for finance capital on the other?

14

CARR

Source: E.H. Carr (1939) *The Twenty Years' Crisis*. London, Macmillan, pp. 67–71 and 75–88. Copyright E.H. Carr, reproduced by permission of Chris Brown Ltd, London.

Following the carnage of the Great War of 1914–18, academics and statespeople had operated on the assumption that only the insane would resort to war in the future. Wars were caused in some way by a series of errors, misunderstandings or misperceptions. In future the security of the world could be assured by creating international organizations like the League of Nations that would provide a forum for mediation, clarification and the resolution of conflicts. Carr attacks this view as utopian. He argues that all appeals to a 'harmony of interests' or some 'cosmopolitan' idea of a universal community of humankind should be seen for what they really are: an attempt to dominate by promoting one's own views as though in the interests of all.

THE RELATIVITY OF THOUGHT

The outstanding achievement of modern realism, however, has been to reveal, not merely the determinist aspects of the historical process, but the relative and pragmatic character of thought itself. In the last fifty years, thanks mainly though not wholly to the influence of Marx, the principles of the historical school have been applied to the analysis of thought; and the foundations of a new science have been laid, principally by German thinkers, under the name of the 'sociology of knowledge.' The realist has thus been enabled to demonstrate that the intellectual theories and ethical standards of utopianism, far from being the expression of absolute and *a priori* principles, are historically conditioned, being both products of circumstances and interests and weapons framed for the furtherance of interests. 'Ethical notions', as Mr Bertrand Russell has remarked, 'are very seldom a cause, but almost always an effect, a means of claiming universal legislative authority for our own preferences, not, as we fondly imagine, the actual ground of those preferences.'[1] This is by far the most formidable attack which utopianism has to face; for here the very foundations of its belief are undermined by the realist critique.

In a general way, the relativity of thought has long been recognised. As early as the seventeenth century Bishop Burnet expounded the relativist view as cogently, if not as pungently, as Marx:

> As to the late Civil Wars, 'tis pretty well known what notions of government went current in those days. When monarchy was to be subverted we knew what was necessary to justify the fact; and then, because it was convenient for the purpose, it was undoubtedly true in the nature of things that government had its original from the people, and the prince was only their trustee. . . . But afterwards, when monarchy took its place again . . . another notion of government came into fashion. Then government had its original entirely from God, and the prince was accountable to none but Him. . . . And now, upon another turn of things, when people have a liberty to speak out, a new set of notions is advanced; now passive obedience is all a mistake, and instead of being a duty to suffer oppression, 'tis a glorious act to resist it: and instead of leaving injuries to be redressed by God, we have a natural right to relieve ourselves.[2]

In modern times, the recognition of this phenomenon has become fairly general. 'Belief, and to speak fairly, honest belief', wrote Dicey of the divisions of opinion in the nineteenth century about slavery, 'was to a great extent the result not of argument, not even of direct self-interest, but of circumstances. . . . Circumstances are the creators of most men's opinions.'[3] Marx narrowed down this somewhat vague conception, declaring that all thought was conditioned by the economic interest and social status of the thinker. This view was perhaps unduly restrictive. In particular Marx, who denied the existence of 'national' interests, underestimated the potency of nationalism as a force conditioning the thought of the individual. But the peculiar concentration which he applied to the principle served to popularise it and drive it home. The relativity of thought to the interests and circumstances of the thinker has been far more extensively recognised and understood since Marx wrote.

The principle has an extremely wide field of application. It has become a commonplace to say that theories do not mould the course of events, but are invented

1. *Proceedings of the Aristotelian Society*, 1915–16, p. 302.
2. Burnet, *Essay upon Government*, p. 10.
3. Dicey, *Law and Opinion* (1905 ed.), p. 27.

to explain them. 'Empire precedes imperialism.'[4] Eighteenth-century England 'put into practice the policy of *laissez-faire* before it found a justification, or even an apparent justification, in the new doctrine';[5] and 'the virtual break-up of *laissez-faire* as a body of doctrine . . . has followed, and not preceded, the decline of *laissez-faire* in the real world'.[6] The theory of 'socialism in a single country' promulgated in Soviet Russia in 1924 was manifestly a product of the failure of Soviet régimes to establish themselves in other countries.

But the development of abstract theory is often influenced by events which have no essential connexion with it at all.

> In the story of political thought [writes a modern social thinker] events have been no less potent than arguments. The failure and success of institutions, the victories and defeats of countries identified with certain principles have repeatedly brought new strength and resolution to the adherents or opponents of these principles as the case might be in all lands. . . . Philosophy as it exists on earth is the word of philosophers who, authority tells us, suffer as much from toothache as other mortals, and are, like others, open to the impression of near and striking events and to the seductions of intellectual fashion.[7]

Germany's dramatic rise to power in the sixties and seventies of the last century was impressive enough to make the leading British philosophers of the next generation – Caird, T.H. Green, Bosanquet, McTaggart – ardent Hegelians. Thereafter, the Kaiser's telegram to Kruger and the German naval programme spread the conviction among British thinkers that Hegel was a less good philosopher than had been supposed; and since 1914 no British philosopher of repute has ventured to sail under the Hegelian flag. After 1870, Stubbs and Freeman put early English history on a sound Teutonic basis, while even in France Fustel de Coulanges had an uphill struggle to defend the Latin origins of French civilisation. During the past thirty years, English historians have been furtively engaged in making the Teutonic origins of England as inconspicuous as possible.

Nor is it only professional thinkers who are subject to such influences. Popular opinion is not less markedly dominated by them. The frivolity and immorality of French life was an established dogma in nineteenth-century Britain, which still remembered Napoleon. 'When I was young', writes Mr Bertrand Russell, 'the French ate frogs and were called "froggies", but they apparently abandoned this practice when we concluded our *entente* with them in 1904 – at any rate, I have never heard it mentioned since that date.'[8] Some years later, 'the gallant little Jap' of 1905 underwent a converse metamorphosis into 'the Prussian of the East'. In the nineteenth century, it was a commonplace of British opinion that Germans were efficient and enlightened, and Russians backward and barbarous. About

4. J.A. Hobson, *Free Thought in the Social Sciences*, p. 190.
5. Halévy, *The Growth of Philosophic Radicalism* (Engl. transl.), p. 104.
6. M. Dobb, *Political Economy and Capitalism*, p. 188.
7. L.T. Hobhouse, *The Unity of Western Civilisation*, ed. F.S. Marvin (3rd ed.), pp. 177–8.
8. Bertrand Russell, *Which Way Peace?* p. 158.

1910, it was ascertained that Germans (who turned out to be mostly Prussians) were coarse, brutal and narrow-minded, and that Russians had a Slav soul. The vogue of Russian literature in Great Britain, which set in about the same time, was a direct outcome of the political *rapprochement* with Russia. The vogue of Marxism in Great Britain and France, which began on a modest scale after the success of the Bolshevik revolution in Russia, rapidly gathered momentum, particularly among intellectuals, after 1934, when it was discovered that Soviet Russia was a potential military ally against Germany. It is symptomatic that most people, when challenged, will indignantly deny that they form their opinions in this way; for as Acton long ago observed, 'few discoveries are more irritating than those which expose the pedigree of ideas'.[9] The conditioning of thought is necessarily a subconscious process.

National interest and the universal good

The realist should not, however, linger over the infliction of these pin-pricks through chinks in the utopian defences. His task is to bring down the whole cardboard structure of utopian thought by exposing the hollowness of the material out of which it is built. The weapon of the relativity of thought must be used to demolish the utopian concept of a fixed and absolute standard by which policies and actions can be judged. If theories are revealed as a reflexion of practice and principles of political needs, this discovery will apply to the fundamental theories and principles of the utopian creed, and not least to the doctrine of the harmony of interests which is its essential postulate.

It will not be difficult to shew that the utopian, when he preaches the doctrine of the harmony of interests, is innocently and unconsciously adopting Walewski's maxim, and clothing his own interest in the guise of a universal interest for the purpose of imposing it on the rest of the world. 'Men come easily to believe that arrangements agreeable to themselves are beneficial to others', as Dicey observed;[10] and theories of the public good, which turn out on inspection to be an elegant disguise for some particular interest, are as common in international as in national affairs. The utopian, however eager he may be to establish an absolute standard, does not argue that it is the duty of his country, in conformity with that standard, to put the interest of the world at large before its own interest; for that would be contrary to his theory that the interest of all coincides with the interest of each. He argues that what is best for the world is best for his country, and then reverses the argument to read that what is best for his country is best for the world, the two propositions being, from the utopian standpoint, identical; and this unconscious cynicism of the contemporary utopian has proved a far more effective diplomatic weapon than the deliberate and self-conscious cynicism of a Walewski or a Bismarck. British writers of the

9. Acton, *History of Freedom*, p. 62.
10. Dicey, *Law and Opinion in England* (2nd ed.), pp. 14–15.

past half-century have been particularly eloquent supporters of the theory that
the maintenance of British supremacy is the performance of a duty to mankind.
'If Great Britain has turned itself into a coal-shed and blacksmith's forge',
remarked *The Times* ingenuously in 1885, 'it is for the behoof of mankind as
well as its own.'[11] The following extract is typical of a dozen which might be
culled from memoirs of public men of the period:

> I have but one great object in this world, and that is to maintain the
> greatness of the Empire. But apart from my John Bull sentiment upon
> the point, I firmly believe that in doing so I work in the cause of Chris-
> tianity, of peace, of civilisation, and the happiness of the human race
> generally.[12]

'I contend that we are the first race in the world,' wrote Cecil Rhodes, 'and that
the more of the world we inhabit the better it is for the human race.'[13] In 1891,
the most popular and brilliant journalist of the day, W.T. Stead, founded the
Review of Reviews. 'We believe in God, in England and in Humanity', ran the
editorial manifesto in its opening number. 'The English-speaking race is one of
the chief of God's chosen agents for executing coming improvements in the lot
of mankind.'[14] An Oxford professor was convinced in 1912 that the secret of
Britain's history was that 'in fighting for her own independence she has been
fighting for the freedom of Europe, and that the service thus rendered to Europe
and to mankind has carried with it the possibility of that larger service to which
we give the name Empire'.[15]

The first world war carried this conviction to a pitch of emotional frenzy. A
bare catalogue, culled from the speeches of British statesmen, of the services
which British belligerency was rendering to humanity would fill many pages. In
1917, Balfour told the New York Chamber of Commerce that 'since August,
1914, the fight has been for the highest spiritual advantages of mankind, without
a petty thought or ambition'.[16] The Peace Conference and its sequel temporarily discredited these professions and threw some passing doubt on the belief
in British supremacy as one of the moral assets of mankind. But the period of
disillusionment and modesty was short. Moments of international tension, and
especially moments when the possibility of war appears on the horizon, always
stimulate this identification of national interest with morality. At the height of
the Abyssinian crisis, the Archbishop of Canterbury admonished the French
public through an interview in a Paris newspaper:

> We are animated by moral and spiritual considerations. I do not think I
> am departing from my role by contributing towards the clearing up of this
> misunderstanding. . . .

11. *The Times*, August 27, 1885.
12. Maurice and Arthur, *The Life of Lord Wolseley*, p. 314.
13. W.T. Stead, *The Last Will and Testament of Cecil J. Rhodes*, p. 58.
14. *Review of Reviews*, January 15, 1891.
15. Spencer Wilkinson, *Government and the War*, p. 116.
16. Quoted in Beard, *The Rise of American Civilisation*, ii. p. 646.

It is . . . no egoist interest that is driving us forward, and no consideration of interest should keep you behind.[17]

In the following year, Professor Toynbee was once more able to discover that
the security of the British Empire 'was also the supreme interest of the whole
world'.[18] In 1937, Lord Cecil spoke to the General Council of the League of
Nations Union of 'our duty to our country, to our Empire and to humanity at
large', and quoted:

> Not once nor twice in our rough island story
> The path of duty is the way to glory.[19]

An Englishman, as Mr Bernard Shaw remarks in *The Man of Destiny*, 'never
forgets that the nation which lets its duty get on to the opposite side to its interest
is lost'. It is not surprising that an American critic should recently have described
the British as 'Jesuits lost to the theological but gained for the political realm',[20]
or that a former Italian Minister for Foreign Affairs should have commented,
long before these recent manifestations, on 'that precious gift bestowed upon the
British people – the possession of writers and clergyman able in perfect good
faith to advance the highest moral reasons for the most concrete diplomatic
action, with inevitable moral profit to England'.[21]

In recent times, the same phenomenon has become endemic in the United
States. The story how McKinley prayed for divine guidance and decided to
annex the Philippines is a classic of modern American history; and this annexation was the occasion of a popular outburst of moral self-approval hitherto more
familiar in the foreign policy of Great Britain than of the United States.
Theodore Roosevelt, who believed more firmly than any previous American
President in the doctrine *L'état, c'est moi*, carried the process a step further. The
following curious dialogue occurred in his cross-examination during a libel
action brought against him in 1915 by a Tammany leader:

Query: How did you know that substantial justice was done?
Roosevelt: Because I did it, because . . . I was doing my best.
Query: You mean to say that, when you do a thing, thereby substantial
justice is done.
Roosevelt: I do. When I do a thing, I do it so as to do substantial justice.
I mean just that.[22]

Woodrow Wilson was less naively egotistical, but more profoundly confident of
the identity of American policy and universal justice. After the bombardment
of Vera Cruz in 1914, he assured the world that 'the United States had

17. Quoted in *Manchester Guardian*, October 18, 1935.
18. Toynbee, *Survey of International Affairs*, 1935, ii. p. 46.
19. *Headway*, November 1937.
20. Carl Becker, *Yale Review*, xxvii. p. 452.
21. Count Sforza, *Foreign Affairs*, October 1927, p. 67.
22. Quoted in H.F. Pringle, *Theodore Roosevelt*, p. 318.

gone down to Mexico to serve mankind'.[23] During the first world war, he advised American naval cadets 'not only always to think first of America, but always, also, to think first of humanity' – a feat rendered slightly less difficult by his explanation that the United States had been 'founded for the benefit of humanity'.[24] Shortly before the entry of the United States into the war, in an address to the Senate on war aims, he stated the identification still more categorically: 'These are American principles, American policies. . . . They are the principles of mankind and must prevail.'[25]

It will be observed that utterances of this character proceed almost exclusively from Anglo-Saxon statesmen and writers. It is true that when a prominent National Socialist asserted that 'anything that benefits the German people is right, anything that harms the German people is wrong',[26] he was merely propounding the same identification of national interest with universal right which had already been established for English-speaking countries by Wilson, Professor Toynbee, Lord Cecil and many others. But when the claim is translated into a foreign language, the note seems forced, and the identification unconvincing, even to the peoples concerned. Two explanations are commonly given of this curious discrepancy. The first explanation, which is popular in English-speaking countries, is that the policies of the English-speaking nations are in fact more virtuous and disinterested than those of Continental states, so that Wilson and Professor Toynbee and Lord Cecil are, broadly speaking, right when they identify the American and British national interests with the interest of mankind. The second explanation, which is popular in Continental countries, is that the English-speaking peoples are past masters in the art of concealing their selfish national interests in the guise of the general good, and that this kind of hypocrisy is a special and characteristic peculiarity of the Anglo-Saxon mind.

It seems unnecessary to accept either of these heroic attempts to cut the knot. The solution is a simple one. Theories of social morality are always the product of a dominant group which identifies itself with the community as a whole, and which possesses facilities denied to subordinate groups or individuals for imposing its view of life on the community. Theories of international morality are, for the same reason and in virtue of the same process, the product of dominant nations or groups of nations. For the past hundred years, and more especially since 1918, the English-speaking peoples have formed the dominant group in the world; and current theories of international morality have been designed to perpetuate their supremacy and expressed in the idiom peculiar to them. France, retaining something of her eighteenth-century tradition and restored to a position of dominance for a short period after 1918, has played a minor part in the creation of current international morality, mainly through her insistence on the role of law in the moral order. Germany, never a dominant Power and

23. *Public Papers of Woodrow Wilson: The New Democracy*, ed. R.S. Baker.
24. *Ibid*. i. pp. 318–19.
25. *Ibid*. ii. p. 414.
26. Quoted in Toynbee, *Survey of International Affairs*, 1936, p. 319.

reduced to helplessness after 1918, has remained for these reasons outside the charmed circle of creators of international morality. Both the view that the English-speaking peoples are monopolists of international morality and the view that they are consummate international hypocrites may be reduced to the plain fact that the current canons of international virtue have, by a natural and inevitable process, been mainly created by them.

The realist critique of the harmony of interests

The doctrine of the harmony of interests yields readily to analysis in terms of this principle. It is the natural assumption of a prosperous and privileged class, whose members have a dominant voice in the community and are therefore naturally prone to identify its interest with their own. In virtue of this identification, any assailant of the interests of the dominant group is made to incur the odium of assailing the alleged common interest of the whole community, and is told that in making this assault he is attacking his own higher interests. The doctrine of the harmony of interests thus serves as an ingenious moral device invoked, in perfect sincerity, by privileged groups in order to justify and maintain their dominant position. But a further point requires notice. The supremacy within the community of the privileged group may be, and often is, so overwhelming that there is, in fact, a sense in which its interests are those of the community, since its well-being necessarily carries with it some measure of well-being for other members of the community, and its collapse would entail the collapse of the community as a whole. In so far, therefore, as the alleged natural harmony of interests has any reality, it is created by the overwhelming power of the privileged group, and is an excellent illustration of the Machiavellian maxim that morality is the product of power. A few examples will make this analysis of the doctrine of the harmony of interests clear.

In the nineteenth century, the British manufacturer or merchant, having discovered that *laissez-faire* promoted his own prosperity, was sincerely convinced that it also promoted British prosperity as a whole. Nor was this alleged harmony of interests between himself and the community entirely fictitious. The predominance of the manufacturer and the merchant was so overwhelming that there was a sense in which an identity between their prosperity and British prosperity as a whole could be correctly asserted. From this it was only a short step to argue that a worker on strike, in damaging the prosperity of the British manufacturer, was damaging British prosperity as a whole, and thereby damaging his own, so that he could be plausibly denounced by the predecessors of Professor Toynbee as immoral and by the predecessors of Professor Zimmern as muddle-headed. Moreover, there was a sense in which this argument was perfectly correct. Nevertheless, the doctrine of the harmony of interests and of solidarity between the classes must have seemed a bitter mockery to the underprivileged worker, whose inferior status and insignificant stake in 'British prosperity' were consecrated by it; and presently he was strong enough to force the abandonment of *laissez-faire* and the substitution for it of the 'social service state', which implicitly denies the natural harmony of interests and sets out to create a new harmony by artificial means.

The same analysis may be applied in international relations. British nineteenth-century statesmen, having discovered that free trade promoted British prosperity, were sincerely convinced that, in doing so, it also promoted the prosperity of the world as a whole. British predominance in world trade was at that time so overwhelming that there was a certain undeniable harmony between British interests and the interests of the world. British prosperity flowed over into other countries, and a British economic collapse would have meant world-wide ruin. British free traders could and did argue that protectionist countries were not only egotistically damaging the prosperity of the world as a whole, but were stupidly damaging their own, so that their behaviour was both immoral and muddle-headed. In British eyes, it was irrefutably proved that international trade was a single whole, and flourished or slumped together. Nevertheless, this alleged international harmony of interests seemed a mockery to those under-privileged nations whose inferior status and insignificant stake in international trade were consecrated by it. The revolt against it destroyed that overwhelming British preponderance which had provided a plausible basis for the theory. Economically, Great Britain in the nineteenth century was dominant enough to make a bold bid to impose on the world her own conception of international economic morality. When competition of all against all replaced the domination of the world market by a single Power, conceptions of international economic morality necessarily became chaotic.

Politically, the alleged community of interest in the maintenance of peace, whose ambiguous character has already been discussed, is capitalised in the same way by a dominant nation or group of nations. Just as the ruling class in a community prays for domestic peace, which guarantees its own security and predominance, and denounces class-war, which might threaten them, so international peace becomes a special vested interest of predominant Powers. In the past, Roman and British imperialism were commended to the world in the guise of the *pax Romana* and the *pax Britannica*. To-day, when no single Power is strong enough to dominate the world, and supremacy is vested in a group of nations, slogans like 'collective security' and 'resistance to aggression' serve the same purpose of proclaiming an identity of interest between the dominant group and the world as a whole in the maintenance of peace. Moreover, as in the examples we have just considered, so long as the supremacy of the dominant group is sufficiently great, there is a sense in which this identity of interests exists. 'England', wrote a German professor in the nineteen-twenties, 'is the solitary Power with a national programme which, while egotistic through and through, at the same time promises to the world something which the world passionately desires: order, progress and eternal peace.'[27] When Mr Churchill

27. Dibelius, *England*, p. 109.

declared that 'the fortunes of the British Empire and its glory are inseparably interwoven with the fortunes of the world',[28] this statement had precisely the same foundation in fact as the statement that the prosperity of British manufacturers in the nineteenth century was inseparably interwoven with British prosperity as a whole. Moreover, the purpose of the statements was precisely the same, namely to establish the principle that the defence of the British Empire, or the prosperity of the British manufacturer, was a matter of common interest to the whole community, and that anyone who attacked it was therefore either immoral or muddle-headed. It is a familiar tactic of the privileged to throw moral discredit on the under-privileged by depicting them as disturbers of the peace; and this tactic is as readily applied internationally as within the national community. 'International law and order', writes Professor Toynbee of a recent crisis, 'were in the true interests of the whole of mankind . . . whereas the desire to perpetuate the reign of violence in international affairs was an anti-social desire which was not even in the ultimate interests of the citizens of the handful of states that officially professed this benighted and anachronistic creed.'[29] This is precisely the argument, compounded of platitude and falsehood in about equal parts, which did duty in every strike in the early days of the British and American Labour movements. It was common form for employers, supported by the whole capitalist press, to denounce the 'anti-social' attitude of trade union leaders, to accuse them of attacking law and order and of introducing 'the reign of violence', and to declare that 'true' and 'ultimate' interests of the workers lay in peaceful co-operation with the employers.[30] In the field of social relations, the disingenuous character of this argument has long been recognised. But just as the threat of class-war by the proletarian is 'a natural cynical reaction to the sentimental and dishonest efforts of the privileged classes to obscure the conflict of interest between classes by a constant emphasis on the minimum interests which they have in common',[31] so the war-mongering of the dissatisfied Powers was the 'natural, cynical reaction' to the sentimental and dishonest platitudinising of the satisfied Powers on the common interest in peace. When Hitler refused to believe 'that God has permitted some nations first to acquire a world by force and then to defend this robbery with moralising theories',[32] he was merely echoing in another context the Marxist denial of a community of interest between 'haves' and 'have-nots', the Marxist exposure of the interested character of '*bourgeois* morality', and the Marxist demand for the expropriation of the expropriators.

The crisis of September 1938 demonstrated in a striking way the political implications of the assertion of a common interest in peace. When Briand proclaimed that 'peace comes before all', or Mr Eden that 'there is no dispute which

28. Winston Churchill, *Arms and the Covenant*, p. 272.
29. Toynbee, *Survey of International Affairs*, 1935, ii. p. 46.
30. 'Pray earnestly that right may triumph', said the representative of the Philadelphia coal-owners in an early strike organised by the United Mine Workers, 'remembering that the Lord God Omnipotent still reigns, and that His reign is one of law and order, and not of violence and crime' (H.F. Pringle, *Theodore Roosevelt*, p. 267).
31. R. Niebuhr, *Moral Man and Immoral Society*, p. 153.
32. Speech in the Reichstag, January 30, 1939.

cannot be settled by peaceful means',[33] the assumption underlying these platitudes was that, so long as peace was maintained, no changes distasteful to France or Great Britain could be made in the *status quo*. In 1938, France and Great Britain were trapped by the slogans which they themselves had used in the past to discredit the dissatisfied Powers, and Germany had become sufficiently dominant (as France and Great Britain had hitherto been) to turn the desire for peace to her own advantage. About this time, a significant change occurred in the attitude of the German and Italian dictators. Hitler eagerly depicted Germany as a bulwark of peace menaced by war-mongering democracies. The League of Nations, he declared in his Reichstag speech of April 28, 1939, is a 'stirrer up of trouble', and collective security means 'continuous danger of war'. Mussolini borrowed the British formula about the possibility of settling all international disputes by peaceful means, and declared that 'there are not in Europe at present problems so big and so active as to justify a war which from a European conflict would naturally become universal'.[34] Such utterances were symptoms that Germany and Italy were already looking forward to the time when, as dominant Powers, they would acquire the vested interest in peace recently enjoyed by Great Britain and France, and be able to get their way by pillorying the democratic countries as enemies of peace. These developments may have made it easier to appreciate Halévy's subtle observation that 'propaganda against war is itself a form of war propaganda'.[35]

The realist critique of internationalism

The concept of internationalism is a special form of the doctrine of the harmony of interests. It yields to the same analysis; and there are the same difficulties about regarding it as an absolute standard independent of the interests and policies of those who promulgate it. 'Cosmopolitanism', wrote Sun Yat-sen, 'is the same thing as China's theory of world empire two thousand years ago . . . China once wanted to be sovereign lord of the earth and to stand above every other nation, so she espoused cosmopolitanism.'[36] In the Egypt of the Eighteenth Dynasty, according to Freud, 'imperialism was reflected in religion as universality and monotheism'.[37] The doctrine of a single world-state, propagated by the Roman Empire and later by the Catholic Church, was the symbol of a claim to universal dominion. Modern internationalism has its genesis in seventeenth- and eighteenth-century France, during which French hegemony in Europe was at its height. This was the period which produced Sully's *Grand Dessin* and the Abbé Saint-Pierre's *Projet de Paix Perpétuelle* (both plans to perpetuate an international *status quo* favourable to the French monarchy), which saw the birth of the humanitarian and cosmopolitan doctrines of the

33. *League of Nations: Eighteenth Assembly*, p. 63.
34. *The Times*, May 15, 1939.
35. Halévy, *A History of the English People in 1895–1905* (Engl. transl.), i. Introduction, p. xi.
36. Sun Yat-sen, *San Min Chu I* (Engl. transl.), pp. 68–9.
37. Sigmund Freud, *Moses and Monotheism*, p. 36.

Enlightenment, and which established French as the universal language of educated people. In the next century, the leadership passed to Great Britain, which became the home of internationalism. On the eve of the Great Exhibition of 1851 which, more than any other single event, established Great Britain's title to world supremacy, the Prince Consort spoke movingly of 'that great end to which . . . all history points – the realisation of the unity of mankind';[38] and Tennyson hymned 'the parliament of man, the federation of the world'. France chose the moment of her greatest supremacy in the nineteen-twenties to launch a plan of 'European Union'; and Japan shortly afterwards developed an ambition to proclaim herself the leader of a united Asia. It was symptomatic of the growing international predominance of the United States when widespread popularity was enjoyed in the late nineteen-thirties by the book of an American journalist advocating a world union of democracies, in which the United States would play the predominant role.[39]

Just as pleas for 'national solidarity' in domestic politics always come from a dominant group which can use this solidarity to strengthen its own control over the nation as a whole, so pleas for international solidarity and world union come from those dominant nations which may hope to exercise control over a unified world. Countries which are struggling to force their way into the dominant group naturally tend to invoke nationalism against the internationalism of the controlling Powers. In the sixteenth century, England opposed her nascent nationalism to the internationalism of the Papacy and the Empire. In the past century and a half Germany opposed her nascent nationalism to the internationalism first of France, then of Great Britain. This circumstance made her impervious to those universalist and humanitarian doctrines which were popular in eighteenth-century France and nineteenth-century Britain; and her hostility to internationalism was further aggravated after 1919, when Great Britain and France endeavoured to create a new 'international order' as a bulwark of their own predominance. 'By "international",' wrote a German correspondent in *The Times*, 'we have come to understand a conception that places other nations at an advantage over our own.'[40] Nevertheless, there was little doubt that Germany, if she became supreme in Europe, would adopt international slogans and establish some kind of international organisation to bolster up her power. A British Labour ex-Minister at one moment advocated the suppression of Article 16 of the Covenant of the League of Nations on the unexpected ground that the totalitarian states might some day capture the League and invoke that article to justify the use of force by themselves.[41] It seemed more likely that they would seek to develop the Anti-Comintern Pact into some form of international organisation 'The Anti-Comintern Pact', said Hitler in the Reichstag on January 30, 1939, 'will perhaps one day become the crystallisation point of a group of Powers whose ultimate aim is none other than to eliminate the menace to the peace and culture of the world instigated by a satanic apparition.' 'Either Europe

38. T. Martin, *Life of the Prince Consort*, iii. p. 247.
39. Clarence Streit, *Union Now*.
40. *The Times*, November 5, 1938.
41. Lord Marley in the House of Lords, November 30, 1938: *Official Report*, col. 258.

must achieve solidarity,' remarked an Italian journal about the same time, 'or the "axis" will impose it.'[42] 'Europe in its entirety', said Goebbels, 'is adopting a new order and a new orientation under the intellectual leadership of National Socialist Germany and Fascist Italy.'[43] These were symptoms not of a change of heart, but of the fact that Germany and Italy felt themselves to be approaching the time when they might become strong enough to espouse internationalism. 'International order' and 'international solidarity' will always be slogans of those who feel strong enough to impose them on others.

The exposure of the real basis of the professedly abstract principles commonly invoked in international politics is the most damning and most convincing part of the realist indictment of utopianism. The nature of the charge is frequently misunderstood by those who seek to refute it. The charge is not that human beings fail to live up to their principles. It matters little that Wilson, who thought that the right was more precious than peace, and Briand, who thought that peace came even before justice, and Mr Eden, who believed in collective security, failed themselves, or failed to induce their countrymen, to apply these principles consistently. What matters is that these supposedly absolute and universal principles were not principles at all, but the unconscious reflexions of national policy based on a particular interpretation of national interest at a particular time. There is a sense in which peace and co-operation between nations or classes or individuals is a common and universal end irrespective of conflicting interests and politics. There is a sense in which a common interest exists in the maintenance of order, whether it be international order or 'law and order' within the nation. But as soon as the attempt is made to apply these supposedly abstract principles to a concrete political situation, they are revealed as the transparent disguises of selfish vested interests. The bankruptcy of utopianism resides not in its failure to live up to its principles, but in the exposure of its inability to provide any absolute and disinterested standard for the conduct of international affairs. The utopian, faced by the collapse of standards whose interested character he has failed to penetrate, takes refuge in condemnation of a reality which refuses to conform to these standards. A passage penned by the German historian Meinecke after the first world war is the best judgment by anticipation of the role of utopianism in the international politics of the period:

> The profound defect of the Western, natural-law type of thought was that, when applied to the real life of the state, it remained a dead letter, did not penetrate the consciousness of statesmen, did not hinder the modern hypertrophy of state interest, and so led either to aimless complaints and doctrinaire suppositions or else to inner falsehood and cant.[44]

These 'aimless complaints', these 'doctrinaire suppositions', this 'inner falsehood and cant' will be familiar to all those who have studied what was written about international politics in English-speaking countries between the two world wars.

42. *Relazioni Internazionali*, quoted in *The Times*, December 5, 1938.
43. *Völkischer Beobachter*, April 1, 1939.
44. Meinecke, *Staaträson*, p. 533.

15

MORGENTHAU

Source: Hans J. Morgenthau (4th edn, 1967) *Politics Among Nations*.
New York, Alfred Knoff, pp. 4–14. Reprinted by permission of
McGraw-Hill Book Company.

Morgenthau's six principles of realism have become the starting point for almost
all undergraduate courses in international political theory. He argues that international relations should be seen as a discrete area of political life where normative, moral and idealistic considerations cannot be used as a guide for action.
In a world of competing sovereign states, where the currency is power, the duty
of each state is to take whatever action is necessary to protect its physical,
political, economic and cultural identity.

This theoretical concern with human nature as it actually is, and with the
historic processes as they actually take place, has earned for the theory presented
here the name of realism. What are the tenets of political realism? No systematic
exposition of the philosophy of political realism can be attempted here; it will
suffice to single out six fundamental principles, which have frequently been
misunderstood.

Six principles of political realism

1. Political realism believes that politics, like society in general, is governed by
objective laws that have their roots in human nature. In order to improve society

it is first necessary to understand the laws by which society lives. The operation of these laws being impervious to our preferences, men will challenge them only at the risk of failure.

Realism, believing as it does in the objectivity of the laws of politics, must also believe in the possibility of developing a rational theory that reflects, however imperfectly and one-sidedly, these objective laws. It believes also, then, in the possibility of distinguishing in politics between truth and opinion – between what is true objectively and rationally, supported by evidence and illuminated by reason, and what is only a subjective judgment, divorced from the facts as they are and informed by prejudice and wishful thinking.

Human nature, in which the laws of politics have their roots, has not changed since the classical philosophies of China, India, and Greece endeavored to discover these laws. Hence, novelty is not necessarily a virtue in political theory, nor is old age a defect. The fact that a theory of politics, if there be such a theory, has never been heard of before tends to create a presumption against, rather than in favor of, its soundness. Conversely, the fact that a theory of politics was developed hundreds or even thousands of years ago – as was the theory of the balance of power – does not create a presumption that it must be outmoded and obsolete. A theory of politics must be subjected to the dual test of reason and experience. To dismiss such a theory because it had its flowering in centuries past is to present not a rational argument but a modernistic prejudice that takes for granted the superiority of the present over the past. To dispose of the revival of such a theory as a 'fashion' or 'fad' is tantamount to assuming that in matters political we can have opinions but no truths.

For realism, theory consists in ascertaining facts and giving them meaning through reason. It assumes that the character of a foreign policy can be ascertained only through the examination of the political acts performed and of the foreseeable consequences of these acts. Thus we can find out what statesmen have actually done, and from the foreseeable consequences of their acts we can surmise what their objectives might have been.

Yet examination of the facts is not enough. To give meaning to the factual raw material of foreign policy, we must approach political reality with a kind of rational outline, a map that suggests to us the possible meanings of foreign policy. In other words, we put ourselves in the position of a statesman who must meet a certain problem of foreign policy under certain circumstances, and we ask ourselves what the rational alternatives are from which a statesman may choose who must meet this problem under these circumstances (presuming always that he acts in a rational manner), and which of these rational alternatives this particular statesman, acting under these circumstances, is likely to choose. It is the testing of this rational hypothesis against the actual facts and their consequences that gives meaning to the facts of international politics and makes a theory of politics possible.

2. The main signpost that helps political realism to find its way through the landscape of international politics is the concept of interest defined in terms of power. This concept provides the link between reason trying to understand

international politics and the facts to be understood. It sets politics as an auto-nomous sphere of action and understanding apart from other spheres, such as economics (understood in terms of interest defined as wealth), ethics, aesthetics, or religion. Without such a concept a theory of politics, international or domestic, would be altogether impossible, for without it we could not distin-guish between political and nonpolitical facts, nor could we bring at least a measure of systematic order to the political sphere.

We assume that statesmen think and act in terms of interest defined as power, and the evidence of history bears that assumption out. That assumption allows us to retrace and anticipate, as it were, the steps a stateman – past, present, or future – has taken or will take on the political scene. We look over his shoulder when he writes his dispatches; we listen in on his conversation with other statesmen; we read and anticipate his very thoughts. Thinking in terms of interest defined as power, we think as he does, and as disinterested observers we understand his thoughts and actions perhaps better than he, the actor on the political scene, does himself.

The concept of interest defined as power imposes intellectual discipline upon the observer, infuses rational order into the subject matter of politics, and thus makes the theoretical understanding of politics possible. On the side of the actor, it provides for rational discipline in action and creates that astounding continuity in foreign policy which makes American, British, or Russian foreign policy appear as an intelligible, rational continuum, by and large consistent within itself, regardless of the different motives, preferences, and intellectual and moral qualities of successive statesmen. A realist theory of international politics, then, will guard against two popular fallacies: the concern with motives and the con-cern with ideological preferences.

To search for the clue to foreign policy exclusively in the motives of statesmen is both futile and deceptive. It is futile because motives are the most illusive of psychological data, distorted as they are, frequently beyond recognition, by the interests and emotions of actor and observer alike. Do we really know what our own motives are? And what do we know of the motives of others?

Yet even if we had access to the real motives of statesmen, that knowledge would help us little in understanding foreign policies, and might well lead us astray. It is true that the knowledge of the statesman's motives may give us one among many clues as to what the direction of his foreign policy might be. It can-not give us, however, the one clue by which to predict his foreign policies. History shows no exact and necessary correlation between the quality of motives and the quality of foreign policy. This is true in both moral and political terms.

We cannot conclude from the good intentions of a statesman that his foreign policies will be either morally praiseworthy or politically successful. Judging his motives, we can say that he will not intentionally pursue policies that are morally wrong, but we can say nothing about the probability of their success. If we want to know the moral and political qualities of his actions, we must know them, not his motives. How often have statesmen been motivated by the desire to improve the world, and ended by making it worse? And how often have they sought one goal, and ended by achieving something they neither expected nor desired?

Neville Chamberlain's politics of appeasement were, as far as we can judge, inspired by good motives; he was probably less motivated by considerations of personal power than were many other British prime ministers, and he sought to preserve peace and to assure the happiness of all concerned. Yet his policies helped to make the Second World War inevitable, and to bring untold miseries to millions of men. Sir Winston Churchill's motives, on the other hand, have been much less universal in scope and much more narrowly directed toward personal and national power, yet the foreign policies that sprang from these inferior motives were certainly superior in moral and political quality to those pursued by his predecessor. Judged by his motives, Robespierre was one of the most virtuous men who ever lived. Yet it was the utopian radicalism of that very virtue that made him kill those less virtuous than himself, brought him to the scaffold, and destroyed the revolution of which he was a leader.

example

Good motives give assurance against deliberately bad policies; they do not guarantee the moral goodness and political success of the policies they inspire. What is important to know, if one wants to understand foreign policy, is not primarily the motives of a statesman, but his intellectual ability to comprehend the essentials of foreign policy, as well as his political ability to translate what he has comprehended into successful political action. It follows that while ethics in the abstract judges the moral qualities of motives, political theory must judge the political qualities of intellect, will, and action.

A realist theory of international politics will also avoid the other popular fallacy of equating the foreign policies of a statesman with his philosophic or political sympathies, and of deducing the former from the latter. Statesmen, especially under contemporary conditions, may well make a habit of presenting their foreign policies in terms of their philosophic and political sympathies in order to gain popular support for them. Yet they will distinguish with Lincoln between their '*official* duty,' which is to think and act in terms of the national interest, and their '*personal* wish,' which is to see their own moral values and political principles realized throughout the world. Political realism does not require, nor does it condone, indifference to political ideals and moral principles, but it requires indeed a sharp distinction between the desirable and the possible – between what is desirable everywhere and at all times and what is possible under the concrete circumstances of time and place.

It stands to reason that not all foreign policies have always followed so rational, objective, and unemotional a course. The contingent elements of personality, prejudice, and subjective preference, and of all the weaknesses of intellect and will which flesh is heir to, are bound to deflect foreign policies from their rational course. Especially where foreign policy is conducted under the conditions of democratic control, the need to marshal popular emotions to the support of foreign policy cannot fail to impair the rationality of foreign policy itself. Yet a theory of foreign policy which aims at rationality must for the time being, as it were, abstract from these irrational elements and seek to paint a picture of foreign policy which presents the rational essence to be found in experience, without the contingent deviations from rationality which are also found in experience.

The difference between international politics as it actually is and a rational theory derived from it is like the difference between a photograph and a painted portrait. The photograph shows everything that can be seen by the naked eye; the painted portrait does not show everything that can be seen by the naked eye, but it shows, or at least seeks to show, one thing that the naked eye cannot see: the human essence of the person portrayed.

Political realism contains not only a theoretical but also a normative element. It knows that political reality is replete with contingencies and points to the typical influences they exert upon foreign policy. Yet it shares with all social theory the need, for the sake of theoretical understanding, to stress the rational elements of political reality; for it is these rational elements that make reality intelligible for theory. Political realism presents the theoretical construct of a rational foreign policy which experience can never completely achieve.

At the same time political realism considers a rational foreign policy to be good foreign policy; for only a rational foreign policy minimizes risks and maximizes benefits and, hence, complies both with the moral precept of prudence and the political requirement of success. Political realism wants the photographic picture of the political world to resemble as much as possible its painted portrait. Aware of the inevitable gap between good – that is, rational – foreign policy and foreign policy as it actually is, political realism maintains not only that theory must focus upon the rational elements of political reality, but also that foreign policy ought to be rational in view of its own moral and practical purposes.

Hence, it is no argument against the theory here presented that actual foreign policy does not or cannot live up to it. That argument misunderstands the intention of this book, which is to present not an indiscriminate description of political reality, but a rational theory of international politics. Far from being invalidated by the fact that, for instance, a perfect balance of power policy will scarcely be found in reality, it assumes that reality, being deficient in this respect, must be understood and evaluated as an approximation to an ideal system of balance of power.

3. Realism does not endow its key concept of interest defined as power with a meaning that is fixed once and for all. The idea of interest is indeed of the essence of politics and is unaffected by the circumstances of time and place. Thucydides' statement, born of the experiences of ancient Greece, that 'identity of interests is the surest of bonds whether between states or individuals' was taken up in the nineteenth century by Lord Salisbury's remark that 'the only bond of union that endures' among nations is 'the absence of all clashing interests.' It was erected into a general principle of government by George Washington:

A small knowledge of human nature will convince us, that, with far the greatest part of mankind, interest is the governing principle; and that almost every man is more or less, under its influence. Motives of public virtue may for a time, or in particular instances, actuate men to the observance of a conduct purely disinterested; but they are not of themselves sufficient to produce persevering conformity to the refined dictates and obligations of social duty. Few men are capable of making a continual sacrifice of all views of private interest, or advantage, to the common good. It is vain to exclaim against the depravity of human nature on this account; the fact is so, the experience of every age and nation has proved it and we must in a great measure, change the constitution of man, before we can make it otherwise. No institution, not built on the presumptive truth of these maxims can succeed.[1]

It was echoed and enlarged upon in our century by Max Weber's observation:

Interests (material and ideal), not ideas, dominate directly the actions of men. Yet the 'images of the world' created by these ideas have very often served as switches determining the tracks on which the dynamism of interests kept actions moving.[2]

Yet the kind of interest determining political action in a particular period of history depends upon the political and cultural context within which foreign policy is formulated. The goals that might be pursued by nations in their foreign policy can run the whole gamut of objectives any nation has ever pursued or might possibly pursue.

The same observations apply to the concept of power. Its content and the manner of its use are determined by the political and cultural environment. Power may comprise anything that establishes and maintains the control of man over man. Thus power covers all social relationships which serve that end, from physical violence to the most subtle psychological ties by which one mind controls another. Power covers the domination of man by man, both when it is disciplined by moral ends and controlled by constitutional safeguards, as in Western democracies, and when it is that untamed and barbaric force which finds its laws in nothing but its own strength and its sole justification in its aggrandizement.

Political realism does not assume that the contemporary conditions under which foreign policy operates, with their extreme instability and the ever present threat of large-scale violence, cannot be changed. The balance of power, for instance, is indeed a perennial element of all pluralistic societies, as the authors of The Federalist papers well knew; yet it is capable of operating, as it does in

1. The Writings of George Washington, edited by John C. Fitzpatrick (Washington: United States Printing Office, 1931–44), Vol. X, p. 363.
2. Marianne Weber, Max Weber (Tuebingen: J.C.B. Mohr, 1926) pp. 347–8.

the United States, under the conditions of relative stability and peaceful conflict. If the factors that have given rise to these conditions can be duplicated on the international scene, similar conditions of stability and peace will then prevail there, as they have over long stretches of history among certain nations.

What is true of the general character of international relations is also true of the nation state as the ultimate point of reference of contemporary foreign policy. While the realist indeed believes that interest is the perennial standard by which political action must be judged and directed, the contemporary connection between interest and the national state is a product of history, and is therefore bound to disappear in the course of history. Nothing in the realist position militates against the assumption that the present division of the political world into nation states will be replaced by larger units of a quite different character, more in keeping with the technical potentialities and the moral requirements of the contemporary world.

The realist parts company with other schools of thought before the all-important question of how the contemporary world is to be transformed. The realist is persuaded that this transformation can be achieved only through the workmanlike manipulation of the perennial forces that have shaped the past as they will the future. The realist cannot be persuaded that we can bring about that transformation by confronting a political reality that has its own laws with an abstract ideal that refuses to take those laws into account.

4. Political realism is aware of the moral significance of political action. It is also aware of the ineluctable tension between the moral command and the requirements of successful political action. And it is unwilling to gloss over and obliterate that tension and thus to obfuscate both the moral and the political issue by making it appear as though the stark facts of politics were morally more satisfying than they actually are, and the moral law less exacting than it actually is.

Realism maintains that universal moral principles cannot be applied to the actions of states in their abstract universal formulation, but that they must be filtered through the concrete circumstances of time and place. The individual may say for himself: 'Fiat justitia, pereat mundus (Let justice be done, even if the world perish),' but the state has no right to say so in the name of those who are in its care. Both individual and state must judge political action by universal moral principles, such as that of liberty. Yet while the individual has a moral right to sacrifice himself in defense of such a moral principle, the state has no right to let its moral disapprobation of the infringement of liberty get in the way of successful political action, itself inspired by the moral principle of national survival. There can be no political morality without prudence; that is, without consideration of the political consequences of seemingly moral action. Realism, then, considers prudence – the weighing of the consequences of alternative political actions – to be the supreme virtue in politics. Ethics in the abstract judges action by its conformity with the moral law; political ethics judges action by its political consequences. Classical and medieval philosophy knew this, and so did Lincoln when he said:

I do the very best I know how, the very best I can, and I mean to keep doing so until the end. If the end brings me out all right, what is said against me won't amount to anything. If the end brings me out wrong, ten angels swearing I was right would make no difference.

5. Political realism refuses to identify the moral aspirations of a particular nation with the moral laws that govern the universe. As it distinguishes between truth and opinion, so it distinguishes between truth and idolatry. All nations are tempted – and few have been able to resist the temptation for long – to clothe their own particular aspirations and actions in the moral purposes of the universe. To know that nations are subject to the moral law is one thing, while to pretend to know with certainty what is good and evil in the relations among nations is quite another. There is a world of difference between the belief that all nations stand under the judgment of God, inscrutable to the human mind, and the blasphemous conviction that God is always on one's side and that what one wills oneself cannot fail to be willed by God also.

The lighthearted equation between a particular nationalism and the counsels of Providence is morally indefensible, for it is that very sin of pride against which the Greek tragedians and the Biblical prophets have warned rulers and ruled. That equation is also politically pernicious, for it is liable to engender the distortion in judgment which, in the blindness of crusading frenzy, destroys nations and civilizations – in the name of moral principle, ideal, or God himself.

On the other hand, it is exactly the concept of interest defined in terms of power that saves us from both that moral excess and that political folly. For if we look at all nations, our own included, as political entities pursuing their respective interests defined in terms of power, we are able to do justice to all of them. And we are able to do justice to all of them in a dual sense: We are able to judge other nations as we judge our own and, having judged them in this fashion, we are then capable of pursuing policies that respect the interests of other nations, while protecting and promoting those of our own. Moderation in policy cannot fail to reflect the moderation of moral judgment.

6. The difference, then, between political realism and other schools of thought is real, and it is profound. However much the theory of political realism may have been misunderstood and misinterpreted, there is no gainsaying its distinctive intellectual and moral attitude to matters political.

Intellectually, the political realist maintains the autonomy of the political sphere, as the economist, the lawyer, the moralist maintain theirs. He thinks in terms of interest defined as power, as the economist thinks in terms of interest defined as wealth; the lawyer, of the conformity of action with legal rules; the moralist, of the conformity of action with moral principles. The economist asks: 'How does this policy affect the wealth of society, or a segment of it?' The lawyer asks: 'Is this policy in accord with the rules of law?' The moralist asks: 'Is this policy in accord with moral principles?' And the political realist asks: 'How does this policy affect the power of the nation?' (Or of the federal government, of Congress, of the party, of agriculture, as the case may be.)

The political realist is not unaware of the existence and relevance of standards of thought other than political ones. As political realist, he cannot but subordinate these other standards to those of politics. And he parts company with other schools when they impose standards of thought appropriate to other spheres upon the political sphere. It is here that political realism takes issue with the 'legalistic-moralistic approach' to international politics. That this issue is not, as has been contended, a mere figment of the imagination, but goes to the very core of the controversy, can be shown from many historical examples. Three will suffice to make the point.[3]

In 1939 the Soviet Union attacked Finland. This action confronted France and Great Britain with two issues, one legal, the other political. Did that action violate the Covenant of the League of Nations and, if it did, what countermeasures should France and Great Britain take? The legal question could easily be answered in the affirmative, for obviously the Soviet Union had done what was prohibited by the Covenant. The answer to the political question depended, first, upon the manner in which the Russian action affected the interests of France and Great Britain; second, upon the existing distribution of power between France and Great Britain, on the one hand, and the Soviet Union and other potentially hostile nations, especially Germany, on the other; and, third, upon the influence that the countermeasures were likely to have upon the interests of France and Great Britain and the future distribution of power. France and Great Britain, as the leading members of the League of Nations, saw to it that the Soviet Union was expelled from the League, and they were prevented from joining Finland in the war against the Soviet Union only by Sweden's refusal to allow their troops to pass through Swedish territory on their way to Finland. If this refusal by Sweden had not saved them, France and Great Britain would shortly have found themselves at war with the Soviet Union and Germany at the same time.

The policy of France and Great Britain was a classic example of legalism in that they allowed the answer to the legal question, legitimate within its sphere, to determine their political actions. Instead of asking both questions, that of law and that of power, they asked only the question of law; and the answer they received could have no bearing on the issue that their very existence might have depended upon.

The second example illustrates the 'moralistic approach' to international politics. It concerns the international status of the Communist government of China. The rise of that government confronted the Western world with two issues, one moral, the other political. Were the nature and policies of that government in accord with the moral principles of the Western world? Should the Western world deal with such a government? The answer to the first question

3. See the other examples discussed in Hans J. Morgenthau, 'Another "Great Debate": The National Interest of the United States,' *The American Political Science Review*, XLVI (December 1952), pp. 979 ff. See also Hans J. Morgenthau, *Politics in the 20th Century*, Vol. I, *The Decline of Democractic Politics* (Chicago: University of Chicago Press, 1962), pp. 79 ff.

could not fail to be in the negative. Yet it did not follow with necessity that the answer to the second question should also be in the negative. The standard of thought applied to the first – the moral – question was simply to test the nature and the policies of the Communist government of China by the principles of Western morality. On the other hand, the second – the political – question had to be subjected to the complicated test of the interests involved and the power available on either side, and of the bearing of one or the other course of action upon these interests and power. The application of this test could well have led to the conclusion that it would be wiser not to deal with the Communist government of China. To arrive at this conclusion by neglecting this test altogether and answering the political question in terms of the moral issue was indeed a classic example of the 'moralistic approach' to international politics.

The third case illustrates strikingly the contrast between realism and the legalistic-moralistic approach to foreign policy. Great Britain, as one of the guarantors of the neutrality of Belgium, went to war with Germany in August 1914 because Germany had violated the neutrality of Belgium. The British action could be justified either in realistic or legalistic-moralistic terms. That is to say, one could argue realistically that for centuries it had been axiomatic for British foreign policy to prevent the control of the Low Countries by a hostile power. It was then not so much the violation of Belgium's neutrality per se as the hostile intentions of the violator which provided the rationale for British intervention. If the violator had been another nation but Germany, Great Britain might well have refrained from intervening. This is the position taken by Sir Edward Grey, British Foreign Secretary during that period. Under Secretary for Foreign Affairs Hardinge remarked to him in 1908: 'If France violated Belgian neutrality in a war against Germany, it is doubtful whether England or Russia would move a finger to maintain Belgian neutrality, while if the neutrality of Belgium was violated by Germany, it is probable that the converse would be the case.' Whereupon Sir Edward Grey replied: 'This is to the point.' Yet one could also take the legalistic and moralistic position that the violation of Belgium's neutrality per se, because of its legal and moral defects and regardless of the interests at stake and of the identity of the violator, justified British and, for that matter, American intervention. This was the position which Theodore Roosevelt took in his letter to Sir Edward Grey of January 22, 1915:

> To me the crux of the situation has been Belgium. If England or France had acted toward Belgium as Germany has acted I should have opposed them, exactly as I now oppose Germany. I have emphatically approved your action as a model for what should be done by those who believe that treaties should be observed in good faith and that there is such a thing as international morality. I take this position as an American who is no more an Englishman than he is a German, who endeavors loyally to serve the interests of his own country, but who also endeavors to do what he can for justice and decency as regards mankind at large, and who therefore feels obliged to judge all other nations by their conduct on any given occasion.

This realist defense of the autonomy of the political sphere against its subversion by other modes of thought does not imply disregard for the existence and importance of these other modes of thought. It rather implies that each should be assigned its proper sphere and function. Political realism is based upon a pluralistic conception of human nature. Real man is a composite of 'economic man,' 'political man,' 'moral man,' 'religious man,' etc. A man who was nothing but 'political man' would be a beast, for he would be completely lacking in moral restraints. A man who was nothing but 'moral man' would be a fool, for he would be completely lacking in prudence. A man who was nothing but 'religious man' would be a saint, for he would be completely lacking in worldly desires.

Recognizing that these different facets of human nature exist, political realism also recognizes that in order to understand one of them one has to deal with it on its own terms. That is to say, if I want to understand 'religious man,' I must for the time being abstract from the other aspects of human nature and deal with its religious aspect as if it were the only one. Furthermore, I must apply to the religious sphere the standards of thought appropriate to it, always remaining aware of the existence of other standards and their actual influence upon the religious qualities of man. What is true of this facet of human nature is true of all the others. No modern economist, for instance, would conceive of his science and its relations to other sciences of man in any other way. It is exactly through such a process of emancipation from other standards of thought, and the development of one appropriate to its subject matter, that economics has developed as an autonomous theory of the economic activities of man. To contribute to a similar development in the field of politics is indeed the purpose of political realism.

16

HERZ

Source: John H. Herz (1957) 'The rise and demise of the territorial state'. *World Politics*, 9: 4, 473–93.

Herz questions the 'old thinking' of scholars like Morgenthau and Carr that the state can be understood as a 'hard shell' protecting the political, cultural and economic values of its population from undesirable foreign intrusion. He argues that advances in technical and scientific knowledge bring the possibility of economic, ideological and military penetration of the state. Specifically, in the age of nuclear weapons our very survival may depend upon nations defining their interests in terms wider than those of self-interest. This, according to Herz, requires that we engage in 'new thinking' in an effort to redefine the language of international politics.

Students and practitioners of international politics are at present in a strange predicament. Complex though their problems have been in the past, there was then at least some certainty about the 'givens,' the basic structure and the basic phenomena of international relations. Today one is neither here nor there. On the one hand, for instance, one is assured – or at least tempted to accept assurance – that for all practical purposes a nuclear stalemate rules out major war as a major means of policy today and in the foreseeable future. On the other hand, one has an uncanny sense of the practicability of the unabated arms race, and a doubt whether reliance can be placed solely on the deterrent purpose of all this preparation. We are no longer sure about the functions of war and peace, nor do we know how to define the national interest and what its defense requires under present conditions. As a matter of fact, the meaning and function of the basic protective unit, the 'sovereign' nation-state itself, have become doubtful. On what, then, can policy and planning be built?

In the author's opinion, many of these uncertainties have their more profound cause in certain fundamental changes which have taken place in the structure of international relations and, specifically, in the nature of the units among which these relations occur. This transformation in the 'statehood' of nations will be the subject of this article.

I. Basic features of the modern state system

Traditionally, the classical system of international relations, or the modern state system, has been considered 'anarchic,' because it was based on unequally distributed power and was deficient in higher – that is, supra-national – authority. Its units, the independent, sovereign nation-states, were forever threatened by stronger power and survived precariously through the balance-of-power system. Customarily, then, the modern state system has been contrasted with the medieval system, on the one hand, where units of international relations were under higher law and higher authority, and with those more recent international trends, on the other, which seemed to point toward a greater, 'collective' security of nations and a 'rule of law' that would protect them from the indiscriminate use of force characteristic of the age of power politics.

From the vantage point of the atomic age, we can probe deeper into the basic characteristics of the classical system. What is it that ultimately accounted for the peculiar unity, compactness, coherence of the modern nation-state, setting it off from other nation-states as a separate, independent, and sovereign power? It would seem that this underlying factor is to be found neither in the sphere of law nor in that of politics, but rather in that substratum of statehood where the state unit confronts us, as it were, in its physical, corporeal capacity: as an expanse of territory encircled for its identification and its defense by a 'hard shell' of fortifications. In this lies what will here be referred to as the 'impermeability,' or 'impenetrability,' or simply the 'territoriality,' of the modern state. The fact that it was surrounded by a hard shell rendered it to some extent secure from foreign penetration, and thus made it an ultimate unit of protection for those within its boundaries. Throughout history, that unit which affords protection and security to human beings has tended to become the basic political unit; people, in the long run, will recognize that authority, any authority, which possesses the power of protection.

Some similarity perhaps prevails between an international structure consisting of impenetrable units with an ensuing measurability of power and comparability of power relations, and the system of classical physics with its measurable forces and the (then) impenetrable atom as its basic unit. And as that system has given way to relativity and to what nuclear science has uncovered, the impenetrability of the political atom, the nation-state, is giving way to a permeability which tends to obliterate the very meaning of unit and unity, power and power relations, sovereignty and independence. The possibility of 'hydrogenization' merely represents the culmination of a development which has rendered the traditional defense structure of nations obsolete through the power to by-pass the shell protecting a two-dimensional territory and thus to destroy – vertically, as it were – even the most powerful ones. Paradoxically, utmost strength now coincides in the same unit with utmost vulnerability, absolute power with utter impotence.

This development must inevitably affect traditional power concepts. Considering power units as politically independent and legally sovereign made sense when power, measurable, graded, calculable, served as a standard of comparison between units which, in the sense indicated above, could be described as impermeable. Under those conditions, then, power indicated the strategic aspect, independence the political aspect, sovereignty the legal aspect of this selfsame impermeability. With the passing of the age of territoriality, the usefulness of these concepts must now be questioned.

Thus the Great Divide does not separate 'international anarchy,' or 'balance of power,' or 'power politics,' from incipient international interdependence, or from 'collective security'; all these remain within the realm of the territorial structure of states and can therefore be considered as trends or stages *within* the classical system of 'hard shell' power units. Rather, the Divide occurs where the basis of territorial power and defensibility vanishes. It is here and now. But in order to understand the present, we must study more closely the origin and nature of the classical system itself.

II. The rise of the territorial state

The rise of the modern territorial state meant that, within countries, 'feudal anarchy' of jurisdictions yielded to the ordered centralism of the absolute monarchy, which ruled over a pacified area with the aid of a bureaucracy, a professional army, and the power to levy taxes, while in foreign relations, in place of the medieval hierarchy of power and authority, there prevailed insecurity, a disorder only slightly attenuated by a power balance that was forever being threatened, disturbed, and then restored. Such has been the customary interpretation.

It is possible to view developments in a somewhat different light. Instead of contrasting the security of groups and individuals within the sovereign territorial state with conditions of insecurity outside, the establishment of territorial independence can be interpreted as an at least partially successful attempt to render the territorial group secure in its outward relations as well. Especially when contrasted with the age of anarchy and insecurity which immediately preceded it, the age of territoriality appears as one of relative order and safety.

Indeed, the transition from medieval hierarchism to modern compartmentalized sovereignties was neither easy, nor straight, nor short. Modern sovereignty arose out of the triangular struggle among emperors and popes, popes and kings, and kings and emperors. When the lawyers of Philip the Fair propounded the dual maxim according to which the king was to be 'emperor in his realm' (*rex est imperator in regno suo*) and was no longer to 'recognize any superior' (*superiorem non recognoscens*), it was the beginning of a development in the course of which, in McIlwain's words, 'Independence *de facto* was ultimately translated into a sovereignty *de jure*.'[1] But centuries of disturbance and real anarchy ensued during which the problems of rulership and security remained unsettled. The relative protection which the sway of moral standards and the absence of highly destructive weapons had afforded groups and individuals in the earlier Middle Ages gave way to total insecurity when gunpowder was invented and common standards broke down. Out of the internal and external turmoil during the age of religious and civil wars, a 'neutralist' central power eventually managed to establish itself in and for each of the different territories like so many *rochers de bronze*.

The idea that a territorial coexistence of states, based on the power of the territorial princes, might afford a better guarantee of peace than the Holy Roman Empire was already widespread at the height of the Middle Ages when the emperor proved incapable of enforcing the peace.[2] But territoriality could hardly prevail so long as the knight in his castle (that medieval unit of impermeability) was relatively immune from attack, as was the medieval city within its walls. Only with a developing money economy were overlords able to free themselves from dependence on vassals and lay the foundations of their own power by establishing a professional army. Infantry and artillery now proved superior to old-style cavalry, firearms prevailed over the old weapons.

As in all cases of radically new developments in military technology, the 'gunpowder revolution' caused a real revolution in the superstructure of economic, social, and political relationships because of its impact on the units of protection and security. A feeling of insecurity swept all Europe.[3] Though a Machiavelli might establish new rules as to how to gain and maintain power, there still followed more than a century of unregulated, ideological 'total' wars inside and among countries until the new units of power were clearly established. Before old or new sovereigns could claim to be recognized as rulers of large areas, it had

1. Charles H. McIlwain, *The Growth of Political Thought in the West*, New York, 1932, p. 268.
2. F.A. von der Heydte, *Die Geburtsstunde des souveränen Staates*, Regensburg, 1952, pp. 103ff., 277, 293ff.
3. Ariosto expressed the feeling of despair which invaded the 'old powers' of chivalry when gunpowder destroyed the foundations of their system, in terms reminding one of present-day despair in the face of the destructive forces loosed upon our own world:

   > Oh! curs'd device! base implement of death!
   > Framed in the black Tartarean realms beneath!
   > By Beelzebub's malicious art design'd
   > To ruin all the race of human kind.

   Quoted from *Orlando Furioso* by Felix Gilbert, in Edward M. Earle, ed., *Makers of Modern Strategy*, Princeton, N.J., 1943, p. 4.

to be determined how far, on the basis of their new military power, they were able to extend their control geographically.[4]

The large-area state came finally to occupy the place that the castle or fortified town had previously held as a unit of impenetrability. But the new unit could not be considered consolidated until all independent fortifications within it had disappeared and, in their place, fortresses lining the circumference of the country had been built by the new central power and manned by its armed forces.[5] If we contrast our present system of bases and similar outposts surrounding entire world regions with what are today small-scale nation-states, perhaps we can visualize what the hard shell of frontier fortifications consolidating the then large-scale territorial states meant by way of extending power units in the age of absolutism. They became, in the words of Frederick the Great, 'mighty nails which hold a ruler's provinces together.' There now was peace and protection within. War became a regularized military procedure; only the breaking of the shell permitted interference with what had now become the internal affairs of another country.

In this way was established the basic structure of the territorial state which was to last throughout the classical period of the modern state system. Upon this foundation a new system and new concepts of international relations could arise. And as early as the second half of the seventeenth century a perspicacious observer succeeded in tying up the new concepts with the underlying structure of territorial statehood.

III. The nature of territoriality

It was hardly a coincidence that this connection was established shortly after the end of the Thirty Years War, when formal sanction had been given to territorial sovereignty in the Westphalian Peace. For here was the turning point, the Great Divide between what were still partially medieval situations reflecting a certain permeability of the rising nation-state (when, for instance, outside powers could still ally themselves with *frondes* within a country against that country's sovereign) and the modern era of closed units no longer brooking such interference.[6]

---

4. On this, see Garrett Mattingly, *Renaissance Diplomacy*, Boston, 1955, pp. 59ff., 121ff., 205ff.
5. See Friedrich Meinecke, *Die Idee der Staatsraison in der neueren Geschichte*, Munich and Berlin, 1925, pp. 241ff.
6. The emergence of 'non-intervention' as a legal concept illustrates this transition. A complete change in the meaning of the term occurred in the brief period between the time of Grotius and that of Pufendorf. Grotius, writing during the last phase of the pre-modern era of religious and 'international civil' wars and still thinking in terms of 'just' and 'unjust' wars, considered a ruler entitled to intervene in the affairs of another sovereign if it was necessary to defend oppressed subjects of the latter; Pufendorf, barely fifty years later, rejected such interference in the 'domestic affairs' of another sovereign as a violation of the sovereign's exclusive jurisdiction over his territory and all it contained. See Walter Schiffer, *The Legal Community of Mankind*, New York, 1954, pp. 34f., 56.

The clarification of the nature of territoriality to which we referred above is found in a little and little-known essay by Leibniz, written for an entirely pragmatic purpose – namely, to prove the right of legation of the territorial ruler (the Duke of Hanover) in whose service the philosopher then was.[7] Leibniz' problem derived directly from the situation created by the Peace of Westphalia. This settlement, for all practical purposes, had conferred sovereign independence upon those princes who formally were still included in the Empire; yet it had not abolished the long-established, essentially feudal structure of the Empire itself, with its allegiances and jurisdictions, its duties of membership, and even its clumsy and scarcely workable framework of government. Thus some of the factually sovereign territorial rulers in Europe were somehow still under a higher authority. Were they now 'sovereign' or not? What accounted for sovereignty?

Leibniz' contemporaries failed to see the problem in this light. The muddled state of affairs was made to order for those jurists and others who argued fine points perennially with the aid of sterile or obsolete concepts. Leibniz, instead, proceeded to study 'what actually happens in the world today,' and as a result could boast of being 'the first to have found the valid definition of sovereignty.'[8]

As he saw it, the first condition for sovereignty was a minimum size of territory. Minuscule principalities, at that time still abundant, could not claim to be on a par with those that recognized each other as equally sovereign in respect to peace and war, alliances, and the general affairs of Europe, because, not possessing sufficient territory, they could at best, with their garrisons, only maintain *internal* order.[9] But there remained the chief problem: how to define the status of those rulers who, because of their membership in the Empire, were subjects of the emperor. Could one be 'sovereign' and 'subject' at the same time? If not, what was the status of these 'subject' rulers as compared with that of their 'sovereign' European brethren? If so, what did their subjection to the emperor amount to? These questions were further complicated by the fact that at every European court, and in the Empire as well, there were certain high dignitaries, often called 'princes,' 'dukes,' etc., who customarily held the rank of 'sovereign.' It was through this maze of relationships that Leibniz arrived at his definitions.

He elaborated his concept of sovereignty by distinguishing it from 'majesty.' Majesty, the authority which the emperor has *qua* emperor over the Empire's members, consists of a number of jurisdictions that confer the right to demand obedience and involve duties of fealty, but it is not sovereignty. Why not? Simply because, with all its supreme authority, majesty does not involve an 'actual and present power to constrain' subjects on their own territories. Their territory, in other words, is impermeable. The subject, on the other hand, if he is a territorial ruler, is sovereign because he has the power to constrain *his* subjects, while not

---

7. 'Entretiens de Philarète et d'Eugène sur le droit d'Ambassade'; quoted here from *Werke*, 1st series, III, Hanover, 1864, pp. 331ff.
8. *Ibid.*, pp. 340, 342.
9. *Ibid.*, p. 349.

being so constrainable by superior power. The decisive criterion thus is actual control of one's 'estates' by one's military power, which excludes any other power within and without. Contrariwise, the absence of such forces of his own on his subjects' territories accounts for the absence of 'sovereignty' in the emperor's 'majesty.' He can enforce his authority or rights only by applying his own or other sovereigns' forces from the outside, 'by means of war.' But in doing so, his condition is no different from that of any other sovereign vis-à-vis *his* fellow-rulers, for war is a contest which can be inaugurated not only by majesties but by any sovereign ruler. And force of arms may constrain a sovereign outside the Empire quite as well as one inside; in fact, war constitutes the only way in which even sovereigns can be constrained.[10] By perceiving that the emperor's power to enforce his authority was actually reduced to means of war, Leibniz was in a position to demonstrate that any and all rulers of impermeable territory, whatever their status in regard to imperial authority, were equal in their sovereign status.

This capacity also distinguished them from those dignitaries who were sovereigns in name only. Leibniz, by way of example, referred to the non-sovereign status of certain papal 'princes,' contrasting it with that of sovereign princes: 'Should His Holiness desire to make . . . [the papal princes] obey, he has merely to send out his "sbirros" [bailiffs], but in order to constrain . . . [the sovereign princes] he would need an army and cannon.'[11] Similarly, if the Empire wants to constrain a sovereign member, 'what would begin as court procedure in an imperial Tribunal, in execution would amount to a war.'[12] In the new age of territoriality, those superior in law no longer could use the machinery of government (courts, etc.) to enforce claims against territorial rulers.[13] In more recent times, this has come to be the relationship between sovereign nation-states as members of international organizations (like the League of Nations or the United Nations) and the organizations as such.

---

10. 'La souveraineté est un pouvoir légitime et ordinaire de contraindre les sujets à obéir, sans qu'on puisse être contraint soy même si ce n'est par une guerre' (*ibid.*, p. 352).

11. *Ibid.*, p. 354.

12. *Ibid.*, p. 358.

13. Leibniz' emphasis on constraint as a primary prerequisite of sovereignty might strike later observers as over-materialistic. But one should remember that the *rocher de bronze* of sovereignty was only then being established, not only against outside interference but also against still recalcitrant feudal powers within the territorial ruler's realm, and even in the latter case frequently by force of arms and armed forces which to the defeated may well have appeared as something very much like occupation forces. As a matter of fact, 'garrisoning' is a key word in Leibniz' arguments: 'As long as one has the right to be master in one's own house, and no superior has the right to maintain garrisons there and deprive one of the exercise of one's right of peace, war, and alliances, one has that independence which sovereignty presupposes (*liberté requise à la Souveraineté*)' (*ibid.*, p. 356).

IV. The territorial state in international relations

From territoriality resulted the concepts and institutions which characterized the interrelations of sovereign units, the modern state system. Modern international law, for instance, could now develop. Like the international system that produced it, international law has often been considered inherently contradictory because of its claim to bind sovereign units. But whether or not we deny to it for this reason the name and character of genuine law, it is important to see it in its connection with the territorial nature of the state system that it served. Only then can it be understood as a system of rules not contrary to, but implementing, the sovereign independence of states. Only to the extent that it reflected their territoriality and took into account their sovereignty could international law develop in modern times. For its general rules and principles deal primarily with the delimitation of the jurisdiction of countries. It thus implements the *de facto* condition of territorial impenetrability by more closely defining unit, area, and conditions of impenetrability. Such a law must reflect, rather than regulate. As one author has rightly remarked, 'International law really amounts to laying down the principle of national sovereignty and deducing the consequences.'[14] It is not for this reason superfluous, for sovereign units must know in some detail where their jurisdictions end and those of other units begin; without such standards, nations would be involved in constant strife over the implementation of their independence.

But it was not only this mutual legal accommodation which rendered possible a relatively peaceful coexistence of nations. War itself, the very phenomenon which reflected, not the strength, but the limitations of impermeability, was of such a nature as to maintain at least the principle of territoriality. War was limited not only in conduct but also in objectives. It was not a process of physical or political annihilation but a contest of power and will in which the interests, but not the existence, of the contestants were at stake. Now that we approach the era of absolute exposure, without walls or moats, where penetration will mean not mere damage or change but utter annihilation of life and way of life, it may dawn on us that what has vanished with the age of sovereignty and 'power politics' was not entirely adverse in nature and effects.

Among other 'conservative' features of the classical system, we notice one only in passing: the balance of power. It is only recently that emphasis has shifted from a somewhat one-sided concern with the negative aspects of the balance – its uncertainty, its giving rise to unending conflicts and frequent wars, etc. – to its protective effect of preventing the expansionist capacity of power from destroying other power altogether.[15] But at the time of its perfection in statecraft and diplomacy, there were even theories (not lived up to in practice, of

14. François Laurent, as quoted by Schiffer, *op.cit.*, p. 157.
15. See my *Political Realism and Political Idealism*, Chicago, 1951, pp. 206–21.

course) about the *legal* obligations of nations to form barriers against hegemony power in the common interest.[16]

More fundamental to the conservative structure of the old system was its character as a community. Forming a comparatively pacified whole, Europe was set off sharply against the world outside, a world beyond those lines which, by common agreement, separated a community based on territoriality and common heritage from anarchy, where the law of nature reigned and no standards of civilization applied. Only recently have the existence and role of so-called 'amity lines' been rediscovered, lines which were drawn in the treaties of the early modern period and which separated European territories, where the rules of war and peace were to prevail, from overseas territories and areas.[17] There was to be 'no peace beyond the line'; that is, European powers, although possibly at peace in Europe, continued to be *homo homini lupus* abroad. This practice made it easier for the European family of nations to observe self-denying standards at home by providing them with an outlet in the vast realm discovered outside Europe. While the practice of drawing amity lines subsequently disappeared, one chief function of overseas expansion remained: a European balance of power could be maintained or adjusted because it was relatively easy to divert European conflicts into overseas directions and adjust them there. Thus the openness of the world contributed to the consolidation of the territorial system. The end of the 'world frontier' and the resulting closedness of an interdependent world inevitably affected this system's effectiveness.

Another characteristic of the old system's protective nature may be seen in the almost complete absence of instances in which countries were wiped out in the course of wars or as a consequence of other power-political events. This, of course, refers to the territorial units at home only, not to the peoples and state units beyond the pale abroad; and to the complete destruction of a state's independent existence, not to mere loss of territory or similar changes, which obviously abounded in the age of power politics.

Evidence of this is to be found not only in a legal and political ideology that denied the permissibility of conquest at home while recognizing it as a title for the acquisition of territorial jurisdiction abroad.[18] For such a doctrine had its non-ideological foundation in the actual difference between European and non-European politics so far as their territoriality was concerned. European states were impermeable in the sense here outlined, while most of those overseas were

16. J. von Elbe, 'Die Wiederherstellung der Gleichgewichtsordnung in Europa durch den Wiener Kongress,' *Zeitschrift für ausländisches öffentliches Recht und Völkerrecht*, IV (1934), pp. 226ff.

17. See Carl Schmitt, *Der Nomos der Erde*, Cologne, 1950, pp. 6off.; also W. Schoenborn, 'Über Entdeckung als Rechtstitel völkerrechtlichen Gebietserwerbs,' in D.S. Constantinopoulos and H. Wehberg, eds., *Gegenwartsprobleme des internationalen Rechts und der Rechtsphilosophie*, Hamburg, 1953, pp. 239ff.

18. On this, see M.M. McMahon, *Conquest and Modern International Law*, Washington, D.C., 1940; M.F. Lindlay, *The Acquisition and Government of Backward Territory in International Law*, London, 1926; and Robert Langer, *Seizure of Territory*, Princeton, N.J., 1947.

easily penetrable by Europeans. In accordance with these circumstances, international politics in Europe knew only rare and exceptional instances of actual annihilation through conquest or similar forceful means.

Prior to the twentieth century, there were indeed the Napoleonic conquests, but I submit that this is a case where the exception confirms the rule. The Napoleonic system, as a hegemonial one, was devised to destroy the established system of territoriality and balanced power as such. Consequently, Napoleon and his policies appeared 'demonic' to contemporaries,[19] as well as to a nineteenth century which experienced the restoration of the earlier system. During that century occurred Bismarck's annexations of some German units into Prussia in pursuance of German unification. As in Napoleon's case, they appeared abnormal to many of his contemporaries, although the issue of national unification tended to mitigate this impression.[20] Besides these, there was indeed the partition of Poland, and considering the lamentable and lasting impression and the universal bad conscience it produced even among the ruling nations in a century used to quite a bit of international skulduggery, again one may well claim an exceptional character for that event.[21]

What, in particular, accounts for this remarkable stability? Territoriality – the establishment of defensible units, internally pacified and hard-shell rimmed – may be called its foundation. On this foundation, two phenomena permitted the system to become more stable than might otherwise have been the case: the prevalence of the legitimacy principle and, subsequently, nationalism. Legitimacy implied that the dynasties ruling the territorial states of old Europe mutually recognized each other as rightful sovereigns. Depriving one sovereign of his rights by force could not but appear to destroy the very principle on which the rights of all of them rested.

With the rise of nationalism, we witness the personalization of the units as self-determining, national groups. Nationalism now made it appear as abhorrent to deprive a sovereign nation of its independence as to despoil a legitimate ruler had appeared before. States, of course, had first to become 'nation-states,' considering themselves as representing specific nationality groups, which explains why in the two regions of Europe where larger numbers of old units stood in the way of national unification their demise encountered little objection. In most instances, however, the rise of nationalism led to the emergence of *new* states, which split away from multinational or colonial empires. This meant the extension of the European principle of 'non-obliteration' all over the world. It is perhaps significant that even in our century, and even after the turmoil of

19. As witness the impression made on contemporaries by the destruction of the first ancient European unit to fall victim to these policies – Venice.
20. See Erich Eyck, *Bismarck*, II, Zurich, 1943, pp. 305ff.
21. Except for these cases, we find only marginal instances of complete obliteration. The annexation of the Free City of Krakow by Russia eliminated a synthetic creation of the Vienna settlement. British conquest of the Boer Republics, if considered as an instance of annihilation of European polities in view of the European origin of the inhabitants, happened at the very rim of the world, as it were, remote from the continent where the practice of non-annihilation prevailed.

attempted world conquest and resulting world wars, a point has been made of restoring the most minute and inconsiderable of sovereignties, down to Luxembourg and Albania.[22]

This hypertrophy of nation-states presented new problems – above all, that of an improved system of protection. For by now it had become clear that the protective function of the old system was only a relative blessing after all. Continued existence of states as such was perhaps more or less guaranteed. But power and influence, status, frontiers, economic interests – in short, everything that constituted the life and interests of nations beyond bare existence – were always at the mercy of what power politics wrought. Furthermore, much of the relative stability and political equilibrium of the territorial states had been due to the extension of Western control over the world. When what could be penetrated had been subjugated, assimilated, or established as fellow 'sovereign' states, the old units were thrown back upon themselves. Hence the demand for a new system which would offer more security to old and new nations: collective security.

I propose to view collective security not as the extreme opposite of power politics, but as an attempt to maintain, and render more secure, the impermeability of what were still territorial states. To an age which took territoriality for granted, replacing power politics with collective security would indeed appear to be a radical departure. From the vantage point of the nuclear age, however, a plan to protect individual sovereignties by collective guarantees for continuing sovereignty appears questionable not because of its innovating, but because of its conservative, nature. Its conservatism lies in its basic objective: the protection of the hard-shell territorial structure of its members, or, as the core article of the Covenant of the League of Nations put it, its guarantee of their 'territorial integrity and political independence' against external aggression. The beginning of air war and the increasing economic interdependence of nations had indicated by the end of World War I that the old-style military barriers might be by-passed. If territorial units were to be preserved in the future, it would be accomplished less by reliance on individual defense potentials than by marshaling collective power in order to preserve individual powers.

But since the idea of organizing a genuine supranational force – an international police force – was rejected, the League had to cling to classical arrangements insofar as the procedures of protection were concerned. The guarantee to the individual states was to be the formation of the 'Grand Coalition' of all against the isolated aggressor, which presupposed the maintenance of a certain level of armed strength by the member states. A member without that minimum of military strength would be a liability rather than an asset to the organization –

---

22. Cf. also the remarkable stability of state units in the Western Hemisphere *qua* independent units; unstable as some of them are domestically, their sovereign identity as units appears almost sacrosanct.

in Geneva parlance, a 'consumer' and not a 'producer' of security.[23] Thus classical concepts (the sovereignty and independence of nationstates) as well as classical institutions (in particular, hard-shell defensibility) were to be maintained under the new system.

Whether there ever was a chance for the system to be effective in practice is beside the point here. It is sufficient to realize how closely it was tied to the underlying structure as well as to the prevailing concepts and policies of the territorial age.

V. The decline of the territorial state

Beginning with the nineteenth century, certain trends became visible which tended to endanger the functioning of the classical system. Directly or indirectly, all of them had a bearing upon that feature of the territorial state which was the strongest guarantee of its independent coexistence with other states of like nature: its hard shell – that is, its defensibility in case of war.

Naturally, many of these trends concerned war itself and the way in which it was conducted. But they were not related to the shift from the limited, duel-type contests of the eighteenth century to the more or less unlimited wars that developed in the nineteenth century with conscription, 'nations in arms,' and increasing destructiveness of weapons. By themselves, these developments were not inconsistent with the classical function of war. Enhancing a nation's defensive capacity, instituting universal military service, putting the economy on a war footing, and similar measures tended to bolster the territorial state rather than to endanger it.

Total war in a quite different sense is tied up with developments in warfare which enable the belligerents to overleap or by-pass the traditional hard-shell defense of states. When this happens, the traditional relationship between war, on the one hand, and territorial power and sovereignty, on the other, is altered decisively. Arranged in order of increasing effectiveness, these new factors may be listed under the following headings: (a) possibility of economic blockade; (b) ideological-political penetration; (c) air warfare; and (d) atomic warfare.

(a) *Economic warfare*. It should be said from the outset that so far economic blockade has never enabled one belligerent to force another into surrender through starvation alone. Although in World War I Germany and her allies were seriously endangered when the Western allies cut them off from overseas supplies, a very real effort was still required to defeat them on the military fronts. The same thing applies to World War II. Blockade was an important

---

23. In League practice, therefore, membership applications of countries without this minimum were rejected (for instance, that of Liechtenstein; cf. Walther Schücking and Hans Wehberg, *Die Satzung des Völkerbundes*, 2nd ed., Berlin, 1924, pp. 252ff.). The decline of genuine collective security in our time is apparent from the fact that, in contrast to this practice, the United Nations pays hardly any attention to the question of defensibility, particularly in connection with membership applications.

contributing factor, however. Its importance for the present analysis lies in its unconventional nature, permitting belligerents to by-pass the hard shell of the enemy. Its effect is due to the changed economic status of industrialized nations.

Prior to the industrial age, the territorial state was largely self-contained economically. Although one of the customary means of conducting limited war was starving fortresses into surrender, this applied merely to these individual portions of the hard shell, and not to entire nations. Attempts to starve a belligerent nation in order to avoid having to breach the shell proved rather ineffective, as witness the Continental Blockade and its counterpart in the Napoleonic era. The Industrial Revolution made countries like Britain and Germany increasingly dependent on imports. In war, this meant that they could survive only by controlling areas larger than their own territory. In peacetime, economic dependency became one of the causes of a phenomenon which itself contributed to the transformation of the old state system: imperialism. Anticipating war, with its new danger of blockade, countries strove to become more self-sufficient through enlargement of their areas of control. To the extent that the industrialized nations lost self-sufficiency, they were driven into expansion in a (futile) effort to regain it. Today, if at all, only control of entire continents enables major nations to survive economically in major wars. This implies that hard-shell military defense must be a matter of defending more than a single nation; it must extend around half the world.

(b) *Psychological warfare*, the attempt to undermine the morale of an enemy population, or to subvert its loyalty, shares with economic warfare a by-passing effect on old-style territorial defensibility. It was formerly practiced, and practicable, only under quite exceptional circumstances. Short periods of genuine world revolutionary propaganda, such as the early stages of the French Revolution,[24] scarcely affected a general practice under which dynasties, and later governments, fought each other with little ideological involvement on the part of larger masses or classes. Only in rare cases – for instance, where national groups enclosed in and hostile to multinational empires could be appealed to – was there an opening wedge for 'fifth column' strategies.

With the emergence of political belief-systems, however, nations became more susceptible to undermining from within. Although wars have not yet been won solely by subversion of loyalties, the threat involved has affected the inner coherence of the territorial state ever since the rise to power of a regime that claims to represent, not the cause of a particular nation, but that of mankind, or at least of its suppressed and exploited portions. Bolshevism from 1917 on has provided the second instance in modern history of world revolutionary propaganda. Communist penetration tactics subsequently were imitated by the Nazi and Fascist regimes and, eventually, by the democracies. In this way, new lines of division, cutting horizontally through state units instead of leaving them separated vertically from each other at their frontiers, have now become possible.

24. See my article, 'Idealist Internationalism and the Security Dilemma,' *World Politics*, II, No. 2 (January 1950), pp. 157ff.; in particular, pp. 165ff.

(c) *Air warfare* and (d) *nuclear warfare.* Of all the new developments, air warfare, up to the atomic age, has been the one that affected the territoriality of nations most radically. With its coming, the bottom dropped out – or, rather, the roof blew off – the relative security of the territorial state. True, even this new kind of warfare, up to and including World War II, did not by itself account for the defeat of a belligerent, as some of the more enthusiastic prophets of the air age had predicted it would. Undoubtedly, however, it had a massive contributory effect. And this effect was due to strategic action in the *hinterland* rather than to tactical use at the front. It came at least close to defeating one side by direct action against the 'soft' interior of the country, by-passing outer defenses and thus foreshadowing the end of the frontier – that is, the demise of the traditional impermeability of even the militarily most powerful states. Warfare now changed 'from a fight to a process of devastation.'[25]

That air warfare was considered as something entirely unconventional is seen from the initial reaction to it. Revolutionary transition from an old to a new system has always affected moral standards. In the classical age of the modern state system, the 'new morality' of shooting at human beings from a distance had finally come to be accepted, but the standards of the age clearly distinguished 'lawful combatants' at the front or in fortifications from the civilian remainder of the population. When air war came, reactions thus differed significantly in the cases of air fighting at the front and of air war carried behind the front. City bombing was felt to constitute 'illegitimate' warfare, and populations were inclined to treat airmen engaging in it as 'war criminals.'[26] This feeling continued into World War II, with its large-scale area bombing. Such sentiments reflected the general feeling of helplessness in the face of a war which threatened to render obsolete the concept of territorial power, together with its ancient implication of protection.

The process has now been completed with the advent of nuclear weapons. For it is more than doubtful that the processes of scientific invention and technological discovery, which not only have created and perfected the fission and fusion weapons themselves but have brought in their wake guided missiles with nuclear warheads, jet aircraft with intercontinental range and supersonic speed,

25. B.H. Liddell Hart, *The Revolution in Warfare*, New Haven, Conn., 1947, p. 36. Suspicion of what would be in the offing, once man gained the capacity to fly, was abroad as early as the eighteenth century. Thus Samuel Johnson remarked: 'If men were all virtuous, I should with great alacrity teach them all to fly. But what would be the security of the good, if the bad could at pleasure invade them from the sky? Against an army sailing through the clouds, neither walls, nor mountains, nor seas, could afford security' (quoted in J.U. Nef, *War and Human Progress*, Cambridge, Mass., 1952, p. 198). And Benjamin Franklin, witnessing the first balloon ascension at Paris in 1783, foresaw invasion from the air and wrote: 'Convincing Sovereigns of folly of wars may perhaps be one effect of it, since it will be impracticable for the most potent of them to guard his dominions. . . . Where is the Prince who can afford so to cover his country with troops for its defense, as that ten thousand men descending from the clouds, might not in many places do an infinite deal of mischief before a force could be brought together to repel them?' (from a letter to Jan Ingelhouss, reproduced in *Life Magazine*, January 9, 1956).

26. See Julius Stone, *Legal Controls of International Conflicts*, New York, 1954, pp. 611ff.

and the prospect of nuclear-powered planes or rockets with unlimited range and with automatic guidance to specific targets anywhere in the world, can in any meaningful way be likened to previous new inventions, however revolutionary. These processes add up to an uncanny absoluteness of effect which previous innovations could not achieve. The latter might render power units of a certain type (for instance, castles or cities) obsolete and enlarge the realm of defensible power units from city-state to territorial state or even large-area empire. They might involve destruction, in war, of entire populations. But there still remained the seemingly inexhaustible reservoir of the rest of mankind. Today, when not even two halves of the globe remain impermeable, it can no longer be a question of enlarging an area of protection and of substituting one unit of security for another. Since we are inhabitants of a planet of limited (and, as it now seems, insufficient) size, we have reached the limit within which the effect of the means of destruction has become absolute. Whatever remained of the impermeability of states seems to have gone for good.

What has been lost can be seen from two statements by thinkers separated by thousands of years and half the world; both reflect the condition of territorial security. Mencius, in ancient China, when asked for guidance in matters of defense and foreign policy by the ruler of a small state, is said to have counseled: 'Dig deeper your moats; build higher your walls; guard them along with your people.' This remained the classical posture up to our age, when a Western sage, Bertrand Russell, in the interwar period could still define power as something radiating from one center and growing less with distance from that center until it finds an equilibrium with that of similar geographically anchored units. Now that power can destroy power from center to center, everything is different.

VI. Outlook and conclusion

It is beyond the compass of this article to ask what the change in the statehood of nations implies for present and future world relations; whether, indeed, international relations in the traditional sense of the term, dependent as they have been on a number of basic data (existence of the nation-state, measurable power, etc.) and interpreted as they were with the aid of certain concepts (sovereignty, independence, etc.), can survive at all; and, if not, what might take their place.[27] Suffice it to remark that this question is vastly complex. We cannot even be sure that one and only one set of conclusions derives from what has happened or is in the process of happening. For, in J. Robert Oppenheimer's words, one of the characteristics of the present is 'the prevalence of newness, the changing scale and scope of change itself. . . .'[28] In the field of military policy, this

---

27. Some of the pertinent questions are discussed in a more comprehensive manuscript, 'Reflections on International Politics in the Atomic Age,' from whose initial chapters the preceding pages were adapted.
28. *The Open Mind*, New York, 1955, p. 141.

means that since World War II half a dozen military innovations 'have followed each other so rapidly that efforts at adaptation are hardly begun before they must be scrapped.'[29] The scientific revolution has been 'so fast-moving as to make almost impossible the task of military men whose responsibility it is to anticipate the future. Military planning cannot make the facts of this future stay long enough to analyze them.'[30]

If this applies to military planning, it must apply equally to foreign policy planning, and, indeed, the newness of the new is perhaps the most significant and the most exasperating aspect of present world relations. Hardly has a bipolar world replaced the multipower world of classical territoriality than there loom new and unpredictable multipower constellations on the international horizon. However, the possible rise of new powers does not seem to affect bipolarity in the sense of a mere return to traditional multipower relations; since rising powers are likely to be nuclear powers, their effect must be an entirely novel one. What international relations would (or will) look like, once nuclear power is possessed by a larger number of power units, is not only extremely unpleasant to contemplate but almost impossible to anticipate, using any familiar concepts. Or, to use another example: We have hardly drawn the military and political conclusions from the new weapons developments, which at one point seemed to indicate the necessity of basing defense on the formation and maintenance of pacts like NATO and the establishment of a network of bases on allied territory from which to launch nuclear weapons 'in case' (or whose existence was to deter the opponent from doing so on his part), and already further scientific and technological developments seem to render entire defense blocs, with all their new 'hard shells' of bases and similar installations, obsolete.

To complicate matters even more, the change-over is not even uniform and unilinear. On the contrary, in concepts as well as in policies, we witness the juxtaposition of old and new (or several new) factors, a coexistence in theory and practice of conventional and new concepts, of traditional and new policies. Part of a nation's (or a bloc's) defense policy, then, may proceed on pre-atomic assumptions, while another part is based on the assumption of a preponderantly nuclear contest. And a compounding trouble is that the future depends on what the present anticipates, on what powers now think and how they intend to act on the basis of their present thinking; and on the fact that each of the actors on the scene must take into consideration the assumptions of the others.[31]

29. Roger Hilsman, 'Strategic Doctrines for Nuclear War,' in William W. Kaufmann, ed., *Military Policy and National Security*, Princeton, N.J., 1956, p. 42.
30. Thomas K. Finletter, *Power and Politics: US Foreign Policy and Military Power in the Hydrogen Age*, New York, 1954, p. 256.
31. The expectations connected with the situation of nuclear deterrence may serve as an illustration. Each side, so we may assume, wants to act 'rationally' – that is, avoid resort to a war which it knows would be suicidal; in this, in fact, is grounded the widespread present belief in the obsoleteness of major – i.e., nuclear – war. However, not knowing for sure that the other side can be trusted to behave rationally, each feels that the possibility of irrational behavior by the opponent must be included in its own calculations. For instance, assuming that

There then evolves the necessity of multilevel concepts and of multilevel policies in the new era. In this we have, perhaps, the chief cause of the confusion and bewilderment of countries and publics. A good deal in recent foreign policies, with their violent swings from one extreme to another, from appeasement or apathy to truculence and threats of war, and also much in internal policies, with their suspicions and hysterias, may be reflections of world-political uncertainties. Confusion, despair, or easy optimism have been rampant; desire to give in, keep out, or get it over with underlies advocacy of appeasement, neutralism, or preventive war; mutually exclusive attitudes follow each other in rapid succession.

One radical conclusion to be drawn from the new condition of permeability would seem to be that nothing short of global rule can ultimately satisfy the security interest of any one power, and particularly any superpower. For only through elimination of the single competitor who really counts can one feel safe from the threat of annihilation. And since elimination without war is hardly imaginable, destruction of the other power by preventive war would therefore seem to be the logical objective of each superpower. But – and here the security dilemma encounters the other great dilemma of our time – such an aim is no longer practical. Since thermonuclear war would in all likelihood involve one's own destruction together with the opponent's, the means through which the end would have to be attained defeats the end itself. Pursuance of the 'logical' security objective would result in mutual annihilation rather than in one unit's global control of a pacified world.

If this is so, the short-term objective must surely be mutual accommodation, a drawing of demarcation lines, geographical and otherwise, between East and West which would at least serve as a stopgap policy, a holding operation pending the creation of an atmosphere in which, perhaps in consequence of a prolonged period of 'cold peace,' tensions may abate and the impact of the ideologies presently dividing the world diminish. May we then expect, or hope, that radically new attitudes, in accordance with a radically transformed structure of nationhood and international relations, may ultimately gain the upper hand over the inherited ones based on familiar concepts of old-style national security,

---

rationally the United States would not permit itself to be provoked into nuclear action, can it rely on Soviet abstention from nuclear attack for similarly rational reasons? Or can the Soviets, who may actually believe that the 'imperialist' powers are ready to inflict the worst on them, rely on Western rationality? And if, knowing that the other side may be swayed by considerations like these, one side takes these amended calculations as yardsticks for its own, what rational considerations remain? Policies then become so dependent on considerations of what you believe the other side believes, etc., ad infinitum, that no sane calculations are any longer feasible. One is caught here in the vicious circle inherent in the problem of the effects of assumptions (in behaviorist parlance, the problem of 'anticipated reactions'), of what David Easton has called the possibility of an 'infinite regress of effects' (*The Political System*, New York, 1953, p. 27). It may be doubted that even the theory of games as applied to international relations can cope with this one. And suppose that, sometime in the future, more than two major units 'play'? In the face of this prospect, as Herbert Butterfield says, 'The mind winces and turns to look elsewhere' (*History and Human Relations*, New York, 1952, p. 23).

power, and power competition? Until recently, advocacy of policies based on internationalism instead of power politics, on substituting the observance of universal interests for the prevalence of national interests, was considered utopian, and correctly so. National interests were still tied up with nation-states as units of power and with their security as impermeable units; internationalist ideals, while possibly recognized as ethically valid, ran counter to what nations were able to afford if they wanted to survive and prosper. But the dichotomy between 'national self-interest' and 'internationalist ideals' no longer fits a situation in which sovereignty and ever so absolute power cannot protect nations from annihilation.

What used to be a dichotomy of interests and ideals now emerges as a dichotomy between two sets of interests. For the former ideal has become a compelling interest itself. In former times, the lives of people, their goods and possessions, their hopes and their happiness, were tied up with the affairs of the country in which they lived, and interests thus centered around nation and national issues. Now that destruction threatens everybody, in every one of his most intimate, personal interests, national interests are bound to recede behind – or at least compete with – the common interest of all mankind in sheer survival. And if we add to this the universal interest in the common solution of other great world problems, such as those posed by the population-resources dilemma (exhaustion of vital resources coupled with the 'population explosion' throughout the world), or, indeed, that of 'peacetime' planetary pollution through radio-active fallout, it is perhaps not entirely utopian to expect the ultimate spread of an attitude of 'universalism' through which a rational approach to world problems would at last become possible.

It may be fitting to conclude this article by quoting two men, one a contemporary scientist whose words on nuclear problems may well apply to other problems of world relations, the second a philosopher whose statement on the revolutionary impact of attitude changes seems as valid today as when it was first made: 'It is a practical thing to recognize as a common responsibility, wholly incapable of unilateral solution, the complete common peril that atomic weapons constitute for the world, to recognize that only by a community of responsibility is there any hope of meeting the peril. It would seem to me visionary in the extreme, and not practical, to hope that methods which have so sadly failed in the past to avert war will succeed in the face of this far greater peril. It would in my opinion be most dangerous to regard, in these shattering times, a radical solution less practical than a conventional one' (J. Robert Oppenheimer).[32] And: 'Thought achieves more in the world than practice; for, once the realm of imagination has been revolutionized, reality cannot resist' (Hegel).

---

32. 'Atomic Weapons,' *Proceedings of the American Philosophical Society*, xc (January 29, 1946), pp. 9f.

17

WALTZ

Source: Kenneth Waltz (1959) *Man, the State and War*. New York, Columbia University Press, pp. 224–37.

Waltz offers three possible images of international relations. He argues that while each of these may possess some explanatory power for international relations, they are also limited in different ways by the types of questions they are capable of answering. The first is the psychological approach, which is to examine the nature and behaviour of humankind. The second is to look at the nature of states themselves, their political system and their ideology. The third, and the one that Waltz thinks is the most fruitful, focuses on the nature and structure of the international system itself.

Throughout the first half of the present century, Norman Angell has argued with persistence, eloquence, and clarity the proposition that war does not pay. Increasingly, under the influence of 'the balance of terror,' one finds men speaking as though the argument Angell first popularized fifty years ago has been made true by recent advances in the technology of warfare. But, in the sense Angell intended, it has always been true. Angell was a rationalist and individualist in the nineteenth-century mold, much less concerned with the relative gains and losses of this or that nation than with the unchallengeable fact that war at best takes men away from the work that produces the necessities and comforts of life, at worst destroys what they have already produced. War may achieve a redistribution of resources, but labor, not war, creates wealth. Perhaps not from the perspective of a nation or a tribe but from the perspective of mankind, war has never 'paid.'

Yet war recurs. The beast in man may glory in the carnage; the reason in man rebels. War and the threat of war stimulate speculation upon the conditions of peace. Seemingly critical thought may, however, embody uncritical reactions to the immediately impressive aspects of the situation faced. Peace programs, whether they would rely for their efficacy upon irenic diplomacy, armed crusade, moral exhortation, or psychic-cultural readjustment, are based at least implicitly on the ideals of the causes of war we entertain. As was argued in the introductory chapter, our estimates of the causes of war are determined by our presuppositions as much as by the events of the world about us. A systematic study of the assumed causes of war then becomes a direct way of estimating the conditions of peace. Our primary concern has not been with building models from which policies promoting peace can be derived but with examining the presuppositions upon which such models are based. This puts the problem in academic terms. Its relevance is much broader, for the policies of statesmen as well as the interests and procedures of scholars are the product of a conjunction of temper, experience, reason, and event. The practice of politics is greatly influenced by the images the politicians entertain.

When Ranke argued that the external relations of states determine their internal conditions, his argument had considerable cogency. So great was the importance of diplomacy in nineteenth-century Europe and so many were the statesmen trained in its ways that even internal governance at times corresponded in method to the techniques by which affairs among states were conducted. One need mention only Metternich and Bismarck. Diplomacy then, as it often has, took on many of the qualities of a game of chess. Perhaps the last illustration of this on the grand scale is provided by Bismarck's manipulations in the Balkan crises of 1885–87. But already by the dawn of the nineteenth century, factors internal to states were becoming more important in international relations. And with their greater importance, one finds a growing tendency to explain relations among states in terms of their internal condition. Most notably among English liberals, the practice of Metternich as well as the dictum of Ranke was reversed. Attempts were made to apply the supposed methods and sanctions of internal governance – judicial settlement, public opinion – to affairs among states.

The vogue of an image varies with time and place, but no single image is ever adequate. Thus Bismarck's skepticism about a possible alliance with Russia was based in part on fear of her internal instability. One who would play a game of chess has to consider the weight of the different pieces as well as the possible moves, and in international politics the weights change with time. Thus John Stuart Mill, writing to an Italian correspondent in June of 1859, expressed England's sympathy for the cause of Italian national freedom but justified England's inaction by pointing out that Austria was the only ally on which England could count should she have to fight for her liberty against France and

Russia united.[1] Mill's thoughts and Bismarck's policies can often be adequately described in terms of the second and third images, respectively, but especially when considering the possibilities of state policy the calculations of each comprehended elements from more than one image. This is generally the case. Yet the firmness with which a person is wedded to one image colors his interpretation of the others. Bismarck was inclined more than Mill to keep his eye on the map of Europe, the chessboard; Mill more than Bismarck to focus upon the qualities of peoples and their governments, the chessmen.

In contrast to Metternich and Bismarck, who were diplomatists in domestic as well as international affairs, statesmen of the twentieth century more frequently transfer the methods of the party politician to external politics. Woodrow Wilson, to cite an example used earlier, saw clearly one of the essential elements of a third-image analysis, that everyone's policy depends upon everyone else's. With many authoritarian states in the world, he realized that even the nonauthoritarian state must on occasion be prepared to use force in order to defend its interests. But, convinced that democratic states are peaceful because their governments reflect the aspirations of the people, he foresaw a day when the internal condition of all states would mean not the constant possibility of war but rather the assurance of perpetual peace. Wilson's emphasis upon the second image led him to particular interpretations of the first and third, rather than to a complete ignoring of them.

According to the third image, there is a constant possibility of war in a world in which there are two or more states each seeking to promote a set of interests and having no agency above them upon which they can rely for protection. But many liberals and socialist revisionists deny, or at least minimize, the possibility that wars would occur in a world of political or social democracies. An understanding of the third image makes it clear that the expectation would be justified only if the minimum interest of states in preserving themselves became the maximum interest of all of them – and each could rely fully upon the steadfast adherence to this definition by all of the others. Stating the condition makes apparent the utopian quality of liberal and socialist expectations. The criticism could be extended by questioning as well their interpretations of the first image. But the point as it applies here – that emphasizing one image frequently distorts, though it seldom excludes, the other two – is perhaps sufficiently clear. It may profit us more to shift our attention briefly to similar effects that may follow from concentration upon the third image.

While from the sociologist's perspective government is simply one of many social institutions, it is at the same time a precondition of society. The first perspective without the second is misleading [as was illustrated in one way in Chapter III, in another way in Chapter VI]. The state of nature among men is a monstrous impossibility. Anarchy breeds war among them; government establishes the conditions for peace. The state of nature that continues to prevail

1. J.S. Mill, *Letters*, ed. Elliot, I, 222.

among states often produces monstrous behavior but so far has not made life itself impossible. The ahistorical analyses of Spinoza, Rousseau, and Kant lay bare the logic of civil society and at the same time make clear why the logic does not carry men past the establishment of separate states to the founding of a world state. Yet in the international as in the domestic sphere, if anarchy is the cause, the obvious conclusion is that government is the cure; and this is true even though the disease in the former case is not fatal. The problem, however, becomes a practical one. The amount of force needed to hold a society together varies with the heterogeneity of the elements composing it. World federalists write as though the alternatives before us were unity or death. 'World government is necessary and therefore possible,' Robert Maynard Hutchins avers.[2] But demonstrating the need for an institution does not bring it into existence. And were world government attempted, we might find ourselves dying in the attempt to unite, or uniting and living a life worse than death.

The third image, like the first two, leads directly to a utopian prescription. In each image a cause is identified in terms of which all others are to be understood. The force of the logical relation between the third image and the world-government prescription is great enough to cause some to argue not only the merits of world government but also the ease with which it can be realized.[3] It is of course true that with world government there would no longer be international wars, though with an ineffective world government there would no doubt be civil wars. It is likewise true, reverting to the first two images, that without the imperfections of the separate states there would not be wars, just as it is true that a society of perfectly rational beings, or of perfect Christians, would never know violent conflict. These statements are, unfortunately, as trivial as they are true. They have the unchallengeable quality of airtight tautologies: perfectly good states or men will not do bad things; within an effective organization highly damaging deviant behavior is not permitted. The near perfection required by concentration upon a single cause accounts for a number of otherwise puzzling facts: the pessimism of St. Augustine, the failure of the behavioral scientists as prescribers for peace, the reliance of many liberals on the forces of history to produce a result not conceivably to be produced by the consciously directed efforts of men, the tendency of socialists to identify a corrupting element every time harmony in socialist action fails to appear. It also helps to explain the often rapid alternation of hope and despair among those who most fully adopt a single-cause approach to this or to almost any other problem. The belief that to make the world better requires changing the factors that operate within a precisely defined realm leads to despair whenever it becomes apparent that changes there, if possible at all, will come slowly and with insufficient force. One is constantly defeated by the double problem of demonstrating how the 'necessary changes' can be

2. Hutchins, 'The Constitutional Foundations for World Order,' in *Foundations for World Order*, p. 105.
3. Cf. Popper, *The Open Society and Its Enemies*, pp. 158–59, 574–79; Esslinger, *Politics and Science*, passim.

produced and of substantiating the assertion that the changes described as necessary would be sufficient to accomplish the object in view.

The contrary assertion, that all causes may be interrelated, is an argument against assuming that there is a single cause that can be isolated by analysis and eliminated or controlled by wisely constructed policy. It is also an argument against working with one or several hypotheses without bearing in mind the interrelation of all causes. The prescriptions directly derived from a single image are incomplete because they are based upon partial analyses. The partial quality of each image sets up a tension that drives one toward inclusion of the others. With the first image the direction of change, representing Locke's perspective as against Plato's, is from men to societies and states. The second image catches up both elements. Men make states, *and* states make men; but this is still a limited view. One is led to a search for the more inclusive nexus of causes, for states are shaped by the international environment as are men by both the national and international environments. Most of those whom we have considered in preceding chapters have not written entirely in terms of one image. That we have thus far been dealing with the consequences arising from differing degrees of emphasis accounts for the complexity of preceding chapters but now makes somewhat easier the task of suggesting how the images can be interrelated without distorting any one of them.

The first and second images in relation to the third

It may be true that the Soviet Union poses the greatest threat of war at the present time. It is not true that were the Soviet Union to disappear the remaining states could easily live at peace. We have known wars for centuries; the Soviet Union has existed only for decades. But some states, and perhaps some forms of the state, are more peacefully inclined than others. Would not the multiplication of peacefully inclined states at least warrant the hope that the period between major wars might be extended? By emphasizing the relevance of the framework of action, the third image makes clear the misleading quality of such partial analyses and of the hopes that are often based upon them. The act that by individual moral standards would be applauded may, when performed by a state, be an invitation to the war we seek to avoid. The third image, taken not as a theory of world government but as a theory of the conditioning effects of the state system itself, alerts us to the fact that so far as increasing the chances of peace is concerned there is no such thing as an act good in itself. The pacification of the Hukbalahaps was a clear and direct contribution to the peace and order of the Philippine state. In international politics a partial 'solution,' such as one major country becoming pacifistic, might be a real contribution to world peace; but it might as easily hasten the coming of another major war.

The third image, as reflected in the writings of Rousseau, is based on an analysis of the consequences arising from the framework of state action. Rousseau's explanation of the origin of war among states is, in broad outline, the final one so long as we operate within a nation-state system. It is a final explanation because it does not hinge on accidental causes – irrationalities in men, defects in states – but upon his theory of the framework within which *any* accident can bring about a war. That state A wants certain things that it can get only by war does not explain war. Such a desire may or may not lead to war. My wanting a million dollars does not cause me to rob a bank, but if it were easier to rob banks, such desires would lead to much more bank robbing. This does not alter the fact that some people will and some will not attempt to rob banks no matter what the law enforcement situation is. We still have to look to motivation and circumstance in order to explain individual acts. Nevertheless one can predict that, other things being equal, a weakening of law enforcement agencies will lead to an increase in crime. From this point of view it is social structure – institutionalized restraints and institutionalized methods of altering and adjusting interests – that counts. And it counts in a way different from the ways usually associated with the word 'cause.' What causes a man to rob a bank are such things as the desire for money, a disrespect for social proprieties, a certain boldness. But if obstacles to the operation of these causes are built sufficiently high, nine out of ten would-be bank robbers will live their lives peacefully plying their legitimate trades. If the framework is to be called cause at all, it had best be specified that it is a permissive or underlying cause of war.

Applied to international politics this becomes, in words previously used to summarize Rousseau, the proposition that wars occur because there is nothing to prevent them. Rousseau's analysis explains the recurrence of war without explaining any given war. He tells us that war may at any moment occur, and he tells us why this is so. But the structure of the state system does not directly cause state A to attack state B. Whether or not that attack occurs will depend on a number of special circumstances – location, size, power, interest, type of government, past history and tradition – each of which will influence the actions of both states. If they fight against each other it will be for reasons especially defined for the occasion by each of them. These special reasons become the immediate, or efficient, causes of war. These immediate causes of war are contained in the first and second images. States are motivated to attack each other and to defend themselves by the reason and/or passion of the comparatively few who make policies for states and of the many more who influence the few. Some states, by virtue of their internal conditions, are both more proficient in war and more inclined to put their proficiency to the test. Variations in the factors included in the first and second images are important, indeed crucial, in the making and breaking of periods of peace – the immediate causes of every war must be either the acts of individuals or the acts of states.

If every war is preceded by acts that we can identify (or at least try to identify) as cause, then why can we not eliminate wars by modifying individual or state behavior? This is the line of thinking followed by those who say: To end war, improve men; or: To end war, improve states. But in such prescriptions the role of the international environment is easily distorted. How can some of the acting units improve while others continue to follow their old and often predatory ways? The simplistic assumption of many liberals, that history moves relentlessly toward the millennium, is refuted if the international environment makes it difficult almost to the point of impossibility for states to behave in ways that are progressively more moral. Two points are omitted from the prescriptions we considered under the first and second images: (1) If an effect is produced by two or more causes, the effect is not permanently eliminated by removing one of them. If wars occur because men are less than perfectly rational and because states are less than perfectly formed, to improve only states may do little to decrease the number and intensity of wars. The error here is in identifying one cause where two or more may operate. (2) An endeavor launched against one cause to the neglect of others may make the situation worse instead of better. Thus, as the Western democracies became more inclined to peace, Hitler became more belligerent. The increased propensity to peace of some participants in international politics may increase, rather than decrease, the likelihood of war. This illustrates the role of the permissive cause, the international environment. If there were but two loci of cause involved, men and states, we could be sure that the appearance of more peacefully inclined states would, at worst, not damage the cause of world peace. Whether or not a remedy proposed is truly a remedy or actually worse than none at all depends, however, on the content and timing of the acts of all states. This is made clear in the third image.

War may result because state A has something that state B wants. The efficient cause of the war is the desire of state B; the permissive cause is the fact that there is nothing to prevent state B from undertaking the risks of war. In a different circumstance, the interrelation of efficient and permissive causes becomes still closer. State A may fear that if it does not cut state B down a peg now, it may be unable to do so ten years from now. State A becomes the aggressor in the present because it fears what state B may be able to do in the future. The efficient cause of such a war is derived from the cause that we have labeled permissive. In the first case, conflicts arise from disputes born of specific issues. In an age of hydrogen bombs, no single issue may be worth the risk of full-scale war. Settlement, even on bad grounds, is preferable to self-destruction. The use of reason would seem to require the adoption of a doctrine of 'non-recourse to force.' One whose reason leads him down this path is following the trail blazed by Cobden when in 1849 he pointed out 'that it is almost impossible, on looking back for the last hundred years, to tell precisely what any war was about,' and thus implied that Englishmen should never have become involved in them.[4] He is falling into the trap that ensnared A.A. Milne when he explained the First World War as a war in which ten million men died because Austria-Hungary sought, unsuccessfully, to avenge the death of one archduke.[5] He is succumbing to the illusion of Sir Edward Grey who, in the memoirs he wrote some thirty years ago, hoped that the horrors of the First World War would make it possible for nations 'to find at least one common ground on which they should come together in

4. Cobden, *Speeches*, ed. Bright and Rogers, II, 165.
5. Milne, *Peace with Honour*, p. 11.

confident understanding: an agreement that, in the disputes between them, war must be ruled out as a means of settlement that entails ruin.'[6]

It is true that the immediate causes of many wars are trivial. If we focus upon them, the failure to agree to settlement without force appears to be the ultimate folly. But it is not often true that the immediate causes provide sufficient explanation for the wars that have occurred. And if it is not simply particular disputes that produce wars, rational settlement of them cannot eliminate war. For, as Winston Churchill has written, 'small matters are only the symptoms of the dangerous disease, and are only important for that reason. Behind them lie the interests, the passions and the destiny of mighty races of men; and long antagonisms express themselves in trifles.'[7] Nevertheless Churchill may be justified in hoping that the fear induced by a 'balance of terror' will produce a temporary truce. Advancing technology makes war more horrible and presumably increases the desire for peace; the very rapidity of the advance makes for uncertainty in everyone's military planning and destroys the possibility of an accurate estimate of the likely opposing forces. Fear and permanent peace are more difficult to equate. Each major advance in the technology of war has found its prophet ready to proclaim that war is no longer possible: Alfred Nobel and dynamite, for example, or Benjamin Franklin and the lighter-than-air balloon. There may well have been a prophet to proclaim the end of tribal warfare when the spear was invented and another to make a similar prediction when poison was first added to its tip. Unfortunately, these prophets have all been false. The development of atomic and hydrogen weapons may nurture the peace wish of some, the war sentiment of others. In the United States and elsewhere after the Second World War, a muted theme of foreign-policy debate was the necessity of preventive war – drop the bomb quickly before the likely opponent in a future war has time to make one of his own. Even with two or more states equipped with similar weapon systems, a momentary shift in the balance of terror, giving a decisive military advantage temporarily to one state, may tempt it to seize the moment in order to escape from fear. And the temptation would be proportionate to the fear itself. Finally, mutual fear of big weapons may produce, instead of peace, a spate of smaller wars.

The fear of modern weapons, of the danger of destroying the civilizations of the world, is not sufficient to establish the conditions of peace identified in our discussions of the three images of international relations. One can equate fear with world peace only if the peace wish exists in all states and is uniformly expressed in their policies. But peace is the primary goal of few men or states. If it were the primary goal of even a single state, that state could have peace at any time – simply by surrendering. But, as John Foster Dulles so often warns, 'Peace can be a cover whereby evil men perpetrate diabolical wrongs.'[8] The

---

6. Grey, *Twenty-five Years*, II, 285.
7. Churchill, *The World Crisis, 1911–1914*, I, 52.
8. 'Excerpts from Dulles Address on Peace' (Washington, April 11, 1955), in New York *Times*, April 12, 1955, p. 6.

issue in a given dispute may not be: Who shall gain from it? It may instead be: Who shall dominate the world? In such circumstances, the best course of even reasonable men is difficult to define; their ability always to contrive solutions without force, impossible to assume. If solutions in terms of none of the three images is presently – if ever – possible, then reason can work only within the framework that is suggested by viewing the first and second images in the perspective of the third, a perspective well and simply set forth in the *Federalist Papers*, especially in those written by Hamilton and Jay.

What would happen, Jay asks, if the thirteen states, instead of combining as one state, should form themselves into several confederations? He answers:

> Instead of their being 'joined in affection' and free from all apprehension of different 'interests,' envy and jealousy would soon extinguish confidence and affection, and the partial interests of each confederation, instead of the general interests of all America, would be the only objects of their policy and pursuits. Hence, like most *bordering* nations, they would always be either involved in disputes and war, or live in the constant apprehension of them.[9]

International anarchy, Jay is here saying, is the explanation for international war. But not international anarchy alone. Hamilton adds that to presume a lack of hostile motives among states is to forget that men are 'ambitious, vindictive, and rapacious.' A monarchical state may go to war because the vanity of its king leads him to seek glory in military victory; a republic may go to war because of the folly of its assembly or because of its commercial interests. That the king may be vain, the assembly foolish, or the commercial interests irreconcilable: none of these is inevitable. However, so many and so varied are the causes of war among states that 'to look for a continuation of harmony between a number of independent, unconnected sovereigns in the same neighborhood, would be to disregard the uniform course of human events, and to set at defiance the accumulated experience of the ages.'[10]

Jay and Hamilton found in the history of the Western state system confirmation for the conclusion that among separate sovereign states there is constant possibility of war. The third image [as constructed in Chapter VI] gives a theoretical basis for the same conclusion. It reveals why, in the absence of tremendous changes in the factors included in the first and second images, war will be perpetually associated with the existence of separate sovereign states. The obvious conclusion of a third-image analysis is that world government is the remedy for world war. The remedy, though it may be unassailable in logic, is unattainable in practice. The third image may provide a utopian approach to world politics. It may also provide a realistic approach, and one that avoids the tendency of some realists to attribute the necessary amorality, or even immorality, of world politics to the inherently bad character of man. If everyone's

---

9. *The Federalist*, pp. 23–24 (No. 5).
10. *Ibid.*, pp. 27–28 (No. 6); cf. p. 18 (No. 4, Jay), and pp. 34–40 (No. 7, Hamilton).

strategy depends upon everyone else's, then the Hitlers determine in part the action, or better, reaction, of those whose ends are worthy and whose means are fastidious. No matter how good their intentions, policy makers must bear in mind the implications of the third image, which can be stated in summary form as follows: Each state pursues its own interests, however defined, in ways it judges best. Force is a means of achieving the external ends of states because there exists no consistent, reliable process of reconciling the conflicts of interest that inevitably arise among similar units in a condition of anarchy. A foreign policy based on this image of international relations is neither moral nor immoral, but embodies merely a reasoned response to the world about us. The third image describes the framework of world politics, but without the first and second images there can be no knowledge of the forces that determine policy; the first and second images describe the forces in world politics, but without the third image it is impossible to assess their importance or predict their results.

18

WALLERSTEIN

Source: Immanuel Wallerstein (1974) 'The rise and demise of the world capitalist system'. *Comparative Studies in Society and History*, 16: 4, 388–94 and 397–406.

Wallerstein challenges the belief that progress, modernization and industrialization will inevitably bring benefits to all, including those nations currently thought of as underdeveloped. He argues that the world capitalist system consists of core, semi-peripheral and peripheral states. He goes on to stress that the relationship between these three positions is necessary if the capitalist world-economy is to continue to run smoothly. The semi-periphery is of particular importance politically because, according to Wallerstein, it acts as a buffer, preventing a unified opposition to the dominance of the core states. This is possible because the semi-periphery states are both exploited and exploiter. Wallerstein's emphasis on economic life places him broadly in the Marxist tradition of thought, although he is at pains to point out where he thinks Marx himself went wrong.

Nothing illustrates the distortions of ahistorical models of social change better than the dilemmas to which the concept of stages gives rise. If we are to deal with social transformations over long historical time (Braudel's 'the long term'), and if we are to give an explanation of both continuity and transformation, then we must logically divide the long term into segments in order to observe the structural changes from time A to time B. These segments are however not discrete but continuous in reality; *ergo* they are 'stages' in the 'development' of a social structure, a development which we determine however not *a priori* but *a posteriori*. That is, we cannot predict the future concretely, but we can predict the past.

The crucial issue when comparing 'stages' is to determine the units of which the 'stages' are synchronic portraits (or 'ideal types', if you will). And the fundamental error of ahistorical social science (including ahistorical versions of Marxism) is to reify parts of the totality into such units and then to compare these reified structures.

For example, we may take modes of disposition of agricultural production, and term them subsistence-cropping and cash-cropping. We may then see these as entities which are 'stages' of a development. We may talk about decisions of groups of peasants to shift from one to the other. We may describe other partial entities, such as states, as having within them two separate 'economies', each based on a different mode of disposition of agricultural production. If we take each of these successive steps, all of which are false steps, we will end up with the misleading concept of the 'dual economy' as have many liberal economists dealing with the so-called underdeveloped countries of the world. Still worse, we may reify a misreading of British history into a set of universal 'stages' as Rostow does.

Marxist scholars have often fallen into exactly the same trap. If we take modes of payment of agricultural labor and contrast a 'feudal' mode wherein the laborer is permitted to retain for subsistence a part of his agricultural production with a 'capitalist' mode wherein the same laborer turns over the totality of his production to the landowner, receiving part of it back in the form of wages, we may then see these two modes as 'stages' of a development. We may talk of the interests of 'feudal' landowners in preventing the conversion of their mode of payment to a system of wages. We may then explain the fact that in the twentieth century a partial entity, say a state in Latin America, has not yet industrialized as the consequence of its being dominated by such landlords. If we take each of these successive steps, all of which are false steps, we will end up with the misleading concept of a 'state dominated by feudal elements', as though such a thing could possibly exist in a capitalist world-economy. But, as André Gunder Frank has clearly spelled out, such a myth dominated for a long time 'traditional Marxist' thought in Latin America.[1]

Not only does the misidentification of the entities to be compared lead us into false concepts, but it creates a non-problem: can stages be skipped? This question is only logically meaningful if we have 'stages' that 'co-exist' within a single empirical framework. If within a capitalist world-economy, we define one state as feudal, a second as capitalist, and a third as socialist, then and only then can we pose the question: can a country 'skip' from the feudal stage to the socialist stage of national development without 'passing through capitalism'?

But if there is no such thing as 'national development' (if by that we mean a

---

1. See André Gunder Frank, Ch. IV (A), 'The Myth of Feudalism' in *Capitalism and Underdevelopment in Latin America* (New York: Monthly Review Press, 1967), 221–42.

natural history), and if the proper entity of comparison is the world-system, then the problem of stage-skipping is nonsense. If a stage can be skipped, it isn't a stage. And we know this *a posteriori*.

If we are to talk of stages, then – and we should talk of stages – it must be stages of social systems, that is, of totalities. And the only totalities that exist or have historically existed are mini-systems and world-systems, and in the nineteenth and twentieth centuries there has been only one world-system in existence, the capitalist world-economy.

[. . .]

Let us therefore turn to the capitalist world-economy. We shall seek to deal with two pseudo-problems, created by the trap of not analyzing totalities: the so-called persistence of feudal forms, and the so-called creation of socialist systems. In doing this, we shall offer an alternative model with which to engage in comparative analysis, one rooted in the historically specific totality which is the world capitalist economy. We hope to demonstrate thereby that to be historically specific is not to fail to be analytically universal. On the contrary, the only road to nomothetic propositions is through the historically concrete, just as in cosmology the only road to a theory of the laws governing the universe is through the concrete analysis of the historical evolution of this same universe.[2]

On the 'feudalism' debate, we take as a starting-point Frank's concept of 'the development of underdevelopment', that is, the view that the economic structures of contemporary underdeveloped countries is not the form which a 'traditional' society takes upon contact with 'developed' societies, not an earlier stage in the 'transition' to industrialization. It is rather the result of being involved in the world-economy as a peripheral, raw material producing area, or as Frank puts it for Chile, 'underdevelopment . . . is the necessary product of four centuries of capitalism itself'.[3]

This formulation runs counter to a large body of writing concerning the underdeveloped countries that was produced in the period 1950–70, a literature which sought the factors that explained 'development' within non-systems such as 'states' or 'cultures' and, once having presumably discovered these factors, urged their reproduction in underdeveloped areas as the road to salvation.[4]

Frank's theory also runs counter, as we have already noted, to the received orthodox version of Marxism that had long dominated Marxist parties and intellectual circles, for example in Latin America. This older 'Marxist' view of

---

2. Philip Abrams concludes a similar plea with this admonition: 'The academic and intellectual dissociation of history and sociology seems, then, to have had the effect of deterring both disciplines from attending seriously to the most important issues involved in the understanding of social transition'. 'The Sense of the Past and the Origins of Sociology', *Past and Present*, No. 55, May 1972, 32.

3. Frank, *op. cit.*, p. 3.

4. Frank's critique, now classic, of these theories is entitled 'Sociology of Development and Underdevelopment of Sociology' and is reprinted in *Latin America: Underdevelopment or Revolution* (New York: Monthly Review Press, 1969), 21–94.

Latin America as a set of feudal societies in a more or less pre-bourgeois stage of development has fallen before the critiques of Frank and many others as well as before the political reality symbolized by the Cuban revolution and all its many consequences. Recent analysis in Latin America has centered instead around the concept of 'dependence'.[5]

However, recently, Ernesto Laclau has made an attack on Frank which, while accepting the critique of dualist doctrines, refuses to accept the categorization of Latin American states as capitalist. Instead Laclau asserts that 'the world capitalist system . . . includes, *at the level of its definition*, various modes of production'. He accuses Frank of confusing the two concepts of the 'capitalist mode of production' and 'participation in a world capitalist economic system'.[6]

Of course, if it's a matter of definition, then there can be no argument. But then the polemic is scarcely useful since it is reduced to a question of semantics. Furthermore, Laclau insists that the definition is not his but that of Marx, which is more debatable. Rosa Luxemburg put her finger on a key element in Marx's ambiguity or inconsistency in this particular debate, the ambiguity which enables both Frank and Laclau to trace their thoughts to Marx:

> Admittedly, Marx dealt in detail with the process of appropriating non-capitalist means of production [N.B., Luxemburg is referring to primary products produced in peripheral areas under conditions of coerced labor – I.W.] as well as with the transformation of the peasants into a capitalist proletariat. Chapter XXIV of *Capital*, Vol. 1, is devoted to describing the origin of the English proletariat, of the capitalistic agricultural tenant class and of industrial capital, with particular emphasis on the looting of colonial countries by European capital. Yet we must bear in mind that all this is treated solely with a view to so-called primitive accumulation. For Marx, these processes are incidental, illustrating merely the genesis of capital, its first appearance in the world; they are, as it were, travails by which the capitalist mode of production emerges from a feudal society. As soon as he comes to analyze the capitalist process of production and circulation, he reaffirms the universal and exclusive domination of capitalist production [N.B., that is, production based on wage labor – I.W.].[7]

---

5. See Theontonio Dos Santos, *La Nueva Dependencia*. (Buenos Aires: s/ediciones, 1968).
6. Ernesto Laclau (h) 'Feudalism and Capitalism in Latin America', *New Left Review*, No. 67, May–June 1971, 37–8.
7. *The Accumulation of Capital* (New York: Modern Reader Paperbacks, 364–5). Luxemburg however, as is evident, lends herself further to the confusion by using the terminology of 'capitalistic' and 'non-capitalistic' modes of production. Leaving these terms aside, her vision is impeccable: 'From the aspect both of realising the surplus value and of producing the material elements of constant capital, international trade is a prime necessity for the historical existence of capitalism – an international trade which under actual conditions is essentially an exchange between capitalistic and non-capitalistic modes of production'. *Ibid.*, 359. She shows similar insight into the need of recruiting labor for core areas from the periphery, what she calls 'the increase in the variable capital'. See *ibid.*, p. 361.

There is, after all, a substantive issue in this debate. It is in fact the same substantive issue that underlay the debate between Maurice Dobb and Paul Sweezy in the early 1950s about the 'transition from feudalism to capitalism' that occurred in early modern Europe.[8] The substantive issue, in my view, concerns the appropriate unit of analysis for the purpose of comparison. Basically, although neither Sweezy nor Frank is quite explicit on this point, and though Dobb and Laclau can both point to texts of Marx that seem clearly to indicate that they more faithfully follow Marx's argument, I believe both Sweezy and Frank better follow the spirit of Marx if not his letter[9] and that, leaving Marx quite out of the picture, they bring us nearer to an understanding of what actually happened and is happening than their opponents.

What is the picture, both analytical and historical, that Laclau constructs? The heart of the problem revolves around the existence of free labor as the defining characteristic of a capitalist mode of production:

> The fundamental economic relationship of capitalism is constituted by the *free* [italics mine] labourer's sale of his labour-power, whose necessary precondition is the loss by the direct producer of ownership of the means of production . . . .
>
> If we now confront Frank's affirmation that the socio-economic complexes of Latin America has been capitalist since the Conquest Period . . . with the currently available empirical evidence, we must conclude that the 'capitalist' thesis is indefensible. In regions with dense indigenous populations – Mexico, Peru, Bolivia, or Guatemala – the direct producers were not despoiled of their ownership of the means of production, while extra-economic coercion to maximize various systems of labour service . . . was progressively intensified. In the plantations of the West Indies, the economy was based on a mode of production constituted by slave labour, while in the mining areas there developed disguised forms of slavery and other types of forced labour which bore not the slightest resemblance to the formation of a capitalist proletariat.[10]

There in a nutshell it is. Western Europe, at least England from the late seventeenth century on, had primarily landless, wage-earning laborers. In Latin

8. The debate begins with Maurice Dobb, *Studies in the Development of Capitalism* (London: Routledge and Kegan Paul, 1946). Paul Sweezy criticized Dobb in 'The Transition from Feudalism to Capitalism', *Science and Society*, XIV, 2, Spring 1950, 134–57, with a 'Reply' by Dobb in the same issue. From that point on many others got into the debate in various parts of the world. I have reviewed and discussed this debate *in extenso* in Chapter 1 of my work cited above.

9. It would take us into a long discursus to defend the proposition that, like all great thinkers, there was the Marx who was the prisoner of his social location and the Marx, the genius, who could on occasion see from a wider vantage point. The former Marx generalized from British history. The latter Marx is the one who has inspired a critical conceptual framework of social reality. W.W. Rostow incidentally seeks to refute the former Marx by offering an alternative generalization from British history. He ignores the latter and more significant Marx. See *The Stages of Economic Growth: A Non-Communist Manifesto* (Cambridge: at the University Press, 1960).

10. Laclau, *op. cit.*, 25, 30.

America, then and to some extent still now, laborers were not proletarians, but slaves or 'serfs'. If proletariat, then capitalism. Of course. To be sure. But is England, or Mexico, or the West Indies a unit of analysis? Does each have a separate 'mode of production'? Or is the unit (for the sixteenth–eighteenth centuries) the European world-economy, including England *and* Mexico, in which case what was the 'mode of production' of this world-economy?

[. . .]

We must start with how one demonstrates the existence of a single division of labor. We can regard a division of labor as a grid which is substantially interdependent. Economic actors operate on some assumption (obviously seldom clear to any individual actor) that the totality of their essential needs – of sustenance, protection, and pleasure – will be met over a reasonable time-span by a combination of their own productive activities and exchange in some form. The smallest grid that would substantially meet the expectations of the overwhelming majority of actors within those boundaries constitutes a single division of labor.

The reason why a small farming community whose only significant link to outsiders is the payment of annual tribute does not constitute such a single division of labor is that the assumptions of persons living in it concerning the provision of protection involve an 'exchange' with other parts of the world-empire.

This concept of a grid of exchange relationships assumes, however, a distinction between *essential* exchanges and what might be called 'luxury' exchanges. This is to be sure a distinction rooted in the social perceptions of the actors and hence in both their social organization and their culture. These perceptions can change. But this distinction is crucial if we are not to fall into the trap of identifying *every* exchange-activity as evidence of the existence of a system. Members of a system (a mini-system or a world-system) can be linked in limited exchanges with elements located outside the system, in the 'external arena' of the system.

The form of such an exchange is very limited. Elements of the two systems can engage in an exchange of preciosities. That is, each can export to the other what is in *its* system socially defined as worth little in return for the import of what in its system is defined as worth much. This is not a mere pedantic definitional exercise, as the exchange of preciosities *between* world-systems can be extremely important in the historical evolution of a given world-system. The reason why this is so important is that in an exchange of preciosities, the importer is 'reaping a windfall' and not obtaining a profit. Both exchange-partners can reap windfalls simultaneously but only one can obtain maximum profit, since the exchange of surplus-value within a system is a zero-sum game.

We are, as you see, coming to the essential feature of a capitalist world-economy, which is production for sale in a market in which the object is to realize the maximum profit. In such a system production is constantly expanded as long as further production is profitable, and men constantly innovate new ways of producing things that will expand the profit margin. The classical economists tried to argue that such production for the market was somehow the 'natural' state of man. But the combined writings of the anthropologists and the Marxists left few in doubt that such a mode of production (these days called 'capitalism') was only one of several possible modes.

Since, however, the intellectual debate between the liberals and the Marxists took place in the era of the industrial revolution, there has tended to be a *de facto* confusion between industrialism and capitalism. This left the liberals after 1945 in the dilemma of explaining how a presumably non-capitalist society, the U.S.S.R., had industrialized. The most sophisticated response has been to conceive of 'liberal capitalism' and 'socialism' as two variants of an 'industrial society', two variants destined to 'converge'. This argument has been trenchantly expounded by Raymond Aron.[11] But the same confusion left the Marxists, including Marx, with the problem of explaining what was the mode of production that predominated in Europe from the sixteenth to the eighteenth centuries, that is before the industrial revolution. Essentially, most Marxists have talked of a 'transitional' stage, which is in fact a blurry non-concept with no operational indicators. This dilemma is heightened if the unit of analysis used is the state, in which case one has to explain why the transition has occurred at different rates and times in different countries.[12]

Marx himself handled this by drawing a distinction between 'merchant capitalism' and 'industrial capitalism'. This I believe is unfortunate terminology, since it leads to such conclusions as that of Maurice Dobb who says of this 'transitional' period:

> But why speak of this as a stage of capitalism at all? The workers were generally not proletarianized: that is, they were not separated from the instruments of production, nor even in many cases from occupation of a plot of land. Production was scattered and decentralized and not concentrated. *The capitalist was still predominantly a merchant* who did not control production directly and did not impose his own discipline upon the work of artisan-craftsmen, who both laboured as individual (or family) units and retained a considerable measure of independence (if a dwindling one).[13]

One might well say: why indeed? Especially if one remembers how much emphasis Dobb places a few pages earlier on capitalism as a mode of *production* – how then can the capitalist be primarily a merchant? – on the concentration of such ownership in the hands of a few, and on the fact that capitalism is not synonymous with private ownership, capitalism being different from a system in which the owners are 'small peasant producers or artisan-producers'.

11. See Raymond Aron, *Dix-huit leçons de la société industrielle* (Paris: Ed. Gallimard, 1962).
12. This is the dilemma, I feel, of E.J. Hobsbawm in explaining his so-called 'crisis of the seventeenth century'. See his *Past and Present* article reprinted (with various critiques) in Trevor Aston (ed.), *The Crisis of the Seventeenth Century* (London: Routledge and Kegan Paul, 1965).
13. Maurice Dobb, *Capitalism Yesterday and Today* (London: Lawrence and Wishart, 1958), p. 21, Italics mine.

Dobb argues that a defining feature of private ownership under capitalism is that some are 'obliged to [work for those that own] since [they own] nothing and [have] no access to means of production [and hence] have no other means of livelihood'.[14] Given this contradiction, the answer Dobb gives to his own question is in my view very weak: 'While it is true that at this date the situation was transitional, and capital-to-wage-labour relations were still immaturely developed, the latter were already beginning to assume their characteristic features'.[15]

If capitalism is a mode of production, production for profit in a market, then we ought, I should have thought, to look to whether or not such production was or was not occurring. It turns out in fact that it was, and in a very substantial form. Most of this production, however, was not industrial production. What was happening in Europe from the sixteenth to the eighteenth centuries is that over a large geographical area going from Poland in the northeast westwards and southwards throughout Europe and including large parts of the Western Hemisphere as well, there grew up a world-economy with a single division of labor within which there was a world market, for which men produced largely agricultural products for sale and profit. I would think the simplest thing to do would be to call this agricultural capitalism.

This then resolves the problems incurred by using the pervasiveness of *wage*-labor as a defining characteristic of capitalism. An individual is no less a capitalist exploiting labor because the state assists him to pay his laborers low wages (including wages in kind) and denies these laborers the right to change employment. Slavery and so-called 'second serfdom' are not to be regarded as anomalies in a capitalist system. Rather the so-called serf in Poland or the Indian on a Spanish *encomienda* in New Spain in this sixteenth-century world-economy were working for landlords who 'paid' them (however euphemistic this term) for cash-crop production. This is a relationship in which labor-power is a commodity (how could it ever be more so than under slavery?), quite different from the relationship of a feudal serf to his lord in eleventh-century Burgundy, where the economy was not oriented to a world market, and where labor-power was (therefore?) in no sense bought or sold.

Capitalism thus means labor as a commodity to be sure. But in the era of agricultural capitalism, wage-labor is only one of the modes in which labor is recruited and recompensed in the labor market. Slavery, coerced cash-crop production (my name for the so-called 'second feudalism'), share-cropping, and tenancy are all alternative modes. It would be too long to develop here the conditions under which differing regions of the world-economy tend to specialize in different agricultural products. I have done this elsewhere.[16]

What we must notice now is that this specialization occurs in specific and differing geographic regions of the world-economy. This regional specialization

14. *Ibid.*, pp. 6–7.
15. *Ibid.*, p. 21.
16. See my *The Modern World-System, op. cit.*, Chap. 2.

comes about by the attempts of actors in the market to avoid the normal operation of the market whenever it does not maximize their profit. The attempts of
these actors to use non-market devices to ensure short-run profits makes them
turn to the political entities which have in fact power to affect the market – the
nation-states. (Again, why at this stage they could not have turned to city-states
would take us into a long dicursus, but it has to do with the state of military and
shipping technology, the need of the European land-mass to expand overseas in
the fifteenth century if it was to maintain the level of income of the various
aristocracies, combined with the state of political disintegration to which
Europe had fallen in the Middle Ages.)

In any case, the local capitalist classes – cash-crop landowners (often, even
usually, nobility) and merchants – turned to the state, not only to liberate them
from non-market constraints (as traditionally emphasized by liberal historiography) but to create new constraints on the new market, the market of the
European world-economy.

By a series of accidents – historical, ecological, geographic – northwest
Europe was better situated in the sixteenth century to diversify its agricultural
specialization and add to it certain industries (such as textiles, shipbuilding, and
metal wares) than were other parts of Europe. Northwest Europe emerged as the
core area of this world-economy, specializing in agricultural production of
higher skill levels, which favored (again for reasons too complex to develop)
tenancy and wage-labor as the modes of labor control. Eastern Europe and the
Western Hemisphere became peripheral areas specializing in export of grains,
bullion, wood, cotton, sugar – all of which favored the use of slavery and
coerced cash-crop labor as the modes of labor control. Mediterranean Europe
emerged as the semi-peripheral area of this world-economy specializing in high-
cost industrial products (for example, silks) and credit and specie transactions,
which had as a consequence in the agricultural arena share-cropping as the mode
of labor control and little export to other areas.

The three structural positions in a world-economy – core, periphery, and
semi-periphery – had become stabilized by about 1640. How certain areas
became one and not the other is a long story.[17] The key fact is that given
slightly different starting-points, the interests of various local groups converged
in northwest Europe, leading to the development of strong state mechanisms,
and diverged sharply in the peripheral areas, leading to very weak ones. Once
we get a difference in the strength of the state-machineries, we get the operation
of 'unequal exchange'[18] which is enforced by strong states on weak ones, by
core states on peripheral areas. Thus capitalism involves not only appropriation
of the surplus-value by an owner from a laborer, but an appropriation of surplus
of the whole world-economy by core areas. And this was as true in the stage of
agricultural capitalism as it is in the stage of industrial capitalism.

---

17. I give a brief account of this in 'Three Paths of National Development in the Sixteenth Century',
    Studies in Comparative International Development, VII, 2, Summer 1972, 95–101.
18. See Arghiri Emmanuel, *Unequal Exchange* (New York: Monthly Review Press, 1972).

In the early Middle Ages, there was to be sure trade. But it was largely either 'local', in a region that we might call the 'extended' manor, or 'long-distance', primarily of luxury goods. There was no exchange of 'bulk' goods, of 'staples' across intermediate-size areas, and hence no production for such markets. Later on in the Middle Ages, world-economies may be said to have come into existence, one centering on Venice, a second on the cities of Flanders and the Hanse. For various reasons, these structures were hurt by the retractions (economic, demographic, and ecological) of the period 1300–1450. It is only with the creating of a *European* division of labor after 1450 that capitalism found firm roots.

Capitalism was from the beginning an affair of the world-economy and not of nation-states. It is a misreading of the situation to claim that it is only in the twentieth century that capitalism has become 'world-wide', although this claim is frequently made in various writings, particularly by Marxists. Typical of this line of argument is Charles Bettelheim's response to Arghiri Emmanuel's discussion of unequal exchange:

> The tendency of the capitalist mode of production to become worldwide is manifested not only through the constitution of a group of national economies forming a complex and hierarchical structure, including an imperialist pole and a dominated one, and not only through the antagonistic relations that develop between the different 'national economies' and the different states, but also through the constant 'transcending' of 'national limits' by big capital (the formation of 'international big capital', 'world firms', etc . . .).[19]

The whole tone of these remarks ignores the fact that capital has never allowed its aspirations to be determined by national boundaries in a capitalist world-economy, and that the creation of 'national' barriers – generically, mercantilism – has historically been a defensive mechanism of capitalists located in states which are one level below the high point of strength in the system. Such was the case of England *vis-à-vis* the Netherlands in 1660–1715, France *vis-à-vis* England in 1715–1815, Germany *vis-à-vis* Britain in the nineteenth century, the Soviet Union *vis-à-vis* the U.S. in the twentieth. In the process a large number of countries create national economic barriers whose consequences often last beyond their initial objectives. At this later point in the process the very same capitalists who pressed their national governments to impose the restrictions now find these restrictions constraining. This is not an 'internationalization' of 'national' capital. This is simply a new political demand by certain sectors of the capitalist classes who have at all points in time sought to maximize their profits within the real economic market, that of the world-economy.

If this is so, then what meaning does it have to talk of structural positions within this economy and identify states as being in one of these positions? And why talk of three positions, inserting that of 'semi-periphery' in between the

19. Charles Bettelheim, 'Theoretical Comments' in Emmanuel, *op. cit.*, 295.

widely-used concepts of core and periphery? The state-machineries of the core states were strengthened to meet the needs of capitalist landowners and their merchant allies. But that does not mean that these state-machineries were manipulable puppets. Obviously any organization, once created, has a certain autonomy from those who pressed it into existence for two reasons. It creates a stratum of officials whose own careers and interests are furthered by the continued strengthening of the organization itself, however the interests of its capitalist backers may vary. Kings and bureaucrats wanted to stay in power and increase their personal gain constantly. Secondly, in the process of creating the strong state in the first place, certain 'constitutional' compromises had to be made with other forces within the state-boundaries and these institutionalized compromises limit, as they are designed to do, the freedom of maneuver of the managers of the state-machinery. The formula of the state as 'executive committee of the ruling class' is only valid, therefore, if one bears in mind that executive committees are never mere reflections of the wills of their constituents, as anyone who has ever participated in any organization knows well.

The strengthening of the state-machineries in core areas has as its direct counterpart the decline of the state-machineries in peripheral areas. The decline of the Polish monarchy in the sixteenth and seventeenth centuries is a striking example of this phenomenon.[20] There are two reasons for this. In peripheral countries, the interests of the capitalist landowners lie in an opposite direction from those of the local commercial bourgeoisie. Their interests lie in maintaining an open economy to maximize their profit from world-market trade (no restrictions in exports and access to lower-cost industrial products from core countries) and in elimination of the commercial bourgeoisie in favor of outside merchants (who pose no local political threat). Thus, in terms of the state, the coalition which strengthened it in core countries was precisely absent.

The second reason, which has become ever more operative over the history of the modern world-system, is that the strength of the state-machinery in core states is a function of the weakness of other state-machineries. Hence intervention of outsiders via war, subversion, and diplomacy is the lot of peripheral states.

All this seems very obvious. I repeat it only in order to make clear two points. One cannot reasonably explain the strength of various state-machineries at specific moments of the history of the modern world-system primarily in terms of a genetic-cultural line of argumentation, but rather in terms of the structural role a country plays in the world-economy at that moment in time. To be sure, the initial eligibility for a particular role is often decided by an accidental edge a particular country has, and the 'accident' of which one is talking is no doubt

---

20. See J. Siemenski, 'Constitutional Conditions in the Fifteenth and Sixteenth Centuries', *Cambridge History of Poland*, *I*, W.F. Reddaway *et al.* (eds.), *From the Origins to Sobieski (to 1696)* (Cambridge: at the University Press, 1950), pp. 416–40; Janusz Tazbir, 'The Commonwealth of the Gentry', in Aleksander Gieysztor *et al.*, *History of Poland* (Warszawa: PWN – Polish Scientific Publ., 1968), pp. 169–271.

located in part in past history, in part in current geography. But once this relatively minor accident is given, it is the operations of the world-market forces which accentuate the differences, institutionalize them, and make them impossible to surmount over the short run.

The second point we wish to make about the structural differences of core and periphery is that they are not comprehensible unless we realize that there is a third structural position: that of the semi-periphery. This is not the result merely of establishing arbitrary cutting-points on a continuum of characteristics. Our logic is not merely inductive, sensing the presence of a third category from a comparison of indicator curves. It is also deductive. The semi-periphery is needed to make a capitalist world-economy run smoothly. Both kinds of world-system, the world-empire with a redistributive economy and the world-economy with a capitalist market economy, involve markedly unequal distribution of rewards. Thus, logically, there is immediately posed the question of how it is possible politically for such a system to persist. Why do not the majority who are exploited simply overwhelm the minority who draw disproportionate benefits? The most rapid glance at the historic record shows that these world-systems have been faced rather rarely by fundamental system-wide insurrection. While internal discontent has been eternal, it has usually taken quite long before the accumulation of the erosion of power has led to the decline of a world-system, and as often as not, an external force has been a major factor in this decline.

There have been three major mechanisms that have enabled world-systems to retain relative political stability (not in terms of the particular groups who will play the leading roles in the system, but in terms of systemic survival itself). One obviously is the concentration of military strength in the hands of the dominant forces. The modalities of this obviously vary with the technology, and there are to be sure political prerequisites for such a concentration, but nonetheless sheer force is no doubt a central consideration.

A second mechanism is the pervasiveness of an ideological commitment to the system as a whole. I do not mean what has often been termed the 'legitimation' of a system, because that term has been used to imply that the lower strata of a system feel some affinity with or loyalty towards the rulers, and I doubt that this has ever been a significant factor in the survival of world-systems. I mean rather the degree to which the staff or cadres of the system (and I leave this term deliberately vague) feel that their own well-being is wrapped up in the survival of the system as such and the competence of its leaders. It is this staff which not only propagates the myths; it is they who believe them.

But neither force nor the ideological commitment of the staff would suffice were it not for the division of the majority into a larger lower stratum and a smaller middle stratum. Both the revolutionary call for polarization as a strategy of change and the liberal encomium to consensus as the basis of the liberal polity reflect this proposition. The import is far wider than its use in the analysis of contemporary political problems suggests. It is the normal condition of either kind of world-system to have a three-layered structure. When and if this ceases to be the case, the world-system disintegrates.

In a world-empire, the middle stratum is in fact accorded the role of maintaining the marginally-desirable long-distance luxury trade, while the upper stratum concentrates its resources on controlling the military machinery which can collect the tribute, the crucial mode of redistributing surplus. By providing, however, for an access to a limited portion of the surplus to urbanized elements who alone, in pre-modern societies, could contribute political cohesiveness to isolated clusters of primary producers, the upper stratum effectively buys off the potential leadership of co-ordinated revolt. And by denying access to political rights for this commercial-urban middle stratum, it makes them constantly vulnerable to confiscatory measures whenever their economic profits become sufficiently swollen so that they might begin to create for themselves military strength.

In a world-economy, such 'cultural' stratification is not so simple, because the absence of a single political system means the concentration of economic roles vertically rather than horizontally throughout the system. The solution then is to have three *kinds* of states, with pressures for cultural homogenization within each of them – thus, besides the upper stratum of core-states and the lower stratum of peripheral states, there is a middle stratum of semi-peripheral ones.

This semi-periphery is then assigned as it were a specific economic role, but the reason is less economic than political. That is to say, one might make a good case that the world-economy as an economy would function every bit as well without a semi-periphery. But it would be far less *politically* stable, for it would mean a polarized world-system. The existence of the third category means precisely that the upper stratum is not faced with the *unified* opposition of all the others because the *middle* stratum is both exploited and exploiter. It follows that the specific economic role is not all that important, and has thus changed through the various historical stages of the modern world-system.

Where then does class analysis fit in all of this? And what in such a formulation are nations, nationalities, peoples, ethnic groups? First of all, without arguing the point now,[21] I would contend that all these latter terms denote variants of a single phenomenon which I will term 'ethno-nations'.

Both classes and ethnic groups, or status-groups, or ethno-nations are phenomena of world-economies and much of the enormous confusion that has surrounded the concrete analysis of their functioning can be attributed quite simply to the fact that they have been analyzed as though they existed within the nation-states of this world-economy, instead of within the world-economy as a whole. This has been a Procrustean bed indeed.

The range of economic activities being far wider in the core than in the periphery, the range of syndical interest groups is far wider there.[22] Thus, it has

---

21. See my fuller analysis in 'Social Conflict in Post-Independence Black Africa: The Concepts of Race and Status-Group Reconsidered' in Ernest W. Campbell (ed.), *Racial Tensions and National Identity* (Nashville: Vanderbilt Univ. Press, 1972), pp. 207–26.

22. Range in this sentence means the number of different occupations in which a significant proportion of the population is engaged. Thus peripheral society typically is overwhelmingly

been widely observed that there does not exist in many parts of the world today a proletariat of the kind which exists in, say, Europe or North America. But this is a confusing way to state the observation. Industrial activity being disproportionately concentrated in certain parts of the world-economy, industrial wage-workers are to be found principally in certain geographic regions. Their interests as a syndical group are determined by their collective relationship to the world-economy. Their ability to influence the political functioning of this world-economy is shaped by the fact that they command larger percentages of the population in one sovereign entity than another. The form their organizations take have, in large part, been governed too by these political boundaries. The same might be said about industrial capitalists. Class analysis is perfectly capable of accounting for the political position of, let us say, French skilled workers if we look at their structural position and interests in the world-economy. Similarly with ethno-nations. The meaning of ethnic consciousness in a core area is considerably different from that of ethnic consciousness in a peripheral area precisely because of the different class position such ethnic groups have in the world-economy.[23]

Political struggles of ethno-nations or segments of classes within national boundaries of course are the daily bread and butter of local politics. But their significance or consequences can only be fruitfully analyzed if one spells out the implications of their organizational activity or political demands for the functioning of the world-economy. This also incidentally makes possible more rational assessments of these politics in terms of some set of evaluative criteria such as 'left' and 'right'.

The functioning then of a capitalist world-economy requires that groups pursue their economic interests within a single world market while seeking to distort this market for their benefit by organizing to exert influence on states, some of which are far more powerful than others but none of which controls the world-market in its entirety. Of course, we shall find on closer inspection that there are periods where one state is relatively quite powerful and other periods where power is more diffuse and contested, permitting weaker states broader ranges of action. We can talk then of the relative tightness or looseness of the world-system as an important variable and seek to analyze why this dimension tends to be cyclical in nature, as it seems to have been for several hundred years.

---

agricultural. A core society typically has its occupations well-distributed over all of Colin Clark's three sectors. If one shifted the connotation of range to talk of style of life, consumption patterns, even income distribution, quite possibly one might reverse the correlation. In a typical peripheral society, the differences between a subsistence farmer and an urban professional are probably far greater than those which could be found in a typical core state.

23. See my 'The Two Modes of Ethnic Consciousness: Soviet Central Asia in Transition?', in Edward Allworth (ed.), *The Nationality Question in Soviet Central Asia* (New York, Praeger, 1973), pp. 168–75.

19

KEOHANE AND NYE

Source: Robert O. Keohane and Joseph S. Nye (1977) *Power and Interdependence: World Politics in Transition*. Boston, Little, Brown, pp. 23–37.

Keohane and Nye challenge the central assumptions of post-Second World War Realist thinking on international relations. While accepting the continued importance of states they argue that increasingly international and transnational actors set the international agenda. Increasing complexity in international life means that power cannot be aggregated but must be understood as distributed across a range of issue-areas. Furthermore, increasing complexity is paralleled with the growth of interdependence such that military force is no longer effective in securing ends. The implications of this are that even states weak in military capabilities may be able to link issues and influence outcomes. Therefore, contrary to Realist thinking, military force becomes both a less effective and less viable means of securing desired outcomes.

One's assumptions about world politics profoundly affect what one sees and how one constructs theories to explain events. We believe that the assumptions of political realists, whose theories dominated the postwar period, are often an inadequate basis for analyzing the politics of interdependence. The realist assumptions about world politics can be seen as defining an extreme set of conditions or *ideal type*. One could also imagine very different conditions. In this chapter, we shall construct another ideal type, the opposite of realism. We call it *complex interdependence*. After establishing the differences between realism and complex interdependence, we shall argue that complex interdependence sometimes comes closer to reality than does realism. When it does, traditional explanations of change in international regimes become questionable and the search for new explanatory models becomes more urgent.

For political realists, international politics, like all other politics, is a struggle for power but, unlike domestic politics, a struggle dominated by organized violence. In the words of the most influential postwar textbook, 'All history shows that nations active in international politics are continuously preparing for, actively involved in, or recovering from organized violence in the form of war.'[1] Three assumptions are integral to the realist vision. First, states as coherent units are the dominant actors in world politics. This is a double assumption: states are predominant; and they act as coherent units. Second, realists assume that force is a usable and effective instrument of policy. Other instruments may also be employed, but using or threatening force is the most effective means of wielding power. Third, partly because of their second assumption, realists assume a hierarchy of issues in world politics, headed by questions of military security: the 'high politics' of military security dominates the 'low politics' of economic and social affairs.

These realist assumptions define an ideal type of world politics. They allow us to imagine a world in which politics is continually characterized by active or potential conflict among states, with the use of force possible at any time. Each state attempts to defend its territory and interests from real or perceived threats. Political integration among states is slight and lasts only as long as it serves the national interests of the most powerful states. Transnational actors either do not exist or are politically unimportant. Only the adept exercise of force or the threat of force permits states to survive, and only while statesmen succeed in adjusting their interests, as in a well-functioning balance of power, is the system stable.

Each of the realist assumptions can be challenged. If we challenge them all simultaneously, we can imagine a world in which actors other than states participate directly in world politics, in which a clear hierarchy of issues does not exist, and in which force is an ineffective instrument of policy. Under these conditions – which we call the characteristics of complex interdependence – one would expect world politics to be very different than under realist conditions.

We will explore these differences in the next section of this chapter. We do not argue, however, that complex interdependence faithfully reflects world political reality. Quite the contrary: both it and the realist portrait are ideal types. Most situations will fall somewhere between these two extremes. Sometimes, realist assumptions will be accurate, or largely accurate, but frequently complex interdependence will provide a better portrayal of reality. Before one decides what explanatory model to apply to a situation or problem, one will need to understand the degree to which realist or complex interdependence assumptions correspond to the situation.

The characteristics of complex interdependence

Complex interdependence has three main characteristics:

1. *Multiple channels* connect societies, including: informal ties between governmental elites as well as formal foreign office arrangements; informal ties among nongovernmental elites (face-to-face and through telecommunications); and transnational organizations (such as multinational banks or corporations). These channels can be summarized as interstate, transgovernmental, and transnational relations. *Interstate* relations are the normal channels assumed by realists. *Transgovernmental* applies when we relax the realist assumption that states act coherently as units; *transnational* applies when we relax the assumption that states are the only units.

2. The agenda of interstate relationships consists of multiple issues that are not arranged in a clear or consistent hierarchy. This *absence of hierarchy among issues* means, among other things, that military security does not consistently dominate the agenda. Many issues arise from what used to be considered domestic policy, and the distinction between domestic and foreign issues becomes blurred. These issues are considered in several government departments (not just foreign offices), and at several levels. Inadequate policy coordination on these issues involves significant costs. Different issues generate different coalitions, both within governments and across them, and involve different degrees of conflict. Politics does not stop at the waters' edge.

3. Military force is not used by governments towards other governments within the region, or on the issues, when complex interdependence prevails. It may, however, be important in these governments' relations with governments outside that region, or on other issues. Military force could, for instance, be irrelevant to resolving disagreements on economic issues among members of an alliance, yet at the same time be very important for that alliance's political and military relations with a rival bloc. For the former relationships this condition of complex interdependence would be met; for the latter, it would not.

Traditional theories of international politics implicitly or explicitly deny the accuracy of these three assumptions. Traditionalists are therefore tempted also to deny the relevance of criticisms based on the complex interdependence ideal type. We believe, however, that our three conditions are fairly well approximated on some global issues of economic and ecological interdependence and that they come close to characterizing the entire relationship between some countries. One of our purposes here is to prove that contention. In subsequent chapters we shall examine complex interdependence in oceans policy and monetary policy and in the relationships of the United States to Canada and Australia. In this chapter, however, we shall try to convince you to take these criticisms of traditional assumptions seriously.

Multiple channels

A visit to any major airport is a dramatic way to confirm the existence of multiple channels of contact among advanced industrial countries; there is a voluminous literature to prove it.[2] Bureaucrats from different countries deal directly with one another at meetings and on the telephone as well as in writing. Similarly, nongovernmental elites frequently get together in the normal course of business, in organizations such as the Trilateral Commission, and in conferences sponsored by private foundations.

In addition, multinational firms and banks affect both domestic and interstate relations. The limits on private firms, or the closeness of ties between government and business, vary considerably from one society to another; but the participation of large and dynamic organizations, not controlled entirely by governments, has become a normal part of foreign as well as domestic relations.

These actors are important not only because of their activities in pursuit of their own interests, but also because they act as transmission belts, making government policies in various countries more sensitive to one another. As the scope of governments' domestic activities has broadened, and as corporations, banks, and (to a lesser extent) trade unions have made decisions that transcend national boundaries, the domestic policies of different countries impinge on one another more and more. Transnational communications reinforce these effects. Thus, foreign economic policies touch more domestic economic activity than in the past, blurring the lines between domestic and foreign policy and increasing the number of issues relevant to foreign policy. Parallel developments in issues of environmental regulation and control over technology reinforce this trend.

Absence of hierarchy among issues

Foreign affairs agendas – that is, sets of issues relevant to foreign policy with which governments are concerned – have become larger and more diverse. No longer can all issues be subordinated to military security. As Secretary of State Kissinger described the situation in 1975:

> progress in dealing with the traditional agenda is no longer enough. A new and unprecedented kind of issue has emerged. The problems of energy, resources, environment, population, the uses of space and the seas now rank with questions of military security, ideology and territorial rivalry which have traditionally made up the diplomatic agenda.[3]

Kissinger's list, which could be expanded, illustrates how governments' policies, even those previously considered merely domestic, impinge on one another. The extensive consultative arrangements developed by the OECD, as well as the GATT, IMF, and the European Community, indicate how characteristic the overlap of domestic and foreign policy is among developed pluralist countries. The organization within nine major departments of the United States government (Agriculture, Commerce, Defence, Health, Education and Welfare,

Interior, Justice, Labor, State, and Treasury) and many other agencies reflects their extensive international commitments. The multiple, overlapping issues that result make a nightmare of governmental organization.[4]

When there are multiple issues on the agenda, many of which threaten the interests of domestic groups but do not clearly threaten the nation as a whole, the problems of formulating a coherent and consistent foreign policy increase. In 1975 energy was a foreign policy problem, but specific remedies, such as a tax on gasoline and automobiles, involved domestic legislation opposed by auto workers and companies alike. As one commentator observed, 'virtually every time Congress has set a national policy that changed the way people live . . . the action came after a consensus had developed, bit by bit, over the years, that a problem existed and that there was one best way to solve it.'[5] Opportunities for delay, for special protection, for inconsistency and incoherence abound when international politics requires aligning the domestic policies of pluralist democratic countries.

Minor role of military force

Political scientists have traditionally emphasized the role of military force in international politics. As we saw in the first chapter, force dominates other means of power: *if* there are no constraints on one's choice of instruments (a hypothetical situation that has only been approximated in the two world wars), the state with superior military force will prevail. If the security dilemma for all states were extremely acute, military force, supported by economic and other resources, would clearly be the dominant source of power. Survival is the primary goal of all states, and in the worst situations, force is ultimately necessary to guarantee survival. Thus military force is always a central component of national power.

Yet particularly among industrialized, pluralist countries, the perceived margin of safety has widened: fears of attack in general have declined, and fears of attacks *by one another* are virtually nonexistent. France has abandoned the *tous azimuts* (defence in all directions) strategy that President de Gaulle advocated (it was not taken entirely seriously even at the time). Canada's last war plans for fighting the United States were abandoned half a century ago. Britain and Germany no longer feel threatened by each other. Intense relationships of mutual influence exist between these countries, but in most of them force is irrelevant or unimportant as an instrument of policy.

Moreover, force is often not an appropriate way of achieving other goals (such as economic and ecological welfare) that are becoming more important. It is not impossible to imagine dramatic conflict or revolutionary change in which the use or threat of military force over an economic issue or among advanced industrial countries might become plausible. Then realist assumptions would again be a reliable guide to events. But in most situations, the effects of military force are both costly and uncertain.[6]

Even when the direct use of force is barred among a group of countries, however, military power can still be used politically. Each superpower continues to use the threat of force to deter attacks by other superpowers on itself or its allies; its deterrence ability thus serves an indirect, protective role, which it can use in bargaining on other issues with its allies. This bargaining tool is particularly important for the United States, whose allies are concerned about potential Soviet threats and which has fewer other means of influence over its allies than does the Soviet Union over its Eastern European partners. The United States has, accordingly, taken advantage of the Europeans' (particularly the Germans') desire for its protection and linked the issue of troop levels in Europe to trade and monetary negotiations. Thus, although the first-order effect of deterrent force is essentially negative – to deny effective offensive power to a superpower opponent – a state can use that force positively – to gain political influence.

Thus, even for countries whose relations approximate complex interdependence, two serious qualifications remain: (1) drastic social and political change could cause force again to become an important direct instrument of policy; and (2) even when elites' interests are complementary, a country that uses military force to protect another may have significant political influence over the other country.

In North–South relations, or relations among Third World countries, as well as in East–West relations, force is often important. Military power helps the Soviet Union to dominate Eastern Europe economically as well as politically. The threat of open or covert American military intervention has helped to limit revolutionary changes in the Caribbean, especially in Guatemala in 1954 and in the Dominican Republic in 1965. Secretary of State Kissinger, in January 1975, issued a veiled warning to members of the Organization of Petroleum Exporting Countries (OPEC) that the United States might use force against them 'where there is some actual strangulation of the industrialized world.'[7]

Even in these rather conflictual situations, however, the recourse to force seems less likely now than at most times during the century before 1945. The destructiveness of nuclear weapons makes any attack against a nuclear power dangerous. Nuclear weapons are mostly used as a deterrent. Threats of nuclear action against much weaker countries may occasionally be efficacious, but they are equally or more likely to solidify relations between one's adversaries. The limited usefulness of conventional force to control socially mobilized populations has been shown by the United States failure in Vietnam as well as by the rapid decline of colonialism in Africa. Furthermore, employing force on one issue against an independent state with which one has a variety of relationships is likely to rupture mutually profitable relations on other issues. In other words, the use of force often has costly effects on nonsecurity goals. And finally, in Western democracies, popular opposition to prolonged military conflicts is very high.[8]

It is clear that these constraints bear unequally on various countries, or on the same countries in different situations. Risks of nuclear escalation affect everyone, but domestic opinion is far less constraining for communist states, or for authoritarian regional powers, than for the United States, Europe, or Japan. Even authoritarian countries may be reluctant to use force to obtain economic objectives when such use might be ineffective and disrupt other relationships. Both the difficulty of controlling socially mobilized populations with foreign troops and the changing technology of weaponry may actually enhance the ability of certain countries, or nonstate groups, to use terrorism as a political weapon without effective fear of reprisal.

The fact that the changing role of force has uneven effects does not make the change less important, but it does make matters more complex. This complexity is compounded by differences in the usability of force among issue areas. When an issue arouses little interest or passion, force may be unthinkable. In such instances, complex interdependence may be a valuable concept for analyzing the political process. But if that issue becomes a matter of life and death – as some people thought oil might become – the use or threat of force could become decisive again. Realist assumptions would then be more relevant.

It is thus important to determine the applicability of realism or of complex interdependence to each situation. Without this determination, further analysis is likely to be confused. Our purpose in developing an alternative to the realist description of world politics is to encourage a differentiated approach that distinguishes among dimensions and areas of world politics – not (as some modernist observers do) to replace one oversimplification with another.

The political processes of complex interdependence

The three main characteristics of complex interdependence give rise to distinctive political processes, which translate power resources into power as control of outcomes. As we argued earlier, something is usually lost or added in the translation. Under conditions of complex interdependence the translation will be different than under realist conditions, and our predictions about outcomes will need to be adjusted accordingly.

In the realist world, military security will be the dominant goal of states. It will even affect issues that are not directly involved with military power or territorial defense. Nonmilitary problems will not only be subordinated to military ones; they will be studied for their politico-military implications. Balance of payments issues, for instance, will be considered at least as much in the light of their implications for world power generally as for their purely financial ramifications. McGeorge Bundy conformed to realist expectations when he argued in 1964 that devaluation of the dollar should be seriously considered if necessary to fight the war in Vietnam.[9] To some extent, so did former Treasury Secretary Henry Fowler when he contended in 1971 that the United States needed a trade surplus of $4 billion to $6 billion in order to lead in Western defense.[10]

In a world of complex interdependence, however, one expects some officials, particularly at lower levels, to emphasize the *variety* of state goals that must be pursued. In the absence of a clear hierarchy of issues, goals will vary by issue, and may not be closely related. Each bureaucracy will pursue its own concerns; and although several agencies may reach compromises on issues that affect them all, they will find that a consistent pattern of policy is difficult to maintain. Moreover, transnational actors will introduce different goals into various groups of issues.

Linkage strategies

Goals will therefore vary by issue area under complex interdependence, but so will the distribution of power and the typical political processes. Traditional analysis focuses on *the* international system, and leads us to anticipate similar political processes on a variety of issues. Militarily and economically strong states will dominate a variety of organizations and a variety of issues, by linking their own policies on some issues to other states' policies on other issues. By using their overall dominance to prevail on their weak issues, the strongest states will, in the traditional model, ensure a congruence between the overall structure of military and economic power and the pattern of outcomes on any issue area. Thus world politics can be treated as a seamless web.

Under complex interdependence, such congruence is less likely to occur. As military force is devalued, militarily strong states will find it more difficult to use their overall dominance to control outcomes on issues in which they are weak. And since the distribution of power resources in trade, shipping, or oil, for example, may be quite different, patterns of outcomes and distinctive political processes are likely to vary from one set of issues to another. If force were readily applicable, and military security were the highest foreign policy goal, these variations in the issue structures of power would not matter very much. The linkages drawn from them to military issues would ensure consistent dominance by the overall strongest states. But when military force is largely immobilized, strong states will find that linkage is less effective. They may still attempt such links, but in the absence of a hierarchy of issues, their success will be problematic.

Dominant states may try to secure much the same result by using overall economic power to affect results on other issues. If only economic objectives are at stake, they may succeed: money, after all, is fungible. But economic objectives have political implications, and economic linkage by the strong is limited by domestic, transnational, and transgovernmental actors who resist having their interests traded off. Furthermore, the international actors may be different on different issues, and the international organizations in which negotiations take place are often quite separate. Thus it is difficult, for example, to imagine a militarily or economically strong state linking concessions on monetary policy to reciprocal concessions in oceans policy. On the other hand, poor weak states are not similarly inhibited from linking unrelated issues, partly because their domestic interests are less complex. Linkage of unrelated issues is often a means of extracting concessions or side payments from rich and powerful states. And unlike powerful states whose instrument for linkage (military force) is often too costly to use, the linkage instrument used by poor, weak states – international organization – is available and inexpensive.

Thus as the utility of force declines, and as issues become more equal in importance, the distribution of power within each issue will become more important. If linkages become less effective on the whole, outcomes of political bargaining will increasingly vary by issue area.

The differentiation among issue areas in complex interdependence means that linkages among issues will become more problematic and will tend to reduce rather than reinforce international hierarchy. Linkage strategies, and defense against them, will pose critical strategic choices for states. Should issues be considered separately or as a package? If linkages are to be drawn, which issues should be linked, and on which of the linked issues should concessions be made? How far can one push a linkage before it becomes counterproductive? For instance, should one seek formal agreements or informal, but less politically sensitive, understandings? The fact that world politics under complex interdependence is not a seamless web leads us to expect that efforts to stitch seams together advantageously, as reflected in linkage strategies, will, very often, determine the shape of the fabric.

The negligible role of force leads us to expect states to rely more on other instruments in order to wield power. For the reasons we have already discussed, less vulnerable states will try to use asymmetrical interdependence in particular groups of issues as a source of power; they will also try to use international organizations and transnational actors and flows. States will approach economic interdependence in terms of power as well as its effects on citizens' welfare, although welfare considerations will limit their attempts to maximize power. Most economic and ecological interdependence involves the possibility of joint gains, or joint losses. Mutual awareness of potential gains and losses and the danger of worsening each actor's position through overly rigorous struggles over the distribution of the gains can limit the use of asymmetrical interdependence.

Agenda setting

Our second assumption of complex interdependence, the lack of clear hierarchy among multiple issues, leads us to expect that the politics of agenda formation and control will become more important. Traditional analyses lead statesmen to focus on politico-military issues and to pay little attention to the broader politics of agenda formation. Statesmen assume that the agenda will be set by shifts in the balance of power, actual or anticipated, and by perceived threats to the security of states. Other issues will only be very important when they seem to affect security and military power. In these cases, agendas will be influenced strongly by considerations of the overall balance of power.

Yet, today, some nonmilitary issues are emphasized in interstate relations at one time, whereas others of seemingly equal importance are neglected or quietly handled at a technical level. International monetary politics, problems of commodity terms of trade, oil, food, and multinational corporations have all been important during the last decade; but not all have been high on interstate agendas throughout that period.

Traditional analysts of international politics have paid little attention to agenda formation: to how issues come to receive sustained attention by high officials. The traditional orientation toward military and security affairs implies that the crucial problems of foreign policy are imposed on states by the actions or threats of other states. These are high politics as opposed to the low politics of economic affairs. Yet, as the complexity of actors and issues in world politics increases, the utility of force declines and the line between domestic policy and foreign policy becomes blurred: as the conditions of complex interdependence are more closely approximated, the politics of agenda formation becomes more subtle and differentiated.

Under complex interdependence we can expect the agenda to be affected by the international and domestic problems created by economic growth and increasing sensitivity interdependence that we described in the last chapter. Discontented domestic groups will politicize issues and force more issues once considered domestic onto the interstate agenda. Shifts in the distribution of power resources within sets of issues will also affect agendas. During the early 1970s the increased power of oil-producing governments over the transnational corporations and the consumer countries dramatically altered the policy agenda. Moreover, agendas for one group of issues may change as a result of linkages from other groups in which power resources are changing; for example, the broader agenda of North–South trade issues changed after the OPEC price rises and the oil embargo of 1973–74. Even if capabilities among states do not change, agendas may be affected by shifts in the importance of transnational actors. The publicity surrounding multinational corporations in the early 1970s, coupled with their rapid growth over the past twenty years, put the regulation of such corporations higher on both the United Nations agenda and national agendas.

Politicization – agitation and controversy over an issue that tend to raise it to the top of the agenda – can have many sources, as we have seen. Governments whose strength is increasing may politicize issues, by linking them to other issues. An international regime that is becoming ineffective or is not serving important issues may cause increasing politicization, as dissatisfied governments press for change. Politicization, however, can also come from below. Domestic groups may become upset enough to raise a dormant issue, or to interfere with interstate bargaining at high levels. In 1974 the American secretary of state's tacit linkage of a Soviet–American trade pact with progress in detente was upset by the success of domestic American groups working through Congress to link a trade agreement with Soviet policies on emigration.

The technical characteristics and institutional setting in which issues are raised will strongly affect politicization patterns. In the United States, congressional attention is an effective instrument of politicization. Generally, we expect transnational economic organizations and transgovernmental networks of bureaucrats to seek to avoid politicization. Domestically based groups (such as trade unions) and domestically oriented bureaucracies will tend to use politicization (particularly congressional attention) against their transnationally mobile competitors. At the international level, we expect states and actors to 'shop among forums' and struggle to get issues raised in international organizations that will maximize their advantage by broadening or narrowing the agenda.

Transnational and transgovernmental relations

Our third condition of complex interdependence, multiple channels of contact among societies, further blurs the distinction between domestic and international politics. The availability of partners in political coalitions is not necessarily limited by national boundaries as traditional analysis assumes. The nearer a situation is to complex interdependence, the more we expect the outcomes of political bargaining to be affected by transnational relations. Multinational corporations may be significant both as independent actors and as instruments manipulated by governments. The attitudes and policy stands of domestic groups are likely to be affected by communications, organized or not, between them and their counterparts abroad.

Thus the existence of multiple channels of contact leads us to expect limits, beyond those normally found in domestic politics, on the ability of statesmen to calculate the manipulation of interdependence or follow a consistent strategy of linkage. Statesmen must consider differential as well as aggregate effects of interdependence strategies and their likely implications for politicization and agenda control. Transactions among societies – economic and social transactions more than security ones – affect groups differently. Opportunities and costs from increased transnational ties may be greater for certain groups – for instance, American workers in the textile or shoe industries – than for others. Some organizations or groups may interact directly with actors in other societies or with other governments to increase their benefits from a network of interaction. Some actors may therefore be less vulnerable as well as less sensitive to changes elsewhere in the network than are others, and this will affect patterns of political action.

The multiple channels of contact found in complex interdependence are not limited to nongovernmental actors. Contacts between governmental bureaucracies charged with similar tasks may not only alter their perspectives but lead to transgovernmental coalitions on particular policy questions. To improve their chances of success, government agencies attempt to bring actors from other governments into their own decision-making processes as allies. Agencies of powerful states such as the United States have used such coalitions to penetrate weaker governments in such countries as Turkey and Chile. They have also been used to help agencies of other governments penetrate the United States bureaucracy.[11] As we shall see in Chapter 7, transgovernmental politics frequently characterizes Canadian–American relations, often to the advantage of Canadian interests.

The existence of transgovernmental policy networks leads to a different interpretation of one of the standard propositions about international politics – that states act in their own interest. Under complex interdependence, this conventional wisdom begs two important questions: which self and which interest? A government agency may pursue its own interests under the guise of the national interest; and recurrent interactions can change official perceptions of their interests. As a careful study of the politics of United States trade policy has documented, concentrating only on pressures of various interests for decisions leads to an overly mechanistic view of a continuous process and neglects the important role of communications in slowly changing perceptions of self-interest.[12]

The ambiguity of the national interest raises serious problems for the top political leaders of governments. As bureaucracies contact each other directly across the national borders (without going through foreign offices), centralized control becomes more difficult. There is less assurance that the state will be united when dealing with foreign governments or that its components will interpret national interests similarly when negotiating with foreigners. The state may prove to be multifaceted, even schizophrenic. National interests will be defined differently on different issues, at different times, and by different governmental units. States that are better placed to maintain their coherence (because of a centralized political tradition such as France's) will be better able to manipulate uneven interdependence than fragmented states that at first glance seem to have more resources in an issue area.

Role of international organizations

Finally, the existence of multiple channels leads one to predict a different and significant role for international organizations in world politics. Realists in the tradition of Hans J. Morgenthau have portrayed a world in which states, acting from self-interest, struggle for 'power and peace.' Security issues are dominant; war threatens. In such a world, one may assume that international institutions will have a minor role, limited by the rare congruence of such interests. International organizations are then clearly peripheral to world politics. But in a world of multiple issues imperfectly linked, in which coalitions are formed transnationally and transgovernmentally, the potential role of international institutions in political bargaining is greatly increased. In particular, they help set the international agenda, and act as catalysts for coalition-formation and as arenas for political initiatives and linkage by weak states.

Governments must organize themselves to cope with the flow of business generated by international organizations. By defining the salient issues, and deciding which issues can be grouped together, organizations may help to determine governmental priorities and the nature of interdepartmental committees and other arrangements within governments. The 1972 Stockholm Environment Conference strengthened the position of environmental agencies in various governments. The 1974 World Food Conference focused the attention of important parts of the United States government on prevention of food shortages. The

September 1975 United Nations special session on proposals for a New International Economic Order generated an intragovernmental debate about policies toward the Third World in general. The International Monetary Fund and the General Agreement on Tariffs and Trade have focused governmental activity on money and trade instead of on private direct investment, which has no comparable international organization.

By bringing officials together, international organizations help to activate potential coalitions in world politics. It is quite obvious that international organizations have been very important in bringing together representatives of less developed countries, most of which do not maintain embassies in one another's capitals. Third World strategies of solidarity among poor countries have been developed in and for a series of international conferences, mostly under the auspices of the United Nations.[13] International organizations also allow agencies of governments, which might not otherwise come into contact, to turn potential or tacit coalitions into explicit transgovernmental coalitions characterized by direct communications. In some cases, international secretariats deliberately promote this process by forming coalitions with groups of governments, or with units of governments, as well as with nongovernmental organizations having similar interests.[14]

International organizations are frequently congenial institutions for weak states. The one-state-one-vote norm of the United Nations system favors coalitions of the small and powerless. Secretariats are often responsive to Third World demands. Furthermore, the substantive norms of most international organizations, as they have developed over the years, stress social and economic equity as well as the equality of states. Past resolutions expressing Third World positions, sometimes agreed to with reservations by industrialized countries, are used to legitimize other demands. These agreements are rarely binding, but up to a point the norms of the institution make opposition look more harshly self-interested and less defensible.

International organizations also allow small and weak states to pursue linkage strategies. In the discussions on a New International Economic Order, Third World states insisted on linking oil price and availability to other questions on which they had traditionally been unable to achieve their objectives.

Complex interdependence therefore yields different political patterns than does the realist conception of the world. (Table 19.1 summarizes these differences.) Thus, one would expect traditional theories to fail to explain international regime change in situations of complex interdependence. But, for a situation that approximates realist conditions, traditional theories should be appropriate. In the next chapter we shall look at the problem of understanding regime change.

Table 19.1 Political processes under conditions of Realism and complex interdependence

	Realism	Complex interdependence
Goals of actors	Military security will be the dominant goal.	Goals of states will vary by issue area. Transgovernmental politics will make goals difficult to define. Transnational actors will pursue their own goals.
Instruments of state policy	Military force will be most effective, although economic and other instruments will also be used.	Power resources specific to issue areas will be most relevant. Manipulation of interdependence, international organizations, and transnational actors will be major instruments.
Agenda formation	Potential shifts in the balance of power and security threats will set the agenda in high politics and will strongly influence other agendas.	Agenda will be affected by changes in the distribution of power resources within issue areas; the status of international regimes; changes in the importance of transnational actors; linkages from other issues and politicization as a result of rising sensitivity interdependence.
Linkages of issues	Linkages will reduce differences in outcomes among issue areas and reinforce international hierarchy.	Linkages by strong states will be more difficult to make since force will be ineffective. Linkages by weak states through international organizations will erode rather than reinforce hierarchy.
Roles of inter-national organizations	Roles are minor, limited by state power and the importance of military force.	Organizations will set agendas, induce coalition-formation, and act as arenas for political action by weak states. Ability to choose the organizational forum for an issue and to mobilize votes will be an important political resource.

Notes

1. Hans J. Morgenthau, *Politics Among Nations: The Struggle for Power and Peace*, 4th ed. (New York: Knopf, 1967), p. 36.

2. See the material referred to in footnotes 9 and 13, Chapter 1; also see Edward L. Morse, 'Transnational Economic Processes,' in Robert O. Keohane and Joseph S. Nye, Jr. (eds.), *Transnational Relations and World Politics* (Cambridge, Mass.: Harvard University Press, 1972).

3. Henry A. Kissinger, 'A New National Partnership,' *Department of State Bulletin*, February 17, 1975, p. 199.

4. See the report of the Commission on the Organization of the Government for the Conduct of Foreign Policy (Murphy Commission) (Washington, D.C.: U.S. Government Printing Office, 1975), and the studies prepared for that report. See also Raymond Hopkins, 'The International Role of "Domestic" Bureaucracy,' *International Organization* 30, no. 3 (Summer 1976).

5. *New York Times*, May 22, 1975.

6. For a valuable discussion, see Klaus Knorr, *The Power of Nations: The Political Economy of International Relations* (New York: Basic Books, 1975).

7. *Business Week*, January 13, 1975.

8. Stanley Hoffmann, 'The Acceptability of Military Force,' and Laurence Martin, 'The Utility of Military Force,' in *Force in Modern Societies: Its Place in International Politics* (Adelphi Paper, International Institute for Strategic Studies, 1973). See also Knorr, *The Power of Nations*.

9. Henry Brandon, *The Retreat of American Power* (New York: Doubleday, 1974), p. 218.

10. *International Implications of the New Economic Policy*, U.S. Congress, House of Representatives, Committee on Foreign Affairs, Subcommittee on Foreign Economic Policy, Hearings, September 16, 1971.

11. For a more detailed discussion, see Robert O. Keohane and Joseph S. Nye, Jr, 'Transgovernmental Relations and International Organizations,' *World Politics* 27, no. 1 (October 1974): 39–62.

12. Raymond Bauer, Ithiel de Sola Pool, and Lewis Dexter, *American Business and Foreign Policy* (New York: Atherton, 1963), chap. 35, esp. pp. 472–75.

13. Branislav Gosovic and John Gerard Ruggie, 'On the Creation of a New International Economic Order: Issue Linkage and the Seventh Special Session of the UN General Assembly,' *International Organization* 30, no. 2 (Spring 1976): 309–46.

14. Robert W. Cox, 'The Executive Head,' *International Organization* 23, no. 2 (Spring 1969): 205–30.

20

BULL

Source: Hedley Bull (1977) *The Anarchical Society: A Study of Order in World Politics*. Basingstoke, Macmillan, pp. 57–74.

Bull claims that order in any society is maintained by its members through a common interest in the elementary goals of social life. This is achieved by accepting certain rules, norms and practices which shape the conduct of individual actors. Although these rules and norms may not always be as formally articulated as they often are in western societies, they are however understood as legitimate and binding. Bull asserts that international society is no different in this respect from any other form of society. Although international society is commonly thought of as anarchical it none the less exhibits a range of institutions which are valued by its members. This position suggests that Grotius is his classical intellectual forebearer.

Order in the modern state

Within the modern state an institution, or set of connected institutions, is available to help make elementary social rules effective: government. A government is distinguished from other institutions within the modern state by its ability to call on physical force. On the one hand, it possesses actual force at its disposal that is overwhelming in relation to that which is commanded by any other group. On the other hand, it possesses a near monopoly of the legitimate use of force: apart from certain residual rights of self-defence that are accorded to the individual, only the government is able to employ force while being regarded by members of the society at large as within its rights in doing so. It is just as important to a government that its use of force should be legitimate as that it should be overwhelming. These two aspects of a government's coercive power are connected inasmuch as the collapse of a government's legitimacy may make possible a combination of force against it such that its force is no longer overwhelming. Insurgent groups show that they understand this interconnection when they devote as much attention to undermining the government's right, in the eyes of the population, to use force, as to combating that force with force of their own.

The government helps to make elementary social rules effective within the modern state by carrying out all the functions that were outlined in the last section. It is not only by the government that these functions are carried out; individuals and groups other than the state also undertake them. But the role of the government in promoting the effectiveness of elementary social rules is a central one.

(i) The government makes rules – not always in the sense that it invents them or first states them – but in the sense that it fixes upon them society's *imprimatur* or stamp of approval. In the modern state this process of rule-making results in a special set of rules which we refer to as 'the law'. While the making of rules in the modern state is formally the function of the legislature, it is familiar that the rule-making or legislative function is carried out not only by legislatures but by administrative bodies, whose formal function is the translation of law into orders, and judicial bodies, whose formal function is the interpretation of laws rather than the making of them.

(ii) The government helps to communicate the rules to those who are bound by them. The publication of statutes and court records, the actual enforcement of the rules by the prosecution of offenders, the work of the police in apprehending, deterring or punishing offenders, all contribute to the spreading of an awareness of what rules are treated by society as rules of law.

(iii) The government also administers or gives effect to the rules, translating them from general principles into requirements that particular persons do or refrain from doing particular things. This is formally the function of the executive branch, but a specialised branch is not necessarily presupposed by this function, which is in fact normally carried out by other arms of the government as well.

(iv) The government is able to interpret the rules – to resolve uncertainties about the validity of rules, their meaning or their relationship to one another – principally through its judicial arm.

(v) The government is able to enforce the law through the use, and the threat of the use, of the police and armed forces and through the sanctions imposed by the courts. Particular legal rules may not be backed up by explicit sanctions, but the legal system as a whole is underpinned by the government's coercive power.

(vi) The government can contribute to the legitimisation of the rules, the acceptance of them as valuable in themselves, by the influence it has over education and public information, the powers of persuasion of its own leaders, and its ability to project itself as the symbolic embodiment of the values of the society and to mould the political culture in a manner favourable to acceptance of the rules as legitimate.

(vii) The government may also adapt the rules to changing circumstances and demands by having its legislature repeal or amend old laws and enact new ones, and by having its administrators execute the law and its judges interpret it in such a way as to change its content.

(viii) The government carries out the function of 'protection' of the rules through the political actions it takes to set the social scene in such a way that the rules will continue to operate. The invocation of armed forces to crush a rising or expel a foreign invader exemplifies this 'protection'. So do measures taken by the government to appease political dissatisfaction, to remove social or economic grievances, to suppress irreconcilable agitators or to heal social cleavages or bridge antagonisms that threaten to bring about the breakdown of society.

What these miscellaneous political acts have in common is that they are all directed towards the preservation of order, not by directly upholding or implementing the rules, but by shaping, moulding or managing the social environment in which the rules operate in such a way that they have the opportunity of continuing to do so. They belong to a sphere of action which the rules themselves may not regulate and may even impede, but which their operation nevertheless presupposes.

Order in primitive stateless societies

Order within the modern state is the consequence, among other things, of government; order among states cannot be, for international society is an anarchical society, a society without government. But primitive stateless societies also present this spectacle of 'ordered anarchy', and it is worth considering the resemblances and differences between the ways in which order is created and maintained in the one case and in the other.

Apart from the attention given by political theorists to notional stateless societies, and the largely speculative accounts of them given by historians such as Maine and Maitland, primitive stateless societies were not subject to empirical observation and systematic analysis until they attracted the attention of twentieth-century anthropologists.[1] Primitive societies that have been identified as stateless by the latter include the Nuer, the Western Dinka and the Mandari of southern Sudan, the Tallensi of Northern Nigeria, the Bwamba of Uganda, the Lugbara of Uganda and Congo and the Konkomba to Togoland. All of these societies are without a government in the sense defined above and are, in addition, without central political institutions – legislative, executive or judicial –

of any kind. Indeed, it is said of some of them that they contain no specialised political roles at all; while there are persons or bodies within them, such as heads of a family or lineage group or a village, that fulfil political roles, these roles are not formally distinguished from the other roles they have. The distinctions which outside observers draw between the political, the local, the kinship or the ritualistic roles of these persons or groups may have no meaning in the culture of the societies themselves.

At the same time these societies clearly exhibit order in the sense that conduct within them conforms to elementary goals of social coexistence. In the shaping of this conduct rules play a vital part, and their effectiveness depends on the carrying out of the order-maintaining functions of making these rules, communicating, administering, interpreting, enforcing, legitimising, adapting and 'protecting' them. In the absence of any central authority, however, these functions are carried out solely by groups – such as lineage groups and locality groups – into which these stateless societies are divided.

Rules do not emanate from any central rule-making authority but arise out of the practice of lineage or locality groups in their relations with one another, become embodied in 'custom' and are confirmed by moral and religious belief. Custom or established practice is of course also a familiar source of rules in centralised political systems; in primitive stateless societies it is the only source of rules.

Conformity to these rules is brought about by conditioning and inertia, by 'moral' sanctions such as public ridicule and reprobation, and by ritual or supernatural sanctions, such as cursing by the elders of a tribe. In societies that are culturally homogeneous, especially if they are small societies, sanctions such as these will often be sufficient in themselves.

Where such sanctions are insufficient to deter or punish violations of rules, there may be a resort to 'self-help' on the part of groups within the society which take upon their own shoulders the responsibility of determining that there has been a breach of the rules, and of attempting to enforce them. The killing of a member of a lineage or locality group, for example, may lead that group to undertake a retaliatory killing of the guilty party or another member of his group. In circumstances in which the bonds between the groups are very strong, the legitimacy of the retaliation may be accepted on both sides and the matter brought to an end. But in others the legitimacy of the act may be disputed, and a sustained conflict, based on both sides on the exercise of subjectively legitimate self-help, may develop.

Since both groups will be interpreting the rules, and the facts of the case, on their own behalf (or on behalf of one of their members) their judgement is likely to be imperfect. Since, moreover, their ability actually to enforce the rules will depend on the amount of force at their command and their will to use it, the enforcement of the rules is bound to be uncertain. Yet the recourse to self-help does not represent disregard of the rules and the descent of the groups concerned into a Hobbesian state of nature; it represents the operation of a system in which these groups are assuming the functions of interpreting, applying and enforcing the rules. Moreover, in doing so they are confined by rules limiting the activity of self-help itself.

Resort to force by these groups in response to what they judge to be a violation of the rules is accepted throughout these societies as legitimate. There is not a general right to self-help, available to any individual or group within the society; only those groups that are entitled to resort to violence may do so. The force which they employ, if it is legitimate, may only be used in response to a violation of rights. The nature of the force employed, moreover, is limited, for example by the principle that retaliation must be proportionate to the offence.

Acts of self-help in primitive stateless societies, in addition to providing rules with a coercive sanction, also serve two further functions, to which Roger Masters has drawn attention: they 'serve to unite social groups and to maintain legal and moral criteria of right and wrong'.[2] Not only do they help, by galvanising a group in support of violent action against an outside group, to maintain its cohesion, they are also, in addition to being an attempt to enforce a rule against this particular violation, a means of restating the rule itself, of underlining its continued validity and enduring importance.

Primitive anarchical societies clearly have important resemblances to international society in respect of the maintenance of order. In both cases some element of order is maintained despite the absence of a central authority commanding overwhelming force and a monopoly of the legitimate use of it. In both cases, also, this is achieved through the assumption by particular groups – lineage and locality groups in primitive stateless societies, sovereign states in international society – of the functions which, in a modern state, the government (but not the government exclusively) carries out in making rules effective. In primitive anarchical society, as in international society, order depends upon a fundamental or constitutional principle, stated or implied, which singles out certain groups as the sole bodies competent to discharge these political functions. In both societies the politically competent groups may legitimately use force in defence of their rights, while individuals and groups other than these must look to the privileged, politically competent groups for protection, rather than resort to force themselves.

In primitive anarchical societies, as in international society, the relations between these politically competent groups are themselves circumscribed by a structure of acknowledged normative principles, even at times of violent struggle. But in both there is a tendency, during these periods of struggle, for the structure of rules to break down, and the society to fall apart to such an extent that the warring tribes or states are better described as a number of contending societies than as a single society. Finally, in both primitive anarchical society and modern international society there are factors operating, outside the structure of rules itself, inducing the politically competent groups to conform to them. These include the factors of mutual deterrence or fear of unlimited conflict, the force of habit or inertia, the long-term interests they have (consciously rationalised in the modern world, and intuitively felt in primitive society) in preserving a system of collaboration, whatever their short-term interest in destroying it.

However, the differences between international society and primitive stateless societies are also remarkable. In the first place there are crucial differences between the units that are politically competent in the two sorts of society. The state in international society is sovereign in that it has supreme jurisdiction over its citizens and its territory. The lineage or locality groups which exercise political powers in primitive society, by contrast, do not have any such exclusive rights in relation to the persons that make them up, and usually have a less clearly defined relationship to territory.

A given lineage group does not necessarily exercise exclusive authority over the persons of which it is composed. In some stateless societies lineage groups are divided into segments, and within them there is a constant process of segmentation and merging. Segments of a lineage which are units at one level merge into larger segments at others. Whereas at one level these units may be in competition, at higher levels they are united as subordinate parts of a larger segment. These shifting combinations and divisions illustrate what has been called 'the principle of complementary opposition' in primitive stateless societies. Politically competent units in primitive anarchical societies are so related that while any two of them are in conflict for certain purposes they are combined for certain other purposes. Thus, on the one hand, each unit engages in conflict sufficient to generate a sense of identity and maintain its internal cohesion, but on the other hand there is no relationship of conflict between units that is not overlaid with some element of co-operation also.

Nor do politically competent units in primitive anarchical societies possess exclusive jurisdiction over precisely defined territories. The view of Sir Henry Maine that in primitive societies political solidarity arose only out of ties of blood and never out of common possession of a tract of territory has been rejected by modern anthropologists, who contend that primitive societies are based on both blood and territory.[3] But the lineage groups that carry out order-maintaining functions in the stateless societies that have been considered do not have exclusive rights to tracts of territory defined by precise, accepted boundaries.

Because the politically competent groups in primitive stateless societies are not sovereign over persons and territory, but are related less exclusively than is the modern state to the persons that belong to them and to areas of land, they appear to have a less self-sufficient existence and to be less introverted or self-regarding than are the members of the society of states.

A second point of contrast is that whereas modern international society, especially at the present time, is culturally heterogeneous, primitive stateless societies are marked by a high degree of cultural homogeneity. By a society's culture we mean its basic system of values, the premises from which its thought and action derive. All primitive societies appear to depend upon a common culture; stateless societies appear to depend upon it to a special degree. Fortes and Evans-Pritchard came to the tentative conclusion, on the basis of the African systems they studied, that a high degree of common culture was a necessary condition of anarchical structures, while only a central authority could weld together peoples of heterogeneous culture.[4] But the society of sovereign states – or, as it has sometimes been called, the inclusive society, today a political fabric that embraces the whole of mankind – is *par excellence* a society that is culturally heterogeneous.

A third point of contrast is that primitive stateless societies rest not simply on a culture that is homogeneous but also on one that includes the element of magical or religious belief. 'The social system', Fortes and Evans-Pritchard wrote, 'is, as it were, removed to a mystical plane, where it figures as a system of sacred values beyond criticism or revision . . . hence the wars or feuds between segments of a society like the Nuer or the Tallensi are kept within bounds by mystical sanctions.'[5] International society, by contrast, is part of the modern world, the secular world that emerged from the collapse of ecclesiastical and religious authority. The various substitutes that have been brought forward in the last three centuries in the attempt to validate or authenticate the rules of international society – the natural law, the customary practice of states, the interests or 'needs' of states, the law common to 'civilised states' – are all inferior to religious authority in terms of their power to produce social cohesion because they are all subject to question and debate. The moral bases of international society may be less brittle than those of primitive societies, not subject to the shattering impact that was made by Christian and Islamic civilisations on sub-Saharan African and Oceanic systems, more able to absorb new intellectual challenges and preserve some measure of continuity. But they do not approach a magical or religious system of values in terms of their social impact.

Finally, there are gross differences in size between international society and primitive stateless societies. The Nuer, the largest-scale society studied by Fortes and Evans-Pritchard, numbered 300,000 in an area of 26,000 square miles. The society of states embraces all mankind and all the earth.

Together, what is shown by these points of contrast is that the forces making for social cohesion and solidarity are very much stronger in primitive anarchical societies than in international society. The less exclusive and self-regarding nature of the political units of which primitive stateless societies are composed, their cultural homogeneity, the underpinning of their rules by magical and religious belief, and their small and intimate nature, all indicate that though government is lacking in these systems, an impressive degree of social solidarity is not. The maintenance of order in international society has to take place not only in the absence of government but also in the absence of social solidarity of this sort.

Order in international society

The maintenance of order in world politics depends, in the first instance, on certain contingent facts which would make for order even if states were without any conception of common interests, common rules or common institutions – even if, in other words, they formed an international system only, and not also an international society. A balance of power, for example, may arise in an international system quite fortuitously, in the absence of any belief that it serves common interests, or any attempt to regulate or institutionalise it. If it does arise, it may help to limit violence, to render undertakings credible or to safeguard governments from challenges to their local supremacy. Within international society, however, as in other societies, order is the consequence not merely of contingent facts such as this, but of a sense of common interests in the elementary goals of social life; rules prescribing behaviour that sustains these goals; and institutions that help to make these rules effective.

Common interests

To say that x is in someone's interest is merely to say that it serves as a means to some end that he is pursuing. Whether or not x does serve as a means to any particular end is a matter of objective fact. But whether or not x is in his interest will depend not only on this but also on what ends he is actually pursuing. It follows from this that the conception of interest is an empty or vacuous guide, both as to what a person does do and as to what he should do. To provide such a guide we need to know what ends he does or should pursue, and the conception of interest in itself tells us nothing about either.

Thus the criterion of 'national interest', or 'interest of state', in itself provides us with no specific guidance either in interpreting the behaviour of states or in prescribing how they should behave – unless we are told what concrete ends or objectives states do or should pursue: security, prosperity, ideological objectives or whatever. Still less does it provide us with a criterion that is objective, in the sense of being independent of the way state ends or purposes are perceived by particular decision-makers. It does not even provide a basis for distinguishing moral or ideological considerations in a country's foreign policy from non-moral or non-ideological ones: for x can be in a country's interest if it serves as a means to a moral or ideological objective that the country has.

However, the conception of national interest or interest of state does have some meaning in a situation in which national state ends are defined and agreed, and the question at issue is by what means they can be promoted. To say that a state's foreign policy should be based on pursuit of the national interest is to insist that whatever steps are taken should be part of some rational plan of action; an approach to foreign policy based on the national interest may thus be contrasted with one consisting simply of the uncritical pursuit of some established policy, or one consisting simply of unconsidered reactions to events. A policy based on the idea of the national interest, moreover, may be contrasted with one based on a sectional interest, or one based on the interests of some group wider than the state, such as an alliance or international organisation to which it belongs. To speak of the national interest as the criterion at least directs our attention to the ends or objectives of the nation or state, as against those of some other group, narrower or wider.

The maintenance of order in international society has as its starting-point the development among states of a sense of common interests in the elementary goals of social life. However different and conflicting their objectives may be, they are united in viewing these goals as instrumental to them. Their sense of common interests may derive from fear of unrestricted violence, of the instability of agreements or of the insecurity of their independence or sovereignty. It may have its origins in rational calculation that the willingness of states to accept restrictions on their freedom of action is reciprocal. Or it may be based also on the treatment of these goals as valuable in themselves and not merely as a means to an end – it may express a sense of common values as well as of common interests.

Rules

In international society, as in other societies, the sense of common interests in elementary goals of social life does not in itself provide precise guidance as to what behaviour is consistent with these goals; to do this is the function of *rules*. These rules may have the status of international law, of moral rules, of custom or established practice, or they may be merely operational rules or 'rules of the game', worked out without formal agreement or even without verbal communication. It is not uncommon for a rule to emerge first as an operational rule, then to become established practice, then to attain the status of a moral principle and finally to be incorporated in a legal convention; this appears to have been the genesis, for example, of many of the rules now embodied in multilateral treaties or conventions concerning the laws of war, diplomatic and consular status, and the law of the sea.

The range of these rules is vast, and over much of this range they are in a state of flux. Here we shall mention only three complexes of rules that play a part in the maintenance of international order.

First, there is the complex of rules that states what may be called the fundamental or constitutional normative principle of world politics in the present era. This is the principle that identifies the idea of a society of states, as opposed to such alternative ideas as that of a universal empire, a cosmopolitan community of individual human beings, or a Hobbesian state of nature or state of war, as the supreme normative principle of the political organisation of mankind. It is emphasised elsewhere in this study that there is nothing historically inevitable or morally sacrosanct about the idea of a society of states. Nor does this idea in fact monopolise human thought and action, even in the present phase; on the contrary, it has always had to do battle with competing principles, and does so now. Order on a world scale, however, does require that one or another of these basic ideas should be clearly in the ascendancy; what is incompatible with order on a world scale is a discord of competing principles of universal political organisation.

On the one hand, the idea of international society identifies states as members of this society and the units competent to carry out political tasks within it, including the tasks necessary to make its basic rules effective; it thus excludes conceptions which assign this political competence to groups other than the state, such as universal authorities above it or sectional groups within it. On the other hand, the idea of international society identifies the relationship between the states as that of members of a society bound by common rules and committed to common institutions; it thus excludes the conception of world politics as a mere arena or state of war.

This fundamental or constitutional principle of international order is presupposed in ordinary state conduct. The daily actions of states – in arrogating to themselves the rights or competences of principal actors in world politics, and in combining with each other to this end, in resisting the claims of supra-state or sub-state groups to wrest these rights and competences from them – display this principle and provide evidence of its central role. The principle is contained in a number of basic rules of international law. Thus it has been the predominant doctrine that states are the only or the principal bearers of rights and duties in international law; that they alone have the right to use force to uphold it; and that its source lies in the consent of states, expressed in custom or treaty. The principle, however, is prior to international law, or to any particular formulation of international law; it is manifest in a whole complex of rules – legal, moral, customary and operational. It is not a static principle, but is subject to constant development. In the formative stages of international society, it had to meet the challenge of doctrines which proclaimed the right of individuals and of groups other than the state to a place in universal political organisation; and at the present time it faces a similar challenge.

Second, there are what may be called 'the rules of coexistence'. Given the guidance supplied by the constitutional principle as to who are the members of international society, these rules set out the minimum conditions of their coexistence. They include, first of all, the complex of rules which restrict the place of violence in world politics. These rules seek to confine the legitimate use of violence to sovereign states and to deny it to other agents by confining legitimate violence to a particular kind of violence called 'war', and by treating war as violence that is waged on the authority of a sovereign state. Furthermore, the rules seek to limit the causes or purposes for which a sovereign state can legitimately begin a war, for example by requiring that it be begun for a just cause, as maintained by the natural-law doctrines of the formative era of the states system, or by requiring that it be begun only after certain other procedures had been tried first, as insisted by the Covenant of the League of Nations. The rules also have sought to restrict the manner in which sovereign states conduct war, for example by insisting that war be conducted in a way proportionate to the end pursued, or in such a way as to spare non-combatants, or so as to employ no more violence than necessary. In addition, the rules have sought to restrict the geographical spread of a war, by establishing the rights and duties of neutrals and belligerents in relation to one another.

There is a further complex of rules of coexistence which prescribes the behaviour appropriate to sustain the goal of the carrying out of undertakings.

The basic rule *pacta sunt servanda*, sometimes seen as a presupposition of the law of nations, and sometimes as a first principle of it, established the presumption on which alone there can be point in entering into agreements at all. Subordinate or qualifying rules concern whether or not good faith need be kept with heretics or infidels, whether or not agreements remain valid in changing circumstances and who is the judge as to whether or not they have changed, whether or not and in what sense agreements are valid that are imposed by force, what the circumstances are in which a party to an agreement can be released from it, what are the principles according to which agreements should be interpreted, whether or not and to what extent a new government succeeds to the obligations of its predecessors, and so on.

The rules of coexistence also include those which prescribe behaviour that sustains the goal of the stabilisation of each state's control or jurisdiction over its own persons and territory. At the heart of this complex of rules is the principle that each state accepts the duty to respect the sovereignty or supreme jurisdiction of every other state over its own citizens and domain, in return for the right to expect similar respect for its own sovereignty from other states. A corollary or near-corollary of this central rule is the rule that states will not intervene forcibly or dictatorially in one another's internal affairs. Another is the rule establishing the 'equality' of all states in the sense of their like enjoyment of like rights of sovereignty.

Third, there is the complex of rules concerned to regulate co-operation among states – whether on universal or on a more limited scale – above and beyond what is necessary for mere coexistence. This includes the rules that facilitate co-operation, not merely of a political and strategic, but also of a social and economic nature. The growth in this century of legal rules concerned with co-operation between states in economic, social, communications and environmental matters exemplifies the place of rules of co-operation and will be considered later (see Chapter 6).

Rules of this kind prescribe behaviour that is appropriate not to the elementary or primary goals of international life, but rather to those more advanced or secondary goals that are a feature of an international society in which a consensus has been reached about a wider range of objectives than mere coexistence. Nevertheless, these rules may be said to play a role in relation to international order, inasmuch as the development of co-operation and consensus among states about these wider goals may be expected to strengthen the framework of coexistence.

This is not the place to expound these three complexes of rules in full, or to examine the problems of interpreting them or reconciling the conflicts between them. Nor is it appropriate here to consider which of them has the status of law, which the status of moral rules, which should be seen as customary or as operational rules, nor to trace the historical evolution through which these rules have passed from one of these embodiments to another, and sometimes back again. It is sufficient to note that the vast and changing corpus of rules and quasi-rules, of which those cited are part of the central core, provide the means whereby international society moves from the vague perception of a common interest to a clear conception of the kind of conduct it requires.

Institutions

In international society it is the members of the society themselves – sovereign states – which are chiefly responsible for performing the functions of helping to make the rules effective; they do so in the absence of either a supreme government, which is able to undertake these functions in the modern state, or the degree of solidarity among themselves that characterises the performance of these functions by politically competent groups in primitive stateless societies. In this sense it is states themselves that are the principal institutions of the society of states.

Thus states undertake the function of making the rules, or legislating, by signifying their consent to them. Rules of general application, like the rules of coexistence, arise out of custom and established practice, and are in some cases confirmed by multilateral conventions. Rules that apply only to particular groups of states may also arise out of custom and established practice – as do the operational rules of crisis avoidance and management now being evolved by the great powers – but they may also be the subject of explicit agreements or treaties.

States communicate the rules through their official words, as when they state that they respect the legal principle of the sovereignty of states, or the moral principle of national self-determination, or the operational rule that great powers should not interfere in each other's spheres of influence. But they also communicate the rules through their actions, when they behave in such a way as to indicate that they accept or do not accept that a particular rule is valid. Because the communication of the rules is in the hands of states themselves, and not of an authority independent of them, the advertisement of the rules is commonly distorted in favour of the interests of particular states.

States administer the rules of international society inasmuch as executive acts ancillary to the rules themselves are performed either by themselves (as when particular states are designated as the depository states for a treaty, or the guarantors of a neutralisation arrangement, or the arbiters of a dispute) or by international organisations which are responsible to them (as when organisations are set up to implement agreements concerning international post and telecommunications, or a host of other matters).

Each state provides its own interpretation of the rules – legal, moral or operational. Even in the case of legal rules, a state relies on its own legal advisers, and there is no conclusive way in which disagreements about interpretation can be settled by an independent authority. The interpretation of moral or of operational rules is even more uncertain.

The enforcement of the rules, in the absence of a central authority, is carried out by states, which may resort to acts of self-help, including acts of force, in defence of their rights under operational, moral or legal rules. Because states are frequently not in a position to carry out effective action in defence of their rights, the enforcement of the rules is uncertain. Because of the low degree of consensus or solidarity among states, actions which the state committing them sees as self-help or rule-enforcement are frequently not viewed as such by international society at large.

States undertake the task of legitimising the rules, in the sense of promoting the acceptance of them as valuable in their own right, by employing their powers of persuasion and propaganda to mobilise support for them in world politics as a whole. At the present time an important means to the legitimisation of rules is to have them endorsed by international assemblies and international organisations.

States undertake the task of changing or adapting operational, moral and legal rules to changing circumstances, but have to do so in the absence of a universal legislative authority competent to rescind old rules and devise new ones, and with the handicap that there is often no consensus as to whether or not, or how, the rules should be changed. States change the rules by demonstrating, through their words or their actions, that they are withdrawing their consent from old rules and bestowing it upon new ones, and thus altering the content of custom or established practice. The operational rules observed by great powers, whereby they respect one anothers' spheres of influence in particular parts of the world, are rescinded or changed when these powers show by what they do or say that they no longer accept them, or regard their boundaries or limiting conditions as having changed. The moral principle of national self-determination – the rule that states should be nation-states – came to displace that of dynastic legitimacy not by enactment of any legislative authority, but by war and revolution. In the changing of legal rules a part is sometimes played by multilateral conventions or treaties, but here also states change the old rules by violating or ignoring them systematically enough to demonstrate that they have withdrawn their consent to them. In other words, while the adaptation of the rules to changed circumstances is part of the process whereby order is maintained, it is itself often accompanied by disorder.

Finally, states undertake the task which, for want of a better term, has been called 'protection' of the rules. The rules which sustain order in international society can operate only if conditions obtain in the international political system that enable them to do so. In particular, they can operate only if that sense of common interests among states, which they seek to translate into a precise guide to conduct, continues to exist. The function of 'protection' of the rules comprises all those things which states may do to create or maintain that state or condition of the system in which respect for the rules can flourish.

The 'protection' of the rules encompasses, first and foremost, those classical acts of diplomacy and war whereby states seek to preserve a general balance of power in the international system (and today a relationship of mutual nuclear deterrence among contending nuclear powers); to accommodate or contain conflicts of ideology; to resolve or moderate conflicts of state interest; to limit or control armaments and armed forces in relation to interests perceived in international security; to appease the demands of dissatisfied states for what they regard as just change; and to secure and maintain the acquiescence of the smaller powers in the assumption by great powers of special rights and responsibilities.

These measures of 'protection' of the rules are not prescribed by the rules of coexistence, or by international law, in which some of the rules of coexistence are stated. Indeed, some of the measures which states take in the course of 'protecting' the rules may bring them into conflict with international law. The activities that go to make up 'protection' of the rules of coexistence are themselves the subject of further bodies of rules, such as those which regulate the balance of power, diplomacy and the special position of the great powers.

In carrying out these functions, states collaborate with one another, in varying degrees, in what may be called the institutions of international society: the balance of power, international law, the diplomatic mechanism, the managerial system of the great powers, and war. By an institution we do not necessarily imply an organisation or administrative machinery, but rather a set of habits and practices shaped towards the realisation of common goals. These institutions do not deprive states of their central role in carrying out the political functions of international society, or serve as a surrogate central authority in the international system. They are rather an expression of the element of collaboration among states in discharging their political functions – and at the same time a means of sustaining this collaboration. These institutions serve to symbolise the existence of an international society that is more than the sum of its members, to give substance and permanence to their collaboration in carrying out the political functions of international society, and to moderate their tendency to lose sight of common interests.

Notes

1. See, for example, M. Fortes and E.E. Evans-Pritchard, *African Political Systems* (Oxford University Press, 1940); John Middleton and David Tait (eds), *Tribes Without Rulers, Studies in African Segmentary Systems* (London: Routledge & Kegan Paul, 1958); and I. Southall, 'Stateless Societies', in *Encyclopaedia of the Social Sciences*, ed. David L. Sills (New York: Free Press, 1968). I am also indebted to Roger D. Masters's penetrating article 'World Politics as a Primitive Political System', *World Politics*, vol. XVI, no. 4 (July 1964).
2. Masters, 'World Politics as a Primitive Political System,' p. 607.
3. See I. Schapera, *Government and Politics in Tribal Societies* (New York: Watts, 1956) ch. 1. For Maine's view see *Ancient Law* (London: John Murray, 1930) p. 144.
4. Fortes and Evans-Pritchard, *African Political Systems*, p. 10.
5. *Ibid.*, p. 18.

21

COX

Source: Robert W. Cox (1981) 'Social forces, states and world orders: Beyond international relations theory'. *Millennium*, 10: 2, 126–55.

Cox argues that international relations can no longer be understood as simply a system where states aggregate power. Furthermore he asserts that the distinction between the state and civil society, which allows the separation of foreign from domestic policy, cannot be maintained. Since it is not tenable to divide politics between the international and domestic, Cox identifies three interrelated spheres of activity – social forces, forms of states and world orders – each of which influences the other two. This allows the integration of normative and historical elements and, importantly, suggests some ways of conceptualizing change in world politics.

Academic conventions divide up the seamless web of the real social world into separate spheres, each with its own theorising; this is a necessary and practical way of gaining understanding. Contemplation of undivided totality may lead to profound abstractions or mystical revelations, but practical knowledge (that which can be put to work through action) is always partial or fragmentary in origin. Whether the parts remain as limited, separated objects of knowledge, or become the basis for constructing a structured and dynamic view of larger wholes is a major question of method and purpose. Either way, the starting point is some initial subdivision of reality, usually dictated by convention.

It is wise to bear in mind that such a conventional cutting up of reality is at best just a convenience of the mind. The segments which result, however, derive indirectly from reality insofar as they are the result of practices, that is to say, the responses of consciousness to the pressures of reality. Subdivisions of social knowledge thus may roughly correspond to the ways in which human affairs are organised in particular times and places. They may, accordingly, appear to be increasingly arbitrary when practices change.

International relations is a case in point. It is an area of study concerned with the interrelationships among states in an epoch in which states, and most commonly nation-states, are the principal aggregations of political power. It is concerned with the outcomes of war and peace and thus has obvious practical importance. Changing practice has, however, generated confusion as to the nature of the actors involved (different kinds of state, and non-state entities), extended the range of stakes (low as well as high politics), introduced a greater diversity of goals pursued, and produced a greater complexity in the modes of interaction and the institutions within which action takes place.

One old intellectual convention which contributed to the definition of international relations is the distinction between state and civil society. This distinction made practical sense in the Eighteenth and early Nineteenth centuries when it corresponded to two more or less distinct spheres of human activity or practice: to an emergent society of individuals based on contract and market relations which replaced a status-based society, on the one hand, and a state with functions limited to maintaining internal peace, external defence and the requisite conditions for markets, on the other. Traditional international relations theory maintains the distinctness of the two spheres, with foreign policy appearing as the pure expression of state interests. Today, however, state and civil society are so interpenetrated that the concepts have become almost purely analytical (referring to difficult-to-define aspects of a complex reality) and are only very vaguely and imprecisely indicative of distinct spheres of activity.

One recent trend in theory has undermined the conceptual unity of the state by perceiving it as the arena of competing bureaucratic entities, while another has reduced the relative importance of the state by introducing a range of private transnational activity and transgovernmental networks of relationships among fragments of state bureaucracies. The state, which remained as the focus of international relations thinking, was still a singular concept: a state was a state was a state. There has been little attempt within the bounds of international relations theory to consider the state/society complex as the basic entity of international relations. As a consequence, the prospect that there exist a plurality of forms of state, expressing different configurations of state/society complexes, remains very largely unexplored, at least in connection with the study of international relations.

The Marxist revival of interest in the state might have been expected to help fill this gap by broadening and diversifying the notion of state and, in particular, by amplifying its social dimensions. Some of the foremost products of this revival, however, either have been of an entirely abstract character, defining the state as a 'region' of a singularly-conceived capitalist mode of production

(Althusser, Poulantzas), or else have shifted attention away from the state and class conflict towards a motivational crisis in culture and ideology (Habermas). Neither goes very far towards exploring the actual or historical differences among forms of state, or considering the implications of the differences for international behaviour.

Some historians, both Marxist and non-Marxist, quite independently of theorising about either international relations or the state, have contributed in a practical way towards filling the gap. E.H. Carr and Eric Hobsbawm have both been sensitive to the continuities between social forces, the changing nature of the state and global relationships. In France, Fernand Braudel has portrayed these interrelationships in the Sixteenth and Seventeenth centuries on a vast canvas of the whole world.[1] Inspired by Braudel's work a group led by Immanuel Wallerstein has proposed a theory of world systems defined essentially in terms of social relations. The exploitative exchange relations between a developed core and an underdeveloped periphery, to which correspond different forms of labour control (e.g. free labour in the core areas, coerced labour in the peripheries, with intermediate forms in what are called semi-peripheries).[2] Though it offers the most radical alternative to conventional international relations theory, the world systems approach has been criticised on two main grounds: first, for its tendency to undervalue the state by considering the state as merely derivative from its position in the world system (strong states in the core, weak states in the periphery); second, for its alleged, though unintended, system-maintenance bias. Like structural-functional sociology, the approach is better at accounting for forces that maintain or restore a system's equilibrium, than identifying contradictions which can lead to a system's transformation.[3]

The above comments are not, however, the central focus of this essay but warnings prior to the following attempt to sketch a method for understanding global power relations: look at the problem of world order in the whole, but beware of reifying a world system.[4] Beware of underrating state power, but in addition give proper attention to social forces and processes and see how they relate to the development of states and world orders. Above all, do not base theory on theory but rather on changing practice and empirical-historical study, which are a proving ground for concepts and hypotheses.

On perspectives and purposes

Theory is always *for* someone and *for* some purpose. All theories have a perspective. Perspectives derive from a position in time and space, specifically social and political time and space. The world is seen from a standpoint defineable in terms of nation or social class, of dominance or subordination, of rising or declining power, of a sense of immobility or of present crisis, of past experience, and of hopes and expectations for the future. Of course, sophisticated theory is never just the expression of a perspective. The more sophisticated a theory is, the more it reflects upon and transcends its own perspective; but the initial perspective is always contained within a theory and is relevant to its explication. There is, accordingly, no such thing as theory in itself, divorced from a standpoint in time and space. When any theory so represents itself, it is the more important to examine it as ideology, and to lay bare its concealed perspective.

To each such perspective the enveloping world raises a number of issues; the pressures of social reality present themselves to consciousness as problems. A primary task of theory is to become clearly aware of these problems, to enable the mind to come to grips with the reality it confronts. Thus, as reality changes, old concepts have to be adjusted or rejected and new concepts forged in an initial dialogue between the theorist and the particular world he tries to comprehend. This initial dialogue concerns the *problematic* proper with a particular perspective. Social and political theory is history-bound at its origin, since it is always traceable to an historically-conditioned awareness of certain problems and issues, a problematic, while at the same time it attempts to transcend the particularity of its historical origins in order to place them within the framework of some general propositions or laws.

Beginning with its problematic, theory can serve two distinct purposes. One is a simple, direct response: to be a guide to help solve the problems posed within the terms of the particular perspective which was the point of departure. The other is more reflective upon the process of theorising itself: to become clearly aware of the perspective which gives rise to theorising, and its relation to other perspectives (to achieve a perspective on perspectives); and to open up the possibility of choosing a different valid perspective from which the problematic becomes one of creating an alternative world. Each of these purposes gives rise to a different kind of theory.

The first purpose gives rise to *problem-solving theory*. It takes the world as it finds it, with the prevailing social and power relationships and the institutions into which they are organised, as the given framework for action. The general aim of problem-solving is to make these relationships and institutions work smoothly by dealing effectively with particular sources of trouble. Since the general pattern of institutions and relationships is not called into question, particular problems can be considered in relation to the specialised areas of activity in which they arise. Problem-solving theories are thus fragmented among a multiplicity of spheres or aspects of action, each of which assumes a certain stability in the other spheres (which enables them in practice to be ignored) when confronting a problem arising within its own. The strength of the problem-solving approach lies in its ability to fix limits or parameters to a problem area and to reduce the statement of a particular problem to a limited number of variables which are amenable to relatively close and precise examination. The *ceteris paribus* assumption, upon which such theorising is based, makes it possible to arrive at statements of laws or regularities which appear to have general validity but which imply, of course, the institutional and relational parameters assumed in the problem-solving approach.

The second purpose leads to *critical theory*. It is critical in the sense that it stands apart from the prevailing order of the world and asks how that order came about. Critical theory, unlike problem-solving theory, does not take institutions and social and power relations for granted but calls them into question by concerning itself with their origins and how and whether they might be in the process of changing. It is directed towards an appraisal of the very framework for action, or problematic, which problem-solving theory accepts as its parameters. Critical theory is directed to the social and political complex as a whole rather than to the separate parts. As a matter of practice, critical theory, like problem-solving theory, takes as its starting point some aspect or particular sphere of human activity. But whereas the problem-solving approach leads to further analytical sub-division and limitation of the issue to be dealt with, the critical approach leads towards the construction of a larger picture of the whole of which the initially contemplated part is just one component, and seeks to understand the processes of change in which both parts and whole are involved.

Critical theory is theory of history in the sense of being concerned not just with the past but with a continuing process of historical change. Problem-solving theory is non-historical or ahistorical, since it, in effect, posits a continuing present (the permanence of the institutions and power relations which constitute its parameters). The strength of the one is the weakness of the other. Because it deals with a changing reality, critical theory must continually adjust its concepts to the changing object it seeks to understand and explain.[5] These concepts and the accompanying methods of enquiry seem to lack the precision that can be achieved by problem-solving theory, which posits a fixed order as its point of reference. This relative strength of problem-solving theory, however, rests upon a false premise, since the social and political order is not fixed but (at least in a long-range perspective) is changing. Moreover, the assumption of fixity is not merely a convenience of method, but also an ideological bias. Problem-solving theories can be represented, in the broader perspective of critical theory, as serving particular national, sectional, or class interests, which are comfortable within the given order. Indeed, the purpose served by problem-solving theory is conservative, since it aims to solve the problems arising in various parts of a complex whole in order to smooth the functioning of the whole. This aim rather belies the frequent claim of problem-solving theory to be value-free. It is methodologically value-free insofar as it treats the variables it considers as objects (as the chemist treats molecules or the physicist forces and motion); but it is value-bound by virtue of the fact that it implicitly accepts the prevailing order as its own framework. Critical theory contains problem-solving theories within itself, but contains them in the form of identifiable ideologies, thereby pointing to their conservative consequences, not to their usefulness as guides to action. Problem-solving theory tends to ignore this kind of critique as being irrelevant to its purposes and in any case, as not detracting from its practical applicability. Problem-solving theory stakes its claims on its greater precision and, to the extent that it recognises critical theory at all, challenges the possibility of achieving any scientific knowledge of historical processes.

Critical theory is, of course, not unconcerned with the problems of the real world. Its aims are just as practical as those of problem-solving theory, but it approaches practice from a perspective which transcends that of the existing order, which problem-solving theory takes as its starting point. Critical theory allows for a normative choice in favour of a social and political order different from the prevailing order, but it limits the range of choice to alternative orders which are feasible transformations of the existing world. A principal objective of critical theory, therefore, is to clarify this range of possible alternatives. Critical theory thus contains an element of utopianism in the sense that it can represent a coherent picture of an alternative order, but its utopianism is constrained by its comprehension of historical processes. It must reject improbable alternatives just as it rejects the permanency of the existing order. In this way critical theory can be a guide to strategic action for bringing about an alternative order, whereas problem-solving theory is a guide to tactical actions which, intended or unintended, sustain the existing order.

The perspectives of different historical periods favour one or the other kind of theory. Periods of apparent stability or fixity in power relations favour the problem-solving approach. The Cold War was one such period. In international relations, it fostered a concentration upon the problems of how to manage an apparently enduring relationship between two superpowers. However, a condition of uncertainty in power relations beckons to critical theory as people seek to understand the opportunities and risks of change. Thus the events of the 1970s generated a sense of greater fluidity in power relationships, of a many-faceted crisis, crossing the threshold of uncertainty and opening the opportunity for a new development of critical theory directed to the problems of world order. To reason about possible future world orders now, however, requires a broadening of our enquiry beyond conventional international relations, so as to encompass basic processes at work in the development of social forces and forms of state, and in the structure of global political economy. Such, at least, is the central argument of this essay.

Realism, Marxism and an approach to a critical theory of world order

Currents of theory which include works of sophistication usually share some of the features of both problem-solving and critical theory but tend to emphasise one approach over the other. Two currents which have had something important to say about inter-state relations and world orders – realism and Marxism – are considered here as a preliminary to an attempted development of the critical approach.

The realist theory of international relations had its origin in an historical mode of thought. Friedrich Meinecke, in his study on *raison d'état*, traced it to the political theory of Machiavelli and the diplomacy of Renaissance Italian city-states, which marked the emergence of a sense of the specific interests of particular states quite distinct from the general norms propagated by the ideologically dominant institution of medieval society, the Christian church.[6]

In perceiving the doctrines and principles underlying the conduct of states as a reaction to specific historical circumstances, Meinecke's interpretation of *raison d'état* is a contribution to critical theory. Other scholars associated with the realist tradition, such as E.H. Carr and Ludwig Dehio, have continued this historical mode of thought, delineating the particular configurations of forces which fixed the framework for international behaviour in different periods and trying to understand institutions, theories and events within their historical contexts.

Since the Second World War, some American scholars, notably Hans Morgenthau and Kenneth Waltz, have transformed realism into a form of problem-solving theory.[7] Though individuals of considerable historical learning, they have tended to adopt the fixed ahistorical view of the framework for action characteristic of problem-solving theory, rather than standing back from this framework, in the manner of E.H. Carr, and treating it as historically conditioned and thus susceptible to change. It is no accident that this tendency in theory coincided with the Cold War, which imposed the category of bipolarity upon international relations, and an overriding concern for the defence of American power as a bulwark of the maintenance of order.

The generalised form of the framework for action postulated by this new American realism (which we shall henceforth call neo-realism, which is the ideological form abstracted from the real historical framework imposed by the Cold War) is characterised by three levels, each of which can be understood in terms of what classical philosophers would call substances or essences, i.e. fundamental and unchanging substrata of changing and accidental manifestations or phenomena. These basic realities were conceived as: (1) the nature of man, understood in terms of Augustinian original sin or the Hobbesian 'perpetual and restless desire for power after power that ceaseth only in death';[8] (2) the nature of states, which differ in their domestic constitutions and in their capabilities for mobilising strength, but are similar in their fixation with a particular concept of national interest (a Leibnizian *monad*) as a guide to their actions; and (3) the nature of the state system, which places rational constraints upon the unbridled pursuit of rival national interests through the mechanism of the balance of power.

Having arrived at this view of underlying substances, history becomes for neo-realists a quarry providing materials with which to illustrate variations on always recurrent themes. The mode of thought ceases to be historical even though the materials used are derived from history. Moreover, this mode of reasoning dictates that, with respect to essentials, the future will always be like the past.[9]

In addition, this core of neo-realist theory has extended itself into such areas as game theory, in which the notion of substance at the level of human nature is presented as a rationality assumed to be common to the competing actors who appraise the stakes at issue, the alternative strategies, and the respective payoffs in a similar manner. This idea of a common rationality reinforces the non-historical mode of thinking. Other modes of thought are to be castigated as inapt, and incomprehensible in their own terms (which makes it difficult to account for the irruption into international affairs of a phenomenon like Islamic integralism, for instance).

The 'common rationality' of neo-realism arises from its polemic with liberal internationalism. For neo-realism, this rationality is the one appropriate response to a postulated anarchic state system. Morality is effective only to the extent that it is enforced by physical power. This has given neo-realism the appearance of being a non-normative theory. It is 'value-free' in its exclusion of moral goals (wherein it sees the weakness of liberal internationalism) and in its reduction of problems to their physical power relations. This non-normative quality is, however, only superficial. There is a latent normative element which derives from the assumptions of neo-realist theory: security within the postulated inter-state system depends upon each of the major actors understanding this system in the same way, that is to say, upon each of them adopting neo-realist rationality as a guide to action. Neo-realist theory derives from its foundations the prediction that the actors, from their experiences within the system, will tend to think in this way; but the theory also performs a proselytising function as the advocate of this form of rationality. To the neo-realist theorist, this proselytising function (wherein lies the normative rôle of neo-realism) is particularly urgent in states which have attained power in excess of that required to balance rivals, since such states may be tempted to discard the rationality of neo-realism and try to impose their own moral sense of order, particularly if, as in the case of the United States, cultural tradition has encouraged more optimistic and moralistic alternative views of the nature of man, the state and world order.[10]

The debate between neo-realists and liberal internationalists reproduces, with up-to-date materials, the Seventeenth century challenge presented by the civil philosophy of Hobbes to the natural law theory of Grotius. Each of the arguments is grounded in different views of the essences of man, the state and the inter-state system. An alternative which offered the possibility of getting beyond this opposition of mutually exclusive concepts was pointed out by the Eighteenth century Neapolitan Giambattista Vico, for whom the nature of man and of human institutions (amongst which must be included the state and the inter-state system) should not be thought of in terms of unchanging substances but rather as a continuing creation of new forms. In the duality of continuity and change, where neo-realism stresses continuity, the Vichian perspective stresses change; as Vico wrote, ' . . . this world of nations has certainly been made by men, and its guise must therefore be found within the modifications of our own human mind.'[11]

This should not be taken as a statement of radical idealism, (i.e. that the world is a creation of mind). For Vico, ever-changing forms of mind were shaped by the complex of social relations in the genesis of which class struggle played the principal rôle, as it later did for Marx. Mind is, however, the thread connecting the present with the past, a means of access to a knowledge of these changing modes of social reality. Human nature (the modifications of mind) and human institutions are identical with human history; they are to be understood in genetic and not in essentialist terms (as in neo-realism) or in teleological terms (as in functionalism). One cannot, in this Vichian perspective, properly abstract man and the state from history so as to define their substances or essences as *prior to* history, history being but the record of interactions of manifestations of these substances. A proper study of human affairs should be able to reveal both the coherence of minds and institutions characteristic of different ages, and the process whereby one such coherent pattern – which we can call an historical structure – succeeds another. Vico's project, which we would now call social science, was to arrive at a 'mental dictionary', or set of common concepts, with which one is able to comprehend the process of 'ideal eternal history', or what is most general and common in the sequence of changes undergone by human nature and institutions.[12] The error which Vico criticised as the 'conceit of scholars', who will have it that 'what they know is as old as the world', consists in taking a form of thought derived from a particular phase of history (and thus from a particular structure of social relations) and assuming it to be universally valid.[13] This is an error of neo-realism and more generally, the flawed foundation of all problem-solving theory. It does not, of course, negate the practical utility of neo-realism and problem-solving theories within their ideological limits. The Vichian approach, by contrast, is that of critical theory.

How does Marxism relate to this method or approach to a theory of world order? In the first place, it is impossible, without grave risk of confusion, to consider Marxism as a single current of thought. For our purposes, it is necessary to distinguish two divergent Marxist currents, analogous to the bifurcation between the old realism and the new. There is a Marxism which reasons historically and seeks to explain, as well as to promote, changes in social relations; there is also a Marxism, designed as a framework for the analysis of the capitalist state and society, which turns its back on historical knowledge in favour of a more static and abstract conceptualisation of the mode of production. The first we may call by the name under which it recognises itself: historical materialism. It is evident in the historical works of Marx, in those of present-day Marxist historians such as Eric Hobsbawm, and in the thought of Gramsci. It has also influenced some who would not be considered (or consider themselves) Marxist in any strict sense, such as many of the French historians associated with the *Annales*. The second is represented by the so-called structural Marxism of Althusser and Poulantzas ('so-called' in order to distinguish their use of 'structure' from the concept of historical structure in this essay) and most commonly takes the form of an exegesis of *Capital* and other sacred texts. Structural Marxism shares some of the features of the neo-realist problem-solving approach such as its ahistorical, essentialist epistemology, though not its precision in handling data nor, since it has remained very largely a study in abstractions, its practical applicability to concrete problems. To this extent it does not concern us here. Historical materialism is, however a foremost source of critical theory and it corrects neo-realism in four important respects.

The first concerns dialectic, a term which, like Marxism, has been appropriated to express a variety of not always compatible meanings, so its usage requires some definition. It is used here at two levels: the level of logic and the level of real history. At the level of logic, it means a dialogue seeking truth through the exploration of contradictions.[14] One aspect of this is the continual confrontation of concepts with the reality they are supposed to represent and their adjustment to this reality as it continually changes. Another aspect, which is part of the method of adjusting concepts, is the knowledge that each assertion concerning reality contains implicitly its opposite and that both assertion and opposite are not mutually exclusive but share some measure of the truth sought, a truth, moreover, that is always in motion, never to be encapsulated in some definitive form. At the level of real history, dialectic is the potential for alternative forms of development arising from the confrontation of opposed social forces in any concrete historical situation.

Both realism and historical materialism direct attention to conflict. Neo-realism sees conflict as inherent in the human condition, a constant factor flowing directly from the power-seeking essence of human nature and taking the political form of a continual reshuffling of power among the players in a zero-sum game, which is always played according to its own innate rules. Historical materialism sees in conflict the process of a continual remaking of human nature and the creation of new patterns of social relations which change the rules of the game and out of which – if historical materialism remains true to its own logic and method – new forms of conflict may be expected ultimately to arise. In other words, neo-realism sees conflict as a recurrent consequence of a continuing structure, whereas historical materialism sees conflict as a possible cause of structural change.

Second, by its focus on imperialism, historical materialism adds a vertical dimension of power to the horizontal dimension of rivalry among the most powerful states, which draws the almost exclusive attention of neo-realism. This dimension is the dominance and subordination of metropole over hinterland, centre over periphery, in a world political economy.

Third, historical materialism enlarges the realist perspective through its concern with the relationship between the state and civil society. Marxists, like non-Marxists, are divided between those who see the state as the mere expression of the particular interests in civil society and those who see the state as an autonomous force expressing some kind of general interest. This, for Marxists, would be the general interest of capitalism as distinct from the particular interests of capitalists. Gramsci contrasted historical materialism, which recognises the efficacy of ethical and cultural sources of political action (though always relating them with the economic sphere), with what he called historical economism or the reduction of everything to technological and material interests.[15] Neo-realist theory in the United States has returned to the state/civil society relationship, though it has treated civil society as a constraint upon the state and a limitation imposed by particular interests upon *raison d'état*, which is conceived of, and defined as, independent of civil society.[16] The sense of a reciprocal relationship between structure (economic relations) and superstructure (the ethico-political sphere) in Gramsci's thinking contains the potential for considering state/society complexes as the constituent entities of a world order and for exploring the particular historical forms taken by these complexes.

Fourth, historical materialism focuses upon the production process as a critical element in the explanation of the particular historical form taken by a state/society complex. The production of goods and services which creates both the wealth of a society and the basis for a state's ability to mobilise power behind its foreign policy, takes place through a power relationship between those who control and those who execute the tasks of production. Political conflict and the action of the state either maintain, or bring about changes in, these power relations of production. Historical materialism examines the connections between power in production, power in the state, and power in international relations. Neo-realism has, by contrast, virtually ignored the production process. This is the point on which the problem-solving bias of neo-realism is most clearly to be distinguished from the critical approach of historical materialism. Neo-realism implicitly takes the production process and the power relations inherent in it as a given element of the national interest, and therefore as part of its parameters. Historical materialism is sensitive to the dialectical possibilities of change in the sphere of production which could affect the other spheres, such as those of the state and world order.

This discussion has distinguished two kinds of theorising as a preliminary to proposing a critical approach to a theory of world order. Some of the basic premises for such a critical theory can now be restated:

(1) an awareness that action is never absolutely free but takes place within a framework for action which constitutes its problematic. Critical theory would start with this framework, which means starting with historical enquiry or an appreciation of the human experience that gives rise to the need for theory;[17]

(2) a realisation that not only action but also theory is shaped by the problematic. Critical theory is conscious of its own relativity but through this consciousness can achieve a broader time-perspective and become less relative than problem-solving theory. It knows that the task of theorising can never be finished in an enclosed system but must continually be begun anew;

(3) the framework for action changes over time and a principal goal of critical theory is to understand these changes;

(4) this framework has the form of an historical structure, a particular combination of thought patterns, material conditions and human institutions which has a certain coherence among its elements. These structures do not determine people's actions in any mechanical sense but constitute the context of habits, pressures, expectations and constraints within which action takes place;

(5) the framework or structure within which action takes place is to be viewed,

not from the top in terms of the requisites for its equilibrium or reproduction (which would quickly lead back to problem-solving), but rather from the bottom or from outside in terms of the conflicts which arise within it and open the possibility of its transformation.[18]

Frameworks for action: historical structures

At its most abstract, the notion of a framework for action or historical structure is a picture of a particular configuration of forces. This configuration does not determine actions in any direct, mechanical way but imposes pressures and constraints. Individuals and groups may move with the pressures or resist and oppose them, but they cannot ignore them. To the extent that they do successfully resist a prevailing historical structure, they buttress their actions with an alternative, emerging configuration of forces, a rival structure.

Three categories of forces (expressed as potentials) interact in a structure: material capabilities, ideas and institutions. No one-way determinism need be assumed among these three; the relationships can be assumed to be reciprocal. The question of which way the lines of force run is always an historical question to be answered by a study of the particular case.

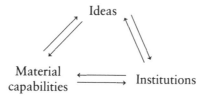

Figure 21.1

Material capabilities are productive and destructive potentials. In their dynamic form these exist as technological and organisational capabilities, and in their accumulated forms as natural resources which technology can transform, stocks of equipment (e.g. industries and armaments), and the wealth which can command these.

Ideas are broadly of two kinds. One kind consists of intersubjective meanings, or those shared notions of the nature of social relations which tend to perpetuate habits and expectations of behaviour.[19] Examples of intersubjective meanings in contemporary world politics are the notions that people are organised and commanded by states which have authority over defined territories; that states relate to one another through diplomatic agents; that certain rules apply for the protection of diplomatic agents as being in the common interest of all states; and that certain kinds of behaviour are to be expected when conflict arises between states, such as negotiation, confrontation, or war. These notions, though durable over long periods of time, are historically conditioned. The realities of world politics have not always been represented in precisely this way and may not be in the future. It is possible to trace the origins of such ideas and also to detect signs of a weakening of some of them.[20]

The other kind of ideas relevant to an historical structure are collective images of social order held by different groups of people. These are differing views as to both the nature and the legitimacy of prevailing power relations, the meanings of justice and public good, and so forth. Whereas intersubjective meanings are broadly common throughout a particular historical structure and constitute the common ground of social discourse (including conflict), collective images may be several and opposed.[21] The clash of rival collective images provides evidence of the potential for alternative paths of development and raises questions as to the possible material and institutional basis for the emergence of an alternative structure.

Institutionalisation is a means of stabilising and perpetuating a particular order. Institutions reflect the power relations prevailing at their point of origin and tend, at least initially, to encourage collective images consistent with these power relations. Eventually, institutions take on their own life; they can become either a battleground of opposing tendencies, or stimulate the creation of rival institutions reflecting different tendencies. Institutions are particular amalgams of ideas and material power which in turn influence the development of ideas and material capabilities.

There is a close connection between institutionalisation and what Gramsci called hegemony. Institutions provide ways of dealing with internal conflicts so as to minimise the use of force. (They may, of course, also maximise the capacity for using force in external conflicts, but we are considering here only the internal conflicts covered by an institution.) There is an enforcement potential in the material power relations underlying any structure, in that the strong can clobber the weak if they think it necessary. But force will not have to be used in order to ensure the dominance of the strong to the extent that the weak accept the prevailing power relations as legitimate. This the weak may do if the strong see their mission as hegemonic and not merely dominant or dictatorial, that is, if they are willing to make concessions that will secure the weak's acquiescence in their leadership and if they can express this leadership in terms of universal or general interests, rather than just as serving their own particular interests.[22] Institutions may become the anchor for such a hegemonic strategy since they lend themselves both to the representations of diverse interests and to the universalisation of policy.

It is convenient to be able to distinguish between hegemonic and non-hegemonic structures, that is to say between those in which the power basis of the structure tends to recede into the background of consciousness, and those in which the management of power relations is always in the forefront. Hegemony cannot, however, be reduced to an institutional dimension. One must beware of allowing a focus upon institutions to obscure either changes in the relationship of material forces, or the emergence of ideological challenge to an erstwhile prevailing order. Institutions may be out of phase with these other aspects of reality and their efficacy as a means of regulating conflict (and thus their hegemonic function) thereby undermined. They may be an expression of hegemony but cannot be taken as identical to hegemony.

The method of historical structures is one of representing what can be called limited totalities. The historical structure does not represent the whole world but rather a particular sphere of human activity in its historically located totality. The *ceteris paribus* problem, which falsifies problem-solving theory by leading to an assumption of total stasis, is avoided by juxtaposing and connecting historical structures in related spheres of action. Dialectic is introduced, firstly, by deriving the definition of a particular structure, not from some abstract model of a social system or mode of production, but from a study of the historical situation to which it relates, and secondly, by looking for the emergence of rival structures expressing alternative possibilities of development. The three sets of forces indicated in Figure 21.1 are an heuristic device, not categories with a predetermined hierarchy of relationships. Historical structures are contrast models: like ideal types they provide, in a logically coherent form, a simplified representation of a complex reality and an expression of tendencies, limited in their applicability to time and space, rather than fully realised developments.

For the purpose of the present discussion, the method of historical structures is applied to the three levels, or spheres of activity: (1) the organisation of production, more particularly with regard to the *social forces* engendered by the production process; (2) *forms of state* as derived from a study of state/society complexes; and (3) *world orders*, i.e. the particular configurations of forces which successively define the problematic of war or peace for the ensemble of states. Each of these levels can be studied as a succession of dominant and emergent rival structures.

The three levels are interrelated. Changes in the organisation of production generate new social forces which, in turn, bring about changes in the structure of states; and the generalisation of changes in the structure of states alters the problematic of world order. For instance, as E.H. Carr argued, the incorporation of the industrial workers (a new social force) as participants within western states from the late-Nineteenth century, accentuated the movement of these states towards economic nationalism and imperialism (a new form of state), which brought about a fragmentation of the world economy and a more conflictual phase of international relations (the new structure of world order).[23]

The relationship among the three levels is not, however, simply unilinear. Transnational social forces have influenced states through the world structure, as evidenced by the effect of expansive Nineteenth century capitalism, (*les bourgeois conquérants*)[24] upon the development of state structures in both core and periphery. Particular structures of world order exert influence over the forms which states take: Stalinism was, at least in part, a response to a sense of threat to the existence of the Soviet state from a hostile world order; the military-industrial complex in core countries, justifies its influence today by pointing to the conflictual condition of world order; and the prevalence of repressive militarism in periphery countries can be explained by the external support of imperialism as well as by a particular conjunction of internal forces. Forms of state also affect the development of social forces through the kinds of domination they exert, for example, by advancing one class interest and thwarting others.[25]

Considered separately, social forces, forms of state, and world orders can be represented in a preliminary approximation as particular configurations of material capabilities, ideas and institutions (as indicated in Figure 21.1). Considered in relation to each other, and thus moving towards a fuller representation of historical process, each will be seen as containing, as well as bearing the impact of, the others (as in Figure 21.2).[26]

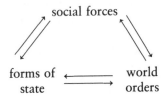

Figure 21.2

Hegemony and world orders

How are these reciprocal relationships to be read in the present historical conjuncture? Which of the several relationships will tell us the most? A sense of the historicity of concepts suggests that the critical relationships may not be the same in successive historical periods, even within the post-Westphalian era for which the term 'state system' has particular meaning. The approach to a critical theory of world order, adumbrated here, takes the form of an interconnected series of historical hypotheses.

Neo-realism puts the accent on states reduced to their dimension of material force and similarly reduces the structure of world order to the balance of power as a configuration of material forces. Neo-realism, which generally dismisses social forces as irrelevant, is not much concerned with differentiating forms of state (except insofar as 'strong societies' in liberal democratic polities may hamper the use of force by the state or advance particular interests over the national interest), and tends to place a low value on the normative and institutional aspects of world order.

One effort to broaden the realist perspective to include variations in the authority of international norms and institutions is the theory of 'hegemonic stability' which, as stated by Robert Keohane, 'holds that hegemonic structures of power, dominated by a single country, are most conducive to the development of strong international regimes, whose rules are relatively precise and well-obeyed.'[27] The classic illustrations of the theory discussed by Keohane are the *pax britannica* of the mid-Nineteenth century and the *pax americana* of the years following the Second World War. The theory appears to be confirmed by the decline in observance of the norms of the Nineteenth century order which accompanied Britain's relative decline in state power from the late-Nineteenth century. Exponents of the theory see a similar decline, since the early 1970s, in the observance of norms of the post-war order, relating it to a relative decline in US power. Robert Keohane has tested the theory in particular issue areas (energy, money and trade) on the grounds that power is not a fungible asset, but has to be differentiated according to the contexts in which a state tries to be influential. He finds that, particularly in the areas of trade and money, changes in US power are insufficient to explain the changes that have occurred and needs to be supplemented by the introduction of domestic political, economic and cultural factors.

An alternative approach might start by redefining what it is that is to be explained, namely, the relative stability of successive world orders. This can be done by equating stability with a concept of hegemony that is based on a coherent conjunction or fit between a configuration of material power, the prevalent collective image of world order (including certain norms) and a set of institutions which administer the order with a certain semblance of universality (i.e. not just as the overt instruments of a particular state's dominance). In this formulation, state power ceases to be the sole explanatory factor and becomes part of what is to be explained. This rephrasing of the question addresses a major difficulty in the realist version signalled by Keohane and others, namely, how to explain the failure of the US to establish a stable world order in the inter-war period despite its preponderance of power. If the dominance of a single state coincides with a stable order on some occasions but not on others, then there may be some merit in looking more closely at what is meant by stability and more broadly at what may be its sufficient conditions. Dominance by a powerful state may be a necessary but not a sufficient condition of hegemony.

The two periods of the *pax britannica* and the *pax americana* also satisfy the reformulated definition of hegemony. In the mid-Nineteenth century, Britain's world supremacy was founded on its sea power, which remained free from challenge by a continental state as a result of Britain's ability to play the rôle of balancer in a relatively fluid balance of power in Europe. The norms of liberal economics (free trade, the gold standard, free movement of capital and persons) gained widespread acceptance with the spread of British prestige, providing a universalistic ideology which represented these norms as the basis of a harmony of interests. While there were no formal international institutions, the ideological separation of economics from politics meant that the City could appear as administrator and regulator according to these universal rules, with British sea power remaining in the background as potential enforcer.

This historical structure was transformed in its three dimensions during the period running from the last quarter of the Nineteenth century through the Second World War. During this period British power declined relatively, losing its undisputed supremacy at sea, first with the German challenge and then with the rise of US power; economic liberalism foundered with the rise of protectionism, the new imperialisms and ultimately the end of the gold standard; and the belated and abortive attempt at international institutionalisation through the League of Nations, unsustained either by a dominant power or a widely-accepted ideology, collapsed in a world increasingly organised into rival power blocs.

The power configuration of the *pax americana* was more rigid than that of the earlier hegemony, taking the form of alliances (all hinging on US power) created in order to contain the Soviet Union. The stabilisation of this power configuration created the conditions for the unfolding of a global economy in which the United States played a rôle similar to that of Britain in mid-Nineteenth century. The United States rarely needed to intervene directly in support of specific national economic interests; by maintaining the rules of an international economic order according to the revised liberalism of Bretton Woods, the strength of US corporations engaged in the pursuit of profits was sufficient to ensure continuing national power. The *pax americana* produced a greater number of formal international institutions than the earlier hegemony. The Nineteenth century separation of politics and economics had been blurred by the experience of the Great Depression and the rise of Keynesian doctrines. Since states now had a legitimate and necessary overt rôle in national economic management, it became necessary both to multilateralise the administrative management of the international economy and to give it an intergovernmental quality.

The notion of hegemony as a fit between power, ideas and institutions makes it possible to deal with some of the problems in the theory of state dominance as the necessary condition for a stable international order; it allows for lags and leads in hegemony. For example, so appealing was the nostalgia for the Nineteenth century hegemony that the ideological dimension of the *pax britannica* flourished long after the power configuration that supported it had vanished. Sustained, and ultimately futile, efforts were made to revive a liberal world economy along with the gold standard in the inter-war period. Even in the post-war period, British policy continued to give precedence to balance of payments problems over national industrial development and employment considerations.[28] Another prime example is the case of the US, where the growth indicators of material power during the inter-war period were insufficient predictors of a new hegemony. It was necessary that US leaders should come to see themselves in ideological terms as the necessary guarantors of a new world order. The Roosevelt era made this transition, including both the conscious rejection of the old hegemony (e.g. by torpedoing the world economic conference in 1933 and abandoning the gold standard) and the gradual incorporation of New Deal principles into the ideological basis of the new world order. There followed US initiatives to create the institutions to administer this order.[29] Neo-mercantilists in the United States now warn against a danger of repeating the British error, urging US policy-makers not to continue to operate according to doctrines appropriate to the *pax americana* when the United States can no longer afford to act as guarantor for a universalist world order. Their persuasive efforts underline the point that in these matters ideology is a determining sphere of action which has to be understood in its connections with material power relations.

Social forces, hegemony and imperialism

Represented as a fit between material power, ideology and institutions, hegemony may seem to lend itself to a cyclical theory of history; the three dimensions fitting together in certain times and places and coming apart in others. This is reminiscent of earlier notions of *virtù*, or of the *weltgeist* migrating from people to people. The analogy merely points to something which remains unexplained. What is missing is some theory as to how and why the fit comes about and comes apart. It is my contention that the explanation may be sought in the realm of social forces shaped by production relations.

Social forces are not to be thought of as existing exclusively within states. Particular social forces may overflow state boundaries, and world structures can be described in terms of social forces just as they can be described as configurations of state power. The world can be represented as a pattern of interacting social forces in which states play an intermediate though autonomous rôle between the global structure of social forces and local configurations of social forces within particular countries. This may be called a political economy perspective of the world: power is seen as *emerging* from social processes rather than taken as given in the form of accumulated material capabilities, that is as the result of these processes. (Paraphrasing Marx, one could describe the latter, neo-realist view as the 'fetishism of power'.)[30] In reaching for a political economy perspective, we move from identifying the structural characteristics of world orders as configurations of material capabilities, ideas and institutions (Figure 21.1) to explaining their origins, growth and demise in terms of the interrelationships of the three levels of structures (Figure 21.2).

It is, of course, no great discovery to find that, viewed in the political economy perspective, the *pax britannica* was based both on the ascendancy of manufacturing capitalism in the international exchange economy, of which Britain was the centre, and on the social and ideological power, in Britain and other parts of northwest Europe, of the class which drew its wealth from manufacturing. The new bourgeoisie did not need to directly control states; its social power became the premiss of state politics.[31]

The demise of this hegemonic order can also be explained by the development of social forces. Capitalism mobilised an industrial labour force in the most advanced countries, and from the last quarter of the Nineteenth century industrial workers had an impact on the structure of the state in these countries. The incorporation of the industrial workers, the new social force called into existence by manufacturing capitalism, into the nation involved an extension in the range of state action in the form of economic intervention and social policy.

This in turn brought the factor of domestic welfare (i.e. the social minimum required to maintain the allegiance of the workers) into the realm of foreign policy. The claims of welfare competed with the exigencies of liberal internationalism within the management of states; whilst the former gained ground as protectionism, the new imperialism and ultimately the end of the gold standard marked the long decline of liberal internationalism.[32] The liberal form of state was slowly replaced by the welfare nationalist form of state.

The spread of industrialisation, and the mobilisation of social classes it brought about, not only changed the nature of states but also altered the international configuration of state power as new rivals overtook Britain's lead. Protectionism, as the means of building economic power comparable to Britain's, was for these new industrial countries more convincing than the liberal theory of comparative advantage. The new imperialisms of the major industrial powers were a projection abroad of the welfare nationalist consensus among social forces sought or achieved within the nations. As both the material predominance of the British economy and the appeal of the hegemonic ideology weakened, the hegemonic world order of the mid-Nineteenth century gave place to a non-hegemonic configuration of rival power blocs.

Imperialism is, thus, a rather loose concept which in practice has to be newly defined with reference to each historical period. There is little point in looking for any 'essence' of imperialism beyond the forms which dominance and subordination take in different successive world order structures. The actual form, whether activated by states, by social forces (e.g. the managements of multinational corporations), or some combination of both, and whether domination is primarily political or economic, is to be determined by historical analysis, and not deductive reasoning.

The expansive capitalism of the mid-Nineteenth century brought most of the world into the exchange relations of an international economy centred in London. The liberal imperialism of this phase was largely indifferent as to whether or not peripheral countries were formally independent or under the political-administrative control of a colonial power, provided that the rules of the international economy were observed.[33] Canada and Argentina, for example, had similar positions in real terms, though one had colonial and the other independent status. In the phase of liberal imperialism, local authorities, who were often pre-capitalist in their relationship to the production process (e.g. traditional agrarian-based rulers), kept their countries in the commercial system. During the second phase, that of the so-called new imperialism following the 1870s, direct state control began to supplant the less formal patterns of the commercial period. Capitalist production relations under this political aegis penetrated the periphery more thoroughly, notably in the extraction of raw materials and the building of the infrastructure (roads, railways, ports and commercial and governmental administrations) required to link the colonies more closely with the metropole.

Capitalist production relations generated new social forces in the periphery. Outsiders came to play important rôles in the local society, some as agents of the colonial administration and of big capital from the metropole, others in smaller businesses, filling the interstices between big capital and traditional local production (for example, the Chinese in southeast Asia, the Indians in east Africa or the Lebanese in west Africa). A local workforce often numerically small and materially better-off than the majority of the population, was drawn into capitalist production. This politically strategic group was opposed to capital on wage and labour issues but aligned with it as regards the development of the capitalist production sector. An indigenous petty bourgeoisie also grew up, occupying the subordinate positions in colonial administration and metropole-based enterprises, as well as in local small business. A local state apparatus emerged under colonial tutelage, encouraging the new production relations by methods ranging from the introduction of compulsory labour or a head tax as a means of generating a labour force, to reproducing, in the colonial context, some of the institutions and procedures of the industrial relations of the metropole.

The existence in the colonial territory of these new social forces, labour and the petty bourgeoisie, which could agree on a nationalist political programme, together with the introduction by the colonial administration of the elements of a modern state apparatus, (control of which could be the aim of this programme) laid the basis for the anti-colonial revolt which swept the colonial world after the Second World War. This movement reacted against administrative control from the metropole, but not continued involvement in capitalist production and exchange relations. The anti-imperialist label on the forces which replaced the structures created by the second phase or new imperialism obscured their rôle in ushering in yet a third phase of imperialism.

James Petras, in his use of the concept of an imperial state system, has posed a number of questions concerning the structural characteristics of states in the present world order. The dominant imperial state and subordinate collaborator states differ in structure and have complementary functions in the imperial system; they are not just more and less powerful units of the same kind, as might be represented in a simple neo-realist model. A striking feature in his framework is that the imperial state he analyses is not the whole US government; it is 'those executive bodies within the "government" which are charged with promoting and protecting the expansion of capital across state boundaries.'[34] The imperial system is at once more than and less than the state. It is more than the state in that it is a transnational structure with a dominant core and dependent periphery. This part of the US government is at the system's core, together (and here we may presume to enlarge upon Petras' indications) with inter-state institutions such as the IMF and the World Bank, symbiotically related to expansive capital, and with collaborator governments (or at any rate parts of them linked to the system) in the system's periphery. It is less than the state in the sense that non-imperial, or even anti-imperial, forces may be present in other parts of both core and periphery states. The unity of the state, posited by neo-realism, is fragmented in this image, and the struggle for and against the imperial system may go on within the state structures at both core and periphery as well as among social forces ranged in support and opposition to the system. The state is thus a necessary but insufficient category to account for the imperial system. The imperial system itself becomes the starting point of enquiry.

The imperial system is a world order structure drawing support from a particular configuration of social forces, national and transnational, and of core and periphery states. One must beware of slipping into the language of reification when speaking of structures; they are constraints on action, not actors. The imperial system includes some formal and less formal organisations at the system level through which pressures on states can be exerted without these system-level organisations actually usurping state power. The behaviour of particular states or of organised economic and social interests, however, finds its meaning in the larger totality of the imperial system. Actions are shaped either directly by pressures projected through the system or indirectly by the subjective awareness on the part of actors of the constraints imposed by the system. Thus one cannot hope to understand the imperial system by identifying imperialism with actors, be they states or multinationals; they are both dominant elements in the system, but the system as a structure is more than their sum. Furthermore, one must beware of ignoring the principle of dialectic by over emphasising the power and coherence of a structure, even a very dominant one. Where a structure is hegemonic, critical theory leads one to look for a counter-structure, even a latent one, by seeking out its possible bases of support and elements of cohesion.

At this point, it is preferable to revert to the earlier terminology which referred to hegemonic and non-hegemonic world order structures. To introduce the term 'imperial' with reference to the *pax americana* risks both obscuring the important difference between hegemonic and non-hegemonic world orders and confusing structurally different kinds of imperialism (e.g. liberal imperialism, the new or colonial imperialism, and the imperial system just outlined). The contention here is that the *pax americana* was hegemonic: it commanded a wide measure of consent among states outside the Soviet sphere and was able to provide sufficient benefits to the associated and subordinate elements in order to maintain their acquiescence. Of course, consent wore thin as one approached the periphery where the element of force was always apparent, and it was in the periphery that the challenge to the imperial system first became manifest.

It was suggested above how the particular fit between power, ideology and institutions constituting the *pax americana* came into being. Since the practical issue at the present is whether or not the *pax americana* has irretrievably come apart and if so what may replace it, two specific questions deserving attention are: (1) what are the mechanisms for maintaining hegemony in this particular historical structure? and (2) what social forces and/or forms of state have been generated within it which could oppose and ultimately bring about a transformation of the structure?

The internationalisation of the state

A partial answer to the first question concerns the internationalisation of the state. The basic principles of the *pax americana* were similar to those of the *pax britannica* – relatively free movement of goods, capital and technology and a reasonable degree of predictability in exchange rates. Cordell Hull's conviction that an open trading world was a necessary condition of peace could be taken as its ideological text, supplemented by confidence in economic growth and ever-rising productivity as the basis for moderating and controlling conflict. The post-war hegemony was, however, more fully institutionalised than the *pax britannica* and the main function of its institutions was to reconcile domestic social pressures with the requirements of a world economy. The International Monetary Fund was set up to provide loans to countries with balance of payments deficits in order to provide time in which they could make adjustments, and to avoid the sharp deflationary consequences of an automatic gold standard. The World Bank was to be a vehicle for longer term financial assistance. Economically weak countries were to be given assistance by the system itself, either directly through the system's institutions or by other states nominally certified by the system's institutions. These institutions incorporated mechanisms to supervise the application of the system's norms and to make financial assistance effectively conditional upon reasonable evidence of intent to live up to the norms.

This machinery of surveillance was, in the case of the western allies and subsequently of all industrialised capitalist countries, supplemented by elaborate machinery for the harmonisation of national policies. Such procedures began with the mutual criticism of reconstruction plans in western European countries (the US condition for Marshall aid funds), continued with the development of annual review procedures in NATO (which dealt with defence and defence support programmes), and became an acquired habit of mutual consultation and mutual review of national policies (through the OECD and other agencies).

The notion of international obligation moved beyond a few basic commitments, such as observance of the most favoured nation principle or maintenance of an agreed exchange rate, to a general recognition that measures of national economic policy affect other countries and that such consequences should be taken into account before national policies are adopted. Conversely, other countries should be sufficiently understanding of one country's difficulties to acquiesce in short-term exceptions. Adjustments are thus perceived as responding to the needs of the system as a whole and not to the will of dominant countries. External pressures upon national policies were accordingly internationalised.

Of course, such an internationalised policy process presupposed a power structure, one in which central agencies of the US government were in a dominant position. But it was not necessarily an entirely hierarchical power structure with lines of force running exclusively from the top down, nor was it one in which the units of interaction were whole nation-states. It was a power structure seeking to maintain consensus through bargaining and one in which the bargaining units were fragments of states. The power behind the negotiation was tacitly taken into account by the parties.

The practice of policy harmonisation became such a powerful habit that when the basic norms of international economic behaviour no longer seemed valid, as became the case during the 1970s, procedures for mutual adjustment of national economic policies were, if anything, reinforced. In the absence of clear norms, the need for mutual adjustment appeared the greater.[35]

State structures appropriate to this process of policy harmonisation can be contrasted with those of the welfare nationalist state of the preceding period. Welfare nationalism took the form of economic planning at the national level and the attempt to control external economic impacts upon the national economy. To make national planning effective, corporative structures grew up in most industrially advanced countries for the purpose of bringing industry, and also organised labour, into consultation with the government in the formulation and implementation of policy. National and industrial corporative structures can raise protectionist or restrictive obstacles to the adjustments required for adaptation of national economies to the world economy in a hegemonic system. Corporatism at the national level was a response to the conditions of the interwar period; it became institutionally consolidated in western Europe just as the world structure was changing into something for which national corporatism was ill-suited.

The internationalisation of the state gives precedence to certain state agencies – notably ministries of finance and prime ministers' offices – which are key points in the adjustment of domestic to international economic policy. Ministries of industries, labour ministries, planning offices, which had been built up in the context of national corporatism, tended to be subordinated to the central organs of internationalised public policy. As national economies became more integrated in the world economy, it was the larger and more technologically advanced enterprises that adapted best to the new opportunities. A new axis of influence linked international policy networks with the key central agencies of government and with big business. This new informal corporative structure overshadowed the older more formalised national corporatism and reflected the dominance of the sector oriented to the world economy over the more nationally-oriented sector of a country's economy.[36]

The internationalisation of the state is not, of course, limited to advanced capitalist core countries. It would not be difficult to make a catalogue of recent cases in peripheral countries where institutions of the world economy, usually as a condition for debt renewal, have dictated policies which could only be sustained by a coalition of conservative forces. Turkey, Peru and Portugal are among those recently affected. As for Zaire, a conference of creditors laid down the condition that officials of the IMF be placed within the key ministries of the state to oversee the fulfilment of the conditions of debt renewal.[37]

The internationalisation of production

The internationalisation of the state is associated with the expansion of international production. This signifies the integration of production processes on a transnational scale, with different phases of a single process being carried out in different countries. International production currently plays the formative rôle in relation to the structure of states and world order that national manufacturing and commercial capital played in the mid-Nineteenth century.

International production expands through direct investment, whereas the rentier imperialism, of which Hobson and Lenin wrote, primarily took the form of portfolio investment. With portfolio investment, control over the productive resources financed by the transaction passed with ownership to the borrower. With direct investment, control is inherent in the production process itself and remains with the originator of the investment. The essential feature of direct investment is possession, not of money, but of knowledge – in the form of technology and especially in the capacity to continue to develop new technology. The financial arrangements for direct investment may vary greatly, but all are subordinated to this crucial factor of technical control. The arrangements may take the form of wholly-owned subsidiaries, joint ventures with local capital sometimes put up by the state in host countries, management contracts with state-owned enterprises, or compensation agreements with socialist enterprises whereby, in return for the provision of technology, these enterprises become suppliers of elements to a globally organised production process planned and controlled by the source of the technology. Formal ownership is less important than the manner in which various elements are integrated into the production system.

Direct investment seems to suggest the dominance of industrial capital over finance capital. The big multinational corporations which expand by direct investment are, to some degree, self-financing and to the extent that they are not they seem capable of mobilising money capital in a number of ways, such as through local capital markets (where their credit is better than that of national entrepreneurs), through the Eurocurrency markets, through infusions of capital from other multinationals linked to technology and production agreements, through state subsidies, and so forth. And yet, particularly since the 1970s, finance capital seems to be returning to prominence through the operations of the multinational banks, not only in the old form of rentier imperialism administering loans to peripheral states, but also as a network of control and private planning for the world economy of international production. This network assesses and collectivises investment risks and allocates investment opportunities among the participants in the expansion of international production, that is, it performs the function of Lenin's 'collective capitalist' in the conditions of late Twentieth century production relations.

International production and class structure

International production is mobilising social forces, and it is through these forces that its major political consequences *vis-à-vis* the nature of states and future world orders may be anticipated. Hitherto, social classes have been found to exist within nationally-defined social formations, despite rhetorical appeals to the international solidarity of workers. Now, as a consequence of international production, it becomes increasingly pertinent to think in terms of a global class structure alongside or superimposed upon national class structures.

At the apex of an emerging global class structure is the transnational managerial class. Having its own ideology, strategy and institutions of collective action, it is both a class in itself and for itself. Its focal points of organisation, the Trilateral Commission, World Bank, IMF and OECD, develop both a framework of thought and guidelines for policies. From these points, class action penetrates countries through the process of internationalisation of the state. The members of this transnational class are not limited to those who carry out functions at the global level, such as executives of multinational corporations or as senior officials of international agencies, but includes those who manage the internationally-oriented sectors within countries, the finance ministry officials, local managers of enterprises linked into international production systems, and so on.[38]

National capitalists are to be distinguished from the transnational class. The natural reflex of national capital faced with the challenge of international production is protectionism. It is torn between the desire to use the state as a bulwark of an independent national economy and the opportunity of filling niches left by international production in a subordinate symbiotic relationship with the latter.

Industrial workers have been doubly fragmented. One line of cleavage is between established and non-established labour. Established workers are those who have attained a status of relative security and stability in their jobs and have some prospects of career advancement. Generally they are relatively skilled, work for larger enterprises, and have effective trade unions. Non-established workers, by contrast, have insecure employment, have no prospect of career advancement, are relatively less skilled, and confront great obstacles in developing effective trade unions. Frequently, the non-established are disproportionately drawn from lower-status ethnic minorities, immigrants and women. The institutions of working class action have privileged established workers. Only when the ideology of class solidarity remains powerful, which usually means only in conditions of high ideological polarisation and social and political conflict, do organisations controlled by established workers (unions and political parties) attempt to rally and act for non-established workers as well.

The second line of cleavage among industrial workers is brought about by the division between national and international capital (i.e. that engaged in international production). The established workers in the sector of international production are potential allies of international capital. This is not to say that those workers have no conflict with international capital, only that international capital has the resources to resolve these conflicts and to isolate them from conflicts involving other labour groups by creating an enterprise corporatism in which both parties perceive their interest as lying in the continuing expansion of international production.

Established workers in the sector of national capital are more susceptible to the appeal of protectionism and national (rather than enterprise) corporatism in which the defence of national capital, of jobs and of the workers' acquired status in industrial relations institutions, are perceived to be interconnected.[39]

Non-established labour has become of particular importance in the expansion of international production. Production systems are being designed so as to make use of an increasing proportion of semi-skilled (and therefore frequently non-established) in relation to skilled (and established) labour.[40] This tendency in production organisation makes it possible for the centre to decentralise the actual physical production of goods to peripheral locations in which an abundant supply of relatively cheap non-established labour is to be found, and to retain control of the process and of the research and development upon which its future depends.

As a non-established workforce is mobilised in Third World countries by international production, governments in these countries have very frequently sought to pre-empt the possibility of this new social force developing its own class-conscious organisations by imposing upon it structures of state corporatism in the form of unions set-up and controlled by the government or the dominant political party. This also gives local governments, through their control over local labour, additional leverage with international capital regarding the terms of direct investment. If industrial workers in Third World countries have thus sometimes been reduced to political and social quiescence, state corporatism may prove to be a stage delaying, but in the long run not eliminating, a more articulate self consciousness.[41]

Even if industry were to move rapidly into the Third World and local governments were, by and large, able to keep control over their industrial workforces, most of the populations of these countries may see no improvement, but probably a deterioration, in their conditions. New industrial jobs lag far behind increases in the labour force, while changes in agriculture dispossess many in the rural population. No matter how fast international production spreads, a very large part of the world's population in the poorest areas remains marginal to the world economy, having no employment or income, or the purchasing power derived from it. A major problem for international capital in its aspiration for hegemony is how to neutralise the effect of this marginalisation of perhaps one-third of the world's population so as to prevent its poverty from fuelling revolt.[42]

Social forces, state structures, and future world order prospects

It would, of course, be logically inadmissible, as well as imprudent, to base predictions of future world order upon the foregoing considerations. Their utility is rather in drawing attention to factors which could incline an emerging world order in one direction or another. The social forces generated by changing production processes are the starting point for thinking about possible futures. These forces may combine in different configurations, and as an exercise one could consider the hypothetical configurations most likely to lead to three different outcomes as to the future of the state system. The focus on these three outcomes is not, of course, to imply that no other outcomes or configurations of social forces are possible.

First, is the prospect for a new hegemony being based upon the global structure of social power generated by the internationalising of production. This would require a consolidation of two presently powerful and related tendencies: the continuing dominance of international over national capital within the major countries, and the continuing internationalisation of the state. Implicit in such an outcome is a continuance of monetarism as the orthodoxy of economic policy, emphasising the stabilisation of the world economy (anti-inflationary policies and stable exchange rates) over the fulfilment of domestic socio-political demands (the reduction of unemployment and the maintenance of real wages levels).

The inter-state power configuration which could maintain such a world order, provided its member states conformed to this model, is a coalition centring upon the United States, the Federal Republic of Germany, and Japan, with the support of other OECD states, the co-optation of a few of the more industrialised Third World countries, such as Brazil, and of leading conservative OPEC countries, and the possibility of revived détente allowing for a greater linkage of the Soviet sphere into the world economy of international production. The new international division of labour, brought about through the progressive decentralisation of manufacturing into the Third World by international capital, would satisfy demands for industrialisation from those countries. Social conflict in the core countries would be combatted through enterprise corporatism, though many would be left unprotected by this method, particularly the non-established workers. In the peripheral countries, social conflict would be contained through a combination of state corporatism and repression.

The social forces opposed to this configuration have been noted above. National capital, those sections of established labour linked to national capital, newly mobilised non-established workers in the Third World, and socially marginal in the poor countries are all in some way or another potentially opposed to international capital, and to the state and world order structures most congenial to international capital. These forces do not, however, have any natural cohesion, and might be dealt with separately, or neutralised, by an effective hegemony. If they did come together under particular circumstances in a particular country, precipitating a change of regime, then that country might be dealt with in isolation by the world structure. In other words, where hegemony failed within a particular country, it could reassert itself through the world structure.

A second possible outcome is a non-hegemonic world structure of conflicting power centres. Perhaps the most likely way for this to evolve would be through the ascendancy in several core countries of neo-mercantilist coalitions which linked national capital and established labour, and were determined to opt out of arrangements designed to promote international capital and to organise their own power and welfare on a national or sphere of influence basis. The continuing pursuit of monetarist policies may be the single most likely cause of neo-mercantilist reaction. Legitimated as anti-inflationary, monetarist policies have been perceived as hindering national capital (because of high interest rates), generating unemployment (through planned recession), and adversely affecting relatively deprived social groups and regions dependent upon government services and transfer payments (because of budget-balancing cuts in state expenditures). An opposing coalition would attack monetarism for subordinating national welfare to external forces, and for showing an illusory faith in the markets (which are perceived to be manipulated by corporate-administered pricing). The likely structural form of neo-mercantilism within core states would be industry-level and national-level corporatism, bringing national capital and organised labour into a relationship with the government for the purpose of making and implementing of state policy. Peripheral states would have much the same structure as in the first outcome, but would be more closely linked to one or another of the core country economies.

A third and more remotely possible outcome would be the development of a counter-hegemony based on a Third World coalition against core country dominance and aiming towards the autonomous development of peripheral countries and the termination of the core-peripheral relationship. A counter-hegemony would consist of a coherent view of an alternative world order, backed by a concentration of power sufficient to maintain a challenge to core countries. While this outcome is foreshadowed by the demand for a New International Economic Order, the prevailing consensus behind this demand lacks a sufficiently clear view of an alternative world political economy to constitute counter-hegemony. The prospects of counter-hegemony lie very largely in the future development of state structures in the Third World.

The controlling social force in these countries is, typically, what has been called a 'state class',[43] a combination of party, bureaucratic and military personnel and union leaders, mostly petty bourgeois in origin, which controls the state apparatus and through it attempt to gain greater control over the productive apparatus in the country. The state class can be understood as a local response to the forces generated by the internationalising of production, and an attempt to gain some local control over these forces. The orientation of the state class is indeterminate. It can be either conservative or radical. It may either bargain for a better deal within the world economy of international production, or it may seek to overcome the unequal internal development generated by international capital.

State classes of the first orientation are susceptible to incorporation into a new hegemonic world economy, and to the maintenance of state corporatist structures as the domestic counterpart to international capital. The second orientation could provide the backing for counter-hegemony. However, a state class is only likely to maintain the second and more radical orientation if it is supported from below in the form of a genuine populism (and not just a populism manipulated by political leaders). One may speculate that this could come about through the unfolding social consequences of international production, such as the mobilisation of a new non-established labour force coupled with the marginalisation of an increasing part of the urban population. The radical alternative could be the form of response to international capital in Third World countries, just as neo-mercantilism could be the response in richer countries. Each projects a particular state structure and vision of world order.

Notes

1. Fernand Braudel, *Civilisation matérielle, Economie et Capitalisme, XVe–XVIIIe Siècle, 3 vols.* (Paris: Armand Colin, 1979). Braudel's theory and method are outlined in his essay first published in 1958 in *Annales E.S.C.* 'Histoire et sciences sociales. La longue durée' (republished in Braudel, *Ecrits sur l'histoire* Paris: Flammarion, 1969).
2. There is now quite a large literature produced by this school. The basic work is I. Wallerstein, *The Modern World-System: Capitalist Agriculture and the Origins of the European World-Economy in the Sixteenth Century* (New York: Academic Press, 1974). A brief summary of the world systems theory is in Wallerstein, 'The rise and future demise of the world capitalist system: Concepts for comparative analysis', *Comparative Studies in Society and History* (vol. 16, no. 4, Sept. 1974), pp. 387–415.
3. Among critics of the world systems approach, note especially Theda Skocpal, 'Wallerstein's World Capitalist System: A Theoretical and Historical Critique', *American Journal of Sociology* (Vol. 82, No. 5, March 1977), pp. 1075–90; and more generally, her major study, *States and Social Revolutions* (Cambridge: Cambridge University Press, 1979). Also see Robert Brenner, 'The Origins of Capitalist Development: A Critique of Neo-Smithian Marxism', *New Left Review* (No. 104, July–August 1977) pp. 25–92.
4. I use the term 'world order' in preference to 'inter-state system' as it is relevant to all historical periods (and not only those in which states have been the component entities) and in preference to 'world system' as it is more indicative of a structure having only a certain duration in time and avoiding the equilibrium connotations of 'system'. 'World' designates the relevant totality, geographically limited by the range of probable interactions (some past 'worlds' being limited to the Mediterranean, to Europe, to China, etc.). 'Order' is used in the sense of the way things usually happen (*not* the absence of turbulence); thus disorder is included in the concept of order. An inter-state system is one historical form of world order. The term is used in the plural to indicate that particular patterns of power relationships which have endured in time can be contrasted in terms of their principal characteristics as distinctive world orders.

5. E.P. Thompson argues that historical concepts must often 'display extreme elasticity and allow for great irregularity'. His treatment of historical logic develops this point in his essay 'The Poverty of Theory' in *The Poverty of Theory and Other Essays* (London: Merlin Press, 1978), esp. pp. 231–242.

6. Friedrich Meinecke, *Machiavellism: The Doctrine of Raison d'État and its Place in Modern History* trans. by Douglas Scott (London: Routledge and Kegan Paul, 1957).

7. This is most clearly expressed in K. Waltz, *Man, the State and War* (New York: Columbia University Press, 1954).

8. *Leviathan*, Part I, chap. xi.

9. Kenneth Waltz, in a paper presented to a panel discussion at the American Political Science Association in August 1980 for which a first version of the present essay was written, asked the question 'Will the future be like the past?', which he answered affirmatively – not only was the same pattern of relationships likely to prevail but it would be for the good of all that this should be so. It should be noted that the future contemplated by Waltz was the next decade or so.

10. A recent example of this argument is Stephen Krasner, *Defending the National Interest: Raw Materials Investments and U.S. Foreign Policy* (Princeton: Princeton University Press, 1978). The normative intent of the new realism is most apparent as a polemic response to liberal moralism. This was also the case for E.H. Carr's *The Twenty Years' Crisis, 1919–1939* (London: Macmillan, 1942) which offered a 'scientific' mode of thinking about international relations in opposition to the 'utopianism' of the supporters of the League of Nations in Britain. Dean Acheson and George Kennan, in laying the foundations for US Cold War policy acknowledged their debt to Reinhold Niebuhr whose revival of a pessimistic Augustinian view of human nature challenged the optimistic Lockean view native to American culture. Krasner's chosen target is 'Lockean liberalism' which he sees as having undermined the rational defence of US national interests.

11. *The New Science of Giambattista Vico* trans. from the third edition by Thomas Goddard Bergin and Max Harold Fisch (Ithaca and London: Cornell University Press, 1970), p. 62, para. 349.

12. *Ibid.*, p. 6, para. 35; p. 22, para. 145; p. 25, para. 161; p. 62, para. 349.

13. *Ibid.*, p. 19, para. 127.

14. See, for instance, R.G. Collingwood's distinction between dialectical and eristical reasoning, *The New Leviathan* (Oxford: Oxford University Press, 1942). Collingwood takes dialectic back to its Greek origins and spares us the assertions of theological Marxism concerning 'Diamat'.

15. Antonio Gramsci, *Selections from the Prison Notebooks* edited and trans. by Quintin Hoare and Geoffrey Nowell Smith (New York: International Publishers, 1971), esp. pp. 158–168. The full critical Italian edition *Quaderni del carcere* (Torino: Einaudi editore, 1975) contains additional passages on this point, e.g. pp. 471, 1321, 1492. Gramsci saw ideas, politics and economics as reciprocally related, convertible into each other and bound together in a *blocco storico*. 'Historical materialism', he wrote, 'is in a certain sense a reform and development of Hegelianism. It is philosophy freed from unilateral ideological elements, the full consciousness of the contradictions of philosophy.' (Einaudi edition, p. 471, my rough translation).

16. As in Krasner, *op. cit.*, and Peter Katzenstein (ed.) *Beyond Power and Plenty. Foreign Economic Policies of Advanced Industrial States* (Madison, Wisconsin: University of Wisconsin Press, 1978). The United States is represented by these authors as a state which is weak in relation to the strength of civil society (or more particularly of

interests in civil society), whereas other states, e.g. Japan or France, are stronger in relation to their societies. Civil society is thus seen in the US case as limiting the effectiveness of the state.

17. The notion of a framework for action recalls what Machiavelli called *necessità*, a sense that the conditions of existence require action to create or sustain a form of social order. *Necissità* engenders both the possibility of a new order and all the risks inherent in changing the existing order ' . . . few men ever welcome new laws setting up a new order in the state unless necessity makes it clear to them that there is a need for such laws; and since such a necessity cannot arise without danger, the state may easily be ruined before the new order has been brought to completion.' Niccolo Machiavelli, *The Discourses* (ed.) Bernard Crick (Harmondsworth, Middlesex: Penguin Books, 1970) pp. 105–106.

18. In this regard, Stanley Hoffmann has written: 'Born and raised in America, the discipline of international relations is, so to speak, too close to the fire. It needs triple distance: it should move away from the contemporary world towards the past; from the perspective of a superpower (and a highly conservative one), toward that of the weak and the revolutionary – away from the impossible quest for stability; from the glide into policy science, back to the steep ascent toward the peaks which the questions raised by traditional political philosophy represent.' In 'An American social science: international relations', *Daedalus* (Summer 1977), p. 59.

19. On intersubjective meanings, see Charles Taylor, 'Hermeneutics and Politics', in Paul Connerton (ed.) *Critical Sociology* (Harmondsworth, Middlesex: Penguin Books, 1965), chap. VI. Also relevant is Peter L. Berger and Thomas Luckman, *The Social Construction of Reality* (Harmondsworth, Middlesex: Penguin, 1971).

20. C. Taylor, *op. cit.*, points out that expectations with regard to negotiating behaviour are culturally differentiated in the present world. Garrett Mattingly, *Renaissance Diplomacy* (London: Cape, 1955) studied the origin of the ideas outlined in this paragraph which are implicit in the modern state system.

21. Collective images are not aggregations of fragmented opinions of individuals such as are compiled through surveys; they are coherent mental types expressive of the world views of specific groups such as may be reconstructed through the work of historians and sociologists, e.g. Max Weber's reconstructions of forms of religious consciousness.

22. Gramsci's principal application of the concept of hegemony was to the relations among social classes, e.g. in explaining the inability of the Italian industrial bourgeoisie to establish its hegemony after the unification of Italy and in examining the prospects of the Italian industrial workers establishing their class hegemony over peasantry and petty bourgeoisie so as to create a new *blocco storico* (historic bloc) – a term which in Gramsci's work corresponds roughly to the notion of historic structure in this essay. The term 'hegemony' in Gramsci's work is linked to debates in the international Communist movement concerning revolutionary strategy and in this connection its application is specifically to classes. The form of the concept, however, draws upon his reading of Machiavelli and is not restricted to class relations but has a broader potential applicability. Gramsci's adjustment of Machiavellian ideas to the realities of the world he knew was an exercise in dialectic in the sense defined above. It is an appropriate continuation of his method to perceive the applicability of the concept to world order structures as suggested here. For Gramsci, as for Machiavelli, the general question involved in hegemony is the nature of power, and power is a centaur, part man, part beast, a combination of force and consent.

See Machiavelli, *The Prince*, Norton Critical Edition (ed.) Robert M. Adams (New York: W.W. Norton, 1977), pp. 49–50; Gramsci, *Selections op. cit.*, pp. 169–170.

23. E.H. Carr, *Nationalism and After* (London: Macmillan, 1945).

24. Charles Morazé, *Les bourgeois conquérants* (Paris: Colin, 1957).

25. A recent discussion of the reciprocal character of these relations is in Peter A. Gourevitch, 'The Second Image Reversed', *International Organization* (Vol. 32, No. 4, Autumn 1978), pp. 881–911.

26. I have been engaged with Jeffrey Harrod in a study of production relations on a world scale which begins with an examination of distinctive patterns of power relations in the production process as separate historical structures and which then leads to a consideration of different forms of state and global political economy. Bringing in these last two levels is necessary to an understanding of the existence of the different patterns of production relations and the hierarchy of relationships among them. One could equally well adopt forms of state or world orders as the point of departure and ultimately be required to bring the other levels in to explain the historical process.

27. Robert O. Keohane, 'The Theory of Hegemonic Stability and Changes in International Economic Regimes, 1967–77', in Ole Holsti, Randolph Siverson, and Alexander George (eds.), *Change in the International System* (Boulder, Colorado: Westview Press, 1981). Keohane cites as others who have contributed to this theory Charles Kindleberger, Robert Gilpin and Stephen Krasner. 'Hegemony' is used by Keohane in the limited sense of dominance by a state. This meaning is to be distinguished from its meaning in this article which is derived from Gramsci, i.e. hegemony as a structure of dominance, leaving open the question of whether the dominant power is a state, or a group of states, or some combination of state and private power, which is sustained by broadly-based consent through acceptance of an ideology and of institutions consistent with this structure. Thus a hegemonic structure of world order is one in which power takes a primarily consensual form, as distinguished from a non-hegemonic order in which there are manifestly rival powers and no power has been able to establish the legitimacy of its dominance. There can be dominance without hegemony; hegemony is one possible form dominance may take. Institutionalised hegemony, as used in this essay, corresponds to what Keohane calls a 'strong international regime'. His theory can be restated in our terms as: dominance by a powerful state is most conducive to the development of hegemony. In the present text, the term 'hegemony' is reserved for a consensual order and 'dominance' *refers only to a preponderance of material power.*

28. Two classic studies relevant particularly to the inter-war period are Karl Polanyi, *The Great Transformation* (Boston, Mass: Little, Brown, 1957) and E.H. Carr, *The Twenty Years' Crisis, op. cit.* The chapter by Stephen Blank, 'Britain: The Politics of Foreign Economic Policy, the Domestic Economy and the Problem of Pluralistic Stagnation', in Katzenstein (ed.), *op. cit.*, comments on post-war British economic policy; as does Stephen Krasner in, 'State Power and the Structure of International Trade', *World Politics* (Vol. 28, No. 3, April 1976). Also see R.F. Harrod, *The Life of John Maynard Keynes* (London: Macmillan, 1951).

29. The international implications of the New Deal are dealt with in several passages in Arthur M. Schlesinger, Jr, *The Age of Roosevelt*, esp. Vol. II, *The Coming of the New Deal* (London: Heinemann, 1960). Charles Meier, 'The Politics of Productivity: Foundations of American International Economic Policy after World War II', in Katzenstein, *op. cit.*, discusses the relationship between the New Deal and the

post-war ideology of world order. Richard Gardner, *Sterling–Dollar Diplomacy: Anglo-American Collaboration in the Reconstruction of Multilateral Trade* (Oxford: Clarendon Press, 1956) shows the link between New Deal ideas and the institutions of world economy set up after World War II in the Bretton Woods negotiations.

30. The basic point I am making here is suggested by a passage in Gramsci's *Prison Notebooks* which reads: 'Do international relations precede or follow (logically) fundamental social relations? There can be no doubt but that they follow. Any organic innovation in the social structure, through its technical-military expressions, modifies organically absolute and relative relations in the international field too.' Gramsci used the term 'organic' to refer to relatively long-term and permanent changes, as opposed to 'conjunctural'. *Selections op. cit.*, pp. 176–177. In the critical Italian edition, the original is to be found in vol. III, pp. 1562.

31. E.J. Hobsbawm writes: 'The men who officially presided over the affairs of the victorious bourgeois order in its moment of triumph were a deeply reactionary country nobleman from Prussia, an imitation emperor in France and a succession of aristocratic landowners in Britain.' *The Age of Capital, 1843–1875* (London: Sphere Book, 1977), p. 15.

32. Among analysts who concur in this are Karl Polanyi, *op. cit.*, Gunnar Myrdal, *Beyond the Welfare State* (New Haven: Yale University Press, 1960); E.H. Carr, *Nationalism and After, op. cit.*; and Geoffrey Barraclough, *Introduction to Contemporary History* (London: Penguin, 1968).

33. George Lichtheim, *Imperialism* (New York: Praeger, 1971) has proposed a periodisation of imperialisms, and I have taken the term 'liberal imperialism' from him.

34. 'The Imperial State System' paper presented to the American Political Science Association, Washington, D.C., August 1980.

35. Max Beloff was perhaps the first to point to the mechanisms whereby participation in international organisations altered the internal policy-making practices of states in his *New Dimensions in Foreign Policy* (London: Allen and Unwin, 1961). R.W. Cox and H.K. Jacobson, et al, *The Anatomy of Influence: Decision-making in International Organisation* (New Haven: Yale University Press, 1972) represented the political systems of international organisations as including segments of states. R.O. Keohane and J.S. Nye, 'Transgovernmental Relations and International Organizations', *World Politics* (Vol. 27 October 1974) pointed to the processes whereby coalitions are formed among segments of the apparatuses of different states and the ways in which international institutions facilitate such coalitions. These various works, while they point to the existence of mechanisms for policy co-ordination among states and for penetration of external influences within states, do not discuss the implications of these mechanisms for the structure of power within states. It is this structural aspect I wish to designate by the term 'internationalisation of the state'. Christian Palloix refers to 'L'internationalisation de l'appareil de l'État national, de certains lieux de cet appareil d'Etat . . . .' (*L'internationalisation du capital*, Paris, Maspero, 1975, p. 82) by which he designates those segments of national states which serve as policy supports for the internationalisation of production. He thus raises the question of structural changes in the state, though he does not enlarge upon the point. Keohane and Nye, subsequent to the work mentioned above, linked the transgovernmental mechanism to the concept of 'interdependence', *Power and Interdependence*, (Boston: Little, Brown, 1977). I find this concept tends to obscure the power relationships involved in structural changes in both state and world order and prefer not to use it for that reason. Peter Gourevitch, *op. cit.*, does retain the concept

interdependence while insisting that it be linked with power struggles among social forces within states.

36. There is, of course, a whole literature implicit in the argument of this paragraph. Some sketchy references may be useful. Andrew Shonfield, *Modern Capitalism* (London: Oxford University Press, 1965) illustrated the development of corporative-type structures of the kind I associate with the welfare-nationalist state. The shift from industry-level corporatism to an enterprise-based corporatism led by the big public and private corporations has been noted in some industrial relations works, particularly those concerned with the emergence of a 'new working class', e.g. Serge Mallet, *La nouvelle classe ouvrière* (Paris: Seuil, 1963), but the industrial relations literature has generally not linked what I have elsewhere called enterprise corporatism to the broader framework suggested here (cf. R.W. Cox, 'Pour une étude prospective des relations de production', *Sociologie du Travail*, 2, 1977). Erhand Friedberg, 'L'internationalisation de l'économie et modalités d'intervention de l'état: la "politique industrielle" ', in *Planification et Société* (Grenoble: Presses universitaires de Grenoble, 1974), pp. 94–108, discusses the subordination of the old corporatism to the new. The shift in terminology from planning to industrial policy is related to the internationalising of state and economy. Industrial policy has become a matter of interest of global economic policy makers, cf. William Diebold, Jr, *Industrial Policy as an International Issue* (New York: McGraw-Hill for the Council on Foreign Relations, 1980) and John Pinder, Takashi Hosomi and William Diebold, *Industrial Policy and the International Economy* (Trilateral Commission, 1979). If planning evokes the spectre of economic nationalism, industrial policy, as the Trilateral Commission study points out, can be looked upon with favour from a world economy perspective as a necessary aspect of policy harmonisation: 'We have argued that industrial policies are needed to deal with structural problems in the modern economies. Thus, international action should not aim to dismantle these policies. The pressure should, rather, be towards positive and adaptive industrial policies, whether on the part of single countries or groups of countries combined. Far from being protectionist, industrial policy can help them to remove a cause of protectionism, by making the process of adjustment less painful.' (p. 50). It may be objected that the argument and references presented here are more valid for Europe than for the United States, and that, indeed, the very concept of corporatism is alien to US ideology. To this it can be replied that since the principal levers of the world economy are in the United States, the US economy adjusts less than those of European countries and peripheral countries, and the institutionalisation of adjustment mechanisms is accordingly less developed. Structural analyses of the US economy have, however, pointed to a distinction between a corporate international-oriented sector and a medium and small business nationally-oriented sector, and to the different segments of the state and different policy orientations associated with each. Cf. John Kenneth Galbraith, *Economics and the Public Purpose* (London: Andre Deutsch, 1974) and James O'Connor, *The Fiscal Crisis of the State* (New York: St. Martin's Press, 1973). Historians point to the elements of corporatism in the New Deal, e.g. Arthur M. Schlesinger, Jr, *op. cit.*

37. The Zaire case recalls the arrangements imposed by western powers on the Ottoman Empire and Egypt in the late-Nineteenth century, effectively attaching certain revenues for the service of foreign debt. See Herbert Feis, *Europe the World's Banker, 1870–1914* (New York: Kelly for the Council on Foreign Relations, 1961), pp. 332–341, 384–397.

38. The evidence for the existence of a transnational managerial class lies in actual forms of organisation, the elaboration of ideology, financial supports, and the behaviour of individuals. Other structures stand as rival tendencies, e.g. national capital and its interests sustained by a whole other structure of loyalties, agencies, etc. Individuals or firms and state agencies may in some phases of their activity be caught up now in one, now in another tendency. Thus the membership of the class may be continually shifting though the structure remains. It is sometimes argued that this is merely a case of US capitalists giving themselves a hegemonic aura, an argument that by implication makes of imperialism a purely national phenomenon. There is no doubting the US origin of the values carried and propagated by this class, but neither is there any doubt that many non-US citizens and agencies also participate in it nor that its world view is global and distinguishable from the purely national capitalisms which exist alongside it. Through the transnational managerial class American culture, or a certain American business culture, has become globally hegemonic. Of course, should neo-mercantilist tendencies come to prevail in international economic relations, this transnational class structure would wither.

39. Some industries appear as ambiguously astride the two tendencies, e.g. the automobile industry. During a period of economic expansion, the international aspect of this industry dominated in the United States, and the United Auto Workers union took the lead in creating world councils for the major international auto firms with a view to inaugurating multinational bargaining. As the industry was hit by recession, protectionism came to the fore.

40. R.W. Cox, 'Labour and Employment in the Late Twentieth Century', in R. St. J. Macdonald, et al, (eds.), *The International Law and Policy of Human Welfare* (Sijthoff and Noordhoff, 1978). This tendency can be seen as the continuation of a long-term direction of production organisation of which Taylorism was an early stage, in which control over the work process is progressively wrested from workers and separated out from the actual performance of tasks so as to be concentrated with management. See Harry Braverman, *Labor and Monopoly Capital* (New York: Monthly Review, 1974).

41. Recent news from Brazil indicates restiveness on the part of Sao Paulo workers whose unions have been subjected to a state corporatist structure since the time of President Vargas.

42. The World Bank promotes a rural development and birth control. The concept of 'self-reliance', once a slogan of anti-imperialism meaning 'decoupling' from the imperial system, has been co-opted by the imperial system to mean self-help among populations becoming marginalised – a do-it-yourself welfare programme.

43. I have borrowed the term from Hartmut Elsenhas, 'The State Class in the Third World: For a New Conceptualisation of Periphery Modes of Production' (unpublished).

22

LINKLATER

Source: Andrew Linklater (1981) 'Men and citizens in international relations'. *Review of International Studies*, 7: 1, 23–37.

Political theory is premised on the idea that the obligations and duties of citizens are owed to the state which, in return, provides security. The concept of the moral life is limited by the boundaries that the state provides. However, as a member of humankind the individual also feels obligations to his or her fellows. Linklater highlights this as one of the enduring problems of international and political theory: the contradiction between viewing individuals as members of humankind or as citizens of particular states. He suggests that the state–citizen relationship is becoming increasingly seen as an obstacle to the individual's capacity for self-realization.

Since Rousseau political theorists have had frequent recourse to a contrast between the fragmented nature of modern social and political life and the allegedly communitarian character of the Greek polis. At the heart of this opposition was the belief that the polis represented a condition of unsurpassable harmony in which citizens identified freely and spontaneously with their public institutions. Unlike their ancient counterparts, modern citizens exhibited less identification with their public world than resolution to advance their separate individual interests and pursue their private conceptions of the good. Nevertheless, the disintegration of the polis was not depicted in the language of unqualified loss. History had not been simply an unmitigated fall, because the individual's claim to scrutinize the law of the polis on rational grounds involved a significant advance in man's self-consciousness. The positive aspect of its decline was man's transcendence of a parochial culture in which neither the right of individual freedom nor the principle of human equality had been recognized. If the modern world had lost the spontaneous form of community enjoyed by the ancients, it surpassed that world in its understanding and expression of freedom.[1]

In the writings of Hegel much is made of the necessity of integrating the ancient ideal of community with the modern principle of individuality. Indeed, for Rousseau, Hegel and the early Marx the modern political problem is how to make good citizens out of modern men, men who are no longer spontaneously citizens.[2] This problematic relationship between man and citizen combines with an equally important, if less discussed, political problem: how should men relate the obligations they acquire as men and the obligations they acquire as citizens? Again, Hegel's account of the experience of Greece is important. Within the polis, only citizens lived properly human lives; neither slaves nor citizens of other states were considered to possess equal worth. Moreover, the citizen's integration into the life of the polis involved an unquestioning acceptance of the roles and responsibilities of membership. This 'immediate' identification dissolved on account of the individual's claim to criticize the life of the polis in accordance with principles of universal reason. A new type of moral consciousness challenged both the exclusiveness of the polis and the supremacy of its civic obligations. Later, it made possible the claim to belong to two societies: the natural society of birth and the universal society embracing all men by virtue of their reason.[3] The distinction between men and citizens created an important problem for international political theory: the problem of how to reconcile the actual diversity and division of political communities with the newly-discovered belief in the universality of human nature.

The conflict between men and citizens is fundamental to the experience of the modern states-system. This is so because the emergence of moral and religious individualism or universalism divided the Western experience of morality between two dominant perspectives.[4] According to one conception of moral life, the individual understands morality as 'an affair internal to a particular community';[5] his separate community is the source of his concrete ethical life and the particular object of his political loyalty; the states-system is the inevitable product of man's division into a variety of particularistic social moralities; the idea of humanity, lacking expession in the roles and responsibilities of a form of life, exerts little or no constraint upon the relations between states. According to the second conception, 'the moral law binds men as men and not as members of any particular community';[6] individuals may employ their rational faculties to determine the rights and duties which necessarily govern them all; the state, moreover, is an incomplete moral community, too limited to satisfy the individual's sense of his wider moral responsibilities, and the states-system is an obstacle to the institutional expression of the human race.[7]

The earliest systematic writings on the modern states-system reveal Western dividedness between these opposed moral traditions.[8] In the history of modern international thought these works comprise the first stage in the understanding of the relationship between men and citizens. As human beings, it was argued, men have obligations to one another which are prior to the formation of separate states; as citizens they acquire specific obligations which they share with fellow-members of their political association alone. Since political obligations are superimposed upon primordial moral ones, the individual has to determine their precise relationship and relative claims upon him. For the classic writers of the states-system 'the services of humanity' ought to survive the establishment of any 'special bond with some particular society';[9] they claimed that 'no convention or special agreement can release (men) from the obligation . . . to fulfil the duties of humanity to outsiders', a responsibility now assumed by the state and its rulers.[10] The classic writings assumed the possibility of men being able to balance the obligations they incurred as human beings and the obligations acquired as members of separate states.

A second stage in the history of international thought highlighted an endemic weakness in these proposed solutions to the problem of relating two types of moral experience. Classic theory itself conceded that the processes of establishing special bonds within states were concluded without contractors conforming with their natural duties.[11] Rousseau and Kant made the more fundamental claim that since competition was inherent in a world of separate, sovereign states the performance of wider ethical obligations was necessarily compromised. Man's condition was transformed totally by the experience of living in and among states. It was necessary now for individuals to behave not as citizens and men, but merely as citizens. Thus, for Rousseau each one of us is

> in the civil state as regards our fellow citizens, but in the state of nature as regards the rest of the world: we have taken all kinds of precautions against private wars only to kindle national wars a thousand times more terrible; and . . . in joining a particular group of men, we have really declared ourselves the enemy of the human race.[12]

The states of Europe exhibit 'glaring contradictions' between 'our fair speeches and our abominable acts, the boundless humanity of our maxims and the boundless cruelty of our deeds'.[13] Extending this theme. Kant wrote that 'the same unsociableness which forced men into (a Commonwealth) becomes again the cause of each Commonwealth assuming the attitude of uncontrolled freedom in its external relations'; citizenship provides men with security whereby a kingdom of ends may emerge within states, but it threatens the possibility of a kingdom of ends between them.[14] Thus, the contradiction between men and citizens came to be regarded as the critical problem of international relations.

Insofar as there has been an impetus for Western political theorists to reflect upon the relations between states, it has been provided by this dichotomy. Theorists have confronted not a world of politics whose 'recurrence and repetition' is alien to a discourse concerned with order and progress, but a world of moral tensions, and their first business has been to discover a means of understanding and overcoming them.[15] This ambition underwent a radically new development when, building on ideas which originated in the late eighteenth century, theorists inaugurated a third phase in the development of international thought.[16] Underlying this new departure was the historicist assault upon both the supposed uniformity of human nature and the alleged timelessness of moral principles. The focus upon the diversity and incommensurability of moral systems was combined with a critique of that realm of human obligation which had been presumed to be in conflict with the special bonds acknowledged among citizens.[17]

Whether defensive or critical of the man–citizen dichotomy, it is unsurprising that theorists of international relations made it their principal concern. Its preeminence corresponds with the view that 'the need for philosophy arises when the unifying power has disappeared from the life of man'.[18] However, what must be at issue since the emergence of historicism, and relativism, is the validity of arguments which seek to defend the claim that the experience of living in and among modern states exhibits unresolved tensions. To consider this problem further, and to specify what turns upon it, I propose to analyse three conceptions of the man–citizen dichotomy. Two of these perspectives have been mentioned – modern natural law and historicism. To these shall be added a third perspective which focused upon the historical development of man's capacity for self-determination. It is to the first of these three perspectives that I now turn.

Rights and duties of citizens

The dichotomy between men and citizens appears in the earliest theories of the modern states-system. These writings reflected a broader development in European culture, the rise of individualism, and its particular expression in political theory, the substitution of an 'ascending' for a 'descending' conception of government.[19] Contractarianism was incorporated to account for political obligations and to justify the primacy of obligations to fellow-citizens. Civil society was to be conceived as the outcome of individual negotiation. Individuals surrendered their inherent, absolute rights to obtain a condition of civility conducive to their 'utility'.[20] Because of their natural equality and liberty, society could be constructed only through free, individual exchanges of equivalent benefits; reciprocity made social life possible, and consent gave force to obligation. Since a society of individuals was more necessary than a society of states, and since a universal political association was unobtainable, contracts were concluded not by the whole of humanity collectively but separately within emergent political groups.[21] Individuals left the state of nature by granting each other determinate rights and duties, the rights and duties of citizens. Between their respective political associations, however, the state of nature continued to exist. As individuals were not parties to contracts with outsiders they were free from specific international moral responsibilities. States, moreover, owed obligations only to those who had consented to their establishment. By their compact individuals had specified the ultimate obligations of citizenship within

associations whose sovereignty expressed the closed nature of moral life.
Classic theorists did not presume that the states-system consisted solely of
insulated moral enclaves. Had they done so the individual would have possessed
a unified moral experience. On this assumption the state would have been the
sole moral constituency and the states-system would have been an unproblem-
atic form of world political organization. That these conclusions were avoided
was a function of the belief that states were artefacts superimposed upon a
primordial moral community co-extensive with mankind. Classic theorists
sought a theoretical integration of contractarianism and moral universalism.
They developed that tradition of thought which originated in one of 'the most
decisive change(s) in political thinking', a change which 'came some time between the days of Aristotle and Cicero, and proclaimed the moral equality of
men'.[22] The doctrine that human reason was endowed with the capacity to
apprehend non-contractual, immutable moral principles inherent in the nature
of things became part of the dualistic foundations of modern international
theory. Thus, 'the universal society of the human race' arose as a 'necessary
result of man's nature'.[23] There was an obligation upon 'the race of men' to
cultivate 'a friendly society' because of 'nature's will' that all men are
'kinsmen'.[24] On account of this primordial, if latent, moral community obligations to citizens could not constitute the outer parameter of the individual's
moral experience; and vertical divisions between states, correspondingly, could
not be the principal characteristics of the states-system.
   The attempt to mediate between two distinct philosophic traditions made it
impossible for those early theories to develop a coherent account of the modern
system of states. Their failure is manifest in their discussion both of the character
of sovereign rights and the principles of statecraft. Ascertained within contractarianism, the constitutive principles of the states-system are rough reproduc-
tions of the principles of conduct observed by individuals within the original
state of nature.[25] The sovereign's right to promote the interests of his association, by force if necessary, is analogous to the right of self-help claimed by men
in their natural state. States must possess these rights until and unless they consent to their amendment or surrender. But, from a perspective inclined to
highlight the unifying capacity of human reason, the attempt to endorse these
absolute, vertical divisions between communities is unjustified. It commits the
error of forming 'a plan of geographical morality, by which the duties of men,
in public and private situations are not governed by their relation to the great
Governor of the Universe or by their relations to mankind, but by climates,
degrees of longitude, parallels not of life, but of latitudes'.[26] Such a 'plan of
geographical morality' violates the existence of a universal moral constituency
supporting moral rights and duties between the individual members of world
society. The rational state cannot regard its rights and responsibilities to be constituted by the transactions between its individual members: the former cannot
emanate from a pact which excludes all but future citizens, since the rights and
duties of insiders and outsiders must be harmonized. Indeed, as Fichte observed,
to avoid being 'in contradiction with the concept of right, a commonwealth . . .

must embrace the whole globe, or at least, must contain the possibility of uniting the whole of mankind'.[27] The dual foundations of classic theory advanced antagonistic methods for ascertaining both the range of the individual's moral sensibilities and their implications for the structure of international society.

Opposed accounts of the morality of statecraft emerge from these diverse philosophical bases. Here a familiar dichotomy between private and public ethics arises alongside the man–citizen division. On the contractarian account, the principle of reciprocity facilitates the development of a society of states, but the reason for states is a constraint upon the level of sociability which can be exhibited in their external relations. Because of the structure of political obligation states cannot allow that international obligations are permanently binding nor can they dismiss out of hand any act of duplicity or violence outlawed within domestic society. Since duties among men cannot be extended indefinitely into the space between states, moral and political experience is bifurcated into the distinct realms of private and public ethics. It is an inevitable product of the compact that the sovereign, as trustee for the welfare of the community, must deny the validity of principles which are normally observed in the conduct of purely private relations. This dichotomy is not objectively-given in the anarchic nature of the states-system; what it depends upon is the prior decision to confine the moral constituency to the boundaries of political association.[28] On account of the apparent rationality of this decision, morality can be separated into two realms without assuming that this disturbs the unity of citizens' moral lives. Nevertheless, if the states-system is an artefact superimposed upon a given international morality the legitimacy of this division of morality must be questioned. For, considered alongside the belief in universal reason, the separation between private and public ethics is a reflection of the incomplete, one-sided nature of moral life. Artificial boundaries between states create an indefensible tension at the heart of the individual's moral experience, whether apprehended or not. What is at issue, therefore, is the existence of particularistic social moralities which concentrate the individual's moral sensibilities upon the immediate, political group. Against this practice moral universalism asserts that a person should be concerned with 'the all encompassing sphere of cosmopolitan sentiment';[29] the moral self-consciousness of individuals and societies ought to develop to that point at which 'a violation of right in one place of the earth is felt all over it'.[30] The sovereign should not be party to a division between the principles of domestic and international political life; as a moral agent he acquires the obligation to collaborate with other sovereigns to control the states-system so that 'it may be brought into conformity with natural right'.[31] The attempt to impose moral principles upon the affairs of states holds the key to overcoming the tension between the obligations of men and the obligations of citizens.

Two conceptions of moral obligation are embedded in the classic reflections upon the states-system. But the corresponding visions of world political organization are not made explicit and the internal contradictions of the argument are suppressed. Typical of these writings is their tendency to relax the force of obligations to humanity. Both Pufendorf and Vattel rely on the argument that these obligations possess an essentially indeterminate status. Pufendorf argued that it is only within civil societies that men have ascertained the precise composition of the rights and duties which are to bind them together; their social contract established what they were uncertain of from their knowledge of the natural law alone.[32] Vattel stated that the content of the natural law is imprecise, that it lends itself to varying interpretations, and that states therefore should refrain from judging each other's conduct.[33] Obligations to citizens are determinate while obligations to men are not. However, neither Pufendorf nor Vattel wished to deny the realm of human obligation with its supposedly moderating impact upon inter-state affairs. Perhaps, the implication to draw is that the states-system is as rational a form of world political organization that men can establish prior to making obligations to humanity more concrete. But, in neither writer's work is there a suggestion that the states-system exhibits only an imperfect or qualified form of rationality. Indeed, the roles and responsibilities of members of sovereign states appear to presuppose the absolute rationality of the state and the finality of the states-system. 'The services of humanity' may survive the formation of special political arrangements, but citizens are urged to hold 'nothing dearer' than the 'welfare and safety' of the state; similarly, sovereigns ought to comply with the imperative that 'the welfare of the people is the supreme law'.[34] 'No convention or special agreement' can cancel 'the duties of humanity', but a constitutive principle of the state-system maintains that 'the liberty of a Nation would remain incomplete if other Nations presumed to inspect and control its conduct'.[35] The attempt to legitimize these propositions reveals that, at best, classic theory equivocated between contractarianism and universalism.

The principal merit of Kant's international theory is the attempt to overcome these inadequacies with earlier international relations theory. In contrast to 'the miserable comforters' (Grotius, Pufendorf and Vattel) Kant aimed to take the principle of equality seriously as a principle of international relations.[36] The conclusions of Kant's theories are well-enough known to make recapitulation unnecessary here. It may be recalled that his theory of politics attempts to establish the absoluteness of reason and to overcome the separation between contractarianism and rationalism.[37] Nevertheless, the dominant trends in social and political thought did not coincide with Kant's individualistic foundation for a universal ethic; they ran counter to doctrines which supposed there was a distinction to be made between the values of any particular place or time, and the values supplied by the existence of an overarching reason. Romanticism, for instance, criticized two key elements in the traditional contractarian theories of society and politics exemplified in the writings of Pufendorf and Vattel: first, the belief that human arrangements were artefacts through which men sought to satisfy pre-social needs; and, secondly, the belief that men possessed, irrespective of their cultural or temporal location, the same set of rational capacities.[38] The second of these criticisms was presumed by later writers to undercut Kant's critique of the states-system.[39] Irrespective of the accuracy of this point, the impact of romanticism and its development was to transform the entire basis upon which traditional international relations theories had rested.

The historicist theory of international relations

Employing the romanticist critique of individualism and rationalism, historicism claimed that the capacities of men were linked inextricably with the forms of life in which they were involved. By claiming that moral capacities were similarly dependent, it was possible to subvert the belief in a universal moral constituency required by the universality of reason. The latter world-view was predicated upon the wrongful abstraction of individuals from their social and historical contexts. Individuals, it was argued, were not men first, and French or German afterwards.[40] Only in the West had thinkers become preoccupied with analysing man's condition as it might have been prior to the development of different social and political practices.[41] Nevertheless, that discourse which aimed to depict the natural characteristics of man simply underlined its own cultural limitations; invariably, existing social categories were imputed to the thought and action of natural man. Culture's unavoidable and irreducible qualities are no more evident than in the theorist's ambition to transcend them.

Therefore, it was argued that the primordial fact about humanity is the existence of cultural individualities. Individuals are not undifferentiated members of a humanity which might attain political unification, but participants within diverse communities of 'intellect and spirit' which have developed in history.[42] The function of states was not to maximize the pre-social requirements of their members but to preserve and enhance the cultures for which they were responsible. Human existence involved cultural pluralism and the necessity of recognizing division into states. But, if there is no moral law which is transcultural, on what basis can international political theory be developed; and what possibilities are there for reasoning about the relations between states? Historicists believed they had established that a theory of obligations to humanity was problematic; the aspiration to specify the duties between all men was immediately to privilege values dominant only within one culture. But the denial of transcultural or suprahistorical values was not a denial, it was supposed, of a genuinely international political theory. Historicism took humanity to be neither an essence shared by all men nor a set of innate natural tendencies, but the totality of cultural configurations.[43] Humanity was revealed in the various, if not infinite, human expressions which could be discerned only through observation of what men had unfolded in their diverse cultural contexts. No single culture could manifest the totality of human possibilities; since every state had a significant role to play in preserving and unfolding human capacities, separate states did not detract from, but enhanced, humanity.

A unique discussion of the presuppositions of a states-system emerged alongside this account of humanity. Each culture had the right of access to its own political form under the rubric that political differentiation was required by cultural pluralism. For the historicist, the state has obligations to enhance its variant on humanity, and moral consciousness need not appear in the form of a tension between internal and external moral requirements. Horizontal moral ties between individual members of world society are deemed illusory; what is objectively necessary is the separation of men into political communities.[44] Unlike classic theory, however, these propositions could be advanced without being vulnerable to Kant's charge of failing inexcusably to apply principles of natural right to the 'wasteland' between states. Historicism had sought to overcome that dichotomy between the state and humanity which had produced internal contradictions in rationalist theories of international relations. By reducing individualism and cosmopolitanism to mere abstractions, historicism sought to overcome the age-old separation between man and citizen.

The historicist critique of modern natural law theory appears to be unanswerable. It is not upon that basis that either the division between the state and humanity or the criticism of the states-system can be established. However, historicism cannot avoid generating its own set of internal contradictions. Rather then dwell on the familiar argument that historicist reasoning is self-refuting,[45] it is important to identify some problems in its attempt to characterize the relationship between culture and humanity.

In order to do this, I shall assume the existence of two cultures which are founded on mutually exclusive principles of international relations. While one culture accepts the historicist's claim that all cultural configurations help to manifest humanity, and acknowledges obligations to other states on this basis, the other confines obligations simply to relations between members of its own, allegedly superior cultural formation. The historicist argument is that each culture is necessary in order to manifest the diverse range of human possibilities. This observation has a highly specific meaning since these cultures negate rather than complement one another, namely that they reveal man's capacity to express himself in wholly antagonistic forms of life. To make a different assertion it would be necessary to choose between these cultures on the grounds that one expressed human potentialities more adequately than the other. Although this point resurrects that very dichotomy which historicism was summoned to deny, it is a division which historicists cannot avoid. For, if we consider the relations between these cultures, on what basis can the first assert that the other should recognize its contribution to human capabilities; and on what basis can it claim that the other should recognize its rightful existence as a sovereign state? It is not possible for the first culture to make its appeal on the basis of the equal validity of cultures. For on the same basis its opponent may claim that its denial of obligations to outsiders is its contribution to the full elaboration of cultural configurations. While historicist reasoning appeared to believe that a principle of the equal validity of cultures was coincidental with a principle that cultures should treat each other as moral equals, it is now apparent that these propositions bear no logical relationship whatsoever. At this point the historicist argument is confronted with a clear choice: either the first principle is advocated with the consequence that there is no longer a defence for the states-system; or the latter principle is advocated at the expense of regarding various cultural systems as equally valid. Since the historicists made the decision to advocate the second principle, they reintroduced that dichotomy which was found in classic theory. In brief, to assert the value of the principle of the equal treatment of cultures in the face of a claim to reject it, is to resurrect a division between a concrete culture and a moral principle which transcends it.

Nevertheless, rather than claim that an ethnocentric culture should acknowledge that all cultures possess equal moral status, the historicist might move to a relativist position. This development would involve affirming the equal validity of all cultural systems, including their different conceptions of international relations. It is assumed that one 'can turn to history as an indefinitely rich compendia of life styles, all of which stand in external relation to one another so that in choosing or rejecting any one I make no comment on the others'.[46] Here, the relativist wishes to endorse two incompatible propositions: firstly, that there are no transcultural criteria which facilitate the rational ordering of cultures, and secondly, that a culture which takes a relativist position has objective grounds for rejecting cultures predicated upon principles which are antagonistic to relativism. Accordingly neither historicism nor relativism can attempt to bridge the gap between men and citizens without engaging in self-contradiction. But if these doctrines are inconsistent, and if natural law doctrine succumbs to the criticism that its account of humanity ignores cultural diversity and historical change, what is to be made of the division between men and citizens?

The philosophers of history

Let us return to the historicist position and begin with the observation that historicism may be made the object of a critique similar to the one it directed at the theory of natural law. If the latter abstracted individuals from historically-evolving cultures, the former abstracted cultures from the wider forms of human experience (including, for example, man's social interaction with nature) through which the development of human capacities takes place.[47] To develop this further, it is important to consider the philosophers of history with their focus upon the emergence and development of the human species itself. What relativism and historicism omitted was consideration of the manner in which unique human powers were developed through the multidimensional aspects of the social world. Within the theory of history there was an attempt to establish a hierarchy of human capacities through a consideration of man's place in the worlds of society and nature. And this attempt has major implications for an understanding of the nature of the dichotomy between man and citizen.

Philosophical historians sought to give an account of the nature and potentialities of historical subjects. Their principal contention was that history was made possible by the existence of creatures which were free. To be free, on this account, was not to be beyond the jurisdiction of the law, to be unconstrained as in the state of nature of the modern natural lawyers, but to have the capacity to initiate action. Man was a unique being which participated within a historical dimension because of his capacity to set his own ends. His uniqueness, however, stemmed not only from this power but also from man's potentiality for self-development. Man was not a static being but one which underwent radical transformation in the course of positing and acting on his freely-determined ends. Philosophers of history wished to highlight the historical development of man's powers and the evolution of his self-knowledge. In brief, they sought to understand the processes which were integral to the creation of the human species.

The *a priori* of history was the existence of a being which was capable of transcending, at least in part, the world of natural determination. What had to be discerned were those characteristics which explained the emergence of a non-natural being. Not surprisingly, this ambition was executed through an analysis of man's early immersion in, or interaction with, the natural world. Theorists of history followed Rousseau's conjecture that early man was a natural being with the latent capacity for free action and self-advancement. Thus, Kant regarded man as that part of nature in an idyllic age with the power of reason and imagination which made possible the establishment of new ends; Hegel emphasized that man's distinctive power was his ability to think and to express his thoughts in a world of his own creation; Marx took human labour to be the instrument whereby non-natural ends and the self-creation of the species were made possible.[48] What history revealed and developed was man's ability to enlarge these distinctive powers. It showed man in a world of his own making, 'a second nature', in which gradual expression was given to his unique potentialities.[49]

This understanding of man as a dynamic, self-constituting being necessarily takes issue with natural law doctrines and historicism alike. The former were wrong to assume that the right ends for man were fixed independently of history, given in his nature or pre-determined by a divine being.[50] The belief in the immutability of human nature and in the static nature of man's rational faculties, which was revealed in the natural law discussion of man in the original state, overlooked his historical transformation. Natural law doctrines abstracted men from the formative role of concrete ensembles of changing social relations.[51] Medieval natural law theories with their conception of the universe as a system of interdependent parts, each possessing its distinctive telos, had confused natural and normative orders. Laws of nature derived their validity from their existence, while laws of social conduct depended for their validity upon human endorsement. The focus upon man's historical development necessitated a division between the repetitive physical world and the potentially progressive world of history.[52] Historicists, moreover, might be accused of having failed to give an account of the character of a being which existed in a cultural and historical dimension, and of failing to make explicit the formation and development of unique human abilities.

Man's capacity for rational self-determination was held to be capable of extension in two respects. First, man could improve the quality of his rational powers and, secondly, he could expand the scope of their operation. What was open to him as an historical being was the ability to enlarge his freedom through ever-increasing rational control of his self and his environment. Through the medium of history, men could come to grasp the adequate goals of free beings together with the conditions for their realization. Gradually, they could gain a form of self-knowledge which was always theirs potentially but which was actualized only within more advanced socio-political arrangements. Since the creation of a world of self-determining beings was a gradual historical process it was inconceivable that all cultures could be conceived to be equally valid. These could be judged by the extent to which their members understood and expressed the nature of rational, self-determination.

Philosophical historians proposed, therefore, a theory of 'historical periodization' which would reveal the main stages of development in man's growth to higher levels of self-consciousness. The urge to place different societies on a scale of ascending types is exhibited both in Hegel's analysis of world-historical peoples and in Marx's consideration of various forms of socially-organized production.[53] It was this aspect of theoretical history which Kant commended to the theorists of international society. A 'minor motive' for attempting a philosophical history was the issue of what various societies had contributed to the growth of world citizenship.[54] In brief, the possibility arises of placing different political associations, or systems of states, on a hierarchy of forms in accordance with their proximity to a condition in which the idea of rational, self-determination is extended into the world of international relations. The execution of this purpose suffered on account of the general disrepute which came to surround philosophical history in the English-speaking world at the beginning of this century. In the writings of T.H. Green, however, there is an attempt to integrate philosophical history and the study of the relations between states.[55] What requires attention, moreover, in the context of the present discussion, is the manner in which the division between man and citizen may be situated within a theory of the historical development of human capacities.

Following Kant, Green maintained that in the course of their history men refined their moral capacities. It was man's deepening and broadening of his understanding of obligation which revealed the growth of his potentiality for rational, self-determination. In early societies rights and duties were attached to persons only as members. A common good was recognized within such societies 'while beyond the particular community the range of obligation (was) not understood to extend'.[56] The essence of man's development was revealed in his ability to recognize 'an ever-widening conception of the range of persons between whom the common good is common'.[57] The culmination of this growth of freedom was contained in the understanding that fundamental obligations were not confined simply to relations between citizens, or to relations between sovereigns and subjects, but ought to extend to all relations between men qua men. The highest development of moral consciousness entailed identifying with a common good of 'a universal society co-extensive with mankind itself'.[58]

For Kant and Green the ideal political environment would be a product of man's ability to live in a world governed by rational principles which men had freely imposed upon themselves. Men transcended nature and expressed their capacity for self-determination most perfectly where they managed the totality of political relations with recourse to self-imposed, universal moral obligations. To use Kantian terminology, the species realizes its potentiality for combining individuality and cosmopolitanism only in a condition in which all men are regarded as colegislators within a universal kingdom of ends. Accordingly, a cosmopolitan culture occupies a higher place on a scale of social types than one in which moral sensibilities are concentrated simply upon insiders. A states-system in which men aim at establishing institutions which express their belief that human beings have 'a claim upon human society as a whole',[59] is more adequate than one in which particularistic social moralities are thought to possess absolute validity. On this basis, philosophical historians sought to criticize plans of 'geographical morality' without succumbing to the criticism that they had superimposed an abstracted, static morality upon diverse societies. While they acknowledged the historical importance of cultural individualities, they did not draw back from positing the existence of transcultural criteria for evaluating human conduct. They sought to derive criteria from man's historical development itself. And in so doing, they thought it possible to regard particularistic moralities as forms of human understanding which would be transcended as men grasped the nature of their capacity for self-determination.

Philosophical historians steered between the contemporary options of ethical absolutism and relativism; immanent within their writings is the belief that these are sides of a false antinomy. What is true of general social and political principles may be taken to be true of the division between men and citizens. This dichotomy is not a feature of an idiosyncratic and relative moral code; nor is it a conflict between a particularistic social morality and the requirements of an immutable ahistorical ethic. Although the dichotomy may arise only within particular cultures at specific points in their evolution, its significance is much deeper. However cast, it expresses a conflict within the experience of the states-system. But when characterized adequately the conflict reveals dissatisfaction of a specific kind, namely with the impediments upon human freedom and rationality which issue both from the character of the sovereign state and the constitutive principles of the states-system.

Here there is a parallel with the division between man and citizen which was so important within Hegel's account of the character of ancient and modern politics. The emergence of individualism within Greek society represented dissatisfaction with the parochial nature of social and political life. The Greek's challenge to a traditional and customary morality expressed his aspiration to live in a social world which embodied individual reason.[60] Social and political morality was not simply 'an affair internal to a particular community'; it had to express the subject's particular sense of the nature of rational conduct. If this more free social world was to develop, Hegel argued, the individual's estrangement from his customary morality was essential.[61] It was necessary to realize a higher understanding of self-determination than that obtained either in those cultures where members thought their social relations rested on natural sanctions or where they enacted their moral obligations uncritically and spontaneously. It was this demand for a higher level of self-determination, expressed in the contrast between man and citizen, which proved to be subversive ultimately of Greek life. Nevertheless, individualism itself could not provide, on Hegel's account, the sufficient condition for a free social world. Individualism, especially when it was the rationale for the pursuit of private interest, became an obstacle to the development of a social environment subject to collective control. The product of individualism was a condition in which individuals were subjected increasingly to impersonal laws operating within their societies.[62] To attain a higher level of self-determination, it was necessary to allow men to pursue their separate individual ends while enjoying integration into a rational state which expressed their capacity for collective self-determination. In this way the reconciliation of that opposition between men and citizens, which had been so necessary to progress beyond the parochialism of Greece, would be accomplished.

Philosophical history provides the resources for characterizing the division between man and citizen in international relations in a similar way. The modern state may offer its citizens freedoms unavailable to members of earlier forms of association; it may make available greater opportunities for individual self-determination and for taking part in the process of controlling the immediate social and political environment. Nevertheless, states separately can only imperfectly realize the human capacity for collective self-determination. The possession of citizenship alone is not sufficient to enable the individual to participate in the control of his total political environment. As Rousseau observed, the citizen's ability to live an autonomous life within states is limited severely by the disruptive power of international events. Refuge from a form of heteronomy, which had its source outside the state, could be found only in autarchic states.[63] Further, as Kant also observed, the world of sovereign states appears to be a world of necessary conflict and competition. Accordingly, theorists have claimed that compared with domestic politics, international politics are 'less susceptible of a progressivist interpretation'; the anarchic nature of the states-system is presumed to subject states to impersonal laws and to limit their ability to engage in moral conduct.[64] However, it is important not to locate resistance to change only in the states-system, thus risking imputing the character of states to their environment. As the discussion of contractarianism sought to show, the fact that states pursue their particularistic interests and insist upon their sovereign rights; the fact that they conduct their external affairs on the basis of a separation between the principles of domestic and international political life, is a function of the nature of the state as a particular system of rights and obligations. Those patterns of behaviour are implicit in the character of the sovereign state itself, implicit in a type of organization which assumes the priority of obligations among fellow-citizens.

Due to this phenomenon the conflict between men and citizens acquires fundamental importance in both the theory and practice of international relations. For, as we have seen, what the existence of a realm of human obligations does, is challenge the state as a particularistic moral community which generates heteronomous relations in its external affairs. It may be suggested that the form of estrangement which is exhibited in the division between men and citizens is as necessary in the experience of the world of states as it was in the life of the Greek polis. It may be regarded as a division which is integral to the movement from attempting to realize autonomy in relations within states to attempting to realize autonomy in relations between them.

The actualization of a higher form of international political life requires that radical critique of the state which historicism was unable to supply and modern natural law theory was unwilling to undertake. We have raised the possibility that the idea of humanity may provide this function if it can be reconstituted within a theory of history which is able to avoid those inadequacies endemic in traditional and modern theories of natural law. It may well be that the existence of a moral community more inclusive than the state can be defended only on the basis of man's capacity for self-determination. If this is indeed so, it may be contended that only within an international political association, which aims at maximizing the conditions for individual and collective self-determination, can men realize their historically-evolved capacities while recapturing morally integrated lives.

Notes

1. The principal exponent of this view was Hegel; see *The Philosophy of History* (New York, 1956), esp. pp. 252–3 and *The Philosophy of Right* (Oxford, 1952), paras 260–1, esp. Additions. For a fuller account see R. Plant, *Hegel* (London, 1973), ch. 1, and C. Taylor, *Hegel* (Cambridge, 1975), chs. 14–15.
2. J.O'Malley (ed.), *Marx's Critique of Hegel's Philosophy of Right* (Cambridge, 1970). Introduction, esp. pp. xi–lxiii.
3. C. Taylor, *op. cit.* esp. pp. 385, 395–7; L. Colletti, *Marxism and Hegel* (London, 1973), ch. 12.
4. This distinction is developed further in W.H. Walsh, 'Open and Closed Morality', *The Morality of Politics*, B. Parekh and R. Berki (eds.) (London, 1972).
5. *Ibid.* p. 19.
6. *Ibid.*
7. The conflict between the two moralities is represented most clearly by the differences between Kantian and Hegelian ethics. See H.B. Acton, *Kant's Moral Philosophy* (London, 1970) and W.H. Walsh, *Hegelian Ethics* (London, 1969). Hegel brought the two moralities (*moralitat* and *sittlichkeit* in his own terminology) into clear opposition as theories of international relations, *ibid.* para 209.
8. The principal texts discussed in this paper are Pufendorf's *The Two Books of the Elements of Universal Jurisprudence* (first published 1660) (Oxford, 1934); *The Law of Nature and Nations* (first published 1672) (Oxford, 1934); *The Two Books on*

the Duty of Man and Citizen According to the Natural Law (first published 1673) (New York, 1927); Vattel *The Law of Nations; or, Principles of the Law of Nature, applied to the Conduct and Affairs of Nations and Sovereigns* (first published 1758) (New York, 1964).

9. Pufendorf, *Elements of Universal Jurisprudence, op. cit.* p. 242.

10. Vattel, *op. cit.* 5–6.

11. See, for example, Pufendorf's remark that 'the just size of a state should be measured by the strength of its neighbours', *The Law of Nature and Nations, op. cit.* p. 968.

12. *Abstract of the Abbe de Saint-Pierre's Project for Perpetual Peace, The Theory of International Relations* M.G. Forsyth. H.M.A. Keens-Soper and P. Savigear (London, 1970), p. 132.

13. *Ibid.* pp. 135–6.

14. *Idea for a Universal History from a Cosmo-Political Point of View*, in Forsyth *et. al. op. cit.* p. 183.

15. For the view that international politics is a world of 'recurrence and repetition,' and its impact upon international relations theory, see M. Wight. 'Why is there no International Theory?' *Diplomatic Investigations* H. Butterfield and M. Wight (eds) (London, 1966), p. 26.

16. See below, pp. 316–18.

17. I. Berlin, *Vico and Herder* (London, 1976), p. xxiii; also 'Herder and The Enlightenment' in the same volume; A. Stern, *Philosophy of History and the Problem of Values* (Hague, 1962), ch. 6.

18. H. Marcuse, *Reason and Revolution* (London, 1969), p. 36.

19. W. Ullman, *Principles of Government and Politics in the Middle Ages* (London, 1961), p. 24.

20. Pufendorf, *Elements of Universal Jurisprudence, op. cit.* p. 103; Vattel, *op. cit.* pp. 9a–10a.

21. Pufendorf, *op. cit.* p. 274; Vattel, *op. cit.* pp. 5–6.

22. A.J. Carlyle, *A History of Medieval Political Theory in the West* (London, 1930), vol. 1, pp. 7–11.

23. Vattel, *op. cit.* pp. 5–6.

24. Pufendorf, *op. cit. The Law of Nature and Nations*, p. 212.

25. Vattel, *op. cit.* p. 7; Pufendorf, *Two Books on the Duty of Man and Citizen, op. cit.* p. 90.

26. *The Philosophy of Edmund Burke* (a selection of his speeches and writings) L.I. Bredvold and R.G. Ross (eds.) (Michigan, 1970), p. 17.

27. Fichte, *The Science of Rights* (Philadelphia, 1869), p. 215.

28. This point is developed below, pp. 320–1.

29. Kant, *The Metaphysical Principles of Virtue* (New York, 1964), p. 140.

30. Kant, *Perpetual Peace,* Forsyth *et. al. op. cit.* p. 216.

31. *Ibid.* pp. 228–9.

32. *Two Books on the Duty of Man and Citizen, op. cit.* p. 48.

33. *Op. cit.* pp. 7–8.

34. Pufendorf *Two Books on the Duty of Man and Citizen, op. cit.* p. 121 and 144.

35. Vattel, *op. cit.* p. 5.

36. W.B. Gallie, *Philosophers of Peace and War* (Cambridge, 1978), ch. 2. Kant's comment appears in *Perpetual Peace, op. cit.* p. 211.

37. J.G. Murphy, *Kant: The Philosophy of Right* (London, 1970), pp. 110–11.

38. A. Lovejoy, 'The Meaning of Romanticism for the Historian of Ideas', *Journal of the History of Ideas*', vol. 2 (1941), pp. 260–78.

39. It may be argued that Kant's later historical and political writings represent 'a point of departure' from his earlier accounts of man as a static being. See C. A. Raschke, *Moral Action, God and History in the Thought of Immanuel Kant* (Dissertation Series No. 5) (University of Montana, 1975), p. 191–2.

40. H. Treitschke, '*Die Politik*'. *The Politic Thought of Heinreich von Treitschke*, H.W.C. Davis (ed.) (New York, 1915), p. 127–8.

41. *Ibid.*

42. For a fuller discussion of this idea see R. Aron, *Peace and War* (London, 1966), pp. 585–91 and R.W. Sterling *Ethics in a World of Power: The Political Ideas of Meinecke* (Princeton, 1958).

43. 'The rays of divine light reveal themselves in a broken form in different peoples, each of whom manifests a new shape and a new conception of the Godhead.' Treitschke, *op. cit.*

44. See Aron, *op. cit.* and Sterling, *op. cit.* for a fuller discussion of these points.

45. 'Historicism claims trans-historical validity for its own thesis, thus refuting it'. Stern *op. cit.* p. 182.

46. G.D. O'Brien, *Hegel on Reason and History* (Chicago, 1975), p. 68.

47. See L. Colletti, *From Rousseau to Lenin* (New York, 1972), p. 39.

48. Rousseau, *A Discourse on the Origin of Inequality, The Social Contract and Discourses,* G.D.H. Cole (ed.) (London, 1968), p. 170: Kant *Conjectural Beginning of Human History. Kant on History* L. Beck (ed.) (New York, 1957), pp. 55–6; Hegel *op. cit.* para 4, addition; Marx *The German Ideology* (London, 1965), p. 39.

49. Hegel, *ibid.* para. 4.

50. Charles Taylor refers to this doctrine as 'expressivism', *op. cit.* esp. pp. 13–29, and pp. 547–52 for its application to Marx's thought.

51. Hegel, *op. cit.* para 145; Marx, *Theses on Fenerbach*, Sixth thesis.

52. Hegel, *op. cit.* Addition to the Preface; *The Philosophy of History*, p. 54.

53. For a discussion of this aspect of Marx's thought, see M. Evans, *Karl Marx* (London, 1975), esp. pp. 72–9 and E. Hobsbawm's introduction to *Marx's Pre-Capitalist Economic Formations* (London, 1964).

54. *Idea for a Universal History*, Forsyth *et. al. op. cit.* p. 191.

55. *Prolegomena to Ethics* (Oxford, 1916), esp. ch. IIIB, 'The Extension of the Area of Common Good.'

56. *Ibid.* p. 238.

57. *Ibid.* p. 237.

58. *Ibid.* pp. 239–40.

59. *Lectures on the Principles of Political Obligation* (London, 1966), pp. 157–8.

60. Hegel, *The Philosophy of History, op. cit.* pp. 251–3.

61. For extended discussion of this theme, see Plant *op. cit.* Schiller's statement is a classic summary: 'If the manifold potentialities in man were ever to be developed, there was no other way but to pit them the one against the other. This antagonism of faculties and functions is the great instrument of civilisation – but it is the only instrument.' *Letters on the Aesthetic Education of Man* (Oxford, 1967), Letter VI, sec. 12.

62. Hegel, *The Philosophy of History, op. cit.* pp. 317–18.

63. S. Hoffmann, *The State of War* (London, 1965).

64. Wight, *op. cit.* p. 26.

SELECTED BIBLIOGRAPHY

Airaksinen, Timo and Bertman, Martin A. (eds) (1989) *Hobbes: War Among Nations*. Aldershot, Avebury.

Annas, Julia (1981) *An Introduction to Plato's Republic*. Oxford: Oxford University Press.

Aron, Raymond (1983) *Clausewitz: Philosopher of War*. London, Melbourne and Henley: Routledge & Kegan Paul.

Beitz, Charles R. (1979) *Political Theory and International Relations*. Princeton, N.J: Princeton University Press.

Brucan, Silviu (1978) *The Dialectic of World Politics*. New York: Free Press.

Bull, Hedley (1977) *The Anarchical Society*. London and Basingstoke: Macmillan.

Bull, Hedley, Kingsbury, Benedict and Roberts, Adam (eds) (1990) *Hugo Grotius and International Relations*. Oxford: Clarendon Press.

Butterfield, Herbert and Wight, Martin (eds) (1966) *Diplomatic Investigations: Essays in the Theory of International Politics*. London: George Allen & Unwin.

Carr, E.H. (1946) *The Twenty Years' Crisis 1919–39: An Introduction to International Relations*. London: Macmillan, 2nd edn.

Ceadel, Martin (1987) *Thinking about Peace and War*. Oxford and New York: Oxford University Press.

Clark, Ian (1989) *The Hierarchy of States: Reform and Resistance in the International Order*. Cambridge: Cambridge University Press.

Claude, Inis L. Jr (1962) *Power and International Relations*. New York: Random House.

Cox, Richard H. (1960) *Locke on War and Peace*. Oxford: Clarendon Press.

Deane, H.A. (1963) *The Political and Social Ideas of St. Augustine*. New York: Columbia University Press.

De Grazia, Sebastian (1989) *Machiavelli in Hell*. New York and London: Harvester Wheatsheaf.

Donelan, Michael (ed.) (1978) *The Reason of States: A Study in International Political Theory*. London: George Allen & Unwin.

Donelan, Michael (1990) *Elements of International Political Theory*. Oxford: Clarendon Press.

Dougherty, James E. and Pfaltzgraff, Robert L. Jr (1990) *Contending Theories of International Relations*. New York and London: Harper & Row, 3rd edn.

Ferguson, Yale H. and Mansbach, Richard W. (1988) *The Elusive Quest: Theory and International Politics*. Columbia, SC: University of South Carolina Press.

Forsyth, M.G., Keens-Soper, H.M.A. and Savigear, P. (eds) (1970) *Theory of International Relations: Selected Texts from Gentili to Treitschke*. London: George Allen & Unwin.

Gallie, W.B. (1978) *Philosophers of Peace and War: Kant, Clausewitz, Marx, Engels and Tolstoy*. Cambridge: Cambridge University Press.

Garnett, J.C. (1984) *Commonsense and the Theory of International Politics*. London and Basingstoke: Macmillan.

Giddens, Anthony (1985) *A Contemporary Critique of Historical Materialism*, Vol. 2, *The Nation-State and Violence*. Cambridge: Polity Press.

Gilpin, Robert (1981) *War and Change in World Politics*. Cambridge: Cambridge University Press.

Harle, Vilho (ed.) (1990) *European Values in International Relations*. London and New York: Frances Pinter.

Held, David (ed.) (1991) *Political Theory Today*. Cambridge: Polity.

Hinsley, F.H. (1963) *Power and the Pursuit of Peace: Theory and Practice in the History of Relations between States*. Cambridge: Cambridge University Press.

Hoffmann, Stanley (1965) *The State of War: Essays in the Theory and Practice of International Politics*. New York and London: Frederick A. Praeger.

Hoffmann, Stanley and Fidler, David P. (eds) (1991) *Rousseau on International Relations*. Oxford: Clarendon Press.

Hollis, Martin and Smith, Steve (1990) *Explaining and Understanding International Relations*. Cambridge: Cambridge University Press.

Holsti, K.J. (1985) *The Dividing Discipline: Hegemony and Diversity in International Theory*. Boston: Allen & Unwin.

Joynt, Carey B. and Corbett, Percey E. (1978) *Theory and Reality in World Politics*. London and Basingstoke: Macmillan.

Kant, Immanuel (1991) *Kant: Political Writings* (ed. H.S. Reiss, trans H.B. Nisbet). Cambridge: Cambridge University Press, 2nd edn.

Kenny, Anthony (1980) *Aquinas*. Oxford: Oxford University Press.

Keohane, Robert O. (ed.) (1986) *Neo-Realism and its Critics*. New York: Columbia University Press.

Keohane, Robert O. and Nye, Joseph S. (1977) *Power and Interdependence: World Politics in Transition*. Boston and Toronto: Little, Brown.

Krombach, Hayo B.E.D. (1991) *Hegelian Reflections on the Idea of Nuclear War*. Basingstoke and London: Macmillan.

Kubalkova, V. and Cruikshank, A.A. (1980) *Marxism–Leninism and Theory of International Relations*. London, Boston and Henley: Routledge & Kegan Paul.

Kubalkova, V. and Cruikshank, A.A. (1985) *Marxism and International Relations*. Oxford: Oxford Unviersity Press.

Linklater, Andrew (1990) *Men and Citizens in the Theory of International Relations*. London and Basingstoke: Macmillan, 2nd edn.

Linklater, Andrew (1990) *Beyond Realism and Marxism: Critical Theory and International Relations*. Basingstoke: Macmillan.

Light, Margot and Groom, A.J.R. (eds) (1985) *International Relations: A Handbook of Current Theory*. London: Frances Pinter.

Little, Richard and Smith, Michael (eds) (1991) *Perspectives on World Politics*. London and New York, Routledge, 2nd ed.

McKinlay, R.D. and Little, Richard (1986) *Global Problems and World Order*. London: Frances Pinter.

Manning, C.A.W. (1962) *The Nature of International Society*. London and Basingstoke: Macmillan, 2nd edn. reissue with a new preface 1975.

Mayall, James (ed.) (1982) *The Community of States: A Study in International Political Theory*. London: George Allen & Unwin.

Midgley, E.B.F. (1975) *The Natural Law Tradition and the Theory of International Relations*. London: Paul Elek.

Morgenthau, Hans J. (1948) *Politics among Nations*. New York: Alfred A. Knopf, and subsequent editions.

Mulgan, R.G. (1977) *Aristotle's Political Theory*. Oxford: Oxford University Press.

Nardin, Terry (1983) *Law, Morality and the Relations of States*. Princeton, N.J.: Princeton University Press.

Navari, Cornelia (ed.) (1991) *The Condition of States*. Milton Keynes: Open University Press.

Olson, William C. and Groom, A.J.R. (1991) *International Relations Then and Now: Origins and Trends in Interpretation*. London: Unwin Hyman.

Onuf, Nicholas Greenwood (1989) *World of Our Making: Rules and Rule in Social Theory and International Relations*. Columbia, S.C.: University of South Carolina Press.

Parkinson, F. (1977) *The Philosophy of International Relations: A Study in the History of Thought*. Beverly Hills and London: Sage.

Roosevelt, Grace G. (1990) *Reading Rousseau in the Nuclear Age*. Philadelphia: Temple University Press.

Rosenau, James N. (1990) *Turbulence in World Politics: A Theory of Change and Continuity*. Hemel Hempstead: Harvester Wheatsheaf.

Sabine, George and Thorsen, Thomas L. (1973) *A History of Political Theory*. Hinsdale, Ill.: Dryden Press, 4th edn.

Smith, Michael J. (1984) *Realist Thought from Weber to Kissinger*. Baton Rouge, La.: Louisiana State University Press.

Taylor, Trevor (1978) *Approaches and Theory in International Relations*. London and New York: Longman.

Thompson, Kenneth W. (1980) *Masters of International Thought: Major Twentieth-Century Theorists and the World Crisis*. Baton Rouge and London: Louisiana State University Press.

Viotti, Paul R. and Kauppi, Mark V. (1987) *International Relations Theory: Realism Pluralism, Globalism*. New York: Macmillan, and London: Collier Macmillan.

Waltz, Kenneth W. (1959) *Man, the State and War*. New York: Columbia University Press.

Waltz, Kenneth N. (1979) *Theory of International Politics*. Reading, Mass.: Addison-Wesley.

Wight, Martin (1979) *Power Politics*. Harmondsworth: Penguin, revised edn.

Williams, Howard (1983) *Kant's Political Philosophy*. Oxford: Blackwell.

Wolfers, Arnold (1962) *Discord and Collaboration: Essays on International Politics*. Baltimore: The Johns Hopkins Press.

Wolfers, Arnold and Martin, Laurence W. (eds) (1956) *The Anglo-American Tradition in Foreign Affairs*. New Haven, Conn.: Yale University Press.

Wright, Moorhead (ed) (1975) *Theory and Practice of the Balance of Power: Selected European Writings 1486–1914*. London: J.M. Dent.

INDEX